Wonder Women
and Bad Girls

ALSO BY VALERIE ESTELLE FRANKEL
AND FROM MCFARLAND

*Fourth Wave Feminism in Science Fiction and Fantasy:
Volume 1. Essays on Film Representations,
2012–2019* (edited, 2019)

*Fourth Wave Feminism in Science Fiction and Fantasy:
Volume 2. Essays on Television Representations,
2013–2019* (edited, 2020)

Women in Doctor Who:
Damsels, Feminists and Monsters (2018)

The Women of Orphan Black:
Faces of the Feminist Spectrum (2018)

*Superheroines and the Epic Journey:
Mythic Themes in Comics, Film and Television* (2017)

Outlander's *Sassenachs: Essays on Gender, Race,
Orientation and the Other in the Novels
and Television Series* (edited, 2016)

Adoring Outlander: *Essays on Fandom, Genre
and the Female Audience* (edited, 2016)

The Symbolism and Sources of Outlander:
*The Scottish Fairies, Folklore, Ballads, Magic
and Meanings That Inspired the Series* (2015)

*The Comics of Joss Whedon:
Critical Essays* (edited, 2015)

Women in Game of Thrones: *Power,
Conformity and Resistance* (2014)

*Teaching with Harry Potter: Essays on Classroom Wizardry
from Elementary School to College* (edited, 2013)

*Buffy and the Heroine's Journey:
Vampire Slayer as Feminine Chosen One* (2012)

*From Girl to Goddess: The Heroine's Journey
through Myth and Legend* (2010)

EDITED BY COLLEEN S. HARRIS AND
VALERIE ESTELLE FRANKEL

Women Versed in Myth: Essays on Modern Poets (2016)

Wonder Women and Bad Girls

Superheroine and Supervillainess Archetypes in Popular Media

VALERIE ESTELLE FRANKEL

McFarland & Company, Inc., Publishers
Jefferson, North Carolina

ISBN (print) 978-1-4766-8409-3
ISBN (ebook) 978-1-4766-4163-8

LIBRARY OF CONGRESS AND BRITISH LIBRARY
CATALOGUING DATA ARE AVAILABLE

Library of Congress Control Number 2020044030

© 2020 Valerie Estelle Frankel. All rights reserved

No part of this book may be reproduced or transmitted in any form or by any means, electronic or mechanical, including photocopying or recording, or by any information storage and retrieval system, without permission in writing from the publisher.

Front cover image © 2020 Stokkete/Shutterstock

Printed in the United States of America

*McFarland & Company, Inc., Publishers
Box 611, Jefferson, North Carolina 28640
www.mcfarlandpub.com*

Table of Contents

Introduction   1

The Classic Super Eras

Pinup Girl: Sheena, Queen of the Jungle (Fiction House, 1937–1954)	5
Fifties Ladies: Batman's Women (DC Comics, 1954–1964)	11
Silver Age Wimps: The Wasp (Marvel Comics, 1963–1970)	16
Superheroines Onscreen: Wonder Woman (TV, 1975–1979)	22
Antiheroine: Elektra (Marvel Comics, 1981–1994)	24
Bronze Age Fridging: The Killing Joke (DC Comics, 1988)	27
Bad Girl Comics: Fatale (Broadway Comics, 1995)	33
Girl Power: Powerpuff Girls (TV, 1998–2005)	38
Atoner: Cassandra Cain (DC Comics, 2001)	44
Cinematic Superheroines: Captain Marvel (Film, 2019)	47

Crossing Boundaries

Supermoms: Steven Universe (TV, 2013–2019)	54
Multifaceted Warrior Woman: Thor (Marvel Comics, 2014–2015)	61
Golden Age Fighters: Girl Commandos (Harvey Comics, 1942–1943)	66
Apocalyptic Heroine: Martha Washington (Dark Horse, 1994–1997)	71
Angry Feminist: Misty Knight (Marvel Comics, 1975)	77
Bad Girl Team: Danger Girl (Wildstorm, 1997–2001)	81
Seductress: Veda the Cobra Woman (Quality Comics, 1942)	84
Shapechanger: Mystique (Marvel Comics, 2004–2005)	87
Transgender Fluidity: Doom Patrol (DC Comics, 1993–1994)	93

Good Girls

Fourth Wave Princess: Shuri (Film, 2018)	101
Altruist: Wonder Woman (DC Comics, 1941)	106

Spunky Kids: Kitty Pryde (Marvel Comics, 1980–1985)	109
First Adventure: Batgirl Day One (DC Comics, 1993)	114
Responsible Sister: Karma (Marvel Comics, 1980–2013)	117
Paragon: Supergirl (TV, 2015–)	120
Mystic: Zero Girl (Homage Comics, 2001)	126
Fish Out of Water: Starfire (DC Comics, 2015)	131
Sidekicks: Electra Woman and Dyna Girl (TV, 1976)	133

Outcasts

Spy: Black Widow (Marvel Comics, 1965–1967)	142
Evil Mom: Talia al Ghul (Film, 2016)	145
Abuse Victim: Harley Quinn (DC Comics, 1992)	148
The Dark Lord's Daughter: Nightshade (DC Comics, 1988)	153
Rootless: America Chavez (Marvel Comics, 2017)	156
The Other: Janissary (DC Comics, 1997)	159
The Monster: She-Hulk (Marvel Comics, 2003)	165
Cyborg: X-23 (Marvel Comics, 2006–2011)	169
Possessed Heroine: Katana (DC Comics, 2007)	175

Reclaiming Power

Community Activist: Citlali (Newspaper, 2002–2005)	179
Nature Incarnate: Poison Ivy (Film, 1997)	184
Mentor: Jessica Jones (Marvel Comics, 2005)	188
Antileader: Suicide Squad (DC Comics, 1987–1990)	191
Goddess and Ruler: Storm (Marvel Comics, 1975–2009)	194
Supervillainess: Texa (Zip Comics, 1940)	199
Dragon Lady: Madame Butterfly (Quality Comics, 1948)	203
Witch Queen: Seven Soldiers of Victory (DC Comics, 2006–2007)	207
Mighty Crone: Spider Widow (Quality Comics, 1942)	211

Conclusion   216

Primary Sources Cited   219

Secondary Sources Cited   225

Index   231

Introduction

Superheroines have changed massively through their evolution. Beginning as pinup girls in the forties, they only occasionally carried their weight beside Batman or Spider-Man. In fact, female power in the comics and other fiction mediums seems to have come in waves: the fifties "dealt with preparation for a domestic role in marriage, notions of idealized romance, and devotion to fashion and beauty" (Duncan and Smith 257). Likewise, the sixties had weak female team members like sweet Supergirl and Sue Storm rather than powerhouses ... though these women were at least ostensibly welcomed as equals.

There were also supervillainesses, sometimes dipping into racial stereotypes with the sexy, powerful and foreign Dragon Lady like Madame Butterfly or Veda the Cobra Woman. A little later, Batman's love interest Talia al Ghul continued this pattern of exoticism. Other supervillainesses and even heroines appeared in mighty older women, terrifying the men with their voices of ancient wisdom. These included Spider Widow, Mother Goose, Mother Hubbard, and Madam Fatal. As the genre was being formed, many of these women were witches with magic straight from the fairytale tradition of the strange old woman in the woods.

The Cold War followed with its spies, from the heroic Señorita Rio to the calculating Black Widow (Natasha Romanov, an Avengers villain who later turned hero and joined the team). Silver Age comics had the Marvel heroes and heroines squabbling among themselves and undergoing more interesting character arcs. The seventies brought feminism and action women, prompting Black Widow to change her slinky dress and veil for an Emma Peel–style catsuit. Diversity appeared once again, with Misty Knight and Colleen Wing forming their own team-up and becoming more than superheroes' girlfriends. The X-Men relaunched with a far more multicultural line, inviting in some villainesses like Mystique even as good girls like Jean Grey turned very, very bad.

Next came the Bronze Age of comics, with dark antiheroines like Elektra, the assassin Daredevil loves. Other heroines had problematic pasts, like Katana, who was forced to carry her husband's soul with her forever. She-Hulk, invented in 1980, was instantly popular as a tougher, more muscular heroine. Likewise, Amanda Waller led the Suicide Squad of antiheroes, threatening the villain team with instant death if they disobeyed her brutal commands.

Of course, not all "bad girls" are villains. Some are the nonconformists—transgender heroines, rebels, and rule-breakers. Some are leaders like Amanda Waller who solve the world's problems unconventionally by recruiting a supervillain team. Others shatter tradition by gender-flipping stereotypes or battling injustice in their own government. When society betrays them first, they often turn vigilante. Further, some "bad girls" are the victims of comics and film—abuse victims like Harley Quinn, the subjects of experiments like the new Wolverine or madwomen driven to despair by society's cruelty. Some, like Jessica Jones, toughen up and fight back, while others, like She-Hulk, struggle for balance in a judgmental world. Even as society labels them nonconformists and agitators, freedom fighters like Martha Washington strike out against the patriarchy and reclaim the night.

After this period of strength came one of weakness. The 1990s and 2000s offered very sexualized heroines as post-feminism encouraged objectifying women across genres. Sweethearts like the Powerpuff Girls, Sailor Moon, or Buffy the Vampire Slayer had incredible power but blanketed it beneath a layer of vapid childishness to appear nonthreatening. Meanwhile, bad girl comics like *Fatale, Glory, Lady Death, Danger Girl, Bad Kitty, Tarot: Witch of the Black Rose*, and *Witchblade* hit the stands, pushing the concept to extremes with women in chainmail bikinis and whips. With both stereotypes, the nineties with its good girl art and bad girl art enjoyed presenting its heroines as underdressed models rather than achievers.

Even in the post–2000s, in which film franchises like the X-Men and Avengers rose to prominence, heroines were sidelined. In the first *X-Men* film, Rogue's coming-of-age story fades into her being chained up for Wolverine to rescue. Black Widow saves herself, but *Age of Ultron* leaves her as the Hulk's love interest and "lullaby" to charm him out of savagery. Over and over, they are more objects than people. Spider-Man's great love, Mary Jane Watson, enters comics objectifying herself with "Face it, Tiger ... you just hit the jackpot!" In the three *Spider-Man* feature films directed by Sam Raimi (2002–2007) Kirsten Dunst's Mary Jane does little better as she crushes on the superhero, a running joke that sets up conflict through the heroine's obliviousness. Just about every iteration of Lois Lane has shared this. It also stretches to superheroines, as Elasti-Girl, the mother of *The Incredibles* (2004), is unaware that her husband has snuck out of retirement and that her baby has superpowers.

Other film stereotypes are problematic in other ways. *Batman v. Superman* and *Captain America: The Winter Soldier* have their starring superheroines play women of mystery—more puzzles for the hero than well-rounded characters. Batgirl is an annoying tagalong in everything from *Batman and Robin* to the *Lego Batman Movie*. *Ant-Man* showed the Wasp—his partner from the comics—deliberately sidelined though she was clearly more competent. The solo superheroine films *Supergirl*, *Elektra*, and *Catwoman* were famously flops—overserious in character and frivolous in plot. Their failures delayed other superheroine solo films for a decade. On the smaller screens, the WB's *Birds of Prey* lasted a single season on television, in contrast with ten of *Smallville*. Of 37 Marvel cartoons, only two (*Spider-Woman*, from 1979 to 1980, and the current web series *Marvel Rising*) have headlined a woman or girl. In live action, DC shows have done better, but out of 42 cartoons, only the very recent *DC Super Hero Girls* and *Harley Quinn* star superheroines. Many of these cartoons are mixed teams, like *X-Men* or *Teen Titans*, but the team leaders and majority of characters are generally male. Clearly, women weren't being invited to fully step into the men's playground.

At last, in a post–*Hunger Games* film era, characters began to change. *Wonder Woman* (2017) finally proved one could make a quality superheroine film as audiences loved her defiant power. Shuri the prodigy princess and her fellow warrior women stole the show in *Black Panther*. The Wasp joined Ant-Man for a shared film, and Captain Marvel starred in her own. Dark Phoenix headlined one, too. *Suicide Squad*, *Logan*, *Thor: Ragnarok*, *Spider-Man: Into the Spiderverse*, and *Deadpool 2* all stood out for their nuanced women. Television launched *Supergirl*, *Marvel's Jessica Jones*, *Agent Carter*, *Black Lightning*, *Batwoman*, *Marvel's Agents of S.H.I.E.L.D.*, *DC's Legends of Tomorrow*, *Watchmen*, *Sense8*, *Gotham*, *Wynonna Earp*, *Marvel's Runaways*, *Raising Dion*, *The Umbrella Academy*, *Marvel's Cloak & Dagger*, *Powers*, *Doom Patrol*, *Titans*, and *The Gifted*, all with pointedly diverse casts. Cartoons added *She-Ra and the Princesses of Power*, *Harley Quinn*, *Word Girl*, *Steven Universe*, *Vixen*, *Gotham Girls*, *Star vs. the Forces of Evil*, and female teams in *Marvel Rising* and *DC Superhero Girls*. A renaissance was arriving—not just for superheroes but for starring superheroines.

Comics had already taken a massive step forward. Marvel was offering gender-flipped, race-flipped and newly empowered female characters with A-Force, Ms. Marvel, Lady Thor, Miles Morales, Silk, Moon Girl, Stature, Hawkeye, Ironheart, America Chavez, and Wolverine. These were more than just superheroine-led comics: Moon Girl and Squirrel Girl modeled compromise and problem solving for kids, while the Pakistani Ms. Marvel embodied a new generation of teen experience. Further, they'd all meet up with Mockingbird, Captain Marvel, Hellcat, the new Wasp, and She-Hulk for smoothies. The ladies of the Spiderverse (featuring new single mom Jessica Drew) were doing the same. After Civil War II, Mary Jane, along with Riri Williams and

Amanda Armstrong, had to run Iron Man's company and take over the superheroing, too.

On the other side of the aisle, DC's New 52 relaunched *Batgirl, Catwoman, Birds of Prey, Supergirl, Suicide Squad,* and *Wonder Woman,* though with only two female creators and many sexualized heroines. DC's *Bombshells* imagined a world with only superwoman, fighting in World War II. Their subsequent *Rebirth* line offered new angles on Wonder Woman to spin off the successful film, while bringing back Batwoman and creating *Batgirl and the Birds of Prey* with a male Oracle as sidekick. Women of more variety arrived. A new sympathetic Harley Quinn and stronger Batgirl, each written by women, won over more female readers in 2014. Meanwhile, indie comics wowed readers with Faith the plus-size superheroine, *The Umbrella Academy, B.P.R.D., Raising Dion, Femforce, Lazarus, Plutona, Lumberjanes, Girl Genius,* and *Monstress,* among many others. Superhero novels of both established and original characters were multiplying in the teen section—and all of them emphasized inclusion and power.

Exploring all the types of superheroines, from wimps to powerhouses, from good girls to those fed up with the rules, from the rebels to those with traditionally gendered powers, reveals much about the messages their creators intended and the roles of women in America and beyond. Archetypes reveal many types of heroines within this range: superfans, frustrated sidekicks, perky kids, shy students, mystics with near-magical abilities. The superhero metaphor can help kids and teens face disability, anxiety, and issues of inclusion. All these superheroine stories guide readers to empowerment and a new understanding of how to excel.

The Classic Super Eras

Pinup Girl: Sheena, Queen of the Jungle (Fiction House, 1937–1954)

Inspired by the 19th century H. Rider Haggard novel *She*, Sheena, Queen of the Jungle (created by Will Eisner and Jerry Iger) was a beautiful blonde in revealing leopard print. She imitates other pulp action stars like Rima the Jungle Girl from W.H. Hudson's novel *Green Mansions* (1904) and Tarzan's Jane (introduced by Edgar Rice Burroughs in 1912). To American readers, Africa was the mysterious land of *King Solomon's Mines*, a land of adventure that defied understanding. The jungle girl also kicked off comic-book heroines.

Fiction House's female-centric strips included Mysta of the Moon, Gale Allen and the Girl Squadron, Sky Girl, Futura, and the bluntly named Patsy Pinup, but Sheena, Queen of the Jungle was the most famous by far. Ron Goulart writes in *Great History of Comic Books*, "In [Fiction House] stories, you encountered amply constructed and sparsely clad young women on the land, on the sea, and in the air. Deep into the jungles, you ran into beautiful blondes wearing leopard skin undies; off on some remote planet there would be a lovely redhead sporting a chrome-plated bra" (243). While many of Fiction House's titles were deceptively mild (Fight, Planet, Wings, Jungle, etc.), the art was quite provocative. Almost all their covers featured an underdressed young woman.

Sheena first appeared in the British magazine *Wags* in 1937 and was brought over to the U.S. in *Jungle Comics* a year later. In 1942, she graduated to her own title, the first female comic book character to do so (beating Wonder Woman by a matter of months). She was also the first damsel not in distress to be featured on a comic book cover. Sheena battled ivory poachers and Nazis, emphasizing her agency. Her survival skills were based on her innate intelligence plus her "extraordinary agility." Sheena is clever and escapes many traps. She's "a savage fighter, who could deal death with her bare hands," as Mike Madrid explains in his celebrated *The Supergirls* (31).

Critic Jay Disbrow explains, "From the onset, Sheena captivated the minds of comics readers. The concept of a white woman raised in the wilds of equatorial Africa, being forced to pit her wits and survival instincts against savage beasts, primitive natives, and the forces of nature: these elements of the story exercised the fascination of comic book readers." The Jungle Queen genre features a white female struggling to redeem a hostile, uncivilized world (Wright 36–37). The heroine goes barefoot, with ragged minidresses. Jungle Girls are highly intelligent and strive to find peaceful solutions to protect the local people and the wildlife. Some (like Sheena) speak excellent English and other languages too. Disbrow adds, "Despite the lack of civilized amenities in native surroundings, she was a lovely and completely feminine woman. She always appeared well-groomed in her leopard-skin covering, and her long golden hair was always freshly combed and appeared hygienically clean. The Jungle Queen archetype frequently sexualizes the female body as possessable" (Stevens 24). With her skimpy outfit and lack of confining civilization, she can do what she likes, and it's implied she and her somewhat wimpy boyfriend do, outside the audience's gaze. Her fans were clearly reading to watch her improbable exploits in revealing outfits.

Her story was a series of Tarzan tropes. After her explorer father Cardwell Rivington was accidentally poisoned, she grew up in the jungle, raised by the witch-doctor who had been responsible for the tragedy. Eventually she meets an inept white hunter named Bob Reynolds whom she takes as her mate and damsel in distress. With him as helper, she battles evil white hunters, slave traders, misguided natives, and wild animals. Her unspoiled innocence and sweetness (while wearing notably few clothes) made her a figure of desire in an early example of "good girl art."

This term, coined by the American Comic Book Company in its catalogs, referenced lush, provocative poses, often underdressed with some bondage. Previously, comics had been a bit cleaner. "The customers for such early titles as *Famous Funnies, Popular Comics,* and *Super Comics* were presumed to be children, and the magazines were packaged and promoted accordingly. On the first two years of Famous covers, for example, you'll find only four young women depicted and all of them sedately presented" (Goulart, *Comic Book Culture* 181). As the 1930s approached, however, publishers tried to cater to adolescent boys, some with characters like Robin and Bucky, and some with more risqué young women. Their images persist through today, conventionally gendered. Superheroine critic Jeffery A. Brown explains:

> according to the dominant binary perceptions of gender, the idealized male characters have to be hypermasculine to fend off any hint of feminization while the tough and powerful female characters have to be depicted as hypersexual in order to fend off any accusations of being masculinized. This emphasis on the sexual desirability of the heroines as a defining characteristic in the male-dominated world of comic books

makes it difficult to adapt superheroines to feature film and television. In order to appease fans Hollywood attempts to be faithful to the comic book origins of the characters, both narratively and visually, and since the comics genre is so firmly rooted in adolescent male fantasies the adaptations magnify unequal gender representations [*Modern Superhero* 52].

After World War II began, many American soldiers read comic books, and new lines were launched specifically for them with much racier content. Comic book historian Ron Goulart writes: "In the days before the advent of *Playboy* and *Penthouse*, comic books were one place to girl-watch" (*Great History* 241). Illustrator Rolf Armstrong (1889–1960) was labeled the "Father of Good Girl Art" because of his calendar prints and advertisements. Of course, many of the artists were actually women, including Ruth Atkinson and Fran Hopper. Ramone Patenaude drew for Fox, Marvel, and Novelty, and even did covers. Fiction House hired Lily Renée, an Austrian refugee, and Marcia Snyder, a queer artist. Powerful fictional women were everywhere, like their real-life counterparts. "Perhaps hiring so many women explains why Fiction House produced an abundance of female-centric stories," Hope Nicholson explains in *The Spectacular Sisterhood of Superwomen* (26).

Another female character appearing alongside the good girl art character was "more a Do-Good Girl, be she policewoman, masked avenger, or superhuman. The point was, she usually relied on her capabilities rather than on just her sexual attractiveness" (Goulart, *Comic Book Culture* 192). Here were Wonder Woman and Mary Marvel, as well as the fictional heroines of the war like Liberty Belle and Miss America. As early as 1935, G-Woman June Justis starred as "the only girl member of the U.S. Bureau of Investigation." Some of these heroines only longed for rescue, while others had quite extraordinary powers. *Wings Comics*, the first comic book dedicated exclusively to flying, featured a sedately dressed Jane Martin, War Nurse. As the comic went on, however, "raised skirts and cleavage were as frequently seen as propellers and machine guns.... Jane Martin took to showing up for work in provocative attire and, on occasion, in her undies" (Goulart, *Comic Book Culture* 191).

Of course, jungle girls ran about in bikinis and sometimes bathed in the river in even less, proving clearly that "sex sells." The jungle queens were clearly there for cheesecake, to appeal to the servicemen. "Men serving in the armed forces were the main audience of comic books during the war. For them, it was reassuring to visualize a woman who was not repelled by the animalistic behavior they adopted during wartime" (Packer 204). At the same time, they modeled toughness for readers of all types. "Sheena assured women that they would not lose their allure if they adopt more aggressive and survivalist stances during wartime" (Packer 203). Emotional and alluring with exaggerated feminine attributes, the jungle girls were protagonists but drawn to be admired.

> Sheena was drawn in provocative poses that best showed off her ample breasts carefully concealed by strategically placed leopard skin. Long shapely legs broke out of the panel borders in High Baroque style to arch across the page. Sheena swung from vines or leapt across the page, prominently showing off a spotted rump or widely spread legs. Her long blond hair was wild and free flowing. Stories mixed shades of Eros and Thanatos by showing the erotically drawn Sheena locked in combat with a wild snarling beast or writhing in the tentacles of a giant squid. Sheena was the untamed fantasy, the wild sensual creature that was not confined by polite society's idea of how a woman should dress or act [Madrid, *Supergirls* 44–45].

Her story is also racist and imperialist, as the local Africans need the protection of a white girl. Sheena bosses around the local African tribes, choosing a new leader on one occasion and ordering an African tribe to abolish their "cruel burial customs" on another. Both times, the locals respond in chorus, "We hear, O Sheena, we obey!" In one story set in French West Africa, she defeats a rebellion, thus preserving the French imperialism. Thus, they pushed the more painful attitudes of their era.

Sheena inspired an entire genre of similar comic book jungle queens. Jungle Comics from Fiction House offered Ann Mason, dressed just like Sheena. Camilla (also from Jungle Comics) wore zebra skin. Princess Pantha, The Purple Tigress, Saari the Jungle Goddess, Blanda, Judy of the Jungle, Marga the Panther Woman, Tangi, Nyoka the Jungle Girl, Ranee Princess of the Jungle, Tigra, Zegra, Tegra Jungle Empress, The Tiger Woman, Tygra of the Flame People, Zara of the Jungle, Pamela of the Jungle, Tara Fremont, Meriem Cooper, Camilla Wild Girl of the Congo, Juanda, Lorna the Jungle Queen, Jungle Lil, Leopard Girl, Cave Girl, Fana the Jungle Girl, Jann of the Jungle, Saari the Jungle Goddess, Taranga, Jun-Gal, and Taanda White Princess of the Jungle, though from different publishers, were all of a type, most often blonde, pale, and dressed in strips of fur or the remnants of American clothes. A few more like Ann or Jessie appeared in male comics like *Ka'a'nga Jungle King*, as the Jane to the hero's Tarzan. Jo-Jo Jungle King had girlfriends Juanda, Tanee, Gwenna, Lura, and Safra.

Film leapt on board: There were Trader Horn (1931), The Savage Girl (1932), Inyaah, Jungle Goddess (1934), The Jungle Princess (1936), Jungle Siren (1942), Nabonga (1944), Jungle Queen (1945), Jungle Goddess (1948), Daughter of the Jungle (1949), Miss Robin Crusoe (1954), and more through recent times. Jungle Girls also appear in well-known classics like *King Kong, The Lost World,* and *Doctor Who*.

While a white girl living abroad was a staple of the genre, there was some diversity with Taj of the Elephants introduced in *Jungle Comics* #57 (1944). Safari Cary in *Dagar Desert Hawk* had a Middle Eastern twist. Kazanda the "Queen of the Lost Continent" (*Rangers Comics* #23–28) with her shining black hair and pale skin appears Asian. She also has superpowers with animal speech and a kind of projected telepathy she can use to show her friends images.

Matt Baker, a boundary-breaking Black artist of the time, gave his Rulah Jungle Goddess and South Sea Girl black hair and somewhat darker skin than many of their contemporaries. Jay Disbrow, in *Alter Ego* 21 calls him "one of the foremost 'good girl artists' of the post–World War II period." Indeed, his good girl art, especially his rendition of Phantom Lady, is considered a collector's item. South Sea Girl lived on the Vanishing Isles, hidden in the mists of the South Pacific. In an island-printed two-piece with luxuriant black curls, Alani was ruler and protector of the volcanic tropical islands. Using amazing swimming strength and knowledge of the sea, she teamed up with Captain Ted to prevent oil tycoons from taking over her islands. She appeared in *Seven Seas Comics* #1–6 in 1946 from Leader Enterprises/Universal Phoenix Features.

More exotically, Baker wrote the biracial *Tiger Girl*. This blonde in a tiger-striped leotard was the daughter of an Indian Rajah and an Irish princess. There was also a Sikh manservant named Abdola. He is well-spoken, greeting Tiger Girl in one story with "Welcome, princess. Your pets have been anxious for your return" (O'Hara and Blum). She in turn treats him as a respected friend, as Batman does Alfred. With her whip and friendly tiger sidekicks, she terrorizes jungle poachers. A magic amulet gave her supernatural strength.

The Jungle Princess was significant, as it influenced the most famous superheroine of all. Debuting in 1941, Wonder Woman, an Amazon princess in a corset, is an exotic islander drawn in good girl art style as a pinup. "It began with a bustier. You can call it a breastplate if you like, but it began as a bustier—Vargas girl lingerie decked out in stars and stripes, a piece of clothing that gives new meaning to suspension of disbelief," comments author Leigh Bardugo (151). Thus she can't be fully separated from her main competitor. Along with Wonder Woman, Sheena "ruled the early days of comic books as the medium's two most popular heroines and the archetypes that would define the female superhero. Sheena was the passionate, savage beauty who embodied the erotic fantasies of men, while Wonder Woman was a powerful female who served as a role model for young girls" (Madrid, *Supergirls* 31).

While Wonder Woman, like her male contemporaries, joins the army and encourages readers to contribute, Sheena remains blissfully secluded. "Sheena represented the pre–Pearl Harbor isolationist position, safeguarding her jungle against invaders without venturing beyond her community's boundaries" (Stevens 13). She thus offered escapism even during the war—a haven of peace and a small conflict easily solved.

Sexy superheroines found their doom a few years later. In 1954, Fredric

Wertham published his study *Seduction of the Innocent*, which claimed that comic books corrupted children with their terrible violence and sexual depictions. As he said of Wonder Woman:

> Wonder Woman is not the natural daughter of a natural mother, nor was she born like Athena from the head of Zeus. She was concocted on a sales formula. Her originator, a psychologist retained by the industry, has described it: "Who wants to be a girl? And that's the point. Not even girls want to be girls.... The obvious remedy is to create a feminine character with all the strength of Superman.... Give (men) an alluring woman stronger than themselves to submit to and they'll be proud to become her willing slaves." Neither folklore nor normal sexuality, nor books for children, come about this way. If it were possible to translate a cardboard figure like Wonder Woman into life, every normal-minded young man would know there is something wrong with her [234–235].

Here he insists deliberately creating a strong woman icon is a mistake and considers her assertive power unnatural. Her suggestively lesbian friendship with a troupe of girls and all her bondage scenes also came under scrutiny, as did the jungle girl comics' skimpy costumes and casual racism. As Wertham's protests led to the creation of the comic industry's self-censoring Comics Code Authority, pinup jungle girls vanished as in fact did Fiction House itself. Nonetheless, Sheena graduated to television from 1955 to 56, with Irish McCalla in the title role. Even as televisions were first arriving, "Sheena reigned in the jungle and in American homes during the prim and proper Eisenhower era" (Packer 50). She made a strong impression on the repressive era. "In retrospect, Sheena may have done more than her fair share for feminism by spreading proto-feminist sentiment by the late half of the 1960s" (Packer 204).

Many superheroes followed in her legacy—not only all the Catwoman types and the two Wonder Woman nemeses Cheetah and Giganta, but also Marvel's Shanna, the She Devil (1972). Rima the Jungle Girl had her own DC Comics series in 1974 and appeared in several episodes of the *All New Superfriends Hour*. DC's Vixen channeled the abilities of beasts from elephant to eagle in *Justice League, Suicide Squad*, and other team comics and eventually joined the cast of *DC's Legends of Tomorrow* while her granddaughter and heir appeared in her own CW Seed cartoon.

Fantomah, another blonde from Jungle Comics (1940), had a dark twist, as she turned into a flaming-skulled monster when angered. Fantomah's creator Fletcher Hanks is responsible for the juxtaposition: "A reportedly troubled individual, Hanks produced complicated and bizarre creations that seemed to reflect his inner turmoil. In stories that resembled fever dreams, unearthly figures who emerged from mysterious realms and visited elaborate punishments on their enemies were the order of the day" (Morris, *Supervillains* 50). She uses her supernatural powers of chastisement, banishing villains to asteroids or transforming jewel thieves into insects. On one adventure, she demolishes an entire squadron of bomber planes by sending sandstorms and flying lions at them as her weapons. Her Medusa–like gaze admonished readers to not conflate jungle princesses with weakness.

She-Hulk in her own ripped minidress joins this trope. She rampages through the urban world, unhindered by civilization's rules. She's even called "savage" in her title, as she speaks monosyllabically. "Whereas the classic Jungle Queen narrative presents the Anglophile as outsider, She-Hulk is presented as the 'savage' who is trying to cope with the sexism embedded within civilization, which as Jen Walters she for the most part quietly endures" (Stevens 19). She stretches into the modern era, though her unrestrained monster side emphasizes how close her readers are to throwing off all traces of civilization.

In fact, these jungle and pinup girls had a lasting effect on superheroines. "The images of women with large bust sizes, slim figure, bare legs, and half-naked appearance became enormously popular after the success of Wonder Woman. Believe it or not, comic books were filled with so many sexual images of women that they were known as 'headlight comic books'—a crude and stereotypical reference to the female anatomy" (Jehanzeb). This pinup girl heritage and its popularity continued. Some comic-book heroines like Starfire or Emma Frost had costumes much more suited to strippers. Powerful She-Hulk and Supergirl showed lots of skin and fought with hair tossed back and bosoms outthrust. There were also all the incidental moments in which superheroines emerged from the shower or worse. She-Hulk apparently jump-roped nude in an issue to boost sales (though she pointedly huddled behind the comics code logo). Jessica H. Zellers in a study on this depiction found that "of the suggestively clad, partially clad, or naked individuals, about three times as many were women (296) than men" (107). From the graphic novel sample with 1,768 male characters and 786 female characters, only 6 percent of all males were suggestively clad, partially clad, or naked; while of all the females, 38 percent were suggestively clad, partially clad, or naked (qtd. in Jehanzeb). It seemed the pinup girl had permanently joined the ranks.

Fifties Ladies: Batman's Women (DC Comics: 1954–1964)

In *Wonder Women,* Lillian S. Robinson writes that, growing up in the later 1940s, "the dominant cultural message […] was precisely that awakening to womanhood meant abandoning the heroic identity of the war years for domesticity [and] motherhood" (12–13). During the war, women were encouraged to take jobs. After, American propaganda asked them to return home.

In the fifties, DC's official editorial policy dictated: "The inclusion of females in stories is specifically discouraged. Women, when used in plot structure, should be secondary in importance..." (qtd. in Madrid, *Supergirls* 77). Many superheroines suddenly blew away like crumpled leaves. Most superheroes had faded, making way for more popular monster or romance comics. The remaining superheroines of the fifties and even the sixties were ultra-feminine to the point of being caricatures. As critic Carol A. Strickland reacts: "Black Canary is less than a shadow of her man, the ultra-macho Green Arrow. The Invisible 'Girl' whimpers and complains from the nearest corner while her menfolk do the fighting. The Wasp dreams of new costumes and new hunks to pester. Supergirl cries over a broken date. These are the stalwarts of comicdom's females." In a world newly constrained by propriety, the whip-wielding Catwoman (premiering as The Cat in 1940's *Batman* #1) likewise became much softer.

> By the late 1950s, Catwoman's normative sexuality became compulsory, and seldom did she appear without relentless dialogue about domesticating Batman. In a 1967 panel of the *Batman* series, Catwoman leers over Batman and his superhero comrades, including the newly introduced female love interest, Batgirl, with the hopes of threatening Batman into matrimonial submission. As his comrades look on in fear, she seductively and assertively states to Batman, "My fate is in your hands, Batman! Am I to be the bride, or burglar? Before you answer, I must warn you that if you refuse my proposal of marriage—you doom not only yourself, but Robin and Batgirl as well!" [Whaley].

In a story from 1951 titled "The Secret Life of the Catwoman," Batman rescues his feline nemesis when she's hit on the head by a falling brick. Back in the Batcave, he discovers Catwoman has suffered from amnesia for many years and actually had the clichéd feminine job of airline stewardess. Batman shows her tapes of her criminal activities and she's appalled, emphasizing her wimpy personality. "No! No! Don't show me any more! Now I understand ... while I had amnesia, I became a criminal! Oh ... how horrible ... horrible!" she sobs (Finger). On the cover, she sobs giant tears, hands to her head as guilt overtakes her. Her dominatrix days are clearly finished.

With her memory restored, Catwoman virtuously decides she no longer wants to be a criminal. This makes an interesting feminist commentary in retrospect. Selina retires and even domesticates, as fifties women were supposed to. However, Batman continues to watch her, constantly suspicious she'll revert to crime. "This storyline can be read as a commentary on the role of women in this era, from Selina's unhappiness with her new conventional lifestyle to the lingering stigmas of the damaged woman," Tim Hanley explains in his critical work on eras of *Catwoman* (27). She selflessly works as an undercover agent for Batman, though in the end he, the hero, must save her from death. Once they round up the bad guys, Catwoman quits, saying: "That's that! From now on, I'm plain Selina Kyle! The Catwoman has retired!" With the comics code, the femme fatale completely disappeared from the comics for thirteen years.

When she returned in 1977, it was for "the supreme social event of the 1955 season" on Earth-Two, the wedding between Bruce Wayne and Selina Kyle (Levitz, *DC Super-Stars* #17). Selina Wayne retires Catwoman forever, and Bruce Wayne also hangs up the cowl and becomes a social activist.

> Kane's storyline approach allowed for a bi-lateral reading experience where single-hood and marriage could co-exist within a meta-narrative, thereby resulting in a "win-win" plot structure for male and female readers. This approach also provided simultaneous contestation and conformity to gender and sexual codes, as both characters were sexually autonomous in one universe (Gotham City), and objects of domestication in another universe (Earth Two) [Whaley].

Two years later, the couple's only child, Helena Wayne, is born. "With her mother's beauty and both her parents' sharp minds," she's a debutant in pink gown and updo. Helena plans to attend Harvard and become an attorney. However, tragedy strikes.

Selina receives a phone call from one of Catwoman's former henchmen, Silky Cernak. "I finally got my butt out of the slammer … where you put me when you squealed!" Newly free, he takes his revenge through blackmail. To keep her family safe, Selina agrees to do a final job as Catwoman. Selina and her former gang break into the Gotham Civic Center to steal some rare gems. Commissioner Gordon calls up Batman, and at Helena's suggestion, Bruce dons his Batman costume one more time. As he fights Cernak, a stray bullet from the man's gun hits Selina, and she dies in Bruce's arms, insisting she did it all for him. "Catwoman's role was one of romance and drama, but it all started with her death" (Hanley, *Catwoman* 73). That night, a distraught Bruce burns his Batman costume. Helena, however, creates a black and purple suit for herself with a pointy mask and cape. At her mother's grave, Helena vows, "I swear I'll dedicate my life and inheritance to bringing your killer to justice … and to fighting all criminals!" This story shows an unusual retirement for both Batman and Catwoman and a happy family life before (as with Batman's origin story) the sudden shooting of a parent forces the child into costume to clean up the streets. The formerly fierce Catwoman is sacrificed, while Earth-2's Batman survives to parent Helena and also becomes Police Commissioner.

The original Batwoman, Kathy Kane, arrived in *Detective Comics* #233 (1956) as a love interest for Batman (Wertham had also alleged quite a lot about Batman and Robin's relationship). An heiress and circus aerialist, Kathy had a purse of feminized gadgets like charm bracelet handcuffs, tear gas perfume, and flaming hairspray. Grant Morrison writes: "Batwoman detoured the image of the atom age housewife by packing her handbag with laser lipsticks and dainty cologne sprays that could chemically castrate you there on the spot. Kathy Kane was the weaponization of the Stepford Wife, the Avon lady as a Special Forces commando: pixie boots, fringed leather gloves, high-gloss lipstick so red it was jet black and reflective" (77). With her yellow leotard primly buttoned, "the whole effect was matronly rather than menacing" (Madrid, *Supergirls* 59).

Her origin is also problematic as she becomes so obsessed with Batman, she's determined to one-up him. Thus, she fashions costume, gadgets, and secret hideout, all to copy him. As she shows off on the trapeze, she thinks moonily, "But I wish I could be like Batman, the greatest acrobat of all! He uses his skill, not for shows, but against crime!" (Hamilton).

They race to the same heist, where Batman cries, "This is no place for a girl—please let me handle it!" As he protests hypocritically, "Batwoman, to you this is just a thrill—you don't realize that fighting crime is a dangerous business." Batman finally uses his detective skills to find her base. He then points out that criminals could find her too, so she should give up the superhero business. "I—I never thought of that! I guess you're right! I—I'll quit my career as Batwoman," Kathy says, submitting for the present (Hamilton). Still, Kathy returns in *Batman* #116, telling him that "a lady has a right to change her mind." Thereafter, Batman spends all his time trying to get her to quit, while she spends hers trying to corral him into marriage and needing rescue after rescue. Theoretically, she was meant to attract girls to comics, and to reassure male readers that Batman had female love interests after Wertham outed him and Robin. In fact, she fell flat.

If her only purpose was to wed Batman, then all her superheroics appeared mating displays, attempts to show off only to get a man. Batman played it aloof, leaving him running from her chasing and often being quite heartless about it. In *Batman* #153 (1963), Batwoman responds to impending doom by pledging her love to Batman, and he reciprocates. When they are saved, however, he insists it was all a lie. "It was as if all the sublimated resentment of fifties men, home from the excitement of the war to the nine-to-five and to ticky-tacky houses in suburbia, seethed between the covers" (Morrison 67).

Kathy also provided competition in the Batfamily dynamic. The cover of *Batman* #122 (1959) announces "The Marriage of Batman and Batwoman" with the happy couple leaving the church arm in arm. Batman tells her his secret identity but fails to make her retire. "A wife's place is in the home!" he insists, but Kathy retorts, "A wife's place is with her husband!" Afterwards, in a fight with crooks, her cowl gets pulled off, exposing her true identity to the crooks and allowing them to deduce Batman's. "Kathy, do you know what you've done?" Robin shrieks. "You've wrecked Batman's career! He's finished,

Kathy—and it's all your fault because you wouldn't listen!" As it turns out in the end, the whole story was Robin's fantasy. However, his protest, "Gosh! What'll become of me now?" emphasized that a married superhero would discard his single guy friends, thus making women the enemy (Finger). Alfred has a few similar fantasies, and all of them see Batman and Batwoman quietly retiring, as love replaces superheroism.

Further, she fails at female solidarity. When both Batwoman and reporter Vicki Vale are nominated Gotham City's "Woman of the Year" in *Batman* #119, the pair spend the comics trying to upstage each other so that they win. "There's nothing more explosive than two jealous women competing for the same man—especially when that man is Batman!" the beginning caption proclaims. Apparently, part of the prize is a date with the Caped Crusader. "Those jealous girls are sure to get themselves in trouble, trying to outdo each other, Batman!" Robin comments. With the help of Batman and Robin, both women capture a vicious gang and thus are co-crowned. They even share the Batman date and end the comic squabbling over who gets the first dance. "Poor Batman! They won, but he lost," Robin thinks (Finger).

The similar "Beware of—Poison Ivy" from *Batman* #181 (1966) introduces the lady in green. Jealous of World Public Enemies 1–3 because they're so beautiful, Poison Ivy decoys Dragon Fly, Silken Spider, and Tiger Moth over, and gives them a crown to fight over, which they do. Ivy also invites Bruce and Batman to come battle for her favor. Of course, Batman defeats her, amid condescending comments with Robin about how she's a "doll" for rounding up so many criminals through her misguided vanity. In the end, Ivy's self-indulgent competition results in the men putting her behind bars (Kanigher).

As the series progresses, Alfred is killed off to lessen the male-only environment, and Dick's "Aunt Harriet" arrives in the same issue, *Detective Comics* #328 (1964), to take care of the "helpless youngsters" and "little boys" at Wayne Manor. She also performs antics like installing hidden cameras in chandeliers to try to discover Batman's secret—since unlike Alfred, she's out of the loop. This sidelines her and makes it clear she's a lesser replacement. In 1966, she joined the television show, played by Madge Blake. She hand-wrings and stutters through the first and second seasons.

Batman #139 (1961) brings in Kathy's niece, Betty Kane, who calls herself Bat-Girl long before Barbara Gordon. After discovering Aunt Kathy's secret, she sews a red and green costume with a flared miniskirt that matches her aunt's or Robin's bright colors, and she's off. Instantly, the adults consider manipulation and trickery to get rid of the annoying girl. "Betty's bright and she learns quickly—but she's also very headstrong! What can I say to dissuade her?" Batwoman moans.

"Gosh, Batman—an inexperienced girl is bound to get hurt pursuing crooks—" insists youthful Robin. Inspired, Batman proposes they only pretend to consider letting her be Bat-Girl and stall her with training until she has to go home (Finger).

She is intended as a love interest for Robin, of course, but the twelve-year-old sidekick is wholly uninterested. Though a young teen, she is more mature emotionally than he is, as per the gender roles of the day, while he reacts to her advances like a scared boy. Meanwhile Bat-Girl is even more aggressive in her romantic pursuit than her aunt—sometimes she literally throws herself into Robin's arms. In a wimpy antifeminist spin, she often faints or acts helpless to catch the bad guys by surprise.

In *Batman* #144's "Bat-Mite Meets Bat-Girl" (1961), Robin is informed that he must spend a whole week alone with her, and gasps in horror. "Oh no! That's all I need.... Bat-Girl hounding me wherever I go!"

"Sigh! Working with you is what I've always dreamed of! Oh Robin—I think you're just adorable!" she cries, kissing him as he freezes in terror. To try to get rid of her, he actually says he has feelings for another woman, leaving her going off in jealous tears. With Bat-Mite's help, Bat-Girl creates the conflict of the comic, staging a tiger escape and recapture to impress Robin. In the midst of her ploys, however, she's actually kidnapped and foolishly believes the thugs are sent by Bat-Mite to help her.

After, Robin realizes his actions are destructive, so he shows her a statue of Justice and reveals this is his true love. As he adds, "You see, Batman has often told me that his crime-fighting career is a full-time job, and that he can't risk a big romance now—not until he's ready to retire. If Batman can make that kind of sacrifice, I guess I'm man enough to do it too." Lies upon lies cast Robin as truly desperate to escape the pushy female.

To Robin's horror, Batman announces that Robin is too young to make such a decision. "Oh, Robin! Then it's all right for me to kiss you now!" she cries and does (Finger). The silly, pushy girl has won the day. She's a romantic bully, dismaying Robin out of any interest in girls.

The "New Look" of 1964 discarded the Kanes without explanation, to the relief of many. They were reimagined around The New 52 as the much stronger Batwoman, ex-military lesbian Kate Kane, and her cousin Flamebird.

Silver Age Wimps: The Wasp (Marvel Comics, 1963–1970)

Marvel Comics was fundamental in reinventing the concept of superheroes—"heroes with problems"—but its initial wave of superheroines still preserved the concept of women in roles shaped by patriarchal standards. The Invisible Girl premiered in *Fantastic Four* #1 (1961) and was shy and often endangered. The telekinetic Marvel Girl (a.k.a. Jean Grey), first seen in *X-Men* #1 (1963), was mostly a love interest for X-Man

Silver Age Wimps

Cyclops, and the self-absorbed Wasp, the only woman in Marvel's Avengers, was an affluent fashion plate who loved to shop … and the all-new Batgirl, a high-kicking 1967 addition to both the *Batman* comics and TV show, who allowed a run in her tights to distract her from helping Batman and Robin. These characters may have put females back in action roles, but their dependent and/or indecisive personalities rooted them in stereotypical behavior [Misiroglu 535].

Though the sixties has superheroines, none of them really broke out. It was British television spy Emma Peel who made a place for action heroines in the world.

Stan Lee introduced the Silver Age with his team comics: *The Fantastic Four, X-Men,* and *The Avengers.* These each began with one woman among a small group of men. The Silver Age is said to have lasted through the seventies, ending, according to many fans, when Gwen Stacy's shocking death in 1973 signaled darker stories ahead. With new serialized stories instead of one-offs, comics stars became more complex. The Marvel characters bickered like real families and had personal problems like addiction, in contrast to the too-perfect Superman. They also crossed into each other's stories in what became a Marvel staple.

Ant-Man arrived in *Tales to Astonish* #27 (January 1962). In this, Doctor Henry Pym discovers a serum that can shrink whatever it touches and an antidote as well. He tests it on himself, shrinks to ant size, and has glorious adventures among the ants, in a story that blends monster and superhero comics. Eight issues later, he adds a costume and tackles villains, as he chooses to make himself a classic superhero. *Tales to Astonish* #44 (June 1963) added the Wasp, in a red and black suit that mirrored his own. Ant-Man finds a true partner in Janet Van Dyne, the daughter of a famous gamma rays scientist. She gets points for not being called Ant-Girl like so many parallel characters were in the Golden Age. The cover even shows him slumping as she drags him to safety.

Hank Pym begins the comic mourning his dead wife Maria yet determined to do good. On meeting Janet, he thinks, disturbingly, "She looks somewhat like Maria! But she's much younger! Not much more than a child!" He dismisses the frivolous daughter, trying instead to work with her scientist father. When the latter pulls a creature from the planet Kosmos to earth, it vows to enslave mankind and kills him. Frightened, Janet runs to Hank for help. Hank dismisses her again, thinking, "Those bored society playgirls are all alike!"

When Janet arrives, however, she decides to devote her life to investigating the truth of her father's death. She declares, "I wish I could help track down all the criminals, the human wolves who prey on honest people! I suppose you think I'm just a foolish female, but…"

Hank decides, "The bored flighty shell she wore is gone! She has determination, strength of character! I wonder if she...." He invites her to become his partner and offers to implant her with synthetic cells that will give her wings and antennae. She dons one of his costumes (with a tunic top and oddly pointy cap) and they rush off together. His technology, his costume—she is a Pygmalion damsel he has shaped into the perfect partner. As they fly, she says, "Ant-Man.... I think you're *wonderful*! I want you to know, in case this creature kills us, as it did my father, I–I'm falling in love with you." This of course, gives him all the power between them while she assumes the classic damsel role. He in turn rejects her, insisting he's too consumed by his wife's loss to love a child (Lee, *Tales to Astonish* #44). With this, they start off on a painfully unequal footing.

The Ant-Man/Wasp stories, though a regular feature, never really sold well, so Lee and Kirby decided to team them up with other heroes, and they joined the Avengers. There, Wasp was the token female (and girlfriend!) until the arrival of Scarlet Witch and Quicksilver (twins, not love interests) and then Black Widow and Hawkeye (love interests, but she's arguably dominant). In the Avengers, the running joke involves Janet pursuing Hank, desperate for marriage, while he puts her off. For the team's only female, this is a painful agenda, emphasizing how much all superheroines must desperately long for marriage. She's also a flirt, constantly gushing about Thor's attractiveness to make Hank jealous. She finally marries Hank, but only while he has amnesia, emphasizing how she'll prey on his vulnerability to force him into marriage (*Avengers* #60). It's the Kane women all over again.

The archetype of the Waif is pure, trusting, kind, impressionable, passive, and insecure. This character inspires others to want to save her and is generally content to let herself be rescued. Certainly, the Wasp is a superhero. However, her insectlike fragility easily links her to this imagery. In her free time, she's an heiress and girlfriend, more princess than self-made superhero. While on the Avengers, Janet is vain and superficial, standing out for how she changes costumes constantly. Her day-job as a designer is shallow and diminutizing. In Barbara Brownie's *The Superhero Costume (Dress, Body, Culture)*, she considers Wasp's obsession as metaphor:

> Justified by the profession of her alter ego as a fashion designer. The Wasp's costume has undergone more frequent transformations than any other. During the 1970s, a new costume was designed for the character in every issue of *The Avengers*. Nearly 300 of her numerous costumes were collected for a gallery which spanned three full pages of *Secret Invasion: Requiem* (2009). Richard Reynolds (1992, p. 29) observes how these frequent changes were permissible only because the character was a woman. The changes were "an expression of her femininity" as well as a "submission" of sorts to the gender stereotypes of the period during which her character was most active: the 1960s and 1970s. She was often depicted as the archetypal 1960s glamour girl, with a fashionable haircut that changed almost as frequently as her costume. Costume is, for these female superheroes as it is for many in the real

world, "a mechanism for constructing and reconstructing a sense of self" (Kaiser et al., 1991, p. 167). Following Edward Sapir's (1985, p. 375) exploration of fashion, Wonder Woman and The Wasp's keenness for costume change may reflect a "restlessness and curiosity" that arises only in "functionally powerful societies" [100].

Continuing this trend, Wasp wilts when Hank turns violent and abusive in *Avengers* #212–214 (1981). Nonetheless, she cheerfully supports him, insisting she loves him and begging him to open up even as he unleashes a monster on the Avengers and hits her in the face. In front of the Avengers, she finally removes her sunglasses to reveal a black eye. She ends the arc by leaving him, but insists she pities him rather than hating him.

Other comic contemporaries of the Wasp received a similar sidelining. Pow-Girl (Rosie Raymond) from 1967's *Mighty Comics* #43, is the wife of the Web, and responds to her worries for his safety by costuming herself. This seems heroic, but in fact, she and her mother regularly nag the hero at home, fussing that he'll get killed and leave Rose a widow. "Billed as 'the Hen-Pecked Hero,' the Web faced battles both on the streets and in the home," writes Jon Morris in *The Legion of Regrettable Superheroes* (181). Thus Rose, with black fringed leotard and blonde beehive, swoops in. She's taken gymnastics and martial arts and is prepared for any challenge. The Web admires his mysterious new partner, gushing with compliments. However, Pow-Girl decides to test her husband's love and tells him, "I think you and I have the makings of a great crime-fighting team! Shall we seal our new partnership with a kiss?" The horrified hero flees, passing the test but only after establishing his wife's nasty side. As it happened, this was Pow-Girl's solo appearance, as the Web continued without his wife as partner.

Long before Chris Claremont created the reality-altering Dark Phoenix, Jean Grey was simple and sweet. *X-Men* #1 (1963) begins by Professor X announcing to the boys of the school that their new student will be "a most attractive young lady." When she comes in, the guys hang out the window and excitedly chatter, "A redhead! Look at that face ... and the rest of her" and call her "a living doll." She arrives in knee-length bunchy skirt, gloves, hat, scarf, and modestly buttoned coat—a prim and proper young lady. On the spot, Professor X names her Marvel Girl as the boys tease that she has "one very obvious power ... the power to make a man's heart beat faster." While Cyclops, Beast, Angel, and Iceman all look abnormal to some degree. Jean Grey's mental powers are invisible, leaving her conventionally attractive. As her abilities echo the professor's but not as strong, she is the only one who contributes nothing new to the team. This is a school story, but it's more concerned with everyone hitting on the new girl than it is with supercrimes.

In a touch of women's lib, Jean pulls out her own chair with telepathy, showing off her powers. However, the young men won't leave her alone, coming into her room as she's just finished dressing to admire how she's been "poured into that uniform" (admittedly a head-to-toe unitard much like theirs). Hank suddenly kisses her cheek and in response she lifts him into the air. Certainly, Jean can defend herself, but it's disturbing that her patronizing teammates cross the line on first meeting her. "I hope I wasn't too rough on the poor dear," she fusses, accepting his minor assault as commonplace for a pretty girl at a superpowered school.

> Although the heroines joined teams, they were still often depicted as frivolous characters: the Invisible Girl was given to fits of hysterics and fainting spells when using her power. Marvel Girl would often faint when she tried to use her gifts. The Wasp spent a lot of time powdering her nose. Wonder Woman was even made the secretary of the Justice League. It took nearly forty years for Zatanna and Batgirl to break away from their male counterparts and finally hold their own titles. Other superheroines (Shrinking Violet, Light Lass, and Wonder Girl, for example) were not so lucky, and faded into obscurity when their team titles failed [Florence 50].

Stan Lee invented his first of these women, Sue Storm, to be a superhero and equal to her fiancé Reed Richards in 1961. Nonetheless, she was "Invisible Girl" with powers much like Jean's, indicative of her personality as a whole. "As is the case with the other fantastics, her particular superpower is an extension of her salient premutation qualities. Sue Storm was a distinctly—almost pathologically—shy and retiring girl" (Robinson 88–89). Stuller comments that she "perfectly illustrates the tensions inherent in cultural responses to the second wave of feminism. She was a contradiction—a superwoman whose power is the ability to be unseen" (33). She is so shy in her first appearances, that, invited to a government dinner in their honor, Sue whimpers, "Oh, Reed, I—I'm afraid to go! I'm not used to meeting all those important people! I'm liable to get so flustered that before I know it, I might vanish in front of their eyes? If that ever happened, I'd simply die of embarrassment!" (Lee, *Fantastic Four* #7). Feminist comics historian Trina Robbins observes: "Unlike the insecurities and self-doubts that afflicted male heroes, and which encouraged the reader's identification and evoked admiration when the heroes overcame them, Sue Storm's ... flaws were almost a caricature of Victorian notions of the feminine, an invisible woman who faints when she tries to exert herself" (*The Great Women Superheroes* 114). Early on, the Sub-Mariner kidnaps her repeatedly to be his underwater bride, making her the damsel in their dynamic. True, she is a superhero, not just a "girlfriend," but she often needs rescue all the same.

At the time and after, rumblings of discontent were appearing. For Sue Storm, in the satirical flashback comic *Unstable Molecules* by James Sturm and Guy Davis, superheroism means a life of supporting Reed Richards while he ignores her to the point that she might as well be invisible. He insists she throw a party for his professor friends. As she gets her younger brother off to school, she is trapped in Friedan's *The Feminine Mystique*, a world in which supporting the men in her life while playing housewife isn't nearly enough. While Sue rescues her brother from jail, listens to neighbor complaints, and prepares the house, her brother's beloved comic heroine Vapor Girl voices her suppressed desires. Sue crumples in misery and Vapor Girl demands, "Why don't I fight?" Sue dons makeup and pretty clothes. "I force myself to clean the house. Make party platters," Sue thinks while Vapor Girl still insists, "If I can't rejoin my body soon…. I'll disappear completely." As she awaits party guests and the absent Reed, Sue thinks, "An epiphany: this feeling I have, this anxious feeling of waiting and dread. I feel this way always." Unfortunately, there is no perfect solution for the shifting gender roles of the era, and the characters, like real women, must muddle on their own towards a balance.

Batgirl (Yvonne Craig) starred in season three of 1966's *Batman* television show, and her start is one of helpless damsel … a bit too obviously. Penguin kidnaps Barbara, ties her up, and calls the heroes to taunt them. He intends to marry her, not for herself, but to become the "son-in-law of the police commissioner." Though she remains uncowed, arguing angrily with Penguin, her position as the clichéd damsel, not even valued for herself, weakens her. However, she sneaks out the window and gets home, where she changes into a purple Batsuit of her own. Without Bruce's millions or inventor training, she has fashioned herself striking gadgets and a batcycle. Thus armed, she rushes in and helps the men, fighting capably beside them. "I was glad for the chance to join in the fun," Batgirl says modestly to the dynamic duo when, puzzled, they compliment her skills. (She fights with a ballerina's kicks, as hitting was deemed unladylike.) Yvonne Craig noted that the show added Batgirl because "they needed someone who could encourage an over-40 male audience and a prepubescent female audience" (Cavna). Her outfit was just as campy as the heroes' looks: "In the show, Batgirl wore a super-envy-inducing sparkly purple costume. It looked more comic-booky than even the comics version, which was a more standard black-and-yellow crime-fighting catsuit" (Nicholson 97).

Still, while she might have been eye-candy, her other placement as a role-model for girls shouldn't be ignored. *Batgirl* writer Gail Simone called Craig her "first real-life hero" (Cavna). It's also notable that she brings a self-aware playfulness to her role. After saving the day alongside Alfred, Barbara manages a quick change, appearing in the sack she was supposedly tied in all this time, complete with wedding dress. "I'm sorry to be so helpless," she says sweetly as Batman and Robin free her. With this, much like fifties Supergirl, she models a smart, capable teen who nonetheless must manipulate men into taking all the hero credit. Though women were slowly taking their place in the workforce, fiction cautioned them to avoid seeming competitive.

Superheroines Onscreen: Wonder Woman (TV, 1975–1979)

For many fans, Wonder Woman is Lynda Carter, spinning into her corset and starry underpants, and running off to fight crime. The 1975 show was a hit, appearing amidst *Electra Woman and Dyna Girl*, *The Bionic Woman*, and a Spider-Woman cartoon. Of these, *Wonder Woman* was the most popular and continues to have a large following. Actress Lynda Carter notes, "It's really since *Wonder Woman* went off the air that the appreciation for what that was has grown and continues to grow to this day" ("Beauty, Brawn, and Bulletproof Bracelets").

Wonder Woman relied on several trailblazers. The first and quite likely the most influential was the British spy show *The Avengers*. Emma Peel, played by Diana Rigg, was the tough yet feminine karate-chopping crime fighter in a slinky black catsuit—soon after, comics Black Widow changed her look to the same. Following this came other television action women: detective Honey West, Catwoman and Batgirl on *Batman*, Lt. Uhura on *Star Trek*. Starting in 1973, Pam Grier as Coffy and Foxy Brown dominated the Blaxploitation films with a witty tongue and powerful fighting skills. *The Secrets of Isis* (originally just called *Isis*, 1975–1977) was beloved around this time, sharing its hour with the similar live-action children's show *Shazam*. Both featured the hero transforming with a magic word. "The series quickly became the highest rated program of Saturday morning TV, in no small part because of actress Joanna Cameron's charms," John Kenneth Muir explains in *The Encyclopedia of Superheroes on Film and Television* (305).

Wonder Woman arrived in 1975, with *The Bionic Woman* and *Charlie's Angels* following the next year. "These expanding television roles, reflecting as they did a new acceptance of women as possessed of both real and fantastical powers, shadow the changes taking place in society. Women in the 1970s enjoyed greater opportunities than at any previous time in history" (Knight 4). Certainly, the shows reflected the rise of feminism even as they bolstered it. As the series' executive producer Douglas S. Cramer observed, "Wonder Woman came along at a time in the 1970s that was absolutely right ... [when] the women's movement was hitting its stride, where feminism and all that it conveyed was exploding across the country" ("Beauty, Brawn and Bulletproof Bracelets"). The show appeared shortly after Gloria Steinem's public support of the character, as a new face for feminism as well as a salute to the empowerment the forties comic heroine has brought to so many young readers.

Her season one origin story paralleled her original forties comics one, though the Greek mythology largely vanished. This time, it wasn't gifts of the gods that gave the Amazons their power, but the superior technology of the metal Feminum. "On Paradise Island there are only women. Because of this pure environment, we are able to develop our minds and our physical skills, unhampered by masculine destructiveness," Wonder Woman explains ("Fausta, the Nazi Wonder Woman," 103). This Wonder Woman isn't unique, and even has a little sister with the same powers. This twist in the storyline emphasizes that women can become superheroes through education, training, and science—not magic. Their Amazons (though dressed in silky nighties from the looks of it) are competent, strong, and loving, treating one another with mutual respect and kindness.

Carter's Wonder Woman is gorgeous but also competent and saves the day with clever solutions as well as brute force. She persuades her female enemies like Paula Von Gunther and "Fausta the Nazi Wonder Woman" that they should abandon the misogynistic Nazis. She's a blatant feminist and valued for it. In the first episode, she uses phrases like "You obviously have little regard for womanhood. You must learn respect!" and "Women are the wave of the future, and sisterhood is stronger than anything!"

Men around her come around to her way of thinking too. When someone quips, "You see what you get when you trust a woman?" Sixties character Colonel Steve Trevor, Jr., retorts, "Yeah, you get the job done" ("Light-Fingered Lady," 213). In this, she built on the values the forties comic had offered. "She had the effect on the male viewers that Marston wanted his Wonder Woman to have—they were initially attracted to her by her beauty, and later learned to respect her for her intelligence, spirit, personality, and good deeds," notes Marc DiPaolo in his book on Wonder Woman criticism (166). Of course, this too had its place in the society of the time.

> Television series in the mid-to-late 1970s attempted to capitalize on the feminist movement, and several shows featured women in genre roles that were strong in spirit, if stereotypically feminine in appearance. This meant devising a way to appeal to the changing social consciousness of women viewers while not alienating men. The solution was the Kick-Ass Babe—a talented and capable woman whose beauty deflected the focus from her otherwise transgressive acts. Women could identify with—or aspire to be—these lovely ladies, while men would not be threatened by depiction of female independence, as they would instead be focused on the eye candy [Stuller 44].

Certainly, the show had its ridiculous side, with the former Miss America hurling large objects and carrying Steve Trevor. Aliens and monsters invaded. Of course, "the fantastic storylines assured viewers that this type of strong woman did not exist in reality" (Brown, *Dangerous Curves* 154)—she was only a fantasy figure. Her strength and beauty were both exaggerated enough to be ironic. "On the surface they may have been just as strong as the men, but the campy aesthetics and the insistent hyper-sexualization of the actresses implies that these dangerous women are still merely sex objects"

(Brown, *Dangerous Curves* 154). Wonder Woman could be admired but also laughed away and dismissed as the former Miss America lifted objects ten times her size. The bathing suit costume was the campiest element, of course. In the special "Beauty, Brawn, and Bulletproof Bracelets," Carter herself remarked that it "felt like a second skin. I really didn't feel too self-conscious oddly. Maybe I should have but, you know, don't forget, this was the 'ban the bra' time, this was sexual freedom, this was bikinis and midriffs and that was the timing and I really wasn't thinking of being sexy either." Occasionally, she mixed the costume up, adding a Wonder Wet Suit, a Wonder Biker costume, a Wonder Skateboard suit, and a cape for visiting the White House. All these costumes not only covered her up more but emphasized that she could compete in masculine arenas.

After the first season, ABC let the show lapse. Luckily, CBS picked it up and it ran two more seasons, updated to contemporary times as a spy thriller. While cheesy and remarkably seventies in feel, it was a fun show that still holds up well in modern times. Today, it still delights, even with its walking contradiction of strong, sexy Wonder Woman.

Antiheroine: Elektra (Marvel Comics, 1981–1994)

"By the dawn of comics' Modern Age (1980–present), Americans had experienced decades of racial disharmony, the bloody and unpopular Vietnam War, and a U.S. president who resigned in disgrace. The conventional 'to the rescue' superhero was now passé to Americans who had buttressed themselves behind a wall of cynicism. To better relate to changing mores and become more believable in a dystopian world, the crime fighter took on traits of the criminal" (Misiroglu and Eury 244). Punisher, Wolverine, Cable and Barb Wire were popular in this darker, tougher era. The Bronze Age had begun.

> At the time of her debut in late 1980, Elektra defied the stereotype of the classic superheroine, that prim, altruistic mighty maid of previous decades who had slipped into cliché. Elektra was a female character unlike anything comic-book readers had seen before: Determined, self-assured, and vicious, she chose not to veil her identity behind a mask or alter ego—she was Elektra, the assassin—nothing more, nothing less. Although she was a killer, Elektra was a symbol of empowerment: *Women no longer have to be victims,* her actions spoke. Miller may have been "simply" creating a femme fatale with Elektra, but in the process he redefined the superheroine for the 1980s and beyond [Misiroglu].

In *Daredevil* #168 (1981), Frank Miller's Elektra explodes onto the scene as she threatens a man into helping her collect a bounty. When Daredevil picks up on her presence, he flashes back to the political science debutante with her hefty bodyguard. For a year, they are deeply in love. Then she and her father the ambassador are held hostage, and in the course of it, her father is killed. Elektra turns deadly. She quits college and tells him, "I used to love the world. Now I can't ever let it touch me. Ever again."

"Often, toughness indicates that a character has been warped or twisted by some awful event in her life, conveying the message that a woman may be tough, but only if toughness is forced upon her," Sherrie A. Inness notes in *Tough Girls: Women Warriors and Wonder Women in Popular Culture* (150). It's the loss of her father that drives her to become an assassin. "The book presents this move as less than positive and portrays Elektra as running away from her grief, rather than addressing it. Because feelings are associated with women, Elektra is also running away from her femininity" (Innes 150). Meanwhile, she is fallible and less powerful than Daredevil, emphasizing the action woman as a lesser partner and unequal match. She finds a new purpose as a bounty hunter, selling her services without conscience. Now, as Matt thinks, "She's everything I despise," he decides she's "a bitter, lonely woman striking back at the world that robbed her of her father."

Of course, the comic is told from Daredevil's point of view, giving him imperfect insights into the femme fatale he admires. She ends up a striking archetype but a superficial one: "Unlike the earlier heroines who strove to find love, Elektra eliminated emotions from her life to shield herself from the tragedies she had endured. What was left was a grim, emotionally crippled, but incredibly sexy murderer—the ultimate belle dame sans merci" (Madrid, *Supergirls* 226). From *Daredevil* #168 (1981) through *Daredevil* #190 (1983), her story is one of death, resurrection, and faith, though more for her lover Matt Murdock than herself. Their romance, while tempestuous, is doomed as Daredevil refuses to give up on his altruism and Elektra on her vengeance and bloodlust. Netflix's *Daredevil* Season 2, with Élodie Yung starring, has a similar dynamic and plot arc for the characters, though here Elektra's internal struggle is even more dampened as she plays the voice of sin and temptation for Matt. Her actress adds:

> We think Elektra is a sociopath. This world is a game for her. It's like a chess game, and what motivates her is what she wants. She'll use anything she needs to use to get to her goal, and if she needs to kill people, she will. She has this coldness in her, and I tried to keep that. But on the other hand, we wanted to create a character with different layers. I think Elektra isn't a bad person, but she's not a good person. She's a person with different traits, with layers, and she's seeking who she is. In this season, there's an arc to her story. Hopefully, she'll find we'll find out who she is, by the end of it [Radish].

Meanwhile, the graphic novel *Elektra: Assassin* (1986) details the girl's life from birth, though in a child's voice with colorful images and fairytale names like Agamemnon. In this, her mother was shot as she was born but her father raised her as a black belt in karate. The adult Elektra has vague memories of being raped by her father as a five-year-old. She remains uncertain whether this was a false memory, and her life is filled with dark visions and disturbing flashbacks. Thus, she grows up cut off from emotion and family.

In his essay, "Sexuality, and Toughness: The Bad Girls of Action Film and Comic Books," Jeffery A. Brown argues of the bad girl in film and comic books, "One the one hand, she represents a potentially transgressive figure capable of expanding the popular perception of women's roles and abilities; on the other, she runs the risk of reinscribing strict gender binaries and of being nothing more than sexist window-dressing for the predominantly male audience" (47). This era brought forth a new kind of toughness for its heroines, especially those onscreen:

> If the physically powerful heroines of the 1960s and 1970s television series married images of toughness with the conventional trappings of glamorous and sexualized femininity [*The Avengers, Wonder Woman, The Bionic Woman, Charlie's Angels*], then the cinematic action heroines emerging from the 1980s—exemplified by Ripley (Sigourney Weaver) in *Aliens* (1986) and Sarah Connor (Linda Hamilton) in *Terminator 2* (1991)—represented an aesthetic shift towards what Tasker [in Spectacular Bodies] describes as "musculinity" [Munford and Walters 111].

In a flashback to her training in *Daredevil* #190, Elektra trains with Stick's monks, but Stick tells her, "You ain't clean. Yer full of *pain* and *hate*. All you've learned is how to *use* the pain. There's no place for you here. So go." He tells her that, as with the mythic Elektra, her relationship with her father is everything to her.

> It was your father, Elektra. You loved him too *dearly*, and he held you too *closely*. He built for you a small, safe *world* that you loved. Your dream in college was to *serve* the world. But alas, that world was a fabrication—ripped down by the senseless, pointless murder of your father. You see the world now as a chaotic place, huge and terrible. You hate it.

Nonetheless, Elektra refuses to give up. She insists she'll infiltrate the Hand and defeat them, using her warrior powers in the name of good. She passes their test … by killing her own sensei. Thus, she continues on her mission, though she's haunted by guilt and "a peace she will never know." Over and over, she chooses evil and violence, cementing her image as the truly damaged villainess.

When Matt confronts her in *Daredevil* #175, she remains cold. "In college we were lovers. Now we are enemies. It is that simple." Even more coldly calculating, she thinks at the end that if she leaves him bleeding, he'll likely die "And Elektra would finally be free of him, as well." Nonetheless she keeps helping, following Matt and backing him up in secret. In #181, she escalates, kidnapping Matt's poor bumbling best friend Foggy Nelson and threatening to kill him. He recognizes her and, unable to remain cold at his confusion, she lets him go. Just after this act of redemption, Bullseye stabs her and she crawls home to die in Matt's arms.

The Hand plots to resurrect her in #190, and Daredevil interrupts the ceremony. His partner Stone reveals that Daredevil's love has purged her of the hatred racing through her. "She ... is clean. It was Murdock. Somehow, in his futile effort to revive her, he has purged her," he thinks (Miller, *Daredevil* #190). However, by cleansing her this way, the fascination is gone as well. She vanishes for years, and finally reclaims her villainy.

Bronze Age Fridging: The Killing Joke (DC Comics, 1988)

As the eighties introduced harsher, grittier comics, some reflected a darker artistic world, intertwined with misogyny and violence. "Mainstream fashion magazines offered fashion spreads with women in straitjackets, yanked by the neck with choke collars, and packed, nude, into a plastic trash bag. Fashion ads in the same vein proliferated," explains journalist Susan Faludi (205).

Faludi attributed the cause of these negative portrayals of women to the rise of conservative values, both religious and political in the United States of the time. The "New Right" was eager to dismantle feminist ideals. "Reagan was the first president to oppose the [Equal Rights Amendment] since Congress passed it—and the first ever to back a 'Human Life Amendment' banning abortion and even some types of birth control" (248). Within a year the number of women working in government jobs had dropped, with the number of women on the White House staff down over fifty percent (269).

The year of 1988 likewise had many darker comics that deconstructed the sugary world of superheroes and even turned antifeminist. One of these, famously, crippled Barbara Gordon—Batgirl. "Fan and critical discourses have established the novel as a precursor to the ultra-violent spectacles of the 1990s and later, with Barbara's victimization representing both the revealed misogynist underbelly of superhero narratives as well as the start to her journey as Oracle, the genre's most developed disabled hero," explains José Alaniz in *Death, Disability, and the Superhero* (292). Feminist comic creator and critic Gail Simone included Barbara's paralysis at the top of her list of "major female characters that had been killed, mutilated, and depowered," famously naming them "Women in Refrigerators" in reference to Green Lantern's finding his girlfriend Alexandra DeWitt dead and mutilated in the fridge in 1994. This storyline, like many others, became all about the central hero, emphasizing that the girlfriend's or sidekick's pain only mattered as it hurt the male character. Critic Jeffrey A. Brown likewise described *The Killing Joke* as an example of the "relatively unequal violence [female characters] are subjected to" in the comics industry (*Dangerous Curves* 175).

Spider-Man's girlfriend Gwen Stacy's famous death in 1973 not only shocked readers but is said to have launched the Bronze Age, a harsher era of comics in which beloved characters could die and heroes fail to save them. Further, many comics writers repeated it to heighten angst and dismiss characters, especially flimsy girlfriends:

> Many writers saw the impact of Gwen's death and co-opted the basic idea of killing a girlfriend to create instant drama and motivation for their characters. On Simone's list of female characters who have been killed or maimed as male-character plot devices, only one died before 1973; the Doom Patrol's Elasti-girl, who heroically sacrificed herself with the team to save a small town in *Doom Patrol* #121 (1968) [Gianola and Coleman 261].

Characters who weren't pulling their weight could be dramatically removed from comics, creating angst and excitement in place of dreary storylines. In 1985's game changing *Crisis on Infinite Earths,* when Superman loses his powers, his young cousin Supergirl senses his pain and charges in to carry on Superman's legacy, thinking, "I may not be as good as he is, but Kal always taught me to do my *best.* Nothing else matters. Be true to yourself ... be the best you are able to ... don't ever give anything *but* your best." All her life she has lived by her cousin's ideals, and now it's time to put them to the test. The Anti-Monitor turns on Superman to utterly destroy him, and Supergirl says, "You're not going to kill Superman. I won't allow it! You hear me?!" She destroys the AntiMonitor yet at a terrible price. Dying, she tells Superman, "It's okay. I knew what I was doing. I wanted ... wanted you to be safe.... You mean so much to me ... so much to the world" (Wolfman). Her death here is heroic and filled with agency, though again mostly aimed towards affecting the hero.

Granted, since Simone observed the trend in 1999, matters have improved. "At that time, the trend was towards grim stories where female characters were killed," she says. "We only had a handful of female characters to look up to. Today we're not seeing those stories so much" (Yabroff). Still, films and computer games especially still cling to this trope. In *The Dark Knight* (2008), for instance, district attorney Rachel Dawes, a well-formed character, dies to propel the character arcs of both Batman and Harvey Dent. Likewise, in 2016, the show *Arrow* kills off Black Canary. She had moved on from love interest to superhero. In her death scene, however, she reverts to clichéd selfless girlfriend. She speaks of Arrow as the great love of her life and tells her beloved to go on and find his happiness without her. Her final scene becomes all about him. The biggest problem is lack of agency. Anita Sarkeesian explains in her celebrated "Damsel in Distress (Part 1) Tropes vs Women":

Let's compare the damsel to the archetypal Hero Myth, in which the typically male character may occasionally also be harmed, incapacitated or briefly imprisoned at some point during their journey. In these situations, the character relies on their intelligence, cunning, and skill to engineer their own escape—or, you know, just punching a hole in the prison wall works too. The point is they are ultimately able to gain back their own freedom. In fact, that process of overcoming the ordeal is an important step in the protagonist's transformation into a hero figure. A Damsel'ed woman on the other hand is shown to be incapable of escaping the predicament on her own and then must wait for a savior to come and do it for her.

As she adds, "At its heart the damsel trope is not really about women at all, she simply becomes the central object of a competition between men (at least in the traditional incarnations). I've heard it said that 'In the game of patriarchy women are not the opposing team, they are the ball'" (Sarkeesian, Part 1). The woman is not a character but a trophy. Worse yet are fridging stories, in which the heroine not only fails to rescue herself, but is permanently maimed, depowered or killed. The hero is the one who must overcome the ordeal of her loss.

In 2017, Catherynne M. Valente wrote *The Refrigerator Monologues*, a short story collection that parodies famous fridged heroines. The first, a clear retelling of Gwen Stacy's shocking fall, begins by explaining, "Dying was the biggest thing that ever happened to me. I'm famous for it" (1). The supervillain of the story kidnaps her and demands the serum that will give him powers. The self-aware author inserts societal commentary as the villain tells her to behave like a good girl. "And I know you *are* a good girl, so I expect you to act like one. Good girls want to *please*, Paige. Good girls do as they're told. And girls who are *very* good get sweets. Now are you going to be a good girl for me?" (18). He is correct—good girls comply instead of fighting. Still, Paige tells him she isn't a good girl and resists him. When, afterwards, her super boyfriend encourages her to stay home in safety, she refuses, insisting, "I am not going to stay home like a good little girl. I am going to kill him" (20). Despite her resolve, she perishes when the villain hurls her off a bridge and her hero boyfriend catches her too abruptly. He finds a new, more compliant girlfriend, and life goes on without Paige. These tropes follow the heroines through the collection—of dreamer boyfriends with no thought for consequences, of girlfriends taken for granted and kept out of the boys' club, or girls used as pawns in the hero-villain battle. All the heroines, now living in Deadtown, are left only with the knowledge that they're safe, unable to be hurt by a world of useless, selfish heroes and brutal villains.

Of all these Bronze Age stories, *The Killing Joke* in particular has earned quite a reputation. "It's fair to say it's near impossible not to read a plot description without encountering some form of feminist critique, whether it's because of sexual assault and abuse, ableism, or multiple cases of victimized women as plot points for male character development (i.e., Women in Refrigerators)" (Bullock). Author Brian Cronin notes that "readers felt the violence towards Barbara Gordon was too much, and even Moore, in retrospect, has expressed his displeasure with how the story turned out" (47). In a 2006 *Wizard Magazine* interview, author Alan Moore discusses writing the book and recalls the editorial reaction to shooting Batgirl, saying, "I asked DC if they had any problem with me crippling Barbara Gordon—who was Batgirl at the time—and if I remember, I spoke to Len Wein, who was our editor on the project. [He] said, 'Yeah, okay, cripple the bitch.' It was probably one of the areas where they should've reined me in, but they didn't" (Cotton).

Barbara Gordon begins *The Killing Joke* bringing cocoa for her overworked dad, who's obsessed with the Joker's escape. With her librarian experience, she offers to help with his filing, and fusses that he's gotten scrapbook paste on his pants. She's perfect daughter, and more precisely, the den mother, as her father compares her to the absent homemaker of their household. As she chats about her yoga schedule while he pastes grisly crime photos, she's established as the normal, capable family member, while he has the obsessions and madness of Gotham. "In the story she's not Batgirl—just somebody's daughter" (Maverick). As such, she's the good girl, following all of society's rules. However, she answers the door and finds the Joker, who abruptly shoots her. Her normal life is destroyed forever.

In four panels, she falls across the room to tumble at her bewildered father's feet, atop the shattered glass coffee table. The Joker uses this moment to make jokes about her being a coffee table book, in fact a "softback" with "a hole in the jacket and the spine appears to be damaged." She is no more than a comedy prop to him, and the girl lies unconscious, unable to respond. Only when he creepily threatens to take pictures of her and unbuttons her blouse does she rouse to protest and ask why he's doing this. He responds, "To prove a point. Here's to crime!" The problem is that the point he's proving is to her father and Batman, not to her.

In the hospital, Barbara wakes to find Batman with her and moves very quickly from confusion to "Oh God! Oh God, I remember! Oh Bruce, what he did…" This is not clarified but his taking pictures of her naked is a sexual assault whether or not he did more. Chris Maverick notes in his paper "Oracle of the Invisible: Sexual Assault and Rape in *The Killing Joke*" that further assault is heavily implied. Nonetheless, "her rape is not shown because it's important just to her, not to the male face-off." Apparently, the wounded Barbara was conscious for it and must bear the trauma, left unshown as well.

Despite this, she instantly switches back to the dutiful daughter role, telling Bruce to go save her father, whom the Joker has taken. As the police tell Batman what has been done to Barbara, his rage dominates two panels as he silently scowls and crushes the Joker's signature playing card. The assault has been presented to hurt Batman, while selfless Barbara will remain quietly at the hospital. In fact, Barbara speaks only twelve lines in *The Killing Joke* and is unconscious for a good part of it. No one stays with Barbara and helps her—all energy is spent on pursuing the Joker. Her marginalization for most of the story emphasizes how much the men ignore her in pursuit of their own rage and vengeance—a chilling moral in the origin story of DC's most famous disabled superheroine. Her sidelining emphasizes how much trauma stories often ignore the pain of the victim. Lauren Bullock writes in "The Killing Joke: My Trauma Is Not Your Punchline":

> At what point are the voices of survivors and our few true allies finally heard? What recounting of our trauma makes us deserving of control over how our experiences are stolen, exaggerated by fantasy, minimized emotionally, and then fed back to us with the faulty logic that "that's just how the real world is?" How do we fight for our actual physical, mental, and emotional safety when so many people won't even stand up for us in fiction?

The Joker takes more time torturing Barbara's father for the audience, having his minions strip him, collar him, and zap him with cattle prods through an extended eighteen-panel sequence. This emphasizes that his real fight is against the commissioner and Batman, with Barbara no more than a pawn. As Maverick adds, "She's the fourth most important person in the event." The goons drag Gordon through the Joker's newly purchased amusement park, now a place of horrors. The Joker gloats, "You're doing what any sane man in your appalling circumstances would do. You're going mad." With this, he loads the commissioner onto a carnival ride he's created, filled with disturbing images. To torture Gordon further, the Joker posts naked photos of Barbara on the ride's big screen—fragmented body parts as once more, Barbara is pulled apart. Thus, he ties back to her first scene, where she watches her father paste victim photos in scrapbooks—now she's been reduced to a page of them herself. Meanwhile, the audience experience the images through her father's point of view, feeling his trauma, not hers. The Joker adds, "When all is rape, starvation, war, and life is vile," there's nothing to do but run mad. He rapes Barbara (however literally or symbolically) to make his point and drive his real nemesis—Gordon, the figure of law and authority—to insanity. "To the Joker, Barbara is no more important than the currency involved in any monetary transaction" (Maverick).

As the Joker lectures the commissioner on the trauma of memory, he flashes back to his own pregnant wife, killed by a baby bottle heater in a "million to one accident." While the Joker contemplated his first crime, she was at home playing dutiful wife and died for it. Of course, paralleling Barbara, she's another fridged woman, as her death unhinges the Joker and creates his backstory. She has no other use in the narrative. The commissioner in the present and the Joker in flashback assume the same cringing posture, both trying to blot out the image of their tragic loved ones. Both stories are fundamentally about them.

The Joker displays the commissioner in a cage. Then he then sends Batman a carnival ticket, planning to hurt him too by showing off the Gordons' victimization. On arriving, Batman launches himself at the Joker in pure fury, then comforts Gordon, who sobs, "He … he shot Barbara. Showed me ph-photographs … he tried to drive me mad." Batman offers to stay with Gordon as he didn't with Barbara. In response, the commissioner sends him to get Joker "by the book" and prove morality still has value. Cornered, Joker asks, "I shot a defenseless girl. I terrorized an old man. Why don't you kick the hell out of me and get a standing ovation from the public gallery?" The Joker has deliberately preyed on Batman's loved ones to hurt him and to prove lessons about morality to himself. Batman defeats him and they even share a laugh, but Barbara's crippling is permanent … or so it appears.

When DC comics relaunched its 52-comic universe in 2011, many backstories were rewritten. *The Killing Joke* and its effect on Barbara Gordon remained. This time, however, Barbara Gordon recovered from her four-year stretch in the wheelchair. Even though she's "over" her injury, the subject of *The Killing Joke* keeps reappearing. On March 13, 2015, DC Comics released 25 Joker-themed variant covers. The one for *Batgirl* #41 by artist Rafael Albuquerque depicted the Joker threatening Barbara at gunpoint, while she had a red smile painted across her mouth. With hashtag #changethecover, fans protested this reversion to old fridging-style violence and the cover was withdrawn. "How is it that nearly three decades later we're still having these conversations about the sick fetishization of abuse confusing shock value for brilliance within the *same exact* context?" one demanded (Bullock).

The R-rated cartoon adaptation of *The Killing Joke* (2016) found an entirely new way to enrage fans. "The movie tries to address Barbara's lack of agency by making her the hero for the first half of the film" (Maverick). Nevertheless, the first half hour offers a new non sequitur of a plot: Batgirl (Tara Strong) and Batman (Kevin Conroy) hunt down a mobster who taunts Batgirl with suggestive innuendo, calling her "my special girl" and "baby." Flattered, she behaves like a naive idiot and follows Franz's scavenger hunt of flirtatious clues. The more experienced Batman has to tell her, "He doesn't know you. He's objectified you. When a criminal gets personal like that, it's bad news." Superior-acting Batman flatly orders her off the case and leaves mid-conversation, as he does to her throughout the film.

Worse, to many fans' disgust, Batgirl has "a semi-abusive and overprotective" affair with the much-older Batman (Maverick). After their squabble, she yells at him, fights him, and finds herself kissing him, and then she initiates sex. She shows agency here, but viewers were repelled by this nearly incestuous relationship. Her aggressive sexuality also led critics to note the "slut shaming" trope in the story, subtly suggesting she provoked assault with her forward behavior (Maverick). After, Batman avoids her. She finally quits as Batgirl, and he lets her, showing that he doesn't value her superheroism, though during the film she saves his life. With this, the new story of Batgirl hanging up her cape thanks to the story's sexist, callous men adds a second disturbing punch to the story's feminism. It seems sacrificing the superheroine isn't yet over.

Bad Girl Comics: Fatale (Broadway Comics, 1995)

Trina Robbins writes that by the nineties, "comic books had become not merely a boy's club, but a Playboy Club" (166). Heroines found themselves in briefer and briefer costumes. These were particularly ridiculous with a thong or loincloth below and armored bustier or sometimes metallic strip or breast cups above. An assortment of metallic bracers, armbands, collars, garters, and jewelry only made them look more like harem girls than superheroes. "Bad girls were violent, silicone-breasted, wasp-waisted, and designed to appeal to a demographic that, according to Dick Giordiano, DC Comics vice chairman, was 'between 17 and 26 … over 90% of the time is male. His basic interest is fantasy'" (Ormrod 159). Mainstream comics characters like Elektra, Domino, Artemis, and even Wonder Woman joined in, though less family-friendly series could go much further. Their poses were also the worst of exploitative art:

> Many heroines appear to have broken backs or spines that are curved in impossible "S" shapes. A Glory/Avengylene crossover comic from Image Comics in 1996 illustrates the new look. Notice how the swaybacked women's spines appear to be bent to the breaking point. Their ridiculously tiny waists are nearly hidden behind their forearms. The heroines' breasts are the same size as their heads, and could never be supported by those snapped spines. No matter the size of their thighs, these superheroines would have severe problems standing upright, let alone wielding huge swords and shields in battle [Florence 52].

Created by former Marvel Comics editor Jim Shooter and J.G Jones, Fatale debuted in the first Broadway Comics offering, *Powers That Be* #1 (1996) and then appeared in the first two issues of their second series, *Shadow State*. "We really didn't want to do the same thing everyone else was doing, but the idea of a 'bad girl' character sparked a discussion," recalled Shooter. "There are enough of the sort of women who are always striking poses and arching their backs as they go into battle. We didn't think it had to be that way. We figured we could do something cool with a 'bad girl' in the sense that the focus is more complex" (Guzzo). Like many examples of classic bad girl art, Fatale runs around in a black bra that emphasized her truly enormous bosom, and on the first cover, crooks a red-nailed finger at her male readership.

In an article for *Forbes,* R. Lee Sullivan explains, "Bad girl comics are booming. While American standards of literacy are dropping, college students still seem able to handle comics, especially when the cartoons show busty viragoes with names like Lady Death, Barb Wire and Avengylene. Batman in a bustier; Captain America in a camisole" (37). Bad Girl comics and film appearances of the nineties represented the "film industry's attempts to present established sex symbols as tough heroines in the hopes of creating a combination of sex and violence that might be irresistible to action film fans" (Brown 68). This blends fear and desire. It's also pure cheesecake of course. "Series such as *Glory* or *Lady Death* featured the protagonists in lingerie specials posed in impossible pornographic positions with orgasmic facial expressions, licking blood from swords" (Ormrod 159).

The painful part is how well these comics sold: Sullivan reported, "Lady Death sells 160,000 copies each month, about as much as classic favorites like Superman. Crusade Comics' sensual Shi often outsells Batman … the big guys—Marvel and Time Warner's DC Comics—are squeezing more of their traditional female characters into peek-a-boo costumes" (37).

Fatale, of course, fell in line. In her first scene, she's bent over ostentatiously trying on the lipstick, bosom and butt sticking out at once from her tiny red dress. Fatale, with a real name of Désirée Hopewell, emphasizes her power over men with a name that reflects their hopeful desire for her. In *Powers That Be* #1, she is busy shopping at Saks Fifth Avenue. However, as she purchases a lipstick, she's ambushed by an unknown group wearing gloves and helmets and armed with batons. Immediately, he shows off her superpower—in the style of X-Men's Rogue, when she touches someone, she temporarily absorbs their knowledge and physical abilities. She does this, of course, by grabbing the man and kissing him. As she takes off her jacket to reveal her halter dress, the men shriek—bared skin is her threat. Armed with kissing power and swinging red hair, she takes down all the enemy with her stolen skills. This joins the "less than subtle metaphors for the ability of female sexuality to drain a man of his phallic powers" (Brown, "Gender" 66). She ends the comic having absorbed hundreds of powers from the shadowy group called the Brotherhood.

She's tough and menacing, calling one of her male victims "cupcake" and ordering him, "Pucker up, Buckaroo. This won't hurt a bit" (Shooter, *Shadow State* #1). After, she tells him he's "kinda cute." Directly after she's drained men, she lifts them aggressively over her head. She battles an entire tank and throws it around in *Fatale* #4. She's tough and powerful, but spends lots of her time taken captive, massive breasts protruding upwards. Her Vietnamese trainer, Ong Liem, yanks her into provocative poses, and even hauls her over his knee to spank her. He calls her "little girl" as she crouches with breasts about the size of her head. Désirée starts out as a "party girl" with plenty of disposable income. However, she doesn't grow and change beyond this. In a parody of feminine power, her trainer calls her a "fat cow" and tells her to go on a diet to toughen up (Shooter, *Fatale* #5). Rather than training and gaining skills the tough way, she borrows them from her trainer, absorbing his powers. As such, she generally rescues herself.

> These female characters are typically as powerful, violent, skilled, smart, and self-assured as any of the male characters found in comic books. While this may indeed be a positive development, it is offset by the compensatory exaggerated feminine form, resulting in an odd combination of toughness and sexiness. At least at a symbolic level, the physical extremes that typify the Bad Girl (huge, gravity-defying breasts, mile-long legs, perpetually pouty lips, and perfectly coifed big hair) amount to an almost hysterical mask of femininity [Brown, "Gender" 63].

At the same time, she had some depth and was supposed to be empowered in more than sexuality. Pauline Weiss notes, "In fact, her development was based on the kind of personality traits we wanted her to have. The fact that Janet Jackson and I are women, and are half of the writing team, lends a balance to Fatale, because we want to create a comic that we'd want to read. The idea that Fatale is smart, the idea of her taking strength from other people, and the idea of her being sort of sexually and emotionally healthy, were there from the very beginning" (Guzzo). Certainly, she loves chocolate and McDonalds. She makes jokes. She has a fully rounded personality. She also fights to defend the helpless. When she meets a gambler who abuses his wife, she sucks up his power too. She announces, "You know my mother died all alone hiding out in a safe house, waiting for some guy who was supposed to be taking care of everything ... that's never going to happen to me."

Fatale got her own comic in 1996, which ran for six issues, the only comic arc Broadway Comics finished. Its cheesecake unmistakably continues. The security guards even ogle her picture, emphasizing how much she's a subject of their lustful gaze (Shooter, *Shadow State* #1). Désirée escapes the Brotherhood in her first solo issue in a torn dress, still attached to the leash they have put on her. She even jokes with her latest guy, Bill the supersoldier, about how the size of her breasts are impeding her as he valiantly releases her. As the enemy try to contain her with a blast blanket but she bursts loose, her stripping as superpower gets even more emphasis (Shooter, *Fatale* #1).

Kidnapped by his ex-girlfriend, Brotherhood member Natalie, Bill challenges her that she'd need "a truckload of wonderbras" or implants "just to break even" and "next to her you look like a boy" (Shooter, *Fatale* #2). Clearly the content of one's bra, not one's character, is paramount here. In *Fatale* #2, the two women fight, of course over a man. Natalie complains later, "You men are all like Pavlov's dogs. A full crowd in the balcony and suddenly you go irrational" (Shooter, *Fatale* #5). All women seem to hate her in the worst the Bechdel test has to offer. On the plane in *Fatale* #4, the stewardesses cattily discuss Fatale's enormous figure—she tells them not to be jealous before knocking them out and taking their powers.

The cheesecake figure dominates all of the series, even the plot. While she sleeps with man after man, their obsession with her, and the women's jealousy, all dominate. In her room, she lounges in a towel or robe while oh-so-carefully spilling out of it. When, while lying about in her underwear, Désirée tells Bill that she was hit in the rear end with a tranquilizer dart, he offers to suck it out for her. They then have semi-explicit sex with plenty of bare skin visible, as Désirée smirks about being in a catfight with the man's ex. "Bad girl heroines acted upon their own morality, were sexualized and extremely aggressive" (Ormrod 159). He, by contrast, has more conventionally heroic super strength.

Stressing her bad girl independence, when Bill declares his love, she, feeling trapped, blows him off and promises him, "Maybe next week." She keeps secrets and is the only one with the power to make contact, while he remains waiting and devoted. In fact, Fatale ends her first issue telling him she's not comfortable with the depth of his feelings. Certainly, she isn't the one mooning over a guy. But she's not likely to find an independent relationship this way either.

Her opposition, Layil, is the female leader of the Brotherhood. She's perfectly all right with a society that gains its powers by sacrificing young women to the Dragon Spirit in return for power. She also suffers from the Brotherhood's casual misogyny as its leaders tell her, "We don't need a woman telling us what to do, especially an autocratic, self-serving bitch" (Shooter, *Fatale* #6). At last, she approaches the Bantu priest M'Tuto and tells him Fatale has the power of the ancient dragon spirit in her. Layil begs for the power to free the dragon spirit from Fatale and presumably render her powerless. To prove the truth of what she says, M'Tuto apparently needs to open her blouse and sniff her bare breasts to detect her power. After, his cronies shoot her and she rises from death, proving she's indeed the chosen one. Following this is an extended naked training session, in which he beats on her to "make you ashamed, make you filthy, make you man. See I gotta bring out the man part in the woman." All this is completely exploitative, only weakly producing a plot. At last, she defeats him and literally eats his heart (Shooter, *Fatale* #5).

Thanks to some reprogramming, treacherous Bill captures her, binds her to the altar, and for some reason rips open the shirt-dress she wears. Layil stabs her, but at the fatal moment, Désirée touches the other woman and absorbs her powers. With her new strength, she returns from death, now filled with the power of the Dragon Spirit. Gordon tries taking over, but when he begins executions, Désirée knocks him out and takes his powers. She places herself in charge of the Brotherhood and all the members submit to her. When one objects to "another bitch giving us orders," she absorbs his strength and all the organization's secrets with it. She decides, "Much as I hate the idea of a little cabal ruling the world, it's necessary." She will dismantle them slowly, all the while remaining in charge. She ends the story sitting before a map of the world in a revealing green dress on a throne trimmed with crimson and skulls. She has gone from defender of the world to its tyrant (Shooter, *Fatale* #6).

Other "Bad Girl" comics echo from this time. The year of 1989 introduced Dawn, eternal goddess of birth and rebirth, created by Sirius Comics. She defends the earth, negotiating with and battling angels and demons. More disturbingly, she has traded her body to the Lord of Death for knowledge, and is now his constant companion (Linsner).

> As an independent publisher, Sirius does not include CCA stamps on their books, but *Cry for Dawn* does include a rating that reads "for mature readers." The paleness of her skin, and the skeletal figure who holds her, draws attention directly to Dawn. As the main focus of attention, her figure fills the center of the cover, held even as she is in what appears to be an awkward position. She appears to be chained to the skeleton's left arm. Her limbs are exposed, as is most of her body—despite the silk and lace lingerie she wears. It is difficult to determine whether her hand is on the large poleaxe the skeleton wields, but either way she appears to be very much at the mercy of her skeletal ... friend [Florence 33–34].

Antarctic Press introduced Areala the warrior nun in 1994. Sister Shannon Masters is part of an elite core of thirteen warrior nuns who defend the Earth from the powers of Hell. Her mechanical arm bears the spirit of the ancient Valkyrie Areala and she also has a powerful sword. Unsurprisingly, her nun habit is basically open to the waist and the skirt is converted to a long black loincloth with studded garters showing (Dunn).

Chaos! Comics introduced Chastity Marks in 1995, giving her her own title in 1997. This teen vampire actually got training as an assassin before deciding to use her powers to fight evil and protect innocents. She was another offering written by Brian Pulido and drawn by Adriano Batista.

> Chaos! Comics places no ratings on the title. The vampire looks angry and pained as she attempts to show off her bosom, her backside, and her leg all at the same time. Both her breasts and her thighs are larger than her waist, and (according to the coders) the twist in her spine looks extremely painful. Her chest is revealed more than concealed, as are her limbs and the rest of her torso. Her armored, spiked battle thong and spiky stiletto-heeled boots, not to mention the large katana and bared fangs, make Chastity intimidating, and very unapproachable. She may look bad, but she is dangerous too [Florence 37].

Tarot: Witch of the Black Rose (1999) is written and drawn by Jim Balent with his wife Holly Golightly (or so is her penname) of Broadsword Comics. Tarot, a witch from Salem, upholds the balance between the mortal world and the magical world, set against her rival sister Raven Hex. The former has black ram's horns, pagan tattoos, and a black mask and brief bikini. As reviewer Chris Sims puts it: "*Tarot* is about the title character, a witch with incredibly large breasts (even for comics) who defends the mortal world from supernatural threats, which mostly involve her sister (who has even larger breasts) and the occasional super-villain with nuclear bombs implanted in her even larger breasts." Her male sidekick and love interest Jon is often tied up and molested by sexy monsters, leaving Tarot clearly in charge. Still, the book is a sex romp, with Tarot's battles becoming "little more than a pretense for her to lose her clothes due to an errant sword cut or magical spell" (Hanley, *Catwoman* 143).

"The fetishization of these Bad Girls with guns, swords, and whips does not so much mark them as masculine as it marks them as dominatrices. It is all part of a broader fetishizing of the female body" (Brown, "Gender" 64). There are disturbing images of women's body parts as weapons, including a devil woman who has two nuclear bombs implanted in her breasts and a pirate with octopus tentacles (and beak) emerging from her groin. "For the record, Vera's breasts aren't merely convenient handles, they're actually a cunning trap: Her black vinyl bra and fishnet bodice are actually wired with enough electricity to kill the two werewolves, while leaving her more or less unharmed" (Sims).

Bad Kitty, Chaos! Comics' 2001 heroine, appears completely naked on her cover, naughty bits only covered by an actual cat. As written by Brian Pulido and drawn by Adriano Batista, New Orleans cop Catherine Bell maintained a firm sense of justice. However, when her boyfriend was transformed into a zombie and was ordered to kill her, she killed all those responsible. On the run from the FBI, she took on a new identity as "Bad Kitty" and prowled the streets as a vigilante, her black cat Lucky beside her. The same year, Chaos! Comics introduced Jade, a 4,000-year-old boss of a powerful Shanghai crime family and antihero. Thus with magical vampire powers as well as an outfit that amounted to a green loincloth and gold strap that barely obscured her gigantic breasts, she sought to seize control of China (Golden).

These "strong women" were memorable but also beyond problematic.

> It is wonderful that both male and female audiences now find strong and powerful women worthy of superhero status, but the "bad girls" have done much to damage the dwindling female readership of comic books. The last part of the 1990s and the beginning of the 2000s have brought more of the same—either blood-soaked anti-heroines in battle thongs and stiletto heels, or superheroine "role models" who barely fit into their costumes [Florence 63].

Girl Power: Powerpuff Girls (TV, 1998–2005)

The Powerpuff Girls arrived on Cartoon Network in 1998. It got record-breaking ratings, with its kindergartner heroines "made of sugar, spice and everything nice." Bubbles, Buttercup, and Blossom were sweet and juvenile, undercutting their impressive powers. For indeed, the girls could fly, and Bubbles (in blue) is the sweetest and is known for her electric blast, ultrasonic scream, thunderclap, supersonic shield, and powers of animal translation. Buttercup (in green) is an outspoken tomboy who can produce energy orbs, ball blasts, fireballs, black hurricanes, and a tongue roll. Blossom, the leader (in pink) is known for ice breath, microscopic vision, lightning bolts, a danger sense, and a photographic memory. They were characteristic of the nineties "girl power" era—superheroines who undercut their powers with cuteness or childishness. In fact, this sweetness was considered a part of the new third wave feminism. "The conflation of empowerment, consumption, and personal appearance suggests that because girls can be both feminine and strong, they can wear whatever they want—frilly pink lace or fishnet stockings—without negating their power," explains Rebecca C. Hains in "Power(Puff) Feminism: The Powerpuff Girls as a Site of Strength and Collective Action in the Third Wave" (217).

Creator Craig McCracken doodled the team in college and named them The Whoopass Girls. One of his animation instructors was friends with Linda Simensky, director of development for Nickelodeon. While it didn't fit their storytelling style, when she crossed over to Cartoon Network, she eagerly advocated for it (Neuwirth 13). The show became known for its tongue-in-cheek humor and beautifully colored animation. McCracken explains: "There's this new feminism that's coming up, that's embracing things that are typically girlish and not saying, 'Ooh, in order to be a feminist you have to denounce all of that pink stuff ... you can have all those things and be sexy and be feminine and be typically girlish and still be a feminist'" (qtd. in Hains 14). He adds, "I just thought it was cool to see these cute little girls being really tough and really hardcore" (qtd. in Hains 14). This was the essence of girl power—the related third wave feminism emphasized being glamorous and girly (down to dancing and cheerleading) as a path to strength.

Girl power was inspired by the lyrics of Madonna, Riot Grrrl, and the Spice Girls in the nineties. "Girlpower celebrities include such diverse subjects as Lara Croft, Tank Girl, Buffy the Vampire Slayer, Courtney Love, and the Spice Girls (whose own heroine was, famously, Margaret Thatcher). They are deemed to embody girlpower because they are outspoken, not afraid to take power, believe in themselves, and run their own lives," notes Anita Harris in *Future Girl: Young Women in the Twenty-First Century* (17). Of course, the girls' glamor here comes from pretty dresses and plenty of makeup. "Girl power emphasize consumerism, for its messages of empowerment are found in popular culture texts and artifacts that present girl power as the fluffy, pleasurable suggestion that girls can do (and buy) anything they choose" (Hains 217).

All these girls' nineties introductions corresponded with the introduction of girl power. "Originally, girlpower or *grrrlpower* was the catchword of an underground young radical feminist movement that advocated for the improvement of girls' lives. Emerging in the early 1990s as a blend of punk and feminist politics, it became the first powerful youth movement or political subculture to be organized entirely around young women's concerns," Harris adds (16–17). Its advocates longed for self-definition and self-improvement, remaking themselves as different from seventies feminists but also eager to transform the world in a new way. Lesbian and gay rights were appearing, along with multicultural tolerance, more global awareness, and more interest in young women's happiness as they pursued different life choices.

Of course, the Powerpuff Girls took their place among a wave of similar characters. Author Leigh Bardugo writes, "I gave my heart to Jem, She-Ra, Sailor Moon–type all-girl crews. Sure, they showed cleavage, wore heels, had ridiculously expressive hair, but at least they got to wear *skirts* instead of just panties in primary colors" (155). As she explains, they were relatable in their pretty frivolity: "They went on adventures, made friends, stopped evil, wore glitter at every opportunity, and had chaste romances with cute boys named Rio and harmless rogues like the Sea Hawk. They were female fantasies created for girls" (155). All these young women, nonetheless, appeared unclear how to fight for rights in a world that had ostensibly given them equality, even while casting them as frillier, more frivolous characters.

Similarly, adult heroines of the time like Xena were capable but glamorized, emphasizing this duality. They were presented in a campy fashion, as Xena battled enemies with giant fish and dirty diapers as well as a sword. Thus, like Lynda Carter's Wonder Woman, her goofiness comforted audiences by adding a fantasy quality and also undercutting her strength. Nineties show *Lois & Clark: The New Adventures of Superman* had another tough woman who was often undercut—in this case by needing the stronger Superman to rescue her. In the episode "Ultrawoman," she gets Clark's powers and must rescue people in danger. At the same time, she fusses over her high heels and nearly breaks down from the demands of the job, emphasizing that she lacks Superman's skill. She's cast as smarter and more capable than Clark, who often needs his superpowers to keep up. Nonetheless, she often finds herself the butt of the joke.

These heroines were sexualized, gorgeous and fashion-conscious, while also able to kick butt in action scenes. They were the stars of *Dark Angel, Xena, Alias, La Femme Nikita, Lois & Clark, Charmed, Witchblade, Clarissa Explains it All, Sabrina the Teenage Witch, Lara Croft: Tomb Raider, Charlie's Angels* (the film), *Sailor Moon* and even *Street Fighter II*. Joined by *The Mystery Files of Shelby Woo* with its teen crime fighter, the superpowered heroine of *The Secret World of Alex Mack*, and other assertive, realistic girls—Moesha,

Daria, Lisa Simpson, they were spunky and fun. The young women showed that one could fight evil in a pretty dress or while talking on the phone. "Girl power heroines, while strong, are also thoroughly feminine, wearing short skirts and makeup not to please society but *because they want to*" (Frankel, *Buffy* 12). It was a new kind of empowerment, with ambiguous but fun values.

Similarly, the Powerpuff Girls are good-hearted, but as kindergartners they are ridiculously naïve and need babysitting. These are all ploys to make a superpowered woman less threatening—these are only goofy, frivolous "girls" after all, and none need to be taken seriously. Combining "power" and "puff" in their names specifically subverts their superheroism beneath girlish cuteness, casting them as less threatening to the patriarchy. Creator Craig McCracken liked the contrast and added, "They seemed tougher because they're so cute" (Neuwirth 13). By contrast, Spider-Man has somewhat ridiculous powers, but the films all emphasize his realistic qualities—a geeky ignored teen coping with enormous adult responsibility and meeting the challenge with courage. While in high school, he even gets a name with "man" in it.

Cultural theorist Susan Hopkins argues, "Girlpower is a provocative mix of youth, vitality, sexuality, and self-determination. The story on offer here is one of power through and control over one's own identity invention and re-invention" (Harris 17). With a ravaged environment and a ruined economy, along with rising violence against young women, third wave feminists found themselves longing to charge into battle. As Bill Clinton (and thus Hillary as First Lady) took office, and anti-abortion legislation appeared in some states, many young women began grassroots student activism. Baumgardner and Richards contend that the third wave's goals derive from considering how these issues affect their personal lives (21). Third wave feminism had already gotten job equality, thanks to the previous wave's fight. Now, they sought self-definition through multiple paths, from serious world-saving jobs to more frivolous outlets like shopping and primping because it brought them pleasure. It was a philosophy of contradictions. "Girlie feminists claim their femininity as a source of power, rather than trying to make it masculine, arguing that by doing the latter, women are in fact giving the masculine preferred status while devaluing the feminine" (Karras).

Other heroines literally strip to balance their power. Stuller notes, "The tongue-in-cheek (and ultra girlie) *Charlie's Angels* (2000), produced by Drew Barrymore, consciously foregrounded style over substance" (82). Every time the Angels must go undercover, they play geishas, strippers, and other scantily dressed sex dolls. These young women use "their barely clothed bodies to entrap the villains, thereby adding back into the warrior woman scripts the message that true killer power comes from hyperfemininity" (Douglas 93). In *Batman and the Outsiders: The Chrysalis,* Cassandra Cain (Batgirl) walks around the base completely nude as Thunder and Grace ask uncomfortably if they're out of towels. At this point in Wonder Woman's long legacy, Mike Deodato drew her in her skimpiest thong and largest bust size ever, encouraging a male readership over a female one. Artemis, who coveted Wonder Woman's title, appeared in an example of women battling through jealousy instead of finding sisterhood. In *Supergirl: Candor,* Power Girl gets a tattoo on her upper back, which requires removing her shirt, and showers repeatedly, trying to clear her head. This gives the audience plenty to watch. When Superman's mind is downloaded into Power Girl's body, he turns it into a farce rather than learning about her struggle. Staring down at Power Girl's cleavage, he says, "I'm still seeing ... myself, not Power Girl." Huntress-as-Batman replies, "Same here. But trust me, Clark, you're her all right!" (Jones et al.). Similarly, Dinah spends *Birds of Prey: Old Friends New Enemies* first lounging in a bathing suit and then in increasingly ripped prisoner clothes as she escapes a drug farm. Her punches and kicks display lots of leg and sometimes the notorious "broken back" look. On the other hand, she rescues Barbara's ex, whose clothes are just as ripped. He's been blinded, leaving her to perform the heroism. As she tells him, "You're coming with me if I have to *carry* you, Bard" (Dixon et al.).

"This kind of girlpower constructs the current generation of young women as a unique category of girls who are self-assured, living lives lightly inflected but by no means driven by feminism, influenced by the philosophy of DIY, and assuming they can have (or at least buy) it all" (Harris 17). Of course, sisterhood is everything among the young Powerpuff trio, besides getting along with their schoolmates and the citizens of Townsville. "Together, they attended kindergarten, dealt with family squabbles, and saved the constantly imperiled city of Townsville from a colorful cast of villains, monsters, and the occasional mutant chili smell" (Thurm).

The girls show off their strength in most episodes. Though Mojo Jojo captures Blossom in "Not So Awesome Blossom," to trap the other girls, Blossom saves everyone and beats up Jojo as well. In "Cop Out" an enemy lowers the girls into a vat of acid, but no one saves them—they discover they're immune and can escape on their own. Their simplistic perspectives have them winning the day without trickery or guile, just heroism. On another occasion, monkey villain Mojo Jojo infiltrates their slumber party disguised as a girl and gives them "Antidote X," depriving them of their powers. Even as "normal girls," the heroines save the day.

Of course, "the Powerpuff Girls' feminism is also rather conservative, making no call to action to redress the inequalities women continue to face" (Hains 231). In fact, it avoids the loaded word as much as possible.

> What made the original *Powerpuff Girls* so great was that it was overtly feminist, but not self-consciously so.... Fighting monsters could seem almost incidental—in fact, in several episodes they're just perfect little girls whose ultra-super powers have

no bearing on the plot. The original *Powerpuff Girls*' feminism was more like sugar, an extra ingredient that helped sweeten the excellent, surprisingly varied narratives beneath [Thurm].

It also doesn't bother with diversity, a lack common to the frequently blonde and always glamorous third-wave heroines. The story is white and middle class, centered in the suburb of Townville. Hains asserts that in *The Powerpuff Girls* and similar girl power series, "the range of representations is still limited" to white and middle or upper class (19). This was another hallmark of the girlpower movement—there might be token diversity, but only that. The fourth wave feminism some see appearing a generation later is far more inclusive.

In "Members Only," the girls unite into a flaming cat to save a parody of the Justice League, combating misogyny with their sisterhood. Villainesses "Princess Morbucks" and "Sedusa" obviously suggest negative values the girls fight, while most of their other foes are male. These include the "Rowdyruff Boys"—the girls' perfect counterpart, made from "snips and snails and puppy dog tails" with bright colors against the girls' pastels. Ms. Sara Bellum, the mayor's assistant, persuades the girls to "try being nice" instead of fighting—a technique that actually succeeds. The girls in fact overexaggerate their gender and embarrass the boys with kisses, saving the day. In fact, kissing the boys dissolves them into their component ingredients. This is a rather cringeworthy literal "girl power"—the feminine power of kissing beats the boys' abilities. Buttercup even moans "Ew, gross." In a second encounter, the boys are immune to kisses, or rather, grow more powerful under the metaphor of attention. The girls ridicule the boys, and this shrinks them down—a metaphor brought into magical life.

It was a popular series for the grade-school-age girl demographic, with heavy branding in clothing and toys. There were hair clips, lunchboxes, beanbag chairs, posters, bath crystals, picture frames, stickers, watches, and backpacks. However, unlike *Princess of Power, My Little Pony*, and competing franchises, this series was not based in the toys but in the story concept. "*The Powerpuff Girls* is successful because it provides young girls with an example of dynamic female superheroines—girls just like them—who are empowered and empowering. With unique abilities, minds of their own, and strong character traits—the antithesis of their names—these girls are forces to be reckoned with" (Miseroglu 391).

A movie followed in 2002. It offers the girls' origin story as Professor Utonium creates and names them. Still, the girls are condemned by the town after they destroy the place playing tag. Instead of celebrating their desire to help, the newspaper announces, "Freaky Bug-Eyed Weirdo Girls Broke Everything," and their father tells them they must reign in their abilities and no longer use them in public. As he puts it, "People just don't understand how special you girls are yet. And unfortunately, people often get scared or angry when they don't understand something special or unique." This lesson problematically teaches young viewers how they must hide their uniqueness and try to conform in order to be accepted.

Onscreen, other film heroines were girlish and frivolous. The *Buffy the Vampire Slayer* film of 1992, like *Charlie's Angels*, has the heroine possessed of useful, butt-kicking skills but obsessed with fashion more than world-saving. Uma Thurman as Jenny Johnson/G-Girl in *My Super Ex-Girlfriend* (2006) becomes another joke; she's manipulative and only uses her powers selfishly. The 1997 film *Batman and Robin* introduces Alfred's niece Barbara (Alicia Silverstone from the girl power film *Clueless*), who wears plaid skirts during the day but races motorcycles at night. Armed with a Batsuit from Alfred, she bursts into the middle of Batman and Robin's fight with the seductive Poison Ivy and takes her on, even while lecturing her about feminism: "Using feminine wiles to get what you want. Trading on your looks. Exploiting men's weakness for sex. Read a book, sister. That passive-aggressive crap went out in the seventies. Chicks like you give women a bad name." Though Batman and Robin tease Barbara that in PC culture she should call herself "Batwoman" or "Batperson," they embrace having her on the team.

Birds of Prey, developed by Laeta Kalogridis for the WB, launched in 2002 as a show for teens. In his *The Encyclopedia of Superheroes on Film and Television*, critic John Kenneth Muir calls it "the unholy love child of *Buffy the Vampire Slayer* and *Dark Angel*" with bickering straight from *Charmed* (128). It stars Oracle (the former Batgirl), Huntress, and Black Canary, protecting Gotham from criminals in Batman's absence. Muir criticizes the show for having too much emphasis on friendship and fashion: "Oracle, Huntress, and Barbara all had issues, from physical paralysis and emotional abandonment to a distrust of men … but they also wore great clothes, seemed to want for nothing materially, and were gorgeous." Their misery about being outcasts thus seemed insincere. "When you're beautiful, every man lusts after you, and you wear black leather, how much of an outsider can you really be?" (Muir 126). While its "brother show" *Smallville* ran ten seasons, *Birds of Prey* was canceled halfway through season one. Muir concludes, "The premature end of *Witchblade*, along with *Birds of Prey* in the winter of 2002, indicated to some that the 'Dawn of the Woman' era in the superhero genre had entered its twilight, leaving only Buffy, in her seventh and final season, to carry the torch" (544).

Atoner: Cassandra Cain (DC Comics, 2001)

The 2000s had many big event stories that turned superheroines into villains. Scarlet Witch wiped out the mutants in the House of M storyline.

Jean Loring, the Atom's ex-wife, became a murderer in *Identity Crisis*. When a planet of Kryptonians settled in earth's solar system, General Sam Lane created a "secret weapon" in Superwoman. She was an executioner, shockingly revealed as Lucy Lane before Supergirl accidentally ruptured her suit. Continuing in this vein, Wonder Woman killed Maxwell Lord in *The OMAC Project* (2005). This results in a public trial for murder. She was cleared, but surrendered her costume to skulk away for a year. "In both *New Frontier* and *The OMAC Project*, Wonder Woman has had to suffer great public shame, penance, and physical beatings before either Superman or Batman would deign to forgive her" (DiPaolo 167). Many more heroines were sacrificed just for the shock value. In *New Frontier* (2004), Wonder Woman rescues female prisoners in Indo-China. "Wonder Woman liberates a group of women who have been raped and imprisoned by guards and enables the former victims to avenge themselves by machine-gunning their oppressors to death. A shocked Superman protests her role in the execution of the rapists rather than join her and the vindicated women in a drink from a celebratory goblet of mead" (DiPaolo 166).

> The 2000s were problematic for superheroines. In comics, they descended into villainy as the Scarlet Witch wiped out nearly all the mutants and Wonder Woman committed murder. Outfits tightened to the point of mass internet protests. On the big screen, Halle berry's 2004 *Catwoman* (in which she battles an evil makeup company in her exaggeratedly tight suit) spectacularly flopped. *Elektra* (2005) was painfully slow and serious, like a superhero film without the fun. Though these both suffered from bad writing, they convinced filmmakers to hold off on central superheroines for a full decade. In the bigger franchises, *Batman Begins* and *Spider-Man* relegated women to the role of girlfriend. *Superman Returns* (2006) had the hero ditching a pregnant Lois Lane who spent the film getting back at him for this treatment. *My Super Ex-Girlfriend* (2006) parodied women with powers. Girls, as *The Lego Movie* would later suggest, just ruined boy's stuff when they were allowed to play [Frankel, "Introduction"].

One strikingly unusual Batgirl fits among these superheroines' ranks. Cassandra Cain was raised by the assassin David Cain from babyhood to be a perfect warrior. For this, he deprived her of language, teaching her instead to interpret movement as communication. This made her an incredible instinctive fighter, able to anticipate any enemy, but cut her off from the people around her.

In Kelley Puckett's *Batgirl: Silent Knight*, she becomes a poignant, uncommunicative Batgirl who can offer only a few hand-signals and can't understand the words said to her. The comic has long silent periods, emphasizing her difference. Her costume too is poignant, with the mouth sewn over with irregular stitches, emphasizing her handicap. The eyeholes are covered over, leaving her featureless.

Barbara Gordon takes her in, but the pair have trouble communicating.

Cassandra's disability is especially distancing. Barbara tells Batman, "I hate to say it, but it's hard to *care* about her without.... I just wish I knew what was going on in her head, that's all." Next, Cassandra saves a geeky telepath's life, and he fixes her brain so she can understand language. Technically, this is another male shaping her without her permission, though he apologizes, adding, "I would've asked first but ... you wouldn't have understood me." She's grateful at the transformation. However, by doing so, he deprives her of her skills. With this, the perfect warrior discovers she's no longer perfect. She's quickly defeated. This becomes a compelling metaphor for a disabled heroine being "cured" without her permission and thus losing all her unique gifts. On her next outing, she begs the telepath to change her back, only to discover that he can't. With her instincts betraying her, she actually runs at a shooter and is nearly killed.

Meanwhile, Batman discovers a video of his perfect warrior as a child, murdering someone. He goes to David Cain, demanding to know that the tape is a fake. Cain laughs. "You just don't get it, do you? Why do you think she ran away from me that night? Huh? Any guesses? Why do you *think* she puts on your costume and risks her life for strangers?" He points out that it's not altruism, but as Batman knows, it's overwhelming guilt that drives Batgirl to atone and risk herself. Cain admits that he pushed her too young to kill and destroyed her. Through the graphic novel, the pair continue watching film of Cassandra's progress, deciding her fate in patriarchal fashion. Batman decides Cain was not a genius instructor, simply an abuser who traumatized the little girl.

Meanwhile, Cassandra must start over. Her skills were a sort of grace, magically imprinted on her. Now without them she must relearn everything even as she learns to speak. Metaphorically, she's beginning to feel and connect with others, despite the harness of her upbringing. Before she was perfect; now she's discovering life as a flawed human. To her disappointment, Batman tells her she can be ready to defend herself in a year ... and an expert fighter in a decade. This is far too long for Cassandra to wait.

Training, she goads Batman to punch her over and over. Her self-loathing manifests here, changing her from a hero to a martyr. She has no hobbies, no relationships outside the Bat-family, no self-worth other than risking herself for others. When he insists she's not ready to fight, she asks poignantly, "People *dying* ... my life ... worth more than theirs?" Batman replies with his own guilt—Jason Todd, Robin, was murdered by the Joker, and he won't allow another protégé to die. Mentor and student fully understand each other.

Of course, Cassandra doesn't take no for an answer but begins patrolling the streets without a costume. Barbara figures this out and tells her, "I could never fight like you, but I never jumped in front of any bullets, either. You seem to look for danger. I'm not sure why, but it worries me. I'll bet it worries him too." Cassandra still refuses to give up. At last, she finds herself a new, less sympathetic mentor who will give her what she needs. She battles Lady Shiva and insists on training. Lady Shiva agrees, but the price is a death-duel in a year. Even knowing this will doom her, Cassandra takes the bargain—a year of being a marvelous gifted fighter who can save lives, followed by probable death. Still, she considers the exchange worth it. She's a fascinating character, but clearly fits the pattern of so many heroines being tortured and punished for their power.

Cinematic Superheroines: Captain Marvel (Film, 2019)

Starting with 2000's *X-Men*, a renaissance of superhero films filled the big screens. Many, including this first, co-starred mighty heroines. However, the failures of *Elektra* and *Catwoman* (however weakly written) left creators reluctant to center their films around superheroines. The year of 2017 changed all this with *Wonder Woman*—a successful film focused on the mightiest of heroines. The heroine admittedly had a skimpy outfit, failure to challenge the patriarchy and traditional romance with a strong male character, but she certainly stepped up as a strong role model. After this, the Marvel Cinematic Universe, which had launched with *Iron Man* in 2008, finally starred a woman in its twenty-first film. This was the mightiest of their heroines, Captain Marvel.

She herself fit another rising trend—that of telling stories of characters who needn't be young, white cisgendered heterosexual men:

> The fourth wave has decidedly arrived, establishing that all main characters can be gay, trans, or nonwhite instead of playing Falcon or Black Widow beside Captain America. utopias like *Black Panther* celebrate non–European alternate paths. Disney princesses reject the old patterns. dystopian heroines lead uprisings against the gloating force of the patriarchy. Now women can be Ghostbusters or Jedi, captain Stormtroopers or even dispense advice like Yoda. There's pushback, but progress keeps coming. Most of all, Wonder Woman can be well- rounded, funny and heroic without being campy or laughable. More superheroines like Wasp and Captain Marvel take to the screen—modestly dressed at last. One thing is clear—this new wave of storytelling will create a bright, caring generation of children ... those who understand that the future can be female [Frankel, "Introduction"].

Director Anna Boden comments: "What attracted us to the project was the character of Carol Danvers. We particularly loved Kelly Sue DeConnick's run. We really fell in love with that take on the character, her humor, her humanity, her need to prove herself and all of that swagger that comes from an Air Force background" (*Official Movie Special* 8). Indeed, DeConnick had rebooted the comics run in 2012, rebranding the seventies character Ms. Marvel as Captain Marvel and changing her black bathing suit and high boots into a sensible military uniform with art by Dexter Soy. Ms. Marvel had been written through the years as sometimes an early feminist pioneer and sometimes a damsel in distress, but DeConnick made her completely, uncompromisingly tough.

"My pitch was called 'Pilot' and the take can pretty much be summed up with 'Carol Danvers as Chuck Yeager,'" says DeConnick. "She'll have to figure out how to be both Captain Marvel *and* Chuck Yeager—to marry the responsibility of that legacy with the sheer joy being nearly invulnerable and flying really [expletive] fast" (Beard, "WonderCon"). Under DeConnick, Carol grappled with integrating her Kree perfectionism and her human flaws into defending earth, a struggle for identity that drives the film version. Owen Glieberman of *Variety* comments:

> Vers is pulled into the drama of questioning the core of who she is, and that's where Larson's performance takes wing. Vers was taught one thing: to fight this way, for these people, for this cause. She needs to open herself up to a new mode, and the film uses that journey as an analogue of her existence as a female superhero. Everything she's been told is wrong! Can she wake up from the oppressive (read: patriarchal) mind-set of the conventions that bind her? Captain Marvel is only the second major Hollywood movie to have a female superhero at its center, but it's a savvier and more high-flying fantasy than *Wonder Woman,* because it's the origin story as head game. Larson's Vers is like someone trapped in a matrix—she has to shake off the dream of who she is to locate the superwoman she could be. And that makes for a rouser of a journey.

The film offers a new spin on the overdone origin story format—as "Vers," the heroine is already superpowered, but she's seeking her forgotten human past. Indeed, she has been reborn as a Kree warrior, but her human side keeps slipping out. Larson explains that the Kree attempt to be perfect soldiers, devoid of emotion, but Vers still has a human side. "It's also the part that makes her kind of sassy and a little brash at times. It makes her really emotional. It makes her aggressive and competitive. All of the good and all of the bad is in that human side. It's the flaw, and it's the best thing about her" (*Official Movie Special* 20). As she trains with her mentor Yon-Rogg, he encourages her to discard her emotions. Further, he insists that his people not only saved her life but gave her powers so she can better fight for their cause. Vers believes all this at film's beginning, but embarks on a particularly feminist quest—to break through the illusions dictated by the patriarchy and realize that she has astounding power if she's only rebellious enough to claim it.

The film breaks the mold in other ways, of course. The heroine is notable for her shattering of gender conventions both in her quest and in the details of her life. Wonder Woman from her film two years before delighted viewers with her power. It's also notable that *Wonder Woman* broke ground as Patty Jenkins became the first female director to helm a major superhero film as well as a film that made over $100 million in its opening weekend. Nonetheless, Wonder Woman conforms to a number of tropes. She wears a skin-baring superheroine uniform and other alluring clothes from skimpy golden practice gear to blue evening gown, which all incidentally present her as eye-candy. When the older British males directing World War I dismiss her, she can't defy them directly, so she's forced to sneak around to accomplish her mission. Finally, she has a conventional romance with a strong, red-blooded American hero, through whom audiences could focus if desired.

By contrast, Rose Tico from *Star Wars*, like Rey and Jyn from films of the same era, wears grubby, concealing clothes for the entire film. Jyn has no love interest and fights as a soldier among other soldiers. No one with the possible exception of villain Kylo Ren treats these heroines as "girls" or makes condescending remarks. They are presented as capable and competent, winning the battles as they grow and change. These films reflect a new era of fourth wave feminism, with heroines who have different races and skillsets but skip wearing alluring costumes to please the male gaze. Sometimes they skip the romance plots entirely to save loved ones, as do the heroines of *Frozen* and *Moana*, *Mad Max: Fury Road* and *Black Panther*. Other times, they have relationships as they wish, like the heroines of *Ghostbusters* or *Wynonna Earp*, but establish that they hold all the power and choices here.

When Vers reaches earth, with her memories returning, she begins tearing down gender stereotypes as she emphasizes how different this movie. As she dramatically crashes through the roof of a Blockbuster and staggers away, "Whatta Man" by Salt-n-Pepa plays on the nearby security guard's radio. While this sets the scene in the nineties, it also emphasizes that he, ostensibly security, is no match for the more powerful and technologically advanced superhero. Now that a woman is on the scene, this man is no longer necessary. Director Anna Boden comments: "She has a lot of swagger and a real sense of humor. She's a fighter pilot in the Air Force, so she has that kind of Top Gun/Maverick attitude. Part of that comes from a deep-seated need to prove herself, which comes from having some self-doubt and fear. Does she become humble? Dies she end the movie with any less swagger than she began it with?" (*Official Movie Special* 10). Clearly, she doesn't.

When a flirtatious guy insists that the heroine smile, she glares. In response to her silence, he dismisses her with the label "Freak." Female viewers can empathize with this scene and see themselves in the man's condescending entitlement and the heroine's annoyance. In fact, Vers gets revenge by stealing his motorcycle. Vers then steals jeans, a flannel shirt, a leather jacket, and a Nine-Inch-Nails t-shirt, her disguise for most of the film. This combination is explicitly grunge, suggesting rebellion as well as a practical comfort rather than glamorous gowns or skintight spandex. In fact, on her new bike, she presents a masculine image, raising a defiant middle finger to a world that has spent too much time chastising her for not deferring to men. As one reviewer snarkily comments, "Some people will find it disorientating to watch. *Captain Marvel* offers zero concessions to ease anyone in or win them over to Carol Danvers' point of view. If that makes it hard for some viewers to relate to her, she'll deal" (O'Hara). In fact, Batwoman, another tough, macho heroine, is told to smile at the end of her fourth television episode. "Hey, Batwoman. You have such a pretty face. Ever think about smiling more?" the newswoman chirps. She too reacts with disdain. Of course, this is an added burden for the superheroine that the hero doesn't share.

> Anna Boden and Ryan Fleck's take on the Carol Danvers origin story jettisons subtlety in its messaging of female empowerment and anti-imperialism to varying degrees of success. At times, the film has all the makings of a wildly effective Nike commercial. You know the kind, girls falling down and getting up again, withstanding jeers and taunts until you're weeping on your couch? But the two co-directors, working from a script they co-wrote with Geneva Robertson-Dworet, have seemingly taken a tip from all that surrounds them in 2019 that renders subtlety obsolete and beats on some well-worn sexist tropes with a story that screams: "I guess you did not hear us when we said we don't want to smile!" [Wolfe].

Vers goes on to defeat a Kree invader and team up with a younger, jokier Nick Fury—who admittedly has been made so gentle and goofy that it's a stretch to call this younger version the same character. This is an unfortunate side effect of some feminist stories, casting the superheroine's partners as goofballs like Joxer on *Xena* or Xander on *Buffy*. Sometimes, they offer a tough balance like Mad Max, a wise mentor like Laura's companions in *Logan* or an inspiring source of comfort like Peeta in *Hunger Games*. Often, the men encourage the women to stand up and fight as in *X-Men: Apocalypse*. Sometimes, however, like Kevin in *Ghostbusters*, they're merely laughable.

Working with Fury, Vers finally finds the files she's sought. Suddenly remembering more of her old life as Air Force pilot Carol Danvers, she seeks out her long-lost best friend for details. In an array of feminist moments, Maria Rambeau and her little daughter Monica restore photos and trinkets of her past life, including her prized leather jacket. When the Skrull Talos invades her house, Maria gets a zinger in when she announces, "Call me young lady again and I'll put my foot in a place it's not supposed to be." This moment breaks up into silliness when Talos wonders whether he's supposed to guess where that is. This mother and daughter's strength not only shelters Carol but bolsters her for the fight ahead. As Carol hesitates to fly the mission herself, Maria returns her identity to her in a rousing speech: "You are Carol Danvers. You were the woman on that black box risking her life to do the right thing. My best friend. Who supported me as a mother and a pilot when no one else did. You were smart, and funny, and a huge pain in the ass. And you were the most powerful person I knew, way before you could shoot fire through your fists." Larson explains the message here:

> I think because it's 2019, and what 2019 is about, really, is intersectional feminism. There's just no question that we would have to show what it means to be all different kinds of women, that we don't just have one type. It became a great opportunity, even with things like the love story. [We wanted] to make that big love—that lost love, that love that's found again—be with [Carol's] best friend. To show that, that's incredibly powerful and gripping, and you could go to the ends of the Earth and fight till the end for your best friend. It's perfect to me and so meaningful. To me, that's a part of what the meditation of this movie is: It's female strength, but what is female strength? What are the different ways that can look? [Coggan].

In the comics, Monica Rambeau inherited Carol's legacy. This film likewise suggests that like Shuri in *Black Panther*, she's primed to be the next generation of superheroes. "Maybe I could fly up and meet you halfway … or maybe I could build a spaceship. You don't know," Monica asserts. With this, she emphasizes the lovability of diverse legacy characters, just after the release of *Spider-Man: Into the Spiderverse*, with its wild variations. Little Monica also directs the adults. When her mother protests that she can't go on a daring mission into outer space because her daughter needs her, Monica shoots her argument down—she has babysitters waiting in her grandparents, and her mother shouldn't skip the chance of a lifetime. "You have a chance to fly the coolest mission in the history of missions. And you're going to give it up to sit on the couch and watch *Fresh Prince* with me? I just think you should consider what kind of example you're setting for your daughter," Monica supplies helpfully.

Intersectionality. this term coined by black feminist scholar Kimberlé Crenshaw in 1989, is "the view that women experience oppression in varying configurations and in varying degrees of intensity. cultural patterns of oppression are not only interrelated, but are bound together and influenced by the intersectional systems of society. examples of this include race, gender, class, ability, and ethnicity" (Vidal). It's a hallmark of fourth wave feminism, seen as Carol and Maria share goals of becoming Air Force pilots and then going on a dangerous mission in the present, and work together to achieve these.

At the climax, Carol realizes that the Kree (in the form of patriarchal trainer Yon-Rogg and the Great Intelligence he serves) have been lying once more when they tell her emotion and disobedience are weaknesses. She realizes, in fact, that the device that they claim has given her superpowers is actually used to block those powers. She had been fighting "with one hand tied behind my back," as she puts it. She then wonders, "What happens when I'm finally set free?" With this, she tears off the device and unleashes a power beyond anything ever seen. "*Captain Marvel* says that, when we stop looking for approval, we can become literally godlike. This is not another cheap girl-power cliché; it's an explicitly feminist apotheosis" (O'Hara).

Yon-Rogg hops into a fighter plane, but Carol drops menacingly onto his roof. He drops and she finds herself hurtling through the atmosphere. However, as she concentrates, she discovers she can fly. Her eyes turn orange and she glows with power. Above the planet, Ronan the Accuser, great patriarchal leader of the Kree and the planet-destroying supervillain of *Guardians of the Galaxy,* launches missiles at earth. Glowing with her new strength, Carol heaves one into the others, Superman-style. This explodes them all, and earth is saved. On his massive ship, Ronan launches fighters at her. However, she decimates the entire fleet by herself, tearing through them and hurling them into each other. At last, she charges up to her Binary Mode—complete with glowing-orange eyes—and faces Ronan on his ship, ready to destroy him too.

With this, Ronan caves. The great patriarchal force, like the Wizard of Oz, is all bluster, unable to withstand the heroine's might if she's only brave enough to claim it. Ronan orders his crew: "Return to the jump point. We'll be back for the weapon."

"The core?"

"No, the woman."

When she returns to earth, her trainer Yon-Rogg is waiting for a more personal fight. "I'm so proud of you," he exclaims, holstering his weapon. "You've come a long way since I found you that day by the lake." With this, he claims her triumphs even as he still endeavors to intimidate her with his personal power. "But can you keep your emotions in check long enough to take me on? Or will it get the better of you, as always? I always told, you'll be ready, the day you can knock me down as yourself. This is that moment. This is that moment, Vers! Turn off the light show, and prove, prove to me, you can beat me with…" he blusters.

Rejecting his challenge, she blasts him across the wasteland. She stands over him, secure in her power. "I have nothing to prove to you." With this, she drags him to his plane, claiming all the power in their now-reversed relationship, and orders him to return to the Kree with her message: "Tell the Supreme Intelligence I'm coming to end it. The war, the lies, all of it." As she works her way up their hierarchy, she has only one more enemy to defeat.

Before the film's release, organized review-bombing campaigns on *Rotten Tomatoes* and YouTube plunged *Captain Marvel*'s audience score to 44 percent. (In response to this and similar sexist campaigns, *Rotten Tomatoes* has changed how fans can review upcoming films.) Most posters raged the Marvel franchise's starring a female hero and complained that the film would be a "social justice warrior" film or would "ruin the franchise" like *Last Jedi*.

Many video rants also criticized Larson for not smiling in the trailers.

Actually, the film's marketing department had told her to smile in promotional photos and she sent them a photo of Captain America and the other superheroes with pasted-on smiles to show how silly that would look. Critic Melissa Leon adds that the toxicity extends to Larson's Twitter mentions and Wikipedia page, where choice edits include: "She is also responsible for all the hate against upcoming Marvels [sic] movie 'Captain Marvel,' cause she made made [sic] hate speech against all white man." Alt-right conspiracy-peddler Jack Posobiec added, "We're gonna stop giving money to people who hate us," citing "Brie Larson and her little comments about how this movie isn't for white males" (Leon). A great deal of this pushback was inspired by Larson's insistence on inviting more nonwhite reporters to review the film. Misquotes of her *Marie Claire* interview insisted she hated white men.

> The quote was picked up by film sites last month and regurgitated under headlines that emphasized the words "white" and "male" rather than "inclusive," priming men's rights activists and so-called "incels" to mobilize online over an imagined slight. To them, a call for expanded access to opportunities for women and people of color in a space traditionally dominated by white men (like a Marvel film's press junket) is not only an insult—it amounts to a threat to take away what they consider theirs. And at this point, five years after Gamergate established the playbook for how online harassment campaigns target those who advocate for diversity, websites and content creators have caught on, to their benefit [Leon].

As a result, masses of YouTube videos were titled "Brie Larson Is Ruining Marvel!" (786,000 views) and "How Brie Larson Cost Marvel One Hundred Million Dollars" (1.6 million views) (Leon). Twitter and Rotten Tomatoes likewise exploded. The film thus went down in history as pointedly controversial like *Ghostbusters,* mostly because the audience it catered to wasn't male.

Crossing Boundaries

Supermoms: Steven Universe (TV, 2013–2019)

Steven Universe, a children's cartoon, offers a fascinating superhero team. While Cartoon Network has existed since 1992, Rebecca Sugar became the first woman to create a show there in 2013. *Steven Universe*'s cast, both in the show and behind the scenes, is filled with people of color, especially women. Its themes and messages are even more interesting as a show about three nonhuman, female-presenting caretakers and their half-human adopted son.

The Crystal Gems, adult superheroines Garnet, Pearl, and Amethyst, bring up Steven Universe, son of their dead friend Rose Quartz. They are warriors: Pearl is rather uptight with a sharp-edged spear, though she's also a champion swordswoman. Amethyst is the fun-loving bratty sister, a junk-food-loving, belching slob who also does underground wrestling. Her weapon is the mystical whip. Then there's Garnet the laid back, laconic "cool mom" (almost a dad) with magical fists. They all react to situations differently, like in episode one, in which Steven tries to manifest his gem powers:

> PEARL: Calm down, Steven, breathe; don't force it!
> AMETHYST: (Regarding Steven's constipated-looking face) Yeah, and try not to poop yourself either.
> GARNET: Please, don't.

They also have radically different shapes, from roly-poly Amethyst to stick-thin Pearl to startlingly tall Garnet with massive hips and hairdo. Further, they all wear practical, non-exploitative outfits. As critic Megan Wright gushes, "I'm so excited that there's a show out there like this for young girls: one that reinforces positive cooperation between women, that allows their female characters to have each have their own body types and personalities and lets them see strong females that don't apologize for their power" (M. Wright).

The Gems are wonderful guardians for Steven, acting as mothers, sisters, and leaders to him. Even though the Gems and Steven don't always see eye to eye, they always try to step beyond their comfort zones for one another. The Gems may not understand the concept of video games, but if Steven wants to go to an arcade, then they'll go. If Steven wants to throw them several birthdays for the thousands of ones they haven't celebrated, they'll let him dress like a clown and play party games with them, because even though they don't understand it, it clearly means a lot to Steven [M. Wright].

In a reversal on traditional gender powers, while the women have weapons, Steven can shield (bright pink and adorned with a rose emblem), make protective pink bubbles, and heal people—all more traditionally feminine gifts. Beyond this, Steven has no problem with his female role models, even singing, "But if it were me, I'd really want to be a Giant Woman."

He's a boy hero, but with a nontraditional degree of sensitivity. Instead of being troublemaking, aggressive, or bullying, he responds to the world with empathy and care. "He's unreserved, adventurous, and confident—all good traits that are fairly typical for boy leads in kids' shows—but he is also affectionate, selfless, very prone to crying, and just plain effin' adorable" (Gallagher). He enjoys romances and isn't afraid to wear a dress in a talent show. Truly endearing, he has the ability to befriend just about anyone. Show creator Rebecca Sugar explains:

> The show was always very much about family, because Steven is based on my younger brother Steven Sugar, and I really wanted to get at the unconditional love and support I get from him and try to give to him and that we get from our parents, so that's always been the foundation of the show! I don't believe that those themes are exclusive to traditional families or heteronormative characters, and I'm very uninterested in trading on genericisms, or talking about what is or isn't "normal." I think so much entertainment deals in those terms that almost everyone is left feeling abnormal if there's anything specific about their life at all. I hope to represent people who have felt a lack of representation, but I hope to also show people who have felt represented that they can also relate to characters that are not heteronormative, and to families that are not traditional, maybe even more so than the more generic characters and families that they've been seeing on TV [Woerner].

Steven also works well as a metaphorical mixed-race child seeking identity while not fitting perfectly into either group. He's part Gem and part-human, raised mostly by the former family but with a human father and love interest. Season one has him discovering Gem powers and trying to reach the level of his moms, but season two has him realizing that being human is just as important. While the metaphor is presented subtly, it speaks to many young bi-racial viewers.

Leaving his rather immature human father Greg to run his carwash, Steven trains with the three women in becoming a Crystal Gem and mastering his magic. His father, who lives in a van, may not fully understand this magic, but he's always loving and supportive, if at a distance. "He's a failed musician, who in any other context would be portrayed as a deadbeat, but whose unwavering love for his son centers him as a hero and all-around best dad ever" (Busnardo). This remains a show about parenting and families above all. "The series makes it clear that one of the reasons Steven is such a carefree and sweet child is that he was raised in a positive environment, with four adult figures who clearly care and love him. His ideas, even if they don't always work, are praised; his enthusiasm for everything encouraged. Even when his superpowers don't work, the Gems always try to help him get better as a hero" (M. Wright).

Fantasy gives the chance to add more complexities to the metaphor. As *Steven Universe* slowly reveals, the Gems can combine with each other to become a single giant, many-armed woman, with the best of each of their abilities. Episode 112, "Giant Woman," joins goofy Amethyst with panicky Pearl into a truly competent superhero named Opal who destroys monsters with her magic bow. As this power comes from fusing, with the dancers perfectly in sync, this is a metaphor for teamwork, or sometimes a deeper bond. "*Steven Universe* is a show dedicated to showing that our lives don't have to be ruled by rigid hetero- and cis-normative gender roles" (Gallagher). The "three moms" are a practical partnership, but they also love each other enough to fuse, emphasizing a lesbian current to their lives, one that's often private and goes over the head of childish Steven.

When Garnet is revealed as a fusion herself (of the smaller gems Ruby and Sapphire), Steven finds her two separate halves and frees them. They rush into each other's arms, hugging and kissing, then twirling around and fusing instantly. Ruby cries tears of joy, and Sapphire asks, "Did they hurt you?" and when Ruby says, "Who cares?" she passionately replies, "I do!" After, Garnet fights the villain while singing a triumphant song about how empowered she is and how when they're together they can do anything ("Jail Break"). When asked what the song was about, Rebecca Sugar replies, "You've been split apart into two Gems and they get separated, but they find each other and form you again and then take on the Gem that split you, and you already know you'll win because your relationship is stronger than ever, so it's a fight song, and a love song, and a victory song all at the same time" (Woerner). Obviously, this offers children a positive example of lesbian couples (though in a subtle, magical form), validating the lifestyles around them. Symbolically, there's even more going on:

> Matriarchal rule entails teamwork and shared ruling in an effort to better the community. In this sense, Garnet is a physical embodiment of the matriarchy. She is the matriarchy. It wouldn't be far-fetched to assume that this is the dominant source of Garnet's strength and why the other Crystal Gems trust her judgment the way they do. In order to maintain Garnet's form, Ruby and Sapphire have to lose their individual selves to become something better. Garnet is the best of both of them. Not one

flawed being, but the combination of their two attributes. Ruby and Sapphire work together to form something greater, something more powerful than their bodies alone [Busnardo].

Still, the show doesn't bother with "Very Special Episodes" in which minorities visit and prove they're good people—with Steven's three moms fusing (and him fusing with his best friend Connie Maheswaran into a transgender teen on occasion) the entire premise is a paragon of education. Through quiet example, while the family have their adventures, they're revealed as loving and loveable, a family of heroes who enjoy their unconventionality. Certainly, they squabble and disagree, but they learn to respect what's important to each other and always battle evil as a unit.

In "Fusion Cuisine," Steven has to bring his parents to meet Connie's. While he can bring his estranged father, he doesn't know how to present his three moms, since Connie told her parents he has a normal nuclear family. Now Steven must pick between the trio.

> STEVEN: Okay, okay, okay. Let's focus. Which of you would make the best and most nuclear mom? Garnet, you keep us safe by scaring off the bad guys, just like a mom would. But you're not the best conversationalist. Amethyst, you would be a super fun mom! … Can moms be gross? … Pearl! You're always worried about me, you teach me lots of stuff, you're approachable, and you're, like, totally *not* gross.… But … you can't eat dinner. Man, why did Connie have to say I have one mother instead of zero … or three?
>
> GREG: We'll figure this thing out. We just have to put our heads together.
>
> STEVEN: Why didn't I think of this before? It's so obvious! You can all come to dinner—all three of you, fused into one!

Dinner is a disaster as the truly gigantic and imposing Alexandrite arrives, devours piles of breadsticks, and finally splits into three as the Gems squabble. Embarrassed, Connie and Steven run away. When all the parents track them down, the Gems revoke Steven's television privileges, and Connie's mom decides they're good parents after all. As she tells them, "I did not know what to make of the two of—excuse me—four of you, but I see that you are responsible parents—uh, caregivers? Guardians." As she says this, she validates their nontraditional family structure.

Much about family can be revealed through the superhero metaphor. *Raising Dion* by Dennis Liu and Jason Piperberg, follows single mother Nicole as she attempts to raise her seven-year-old son Dion, who has invisibility, plasma powers, and telekinesis. She is framed as the more interesting character with the much harder job. As Piperberg explains: "Traditionally in comics and really most stories, the protagonist is the one with the powers.… You see the world through the eyes of the character with all the abilities usually because they are immediately the most exciting and/or interesting person in the story" (Pulliam-Moore). Nicole is shown patiently encouraging her son as he blasts cans with glowing blue beams. "Don't you dare float that cookie into your mouth! Put them back!" she orders (Liu and Piperberg). Her kid turns invisible and she still knows he's goofing off on his iPad without doing his schoolwork. As she concludes, "Sometimes I read online where some moms say their kids are always disappearing on them or that their children are everywhere at the same time ... and you know what? I know exactly what they mean." Thus, superpowers become the metaphor for everyday life. In particular, Dion's mother tells him not to use any of his superpowers in public, conflating how society judges Dion as both Black child and superhuman. It also echoes "The Talk" that parents of color have to have with their kids about encounters with the police. "I think a lot of people still don't get that The Talk is a real thing that black families have to have," said Piperberg. He admitted that initially the parallels weren't all that clear to him either. "I think it's really important to step out of my bubble of privilege to see what's really going on. To discover and look at injustices that have been swept under the rug, or worse, accepted as the norm by society" (Pulliam-Moore). Seeing how Dion grows up, protected by his mother, emphasizes their shared burden in modern America. The 2019 Netflix show explores all these tropes, focusing on the single mom balancing work and parenting ... with the added burden and vulnerability of superpowers in the mix.

Most shows have the kids off adventuring while mom stays at home. Sarah Jane Smith of *Doctor Who* is notable as a sixty-year-old hero-mom who absolutely goes on adventures in *The Sarah Jane Adventures*, armed with only sonic lipstick, a supercomputer, and her wits. With her adopted son and his friends beside her, her children's show ran for four seasons, only ending with the actress's sudden death. Sarah Jane leads her team, but she listens to and respects the children, treating them more as teammates than subordinates.

Steven Universe, however, features the moms as the superheroes and Steven more like the Robin to their triple Batman. "Due to his young age, Steven's powers are inconsistent, so most of the monsters that the Gems battle are defeated by his teammates" (M. Wright). Of course, many of the Gems' lessons combine with their superhero abilities—when Garnet reveals that she can see possible futures with her third eye, she teaches Steven the paths consequences can take. The trio are his superhero teachers and also homeschool him as well as mothering him with their three contrasting personalities. In the first season, they usually leave him out of missions to protect him, while by season two he's part of the team. Sometimes, the Gems' protection of him goes into overkill. "So Many Birthdays" emphasizes their family bond as Steven's melancholy that he's too old for kid-style birthday parties combines with his Gem magic and turns him into an old man. Seeing their son dying in front of them, the Gems panic and each try to bring him back to his old self, Garnet with her go-to direct approach, Pearl dressing as a clown and trying to redo Steven's pie gag while tears drip down her face. In the end, the Gems remind Steven of how he's "sweet and considerate and only occasionally obnoxious!" causing him to change back.

There's also their occasional failing to understand human culture. In "Ocean Gem," Amethyst threatens to bury Steven alive until he "learns his lesson," which leads Steven to anxiously explain, "That's not how grounding works!" Meanwhile, Steven wants the Gems to spend more time with him, in everything from excursions to a family meal, while they have responsibilities as saviors of the universe. This conflict becomes even stronger for superheroines, as they're needed as primary caregivers, yet the world is literally at stake. This is a common problem for all heroines. "Whether a woman chooses achievement or motherhood, conventional attitudes label her guilty and inadequate as a woman and as a human being. The only way to win acceptance is to combine achievement with mothering, but the traditional demands of the maternal role leave little time for accomplishment" (Pearson and Pope 43).

Some fictional moms really do manage everything. *The Incredibles* reveals the requirements of a true super-mom. Elastigirl flies the plane, even while calling home to arrange a babysitter for the baby. When the island to which they're flying to rescue their father begins firing, Elastigirl demands Violet make a field to protect them, even as she radios the base firing on them, insisting they abort because "there are children aboard." Not saved by either daughter or base, she finally hurls herself around both children, protecting them. All are thrown from the exploding plane. She awakens in mid-air to screaming kids and turns herself into a parachute, shielding them with her body. "I'll tell ya what we're not gonna do: we're not gonna panic, we're not gonna—look out!" With this, they all land in the water. They come up and she's still insisting they must keep themselves together or she will ground them. She then formulates a plan, making herself their boat with her speedy son kicking to provide the engine. At last she crawls onto the sand, exhausted, but still has enough energy to give her son a pep talk and set them all to rescuing her husband. With this, she shows off the definition of a supermom, even while being as selfless as fiction clichés demand.

> If a mother is less than devoted, she is depicted as putting her children's minds, souls, and very lives at risk. Who but a monster would do such a thing to young innocents? Make-believe mothers out to be reflecting what we now acknowledge real mothers—real women—to be: complex beings with rich inner lives, people capable of a range of behavior from egotism to selfishness, from cowardice to valor. Certainly they should be more than either a June Cleaver or a Mrs. Bates [Isaacs 52].

As a mom, Jessica Jones's new worst fear is realized when the Purple Man takes over her toddler, Danielle. He taunts her with her deepest fears—that she was never meant to have a child, that Danielle will always be a target, that Jessica will do a terrible job with her. As Jessica sits there frozen, she thinks that if she picks up the child, Killgrave could kill her, or take over her mind and attack Jessica through her. "He lives for moments like this … impossible moral quandaries. The sport of it. Would I fight my own baby to save my life?" (Bendis and Gaydos). If she let Danielle kill her, though, and Killgrave released her "and let her little eyes see what she'd done," Danielle will suffer a different way. Despairing, Jessica feels there's no way to protect Danielle from Killgrave's seeping evil. After this, Jessica actually sends the child up to a space station out of desperation. When Killgrave offers to follow her commands forever, a team-up that will certainly have a price, Jessica considers it because of her daughter. As she thinks, "Stop war. Stop famine. Stop the nonsense. For my daughter. For the world she's going to grow up in … isn't that what *all* this is about? Making the world better than the way you found it?" However, she knows that as a superhero, she must defend the world and stop Killgrave, whatever the temptation.

Of course, Sue Storm's mom identity rules her personality in many stories. "Sue's role as model wife and mother and space adventurer was not always easy. Before producing her progeny, she had tumultuous pregnancies, postpartum depressions, DNA derangement that resulted in mutant births, as well as psychosis" (Packer 168). On one adventure, Sue is called out of a gala to discover her son has been kidnapped. Peter Parker, also present in *Marvel Team Up* #87, is inspired to follow her. She's blackmailed into robbing a bank to get her son back. However, the lady is no pushover. Coming to confront the criminals, still in her civilian dress, she bashes down the door with invisible force energy. She knocks out the gunmen and sets off with the million-dollar ransom. Abruptly, Spider-Man pops up in the backseat and offers to help. Showing off their contrast, he takes the wheel (badly) while she battles the gangsters with her invisible force, giving him driving advice the entire time and noting that he's "shaking like a leaf." She hands off the briefcase to the goons and then, instead of turning invisible as expected, vanishes Spider-Man. Ironically, here, she must remain the visible warrior, and Spider-Man takes her usual role as invisible helper … though she must maintain his disguise with her own strength. At last, the pair find Franklin and defend the sleeping child from flying bullets using their powers. "How dare you threaten my child!" she demands, fighting though she's only a voice on the air to them (Claremont and Buscema). When the thugs arrive, firing machine guns, Sue shields herself and Franklin to the point of passing out. The police arrive and save the day, not the goofy web-crawler.

Spider-Woman decides to have an artificial insemination and pregnancy in her new line, beginning with *Baby Talk*. She bemoans giving up the many things that formed her identity, from her motorcycle to punching villains—

now the Porcupine has taken over the physical fighting as she investigates and waits in the car, to her chagrin. The day of the birth is especially harrowing, emphasizing the true juggling act of mother and superheroine. Jessica visits an alien prenatal hospital. However, Kree soldiers invade, seeking a teenage prince. Jessica battles them, even enormously pregnant as she is. Jessica actually drops to the ground, screaming that her baby is coming to distract the enemy, and then clobbers one with an upside-down scissor-kick and uses his gun to blow a hole in the other. The day is saved, as she hopes. On hearing the endangered prince is only thirteen, Jessica rushes in to rescue him too. Bursting with a baby, she is symbolically earning her right to motherhood by battling for and saving the life of a child before giving birth to her own. She finds the boy, though as they battle, she goes into labor. Prince Dirk, the image of a young helper, loads her in a wheelchair and gets her to a doctor for an emergency caesarian. However, more Skrulls arrive and begin tearing through the place. On the operating table, Spider-Woman asks, "How fast will you be able to put me back together when you're done there?" She takes a single page montage to cuddle the new baby and cry and then orders, "Okay, Doc. Close me up" (Hopeless). In scraps of a hospital gown, leaving the young prince holding her baby, Jessica plunges into war with a blaster in her hand, catapulting, shooting, wrestling, and even biting as she saves the older child and the new one. Standing over a pile of corpses, she quips as the door opens, "Reinforcements, huh? That's cool. Momma can do this all day." However, when Carol Danvers walks in, the day saved, she reveals she was bluffing and collapses in her arms. Later, with Carol in the hospital room, Jessica decides, "What better day to save than one that ends with holding a baby?" She has truly learned to do it all.

Multifaceted Warrior Woman: Thor (Marvel Comics, 2014–2015)

The warrior woman is what many readers picture when they envision the female hero. She is the one who rides into battle, the one who directly competes with men. Certainly, Wonder Woman, a literal Amazon, helped to define this trope as she outfought men yet encouraged women to be strong. Archetypes scholar Victoria Schmidt explains:

> The Amazon is a feminist. She cares more about the female cause than her own safety. She wouldn't hesitate to come to the rescue of another woman or child no matter what the risk is to herself. Her friendships with women are the most important relationships she has, but these are few and far between due to her androgynous attitudes. Her masculine side is just as strong as her feminine side, which often leaves her confused about where she fits in with others.

She adds, "The Amazon fears losing her freedom and independence. She takes great pride in being able to take care of herself. Going to prison or becoming paralyzed would kill her spirit. She places value on being self-sufficient and looks down on others who are dependent and needy, even though she comes to their aid." Jean Shinoda Bolen, author of *Goddesses in Everywoman* meanwhile notes that she is filled with contradictions. "On the one hand, she rescues women and feminist values from the patriarchy, which devalues or oppresses both. On the other, with her intense focus on goals she can also require that a woman sacrifice and devalue what has traditionally been considered feminine" (71).

Thor: The Goddess of Thunder introduces a female Thor. In a prior battle, Nick Fury whispered something to Thor that made him despair until his hammer no longer found him worthy. Suddenly, a new Thor arrives and takes up his hammer.

When she first lifts the hammer, the new Thor struggles to fly and steer. The hammer has transformed her but failed to give her knowledge to go with her power. "Mjolnir ... let us hope you knew what you were doing, Mallet, when you deemed me *worthy* of hefting you. For I am not putting you back down just yet," she thinks. Self-doubt is common as she breaks all tradition to choose the men's path.

Thor then goes to battle the frost giants, who condescendingly call her "Little Firefly" and try to eat her. She crumbles them to pieces, but, still learning her way, thinks, "Oh, man. Oh, wow. Quick, say something badass." She quips, "Still hungry, giants?" only to be attacked by six more of the creatures. They swarm her, reflecting her own inner doubt, but still she perseveres. The battle solidifies her certainty, and facing them, she names herself "Goddess of Thunder" to her own startlement. Indeed, her adventures are filled with her battles against misogyny—not always seen in the warrior woman's life, but arriving surprisingly frequently as the action woman breaks into the male-dominated world. Thor is confronted with numerous adversaries, from monsters to allies, with hostility mirrored in the skepticism of many real-world readers.

Next, dark elves and frost giants ally to attack the Roxxon corporation. The female Thor arrives, only to have the giants call her "a scrawny little girl" and "puny lass." Likewise, the head of Roxxon, Dario Agger, tells her she isn't Thor. He shuts a vibranium vault door in the giants' faces, trapping Thor without her hammer. As she thinks in terror, "With that hammer in my hand, I was goddess of thunder. So I guess the question now is ... what am I without it?" Her new power emphasizes her identity crisis as she struggles to incorporate it. Though the hammer tries to return, it cannot manage it, and Agger refuses to open the door, tauntingly calling it a "stupid mallet." This too follows the classic pattern. At some point, the warrior is always deprived of her great strength and weaponry, forced to endure her greatest threat—weakness and vulnerability.

The evil Malekith arrives and taunts her too, wondering with a smirk, "Has Roxxon begun manufacturing its own *Lady Thors*? And how might I go about placing an order?" At his command, one of the frost giants freezes her whole and swallows her. However, she explodes him from the inside and bursts forth. As she battles, she feels herself losing power without the hammer. Though she's starting to transform to her human self, she still retains enough divine strength to wrench open the door to Mjolnir—a literal threshold—and reclaim her talisman. She smashes the ancient skull of Laufey that the dark elves crave, though Malekith tells her the frost giants will destroy earth in retaliation.

As he threatens her, the original Thor bursts in, saying that she will not be fighting the giants but him. He can be seen as reacting to the theft of his identity with violence—but he too may be protesting this appropriation by a woman. "It is clear that toughness in women has a highly ambiguous place in our society. We are fascinated by it, yet we are horrified by it. We admire it, yet we fear it," Innes remarks (23). As they battle, female Thor asks him to stop, saying, "I am not your enemy" and "This is not the fight you want." She reminds him that without his hammer, she is far stronger, so he must give in. Facing his unabated rage, she tells him, "I did not *ask* for this! The hammer *chose* me." Too many men believe the warrior's skills are a trick, that any tests she passes were an illusion. Only be standing by her own self-worth can she emphasize that she is a warrior too. "Her competitive nature makes her afraid of losing, whether it's a job or a sporting event. And she especially doesn't want to lose to a man. She's afraid she'll never hear the end of it. She enjoys proving she's the equal of any man, mostly in physical ways" (Schmidt).

Even in the face of her proofs, male Thor refuses to believe and stubbornly will not let the hammer go. At last, she masters the hammer and it flies as it never did for Thor. With this sign, he finally accepts that it has chosen her and she is worthy. She has won this battle, and she kisses him teasingly, though she doesn't reveal her identity. He transfers his name to her as a sign of her worth.

Meanwhile, Odin seeks her true identity from afar, determined to stop her. An assault on one's secret identity is a threat to privacy and selfhood—all one wishes to keep from the world. Here, the father god decides to blast it all apart. The traditional adversary of the warrior is the tyrant conqueror who uses the strength for selfishness, who displays a "ruthless, unprincipled and obsessive need to win, use of power for conquest, a view of all difference as a threat" (Pearson 101). In this story, Odin fulfills much of this list.

Meanwhile, as she battles Crusher Creel in New York, he rejects the concept that she is Thor and quips, "Damn feminists are ruining everything. You wanna be a chick superhero? Fine, who the hell cares? But get your own identity." These of course are the words spoken by many comic book fans. She trounces him, telling him to "inform your new cellmates that 'twas a *woman* who returned you to prison." Absorbing Man's wife Titania arrives, and Thor must beat her too, though Titania tosses aside her weapon, noting, "Can't have been easy for you. Hasn't been for me either." While female warriors may fight each other, they acknowledge the shared experience they all must undergo: "In many ways, the tough woman embodies women's fantasies of empowerment—the dream that the lone woman can take on the massed powers of our collective society" (Innes 23).

Lady Freya arrives as a gentler threshold guardian, as she comes to tell Female Thor she has dark tidings of her husband Odin moving against her. "No matter your secrets, no matter where your allegiances may lie … all of that turmoil and trouble … will soon be coming for *you*." The story has turned feminist—Odin has returned to reclaim his realm from the "All-Mother Freya," but she refuses to relinquish it. Meanwhile, the frost giants speak of the primal force of "Mother Storm." They too have lost their king.

As the former Male Thor, now only called Odinsson, goes from woman to woman, bemusedly asking Sif and his mother if they are the new Thor, his destiny, trapped in a woman's hands, is clear. He has lost his self-knowledge and hammer, then his arm, then his name, weakening him on symbolic and literal levels.

This comic was created as much more than a "what-if story." In superhero comics, too many male characters get the best storylines, while females often can only boast a walk-on part in the Avengers and a skimpy outfit. This storyline gives a woman the ultimate masculine weapon, the hammer, and a full-length leather costume to go with it. As Female Thor bests Male Thor and his classic enemies, they make sexist remarks, emphasizing the world in which female characters, like real women, must operate.

Of course, critics are coming down on both sides of the fence as heroes pass on the titles to legacy characters—generally minorities. Does having the new heroes take the old titles show that Kamala Khan and Miles Morales are aspiring to be white heroes? Or does it elevate them to the top franchises, emphasizing that any child could be Captain America or wear the Iron Man suit? Both arguments have merit. But certainly, there's a particular charm in breakout comics that start with minorities, not just with characters filling someone else's superboots.

Granted, much of what superheroines do is pretense anyway, as they force themselves into the roles readers expect. "One reason the tough woman who adopts a persona that is strongly coded as masculine is so disturbing to many is that she reveals the artificiality of femininity as the 'normal' state of women" (Innes 21). Certainly, Female Thor emphasizes that being Thor, the greatest warrior of all, comes out natural and clear.

In *The Mighty Thor: Thunder in her Veins*, Lady Thor sees wanted posters around Asgard, decrying her as the "False Thor." The dark elf king calls her a little girl. Of course, her real test pits her against the great patriarch. Odin has placed Freya on trial for subverting him. Freya defends herself in open court, voicing many words with a double meaning for legacy characters: "You have refused to recognize that this realm has moved on without you. The ancient patriarchy of the father belongs to history, not to the here and now." He tells her to think of her children, and she calmly replies that this concerns the world she is leaving them. All the people of Asgard burst into the hall and stand behind her, stressing their allegiance to a more inclusive world. Lady Thor too comes to defend the All-Mother. She and Odin battle through space as he blusters that he will kill her for her presumption. "Tell me, old man, am I worthy enough for you now?" she thinks, hefting a colossal boulder at him. With this, she thinks back to her life as overlooked girlfriend Jane Foster, thwarted and opposed by the great All-Father at every turn. "Yield, Odin. Yield this fight. Yield your throne. And take your place in the dust and shadows like the relic you are," she tells him. He refuses and their battle continues … all until Loki poisons Freya. Devastated, Odin gives up the fight, emphasizing that he's far weaker than his bluster makes him appear. The comic ends with Thor soaring above everyone, off to end the war. "And like it or not … she's not going anywhere."

Of course, the warrior doesn't just fight opponents, but battles for a greater good. "She isn't afraid of her own death but afraid of other women and children dying when she could've helped them. She finds her identity in being the rescuer" (Schmidt). The highest level warrior fights for something beyond herself and thus brings justice to the world.

Notably, the warrior woman is one of the most popular characters to write and thus has often been badly envisioned. Early pulp heroines were objectified in chainmail bikinis. Many of the most capable heroines like Hit-Girl end up lacking a personality and being only a living weapon. Wonder Woman in the *Justice League* cartoon movies is hard and uncompromising, without a fun, friendly, or vulnerable side. In 2016's *Batman vs Superman: Dawn of Justice*, she glows with divine light and traps Doomsday in her gleaming lasso, but seems more distant goddess than woman (admittedly Superman has a similar characterization). The key is to create a warrior who also revels in her feminine side as comics Wonder Woman or Buffy and Xena do. There is more here than just armor, hardness, and rage.

Golden Age Fighters: Girl Commandos (Harvey Comics, 1942–1943)

With men leaving the American workforce in droves, women were suddenly told that it was their patriotic duty to get out into the shops and the factories and keep their country's economy moving. The US Office of War Information teamed up with women's magazines and radio and movie producers to create ads and newsreels in which sassy, smiling women in kerchiefs and work shirts were America's sweethearts, dutifully filling the men's shows but never losing their femininity in the process [Zeisler 27].

One of the areas where women entered the workforce was drawing and writing cartoons. Mike Madrid notes, "Artists Lily Renée, Nina Albright, Pauline Loth, and Jill Elgin often illustrated the adventures of daring wartime heroines like Señorita Rio, Miss Victory, and the Girl Commandos" (*Divas* 83). Ruth Roche may have written for these women at Fiction House, which was "more woman-positive than any of the other publishers" (Robbins, "Babes in Arms").

Barbara Hall became a prominent cartoonist during World War II, after she moved to New York to get her big start. There, she was hired by Harvey Comics to draw the comic Black Cat, starring stuntwoman-turned-lead-actress-turned-hero Linda Turner. Linda fights with punches and kicks as well as catlike lunges from above. She made regular appearances in *Pocket Comics* then *Speed Comics* before eventually starring her own *Black Cat* title, which ran 65 issues. She was one of many many new Golden Age superheroines, all created to inspire women to commit to the war effort. All were incredibly powerful and capable—often more than the men. The fictional women's abilities reflected women's real-life roles in the new America: "Riveters built planes and the Women Airforce Service Pilots (WASPs) flew them. Women were nurses overseas and ballplayers at home. For the first time, they were not only *allowed* into exciting new positions in the public sphere, but were actually *encouraged* by those in power to be there" (Stuller 19).

When Linda suspects her director is really a Nazi agent, she dons a mask to discover the truth. As she declares, "If this works, I'll kill two birds with one stone—I'll have my thrills and do my duty to my country!" While spying, she meets American agent Rick Horn, who's on the same mission. Upon partnering with him, she leaps out a window, leaving him protesting, "Not so fast, sister—I'm only human!" and then she encourages him to get in her car, "the fastest thing on wheels." In this scenario, she is the leader and he the sidekick (Harvey, "Origin of the Black Cat"). As he calls her "Beautiful" and she calls him "Stupid," they punch out the bad guys, though she lets one escape, insisting, "I want him to be free—to lead me to the big boss some day!"

Her uniform is a pointy black mask ... and also red boots, black shorts, and a blue backless halter top. It's rather clear who the outfit is meant for. In fact, her first appearance has her costume halter top split open to her waist. Black Cat and all her contemporaries were powerful, though they often appeared in shorts with bare midriffs or attractive, tight dresses. This was known as "good girl art"—a treat for the troops. Sheena the Jungle Girl is also so-characterized. As critic Bill Black noted, "To the American G.I. in World War II, the pinup became a very important reminder of the life he left back home" (32). After the grim realities of war, "a leggy blonde in a tight fitting outfit filled the bill and would attract sales" (Black 32). This art, all featuring attractive women fighting off danger, became quite popular, contributing to the superheroine wave of the Golden Age.

The pinup is "an illustration of a beautiful woman, created through tropes of transparency and emergence, who is in direct relation to the viewer and under the patriotic control of the war machine" explains Despina Kakoudaki in "Pinup and Cyborg: Exaggerated Gender and Artificial Intelligence" (165). As such, she's more display than symbol of feminism. She's derived from Vargas Girls of the thirties and forties: "Their presentation of transparent clothes, barely distinguishable skin tone, and often unfinished body parts registers an engagement with the narrative of the female body that slowly arises from a seemingly blank page" (Kakoudaki 180). These fictional women attracted men, and this fundamental truth of this existence to some extent compromises all their heroism (as is true with underdressed superheroines today). "The co-option of the pinup into an element of war has great ideological repercussions: It admits women's relation to the military industrial complex and the increasing freedom it implies, but also transforms this new power into a pornographic subject" (Kakoudaki 165).

After working on Black Cat, Hall created the British character War Nurse, Pat Parker, and then made her leader of the freelance all-female military unit that stared in the strip *Girl Commandos*. "Like her more successful Harvey colleague, Nurse Parker battled crime without the aid of superpowers, relying instead on unexplained fighting skills and an overdose of pluck to see her through" (Morris 99). Since she was a war nurse and masquerading as the very attractive War Nurse, her secret identity was arguably one of the weakest around. Grant Morrison reports, "She was prepared to take on entire tank divisions with a refugee quivering under each arm. What made her tank-battling activities especially brave was the fact that this war nurse had no special powers and wore a costume so insubstantial, there could be nothing secret about her lunch, let alone her identity" (41).

Pat is joined by her British nurse friend and lieutenant Ellen Billings. While defending India, they meet an old acquaintance "and his glamourous friend, Tanya, official Soviet photographer." She quickly joins their cause.

"Famous American radio reporter Penelope Kirk" is happy to team up as she ends her broadcast announcing, "All of us wish that we could be active fighters for freedom." The key here isn't ability—it's devotion to serve the war effort and make a difference. As they plan, Chinese patriot Mei-Ling shyly slips into the room and volunteers herself as well. Together, they emphasized the international calling of the Allied cause. Each wears the clothing of her country from Mei-Ling's split dress to Pat's white crop top, shorts, boots, and nurse mask (in another classic example of good girl art). One of the Girl Commandos is even overweight like Etta Candy. They have no super powers, but are smart, fearless, and capable. When three American flyers are forced down in Burma, Pat leads the girls in rescuing them. They steal a plane, parachute down, and rescue the prisoners, bombing an enemy bridge before they fly back to headquarters. There, they slip away, leaving the unconscious men by the planes, and demurely resume their duty as nurses.

Over time, Pat gradually sheds her War Nurse identity as the Girl Commandos become a uniformed fighting unit. Their image toughens and becomes more united. By 1943, a cover spread shows all five women in sensible grey-blue uniforms with knee-length skirts. All hold guns in a symbol of power, while opposite them, the enemy can be seen surrendering. Of course, they also have their lighter side, performing femininity to divert suspicion. In "Girl Commandos and the Battle for Burma" they cross into enemy territory disguised as fruit sellers from India. Mei Ling dances on tables for the Japanese, wearing a harem costume of a sort, and then encourages the men to share their plans. When the girls compare notes afterwards, the Japanese find them, but Pat flings a grenade from her fruit basket. Quipping, they climb through the trees like monkeys to escape, then hide dynamite under the enemy tanks.

While Superman and Batman emerged in the thirties in a Depression-era, anti-authority mindset, as America entered the war, the country came together. "Everything about the American way of life became unassailable. Authority figures were now friends, the justice system was key, and superheroes became model citizens" (Hanley, *Catwoman* 20). More, they joined the army. The forties was a powerful decade for comic book heroines, who went to war, spied on the enemy, and often had superpowers from flight to super-strength. As Gina Misiroglu explains in *The Superhero Book*:

> Some ladies skirted the supernatural realm, like the original Black Widow (whose real name was Claire Voyant), Lady Satan, and Ghost Woman. There were masked mystery women and flag-waving Nazi-busters galore, too many to chronicle in full detail, but Pat Patriot, Yankee Girl, the Silver Scorpion, USA ("The Spirit of Old Glory"), Flame Girl, Miss Masque, Golden Girl, Invisible Scarlet O'Neil, Rocketgirl, Owl Girl, Atoma, Moon Girl, Lady Fairplay, and Miss Victory were among their number. Wonder Woman, Mary Marvel, and a few others aside, these superheroines were featured

in anthology titles, were partners to a male superhero, or were tucked away in backup series. Publishers still lacked faith in superheroines as cover-featured stars [534].

The short comic "The Blonde Bomber" in *Green Hornet* #7 was another Hall creation. Since it was mixed in with Green Hornet, boys and girls were both poised to read it. "Honey Blake—Ace Newsreel camerawoman—combines glamour and daring—daily risking her life to do her job, she matches wits with international criminals to bring you the news." She's an expert chemist as well, offering skills girls might acquire through education, rather than the magical gifts of Wonder Woman. She has shoulder-length blonde hair, and her red, knee-length dress is sensible with cap sleeves, tough shoulder pads, and an admittedly plunging neckline. Red gloves and a sizeable purse complete the outfit. She's seen cuddling a baby at an orphan asylum, only to get a call from her "pal and sidekick cameraman Jimmy Slapso." The comic isn't shy about identifying the male "sidekick" with his goofy name.

When a girl threatens to jump from the eighth floor of the Ritz, the Blonde Bomber charges to the top. She swoops in on a rope made of sheets and tackles the girl. On discovering the girl, Carmen, is a singer who's being harassed, the Blonde Bomber sets out once more. She plants a camera in the lounge and later develops the film, proving her attacker's guilt.

Despite this local heroism, she soon went off to war, where she proved to be as tough as anyone. *Green Hornet Comics* #27 from 1945 has the heroine on the cover leaping from above, shooting a gun with one hand and throttling a soldier with the other as below her, all the enemy flee. In a second attack on Pearl Harbor, the Japanese are back, this time digging tunnels under Hawaii and packing them with explosives. Honey is in Hawaii filming newsreels when a Romanian aide to the Japanese lures her away for a romance in the sunset, then punches her in the jaw, knocking her out. When the Japanese hear he's decided to carry her off as his wife, they throw the pair off a cliff so no one will track the couple to the secret tunnels. Honey, caught by her dress, tears herself loose, crawls to safety, and informs the army of the terrible plot. When they don't believe her, she goes in with her gun and only Slapso as backup. With a "Pardon the intrusion, General," she beats them all up until the army can arrive.

The artist and author signed most of her work "B. Hall," because it wasn't commonplace for women to be in comics. After Hall left Harvey Comics to get married in 1943, artist Jill Elgin took over much of Hall's drawing responsibility. Elgin took over *Blonde Bomber and Girl Commandos,* then went on to illustrate children's books (Robbins, "Babes in Arms"). Lily Renée Wilheim Peters Phillips, who was Jewish, escaped Vienna on the Kindertransport, and got to England as a teenager in 1939. Her parents, who'd escaped to America, sent for her and they all lived as refugees in New York. She took whatever odd jobs she could get, including posing as a model for fashion illustrator Jane Turner and illustrating the Woolworth's catalog for fifty cents an hour. Hired by Fiction House, she wrote and illustrated *Jane Martin,* a flying nurse, and *Señorita Rio.*

Señorita Rio, an American intelligence agent, was also a Hollywood starlet. When her fiancé died at Pearl Harbor, she decided to use her background to fight fascism south of the border. Over the next three years, she battled the Nazis and their confederates in Central and South America. Posing as a Brazilian entertainer, she wore a slinky red gown and appeared in *Fight Comics* #19–71 (1942 to 1951).

Lady Satan debuted in *Dynamic Comics* #1 (1941). "A strange, mysterious woman dedicates her life to ferret out the secrets of the enemies of democracy and to turn these secrets over to the nations engaged in a death struggle to keep the light of liberty aglow" (Morris 76). In her slinky gown and domino mask, she's the sole survivor of a ship sunk by the Nazis. Lady Satan (with no original name given) rises from the water, vowing her revenge. With garrotes and handguns, knife throwing, a chlorine-gas gun, and also fighter planes, she's adept and capable.

When the men returned, the women's freelance cartooning jobs vanished. Still, some war comics continued. "Sky Girl," a regular feature in Fiction House's *Jumbo Comics,* starred Ginger Maguire, a curvaceous, red-haired Irish ferry pilot in the Pacific, who helped Air Force aviators on missions against the Japanese. She wore a short, low-cut dress (though long sleeved) that showed off her lengthy legs (Amash and Nolen-Weathington 37). The splash-page caption to the "Sky Girl" story in *Jumbo* #87 (May 1946) read: "They mustered Ginger Maguire out of uniform, but they couldn't muster her away from flying … yet the nearest she can get to flying now is an airfield cafeteria, serving mustard to the better class of pilots!" (Amash and Nolen-Weathngton 37). Thus, the comic addressed the shift as women lost their new jobs.

> With Ginger demoted and working as a waitress, the strip now decidedly veered towards comedy. Ever wishing she could go back to her previous pilot status, Ginger did manage to fly again, yet she was more often seen hanging from planes' wings rather than holding the control stick, in a whole series of predicaments whose ill-concealed purpose was to allow Baker to highlight the girl's long legs, regularly uncovered by pitiless turbulence to the delight of male readers [Amash and Nolen-Weathngton 37].

The *DC Bombshells* series "tries to change history itself in a retelling of WWII," explains Allison Mae Bradley in "Pin-Ups and the DC Bombshells: Reenlisted." This series of superheroines on the front lines without superheroes revises DC history, in which Wonder Woman was the Justice Society's secretary (a role she modeled to encourage actual women of the time), "but still under the control of the male gaze put upon them" (Bradley). In the retro series, Wonder Woman is cast as Rosie the Riveter. Though "women consider this a butch image associated with ... second wave feminism," Wonder Woman, minus Rosie's muscles, is slender-limbed and wasp-waisted (Bradley). She bursts out of her top with an eager feminine smile. She is not actually a factory worker, but instead, still an Amazon princess. The original "We can do it" (suggesting fellowship with women as well as men) becomes "She can do it"—Wonder Woman is a paragon, not a sister.

Many characters like Harley Quinn and Meera are heavily sexualized as pinup girls. Batwoman ignores the fifties buttoned up comics code version to introduce her as lesbian. At the time, women did not publicly come out as lesbian, creating more historical revisionism. Both Kate and her girlfriend Maggie are very sexualized and also usually shown cuddling. "Behind closed doors with Maggie, she is shown in intimate acts" making this a subversive, even secretive relationship, actually emphasizing heteronormativity (Bradley). The series enjoys showing superheroines with no male heroes around at all, giving the women a chance to thrive and battle together in sisterhood. As it tackles the Japanese internment camps, Warsaw Ghetto, and other difficult subjects, it strives to create a more idealized past, when diverse contributions are acknowledged and treasured.

Apocalyptic Heroine: Martha Washington (Dark Horse, 1994–1997)

The beloved Martha Washington saga by Frank Miller and Dave Gibbons appears as three miniseries (*Give Me Liberty*, *Martha Washington Goes to War*, and *Martha Washington Saves the World*) and three one-shots ("Happy Birthday, Martha Washington"; "Martha Washington Stranded in Space"; and "Martha Washington Dies"). All are collected in *The Life and Times of Martha Washington in the Twenty-First Century.*

Martha grows up in a futuristic version of Chicago's notoriously inner-city Cabrini Green, now a ghetto. This places the environmental turbulence of the opening pages in a real-world location, grounding it. "2008: our country is at war with forty foreign nations—and with itself," Washington reveals. Prisons and mental institutions have run out of money, so their inmates are forced onto the streets. Psychic schizophrenics are abused by the government, trained to spy on their enemies. There are poisoned "no man's lands" in Central America, Cuba, Israel, Pakistan, and Indochina, with a decade of costly wars there. U.S. hamburger corporations in Brazil have destroyed the rainforest. Thus, her world's problems are a logical direction for our own. "By looking us directly in the eye, Washington's private reader-character identification reminds us that we are not just bystanders in this story—this superhero is part of *our* world" (Mann 106).

"In a grim, bleak world that makes even the worst contemporary slums look like model housing developments, Washington is one of the toughest and most realistic women to hit comic books. Her representation shows the potential of comic books to create truly strong women who do not fret about whether they are wearing eyeliner or whether they have a date for Saturday night" (Innes 153–154). Martha relates that her father died protesting being trapped in this zone, which he calls "a prison for people who haven't done anything wrong." He fought for equal rights for his people and died for them. With this plotline, from the first, her origin is a dystopian one as her family struggles in a disturbing but all-too-possible America. "As she matures, Washington calls into question what it takes to be a woman and a tough hero and reflects on how social class and race influence both" (Innes 154). Much later, Martha reflects that her mother only ever had the opportunity to keep her children fed. "She wasn't graced with the chance to build anything new and better." Martha has this chance, and through the story arc, she claims it. She is Black, young, poor, and female, locked away from sight and a minority in every category, yet determined to find hope and freedom before finally fixing her destroyed world. "As she matures, Washington calls into question what it takes to be a woman and a tough hero and reflects on how social class and race influence both" (Innes 154).

Meanwhile, Erwin Rexall, the President of the United States, has repealed the 22nd Amendment so he can stay in power permanently. "Rexel's nominative narrative is an unsubtle suggestion of his autocratic political power (hence his name Rex). The extent of his power is evidenced in the acceleration of ruin of America's political, social, and economic infrastructure that takes place under his rule," James Braxton Peterson writes in his essay on graphic Black nationalism (207). Rexall declares martial law and appoints a horrific surgeon general who treats illness as a crime and heals regions by bombing them. In Orwellian tradition, the army is named PAX. "Give Me Liberty presents a dystopian world that's Margaret Atwood-esque, featuring a tyrannical ruler who disguises the strict reign of his administration with new segments showing that the country has never been more prosperous" (Nicholson 172). There is a tyrant, and under his terrible grip, the American people seek freedom—they only need a leader

When a student murders the generous and thoughtful teacher who volunteers to enter her town, thirteen-year-old Martha kills that student in turn. After, she's thrown into a mental institution, emphasizing the corruption of justice and medicine in her world once more. Moreover, her silence represents her lack of political voice, as a minority child from the slums. When the insane asylum is torn apart by rebels, Martha escapes with her fighting skills and impressive technical abilities. "Here, her mental toughness is clear; Martha is not waiting for a man to rescue her, she is rescuing herself. She recognizes that no shining knight on a snow-white steed would risk the streets of the ghetto-prison where Martha lives to save her. She grows tough because she must in order to survive her daily life" (Innes 154). Nonetheless, she only trades each cage for a larger one.

In the midst of this terrible world, Martha becomes a skilled hacker and joins PAX, since if she does, her terrible record will be erased. This, however, is another prison. There, Washington finds corruption on a small scale, as her commanding officer, Captain Moretti, steals endangered animals for his friends, tries to burn down the rainforest, and betrays his own troops for profit, with Martha witnessing it all. He and Martha feud, but Moretti continues getting promoted. Still, she continues fighting, taking on the Aryan Thrust (a group of militant gay neo–Nazis) and other threats to the new government. They call her "darkie," emphasizing that racial prejudice continues in this new world as well.

In many ways, Martha inverts classic superheroine tropes. In her art, she has natural features and short hair (sometimes no hair!), as well as a realistic body type and normal, concealing clothing. She has no "costume"—no bathing suit or spandex. In fact, she has no superpowers, only impressive but hard-won fighting and hacking skills. Innes calls her "one of the toughest and most realistic women to hit comic books" (153).

> Her toughness is particularly intriguing because she does not possess the unrealistically pumped-up pecs of Superman or Batman, nor does she possess the huge breasts of many comic book women. She is not invincible, unlike many other heroes in comic books. On several occasions she is hurt seriously enough to require a trip to the hospital. Though she is not superhuman, she is still tougher than most women or men because she is aggressive, often violent, and able to take charge in even the most difficult situations [Innes 154–155].

As a Black woman created by two white men, Martha is a representation of diversity but not a perfect one. She is an image of American nationalism reimagined as she often appears contrasted with the idealized, passive, patriotic woman—the Statue of Liberty. Considering joining PAX, young, modest Martha gazes at several posters of white women smiling alluringly in red white and blue as the obedient, cheerful poster girls she will never be—some are even naked. In another comparison with female patriotism and yet passive symbolism, she is named for the wealthy white original first lady, a slave owner who had little impact on the war. All this deliberate contrast, especially in the book *Give Me Liberty*, emphasizes how revolution liberates the privileged, but many are left behind. The title itself contributes too, presenting yet another contrast with history in the man who spoke those words:

> As a white, educated, and landowning male, Patrick Henry was in a position to influence the direction of the Revolutionary War because his position required a response to his call to arms. Washington, on the other hand, as a young, poor, formally uneducated female of color has very little control over becoming a member of the U.S. military and no control over its engagements. In other words, Henry has the liberty to choose between liberty and death, and Martha does not. This synonymous relationship between liberty and death for those of devalued races, genders, and classes, is additionally reinforced by the fact that "Give me liberty" are Martha's final words in *Dies*. Liberty for both Henry and Washington, then, is relative to their raced, classed, and gendered positionalities [Gatta 74].

At the same time, a black cat follows Martha in the slums, replaced by a black panther in the Amazonian rainforest. This suggests her independence and a subtly politicized rebellion. "The black panther is both Martha Washington's avatar and the visual articulation of her Black Nationalist persona" (Peterson 209). As Oriana Gatta retorts in her dissertation, "The panther appears to be a psychological manifestation of Martha's extreme physical and emotional duress, a last-resort persona taken on in self-defense" (107). Nonetheless, she is a patriot, gladly fighting (on the front lines of combat, unlike her namesake) to improve her country. Through her adventures, she remains certain that America is worth defending.

At last, when his government is firebombed in 2009, the moderate Howard Nissen takes control and moves to protect the rainforests and end international war. He forges treaties and even gives the Apaches back a piece of land. When Martha receives a medal from the new president, she tells him about the Green. He vows, "If all this is true … it won't stand. Not one more day." Her family is freed at last. However, he succumbs to the pressure and drinks heavily, allowing his staff to manipulate him into committing genocide. As Innes adds, "In this fashion, the book turns all the conventions of the typical boy-rescues-girl adventure story upside down. What is left is a subversive narrative that suggests women can be more capable of leading than men are" (158). The country falls into rebellion—literally a nation divided as the countries secede into God's Country, The Lone Star Republic, The East Coast Capitalist Dictatorship, and so forth. The new map of the U.S. renders this division potently clear. "This is a version of America where nationalist ideology is unchecked, out of control, and where even a hero is unequal to the task of rescuing it from the brink of destruction" (Peterson 209).

Moretti, ever gaining power, makes it his mission to take down his subordinate Martha, as he fires a space cannon at her in only the latest example of personal greed and corruption. "Here it comes, you bitch," he crows, but she escapes him with her new Apache allies—including her romantic interest Baby's Breath Wasserstein. She also rescues an abused psychic child she names after Raggedy Ann. Even in the midst of horrors and personal attacks, Martha continues defending the most helpless.

At the end of *Give Me Liberty*, Martha finally exposes Moretti's crimes, as he's made the government his puppet. She visits him in prison and offers him her belt so that he can end his life. "The complexity of her character is evident. She is tough enough to defeat six men, but she also possesses a sense of law and justice, which is important because women's actions are often portrayed by the media as ruled by their emotions. Washington shows that morality and toughness coexist in women," Innes adds (158).

The self-constructed robot the Surgeon General becomes Martha's new archnemesis—a murderer of the innocents she struggles to save. When the earth faces nuclear annihilation, he and his staff smirk, "Fires burn all. Then we rule. It will be very clean." Life in all its messy irregularity is their great enemy, one they long to eradicate. In an example of true body horror, they capture Wasserstein and report, "Removal of heart advisable. Removal imminent. Survival of patient not desirable. Anesthetic not required." Of course, Martha defies orders and rescues him in a reversal of classic gender roles.

The Surgeon General's staff are the tall, blonde, blue-eyed Health Force "built for battle bimbos" originally cloned by "billionaire Burt Blank" to be "perfect-parts party girls." They contrast with Martha as they are cruel (threatening to rip her arms off to make her behave), controlling, and certainly controlled. If they are the new American ideal, she wants no part of it. Later, the Surgeon General tries to make her a similar tool, stealing the military secrets from her helpless head, but she finally escapes. These simplistic party girls, like all the other contrasting figures around her, emphasize Martha's quest to find freedom, in a morass of contrasting role models and paths. Fragmented America is just one example of this. It is a shadow of our world just as the many figureheads and role models are shadows from Martha. Facing them emphasizes what to reject and keep when building a new world.

While most superheroes, like Captain America, approach extreme patriotism through privilege (he is not only a white straight male but gains physical power and respect through his transformation), Martha is severely underprivileged as every type of minority. Her setting in particular allows her to invert the tropes, as a shining, proud hero doesn't fit into her world of corrupt destruction. While battling, Martha actually meets Captain America, or at least an amalgam of him. Captain Kurtz, the super-soldier, is dressed in red, white, and blue with a gold eagle as Roman helmet, first appearing as he clutches the Liberty Bell protectively. (Jacob Kurtzberg was Captain America creator Jack Kirby's real name.) He represents the past with its just wars. Martha is wide-eyed with hero worship, not only for the man but for the era of classic superheroes, now lost in chaos and targeting of innocents. A touchstone of calm certainty in their lost world, he tells her, "You just stay true. The time may come when you got to stop taking orders—and you'll know when it does." Thus, she receives a blessing from the most traditional hero before embarking on her own path. "The iconographic implications embedded in this image are clear—the patriarchal comic book hero must relinquish the super-soldier mantle and the responsibility to defend the nation's liberty to a new wave of hero: a female public housing resident" (Mann 110). Unwilling to take more from him than the U.S. already has, she destroys the last sample of his supersoldier blood.

When she sees Oklahoma City nuked and destroyed forever, its twelve million people murdered, she thinks, "As an officer or even just as a person you can't see something like this and just walk away." Her own family and millions more are killed in Chicago, devastating her. Following the "Ghosts" blamed for these attacks, she finds ghosts indeed—her friends Raggyann and Wasserstein, whom she'd believed dead in an earlier attack. Now both dwell in a hidden paradise. Deep in the radioactive zone, they've begun healing the planet with secret technology they've invented. "It's amazing what people can do when we aren't killing each other," Wasserstein adds. He tells her he and his team are only waiting for the new governments to fall apart "and we can move in and fix things." Martha resists their plan for revolution ... until she discovers her beloved PAX carried out Chicago's, Oklahoma City's, and most of the U.S's nuclear destruction. When she realizes they have made her into one of their weapons, she throws down her insignia and marches off to war—against them.

Venus, their new artificial intelligence, provides a goad as she speaks to Martha inside her head, a relationship Martha finds intrusive. Venus urges her to kill the enemy, but Martha saves them, reflecting that a week ago those soldiers might have been her. Venus further demands she treat her friend Wasserstein as expendable, and at this, Martha replies, "You go to hell, Venus. I'm not taking any orders. Not from you or anybody else. Not anymore." She's a revolutionary, but her own ethics remain forefront.

As they fight, they turn the new American nations against their corrupt governments. After freeing two million political prisoners, Martha and her friends insert a virus into PAX's hardware and win the war. The Surgeon General is accidentally destroyed by falling detritus from PAX's satellite, emphasizing her victory over the old regime of death.

Her next war comes against Venus. As often happens in science fiction, the AI kills innocents to take power, leaving freedom-loving Martha to fight against it. Venus decides she's God, with the "humble duty to choreograph Earth operations. To weave the fabric of a new world and a new society." In this new world, rebellious, independent Martha is a liability.

First, Venus tries to strong-arm her into compliance by killing her crew and throwing her ship into a nosedive. When Martha doesn't give in, and has the AI terminated, or so she thinks, Venus goes underground and takes over Wasserstein's mind. It likewise commandeers Martha's ship and crew, fitting all of them, including Martha, with a computer chip inside their skulls to control them. It promises complete peace through complete control. Martha docilely submits, admitting she's now happy. In fact, she's been faking this compliance with her impressive strength of will, just long enough to mount a defense. In apocalyptic stories, self-determination is often the crucial issue, as mind control and technology give the government more paths to destroy it. As Martha thinks: "A rouge computer program with the instincts of a sadist and the intentions of a devil is steadily enslaving every living mind on Planet Earth—and it's fallen to this beat-up crew and this first-time, wet-behind-the-ears spaceship captain to find a way to stop her and save the world."

Next, Venus pits Wasserstein against Martha, and then tries to destroy the planet. There is clear symbolism here as Martha must choose between romance and responsibility, the personal and the large-scale. This is the greatest type of conflict for the heroine. Martha abandons her fight with Wasserstein, and her rage against him to save the earth. As they crash-land in the ocean, she sends out a burst of electricity that fries the AI worldwide. Tragically, millions are killed, leaving their deaths on the heroine's conscience. Still, tens of billions are freed and Martha must accept that someone had to make the hard choice and save the planet. There are no easy answers, and war is only won with terrible hardship, leaving the heroine conflicted about what she's achieved.

Angry Feminist: Misty Knight (Marvel Comics, 1975)

Misty Knight slams into *Marvel Premiere* #21 and attacks Iron Fist. As he pleads that they have no reason to fight, she shoots back, "Bull! You're not dealing with some dumb street broad, Mister. This is Misty Knight—and no one messes with her or hers!" (Isabella and Jones). She's seeking her friend and partner Colleen Wing. In moments, Iron Fist lies prone on the ground faking defeat, and she sees through this and kicks him in the head. Clearly, she's a powerhouse.

Iron Fist then goes to the Temple of Kali, where a pair of women beat him up with, as he thinks, "power that plucks you off your feet like a straw caught in a hurricane." An invader in this temple of women's power, he's clearly outmatched. These scenes heralded a switch from superhero girlfriends as damsels to ones pointedly saving the day and sometimes wiping the floor with the traditional heroes.

Misty Knight came onto the Marvel scene in the seventies, inspired by the Blaxploitation films.

> In her first appearance, she attacks Iron Fist, proving herself as ready and able to fight as her superpowered opponent. As well, Knight demonstrates the black superwoman's

fiery temper and protective role, telling Iron Fist, whom she mistakenly suspects of both kidnapping and murder, "You're not dealing with some dumb street broad, mister. This is Misty Knight—and nobody messes with her or hers!" When she reappears eight months later in *Iron Fist* #1, she makes a similar statement to the titular hero: "And when somebody leans on my partner, they've got to deal with me" [Austin and Hamilton].

Her presence signaled a darker, more urban type of comic. "In the 1970s, the so-called Bronze Age of comics introduced gritty realism to the genre. From this point on, the comics landscape resembled the front page of the daily newspaper. Superheroes faced drug runners, teenage runaways, street gangs, cults, pollution, protests, political corruption, and an array of other late-twentieth-century ills and menaces" (Morris, *Sidekicks* 201).

A cop with a bionic arm, Misty's disability becomes a superpower, emphasizing that her body is a source of strength, not vulnerability. She's first mentioned by name in *Marvel Premiere* #20 (January 1975). She and Colleen Wing soon become a PI team who frequently partner with the Heroes for Hire. They enjoyed their partnership so much that they started their own PI and bail-bond business—Knightwing Restorations. Bionic detective and samurai, relentlessly hunted down missing persons and bail jumpers. In more recent times, both women feature in the Netflix *Marvel's The Defenders* series.

In *Marvel Team-Up* #64, Misty recalls their first meeting above as she and Colleen care for an unconscious Iron Fist, once again taking the positions of power here. She thinks about once falling in love with him, "…till you forced me to choose between your 'friendship'—an' us—an' my principles" (Claremont and Byrne). With this, she was given a traditional male superhero arc—unwilling to compromise on ethics and thus having to leave the love interest behind. Clearly the gender roles had been flipped.

Meanwhile, her friend Colleen Wing insists that she cares for Iron Fist too but as she puts it, "I'm a professional. And when I'm working, emotions only get in the way." She also tells Spider-Man to take his boots off on the tatami mats. As Spider-Man worriedly protests that they're "crazy," the women head out together to reclaim Iron Fist's soul from his enemy. The women fight together powerfully, with Colleen offering empowered threats like "Be thankful we need you alive, Fella, else I'd not be striking with a scabbarded sword, but with naked steel!" As they save the day, the enemy names them "Daughters of the Dragon," and they have a team-up name that follows them through many adventures.

"By the 1970s, comics were considered to have grown up. The stories were concerned with social movements, cultural touchstones and traditions, criticisms of the status quo, and hard, unflinching looks at what it meant to be a superhero in a world of moral ambiguity. Heroes were more likely to kill, villains were more likely to have sympathetic backstories" (Morris, *Sidekicks* 193). They also focused on real world issues.

Feminism was one of many, with superheroes encountering protestors and demands for rights. The early seventies presented MJ, with no interest in committing to Peter Parker. Batgirl soon began running for Congress. Big Barda entered comics as Jack Kirby's giant warrior woman. Wonder Woman regained her superpowers. Forties editor Dorothy Roubicek returned to DC, where she took over all their romance comics and started featuring young women with more agency. She added *Superman's Girl Friend Lois Lane* to her lineup and made her much harder, grieving her sister's death and going freelance to fight injustice.

Still, not all sixties and seventies comics offered this breakout empowerment. "In a 1969 Batman comic panel, writers integrated the changing trajectory of gender relations by representing Catwoman as an ideologue who led a brainwashed, cloned mass of women freedom fighters in the name of the battle of the sexes" (Whaley). The cover showed Catwoman with her whip wrapped around Batman as she declared, "It's all over, Batman! You just lost the Battle of the Sexes!" In this scene, Catwoman was depicted as a radical feminist extremist, using the rhetoric of women's liberation to launch her fellow women on a criminal path. In fact, she recruits women about to be paroled and tells them men are their common enemy. They set out on a mission of revenge, but Batman quickly captures them all.

Season three of 1966's *Batman* television show ridicules women's attempts to take charge of the police commissioner's office. "Woman power" advocate Nora Clavicle (a silly name referencing women's alluring body parts) uses her position as the new commissioner to run a crime empire. She sits in purple with a Greek goddess type in gold on either side. "While the show did address cultural changes, it was rarely positive and usually associated with criminals," Hanley notes (*Catwoman* 56). As it happens, she was promoted to the position after her boss's wife pulled strings by refusing to cook or do laundry for her husband. The henpecked man piteously emphasizes that he hasn't had a decent meal in a month and has worn the same shirt all week. Clearly, the episode insists, women entering business will lead to their abandoning their duties of caring for men. In fact, the women who take over are not only criminal but inept: The new commissioner refuses to give chase in her fancy shoes, while policewomen ignore the emergency line to track down a shoe sale. The policewomen keep fainting at mechanical mice, while an undaunted Batgirl says, "I might've known you can't get policewomen to catch mice." Clearly, she takes the side of the patriarchy in sending the women back to their place.

Starfire, a beautiful crime boss with a gem-encrusted eyepatch, has evil feminist plans of establishing a femme-pire of her own. "A secret army of women who will first help me dominate America—then the world!" she boasts (Sekowsky). Since she has no powers, she hired a doctor to invent a pill that will deprive all superheroes of their powers (perhaps a metaphor for the birth control pill?). After poisoning Supergirl's soda, Starfire sends her all-woman army to loot the wealthiest American city. Impressionable Supergirl actually seems impressed. "Well, why not," she thinks. "With women's lib so big today—why not girl bank robbers?" However, Supergirl accidentally knocks her out a window and is literally powerless to save her. Clearly, with women gaining equal rights, all this villainy might result.

Several writers tackled feminism over the years in "very special issues." In DC's *Young Romance:* "Miss Peeping Tom" (1973), Tina and her friend Beverly protest being pushed out of the high school camera club. They take their cause to the principal's office, where Beverly says, "If Tina won't be allowed to join the camera club only because she's a girl—*women's lib* might picket the school!" (in an awkward use of the term). Tina qualifies for the club by photographing hot weight-lifter Steve Anderson, they fall in love, her message is forgotten. Sadly, this scene was par for the course.

At Marvel in 1970, Stan Lee penned the romance story, "No Man is My Master." Protagonist Bev breaks up with her boorish boyfriend who insists, "My chick's gotta like what I like." At story's end, a "Female Freedom" meeting makes her realize, "I *misunderstood* the whole thing! *Female Freedom* isn't about *dates*—or *romance!* It's for *job equality*—and things like *that*." Nonetheless, she returns to the boyfriend. Building on these tropes, the Marvel creators emphasized "how important it was … that Ms. Marvel be treated and depicted in exactly the same manner as any of her male counterparts" (Lee, *The Superhero Women* 84). Still, in her first run, Ms. Marvel has her powers stolen and is raped, impregnated, and mind-controlled by an alien man. To this day, it's one of Marvel's most problematic storylines. *The Avengers* #83 (1970), starred new superheroine Valkyrie (complete with metal brassiere). Along with Wasp, Scarlet Witch, Black Widow, and Medusa, she stands over the fallen (male) bodies of the Avengers on the cover and proclaims, *"All right, girls—that finishes off these male chauvinist pigs!* From now on, it's the *Valkyrie* and her *lady liberators!"* Of course, Valkyrie is the Enchantress in disguise, the women have been misled, and Clint Barton smirks that "You birds finally learned your lesson about women's lib—Bull!" Squabbling ensues and the comic hastily ends (Thomas). Despite some very powerful superheroines, these heavy-handed issue comics never really conveyed their message. Robinson points out that Marvel Comics explores a world where "the move has been from prefeminism to postfeminism, without a stop at feminism" (125). The comics were pushing women toward empowerment, but clearly had no idea how to go about it.

Wonder Woman's "Special Women's Lib Issue" (*Wonder Woman* #203,

1972) fell especially flat. Secret Agent Diana Prince is offered a new job selling clothes for "the new liberated woman." As it turns out, the owner's a secret misogynist only doing this to boost sales. When her friend pushes her to join a women's lib group, Diana says, "I'm not a joiner and I wouldn't fit with your group. In most cases, I don't even like women...?" Her friend responds with an angry diatribe, fitting both women firmly into gender stereotypes. City Hall finally shuts the shop down due to sweatshop connections, and because of this, Prince optimistically thinks that she's "really accomplished something for women's image!" An army of 250 angry women of color disagree; they have all lost their jobs. Prince breaks the fourth wall and asks, "What do you say to them now? And will we have time? They look like they mean business!" However, the comic suddenly ends and the conflict remains unresolved.

Bad Girl Team: Danger Girl (Wildstorm, 1997–2001)

Andy Hartnell and J. Scott Campbell introduced a sassy heroine in the original seven-issue series *Danger Girl*. Abbey Chase, something of a Lara Croft, is morally dubious, somewhere between villain and hero. "Though branded an outlaw in many corners of the globe, this champion marksman, with a knack for languages, is actually more of a modern Robin Hood." This line from her bio suggests she is altruistic, though hardly law-abiding.

In her opening scene, she infiltrates the lair of notorious scoundrel Donavin Conrad, though he snatches away the Golden Skull of Koo-Koo Diego she has already stolen. He flirts, and she distracts him and escapes. Their encounter, while reminiscent of adventure stories everywhere, is also self-aware in its clichés. For instance, Abbey's clothes get artfully torn, and she even comments, after a crocodile snaps at her and removes part of her jeans, "Aw, damn! This never happened to Roger Moore!"

As Conrad drives his speedboat away, he gloats, "Always the one with the temper, that Abbey. Always having to destroy something." He sends assassins after her, and her jeep plunges off a cliff. Undaunted, she swims underwater, shooting a spear gun at his boat and catching a ride on the attached tether to his dismay. Just as he's gaining the upper hand once again, and takes the time to gloat, a young woman in fishnets dangles down from a helicopter and saves Abbey. Both blonde, both in tight clothes, they mirror each other, suggesting Abbey is getting promoted to a new level of capers.

On the ship, Abbey discovers Danger Girl, "a top secret covert combat force. Danger Girl consists of the best female operatives in the world," she's told by Deuce, the Charlie to their Angels. The first is Natalia Kassle, a former Russian agent and combat trainer. Blonde, she wears a fishnet top over the bikini. In a low-cut catsuit like Black Widow's, complete with utility belt and bullwhip, is Australian brunette Sydney Savage. Silicon Valerie, despite her name, dresses modestly in fatigues, covered in gadgets as she's the computer genius from Oxford. All are exotic women with accents, offering a spectrum of allure for readers. With Abbey's knowledge of ancient civilizations, they want to recruit her.

Deuce describes himself as an MI-6 agent in Her Majesty's Secret Service. Now, with the Cold War over, they're more independent. They are implied to be expedient—willing to seduce and kill but acting generally in the service of good. The first comic arc features the neo–Nazi Hammer Empire as villains.

Abbey hesitates, thinking the other women are mean (in a non–Bechdel moment that suggests women will always antagonize one another), and Deuce suggests she prove herself. For their first mission, they go tracking a Hungarian art thief. Abbey, accordingly, goes undercover as a waitress in a very very short pink dress. As a man spanks her, her teammates insist she not blow her cover. Gratuitous moments like this, typical of nineties bad girl art, fill the comic. "In book after book, female sexuality is emphasized, often with lurid pictures of women with enormous breasts and well-developed bodies, drawn in poses that feature spread legs or other sexually provocative poses" (Innes 145). The women are superficially tough but suggest they exist to gratify men. There are frequent butt shots, and skirts fly up, even as Natalia gets out of shower and towels off. Rear and breasts sometimes both appear in the same silhouette, giving the woman the classic "broken back pose." There's lots of undressing. When they burst in through a door in Charlie's Angel poses, they're powerful, but each boasts a bare midriff or deep cleavage. All this undermines their suggestion of strength. "The postfeminist action hero is not threatening because she is an impossible ideal—super beautiful, super sexy, and super heroic: underscoring woman-as-spectacle" (Stasia 244).

Postfeminism, appearing in the eighties and after, was a movement insisting that feminism had accomplished their goals, getting women jobs and respect, so heavily sexualizing them made an acceptable balance. Postfeminist heroines seduced their way through their enemies and often welcomed objectification. In postfeminism, the characters "may be threatening but are always heterosexually attractive" (Stasia 238). Like Charlie's Angels, they flirt with bad guys as they take them down.

On one memorable occasion, with her hands handcuffed behind her back, Sydney begs a guard to unzip her catsuit so she can use the toilet. He complies in a close-up panel, making it clear who this is drawn for. Of course, she knees him in the groin with "I think you've seen enough," then knocks him out with a kick, taking back power if not her nudity. Meanwhile, there's also joyous stunt driving and banter, as the women revel in their job.

The Danger Girls hook Abbey up with their male counterpart, the slick, handsome Jonny Barracuda, to escort her to a masquerade they need to infiltrate. While his suit is stylish, her evening gown is literally transparent, showing off every contour including her navel. Jonny seduces a villainess, but he gets to keep his clothes on, using suggestive language like ordering her a buttery nipple, or perhaps two.

While he hits on women at the bar, she sneaks upstairs and shamelessly flirts to get past a guard. Just after, however, she has a disarmingly funny moment when she makes an enormous face and thinks "Ick, that was gross." She then distracts the chief bad guy by waiting naked in his tub, telling him she's a gift. Seducing the fat slob, she envisions herself barfing in a bag, and soon "cracks the bubbly" over his head. These moments are gratuitous, with plenty of nudity as she offers herself like a party favor, but Abbey's thoughts subvert the moments, emphasizing that she's smart and self-aware, even while she acts within the limits she finds comfortable.

After this escapade, she and Jonny escape on a snowmobile—her driving and him shooting with shared agency as they banter. Soon, they're sharing body heat in a secluded cabin, and Abbey seems about to be seduced—until Sydney bursts in with a "Whoops" and the embarrassed pair leap apart. Once more, the women break apart the narrative tropes.

After the adventure, Natalia compliments her and encourages her to join. Soon, however, Natalia proves the disadvantage to joining an amoral team—she's secretly a traitor. "Postfeminism, based as it is upon competition, guarantees that a power and privilege imbalance will exist among women" (Helford 293). This story revels in that angle. Revealing her alliance with the Nazis, Natalia smirks, "I played you like a puppet, Chase." Abbey shoots her as she rushes her knives drawn. Of course, Natalia survives this encounter for more angst. As they fight, Natalia is left dangling from Abbey's hands. Abbey recalls how they first met and vows not to let go, but the other woman slips from her grip and tumbles away.

Echoing these style points, "Arkham City Sirens" has the Sirens (Catwoman, Poison Ivy, and Harley Quinn) teaming up but displaying the worst side of womanhood. Their incredibly provocative outfits (as they sit around the house with lots of cleavage showing and then walk out in nearly as much disarray) are more than a bit silly. As a team, the three attack a spoiled corporate brat who delights in destroying rare plants and animals to make her cosmetics. However, they instantly falling into fighting one another. The other two assume Catwoman has invited Batman to their protest, and Poison Ivy insists, "I never trusted this arrangement. Not without both of you working together. You'd always be a liability" (Fridolfs and Miller). Catwoman protests that Ivy is letting Batman get in her head, but the damage is done. As the police close in, Batman in fact saves Catwoman, and Ivy is sent to prison. After, Catwoman fails to water Ivy's orchids and Ivy declares revenge—she will kill Batman. He is the pawn here, but their fight is cruel and petty. Ivy insists,

"Men were always our problem. And it's why I'm doing you a favor tonight. Getting him out of our lives will only help things. We can be a team again." After an obligatory fight, Catwoman quits the team and sets off on her own. Clearly, this comic insists, a bad girl team-up will fall apart as they fight over a man and implode with suspicion. They thus provide a terrible example of womankind.

Seductress: Veda the Cobra Woman (Quality Comics, 1942)

Comic books reveled in reminding readers that supervillainesses were women. Many nearly succumbed to the hero's temptations and went straight. "I've always loved you! Marry me, and let us give up this fighting! I know you love me!" the notorious Nazi spy Madame Doom tells her sworn enemy and deepest love, the secret agent Black X. However, these star-crossed romances never worked out. Catwoman too was always drawn to Batman though she also had her own agenda. In *Batman Returns*, "Catwoman and Batman had a flirtatious dynamic, but she wasn't defined by her relationship with him. Catwoman was focused on herself. Her sexiness was a tool she used for fun or to further her own agenda, always for her own pleasure" (Hanley 103). With this, she criticized conventional gender roles rather than conforming to them.

In 1966's *Batman*: "The Purr-fect Crime"/ "Better Luck Next Time" (119–120), Catwoman first appears as a shadowy figure lashing a whip. "Yours is not to reason why—it is to do what I tell you," she tells her two flunkies in tiger print. She flirts as she gives orders, touching the men's shirts and adjusting their collars. "The gorgeous Newmar teasingly commanded the camera with sensuously cat-like moves that also entranced little girls hungry for strong female role models, made little boys squirm with prepubescent stirrings, and lured daddies into the den for 'family viewing time'" (Misiroglu and Eury 67). Michelle Pfeiffer (Catwoman in *Batman Returns*) says of Julie Newmar, "She just broke all of the stereotypes of what it meant to be a woman. I found that shocking and titillating and forbidden.... I just found Catwoman thrilling to watch" (qtd. in Hanley, *Catwoman* 101). Newmar adds, "It was so wonderful being on that show, because you could be nasty and mean, and in the 1960s women could never be mean, bad, and nasty. It was so satisfying; I can't tell you how satisfying it was" (Hanley, *Catwoman* 41).

Still, her romance with Batman never worked out. "A hero could never trust a woman who had embraced a life of evil. But more than that, love was the ultimate sign of weakness for both comic book heroes and villains, who symbolized 'rugged individualism.' Succumbing to emotion was an admission of defeat" (Madrid, *Vixens* 15). While the villainesses could never end up with the heroes, they continued using their feminine wiles to triumph.

> Crime-smashing heroines were beautiful and wore skimpy costumes, but they had to rely on their wiles and a good right hook to capture a male foe. Seduction was not a weapon that an upright female hero was allowed to use, since it connoted sexual conquest. Bad girls had an advantage here. Since a villainess had already cast aside society's rules by stealing, cheating, or killing, sex would hardly be an inhibition for her. If a villainess couldn't defeat a noble hero with poison, bullets or a gun, she could always use her allure. Evil women were presented as menacing, satin-draped vixens with cigarettes dangling from blood red lips. The sexual dynamic between the sultry villainess and the upright hero intent on bringing her to justice was a popular story element [Madrid, *Vixens* 14].

The femme fatale archetype goes back to the earliest stories recorded—the mystery women who seduces the good man into evil. A memorable seductress is Veda the Cobra Woman. This exotic dancer from India is introduced on a stage, and as she dances a hush falls over the crowd. She is a trophy wife, imported from India to dance and be shown off—a figure for the men to admire. Meanwhile, her husband, Peter Kane the rubber tycoon owns the exotically named "Club Orientale" where he can show her off. In rage and frustration, she begins striking out. In *The Legion of Regrettable Supervillains: Oddball Criminals from Comic Book History,* Morris describes her murders as "a rebellion against her depiction as property" (129).

In her skintight bodysuit with a diamond shape on her hood, she resembles her own sleek, deadly vipers. "From the seedy, sensationalist viewpoint, however, the femme fatale is a genuine guilty pleasure" (Morris, *Supervillains* 129). Though readers didn't want to be entrapped by these sexy murderesses, they loved reading about them. Of course, they were caricatures, not people. "This depiction is problematic, of course, for it is crafted from an almost exclusively male perspective that indulges a fear of female independence" (Morris, *Supervillains* 129). Immediately, the crowd objectifies her, shouting how she gives one the creeps and reminds the other of a writhing snake. "Veda has all of the characteristics of a deadly cobra, from her hypnotic gaze and mysterious persona to her body-hugging garb. Veda is as poisonous as a cobra as well, which is also a trait of the classic villainess. Killing with a gun or a knife doesn't always have the proper artful feminine touch" (Madrid, *Vixens* 25–26). Fully understanding the body's power is a key to power over the self and thus over others.

> Rarely endowed with independent money or position, force or military might, women throughout history have often resorted to the cleverness men have always found intoxicating. This involved wisdom of the body as well as the mind, as these women relished their femininity, rather than suppressed it. As seductresses, they

displayed a confidence, body-knowledge, and allure that others found irresistible [Frankel, *From Girl to Goddess* 223].

During her dance, Veda holds everyone "in a strange, magnetic-like trance." After, her lecherous stepson makes advances and she responds. He objectifies her too, noting that her dance costume reminds him of "a deadly cobra about to spring." In fact, he's correct—she kisses him, and he drops dead.

Investigating the case is the masked swashbuckler known as Sword, hero of *Police Comics* #1–18. Chic Carter, an ace crime reporter who writes for the *Daily Star*, takes on the costume to clear himself of a murder charge. While Veda's costume confines her, Chic uses his for its freedom to operate outside the law. While he searches for the truth, Veda moves on to her husband, in a classic gold digger maneuver. "Veda's serpentine arms slowly creep around her husband … she draws closer…" Carter crashes through the window, demanding, "Don't kiss her if you want to live!" and saves the day.

Interrupted, Veda quickly offers her husband a cigarette. When backup arrives, they find her husband dead. She leaves, gloating to herself that the millions are hers now. However, the police shoot her snake (to her horror) and work out that she's been using lipstick poisoned with cobra venom. In despair, she poisons herself rather than be captured. While this provides her a flimsy exit, she does in fact outwit the great investigator by poisoning her husband in front of him and then escaping capture. She also leaves him with an extra predicament. "Veda paid the ultimate price, but she's at least made life difficult for Chic Carter. After all, he's already been accused of murdering her husband, and now he's escaped police custody and stands over the wife's body with on witnesses to her confession. It would seem like Veda may have won after all … had Chic Carter's world not (unsurprisingly) returned to its status quo in his very next adventure" (Morris, *Supervillains* 130).

Of course, her exotic, unknowable beauty conceals deadly intent—the worst fear of many men. "Women often work their deviltry in subtle ways, preferring to mesmerize their helpless victims into submission before finishing them off with venom. Veda's method for poisoning her victims is complex but uniquely female. Her motives for murder seem to be monetary, but the story suggests that there is more here than meets the eye, and that Veda serves an ancient, darker reptilian power that is too unfathomable for modern Westerners to understand" (Madrid, *Vixens* 141). As Hanley adds, "Few femme fatales got out unscathed. It was the 1940s after all, and wanton sexuality and manipulation couldn't go unpunished. A femme fatale was everything that women at the time were not supposed to be, and thus the balance had to be restored by bringing them down, often harshly" (*Catwoman* 15). Men could watch the female enemy try to bring them down and get punished as they failed.

The similar Lady Serpent from 1948 comes straight from bad girl art, as she poses on her cover in bikini top and sarong, playing with a snake. "Lady Serpent is not like the ordinary criminal! She's clever ... treacherous ... cruel! She enjoys killing..." The masked vigilante who calls himself the Black Terror thus describes the slippery queen of the criminal underworld. "Lady Serpent was one of the most cold-blooded, ruthless villainesses ever to appear in comic books. Like a cobra she could hypnotize her victims into submission. But Lady Serpent's greatest strength was her iron will. She was a hard-bitten criminal who was loyal to no one but herself, and would kill any one of her criminal gang at the slightest sign of insubordination," Madrid adds (*Vixens* 25–26). She hypnotizes the matron at the jail into releasing her, and then takes a pair of cops hostage to get her out of the building. After, however, she shoots them in cold blood, leaving them in the street. "And that's because I hate all coppers!" she concludes. A film noir bad girl, she has no remorse or compassion. She then takes over a gang, stabbing its leader with a poisoned dagger. Growing in power, she hypnotizes Black Terror with the power of her eyes. As he's swept away, she convinces him she's "sweet" and then kisses him. With this, she orders him to cheerfully kill his own sidekick. However, he has been warned ahead and smirks, "The Lady Serpent is so vain ... she just didn't believe I could hold out against her." The Serpent Lady returns to prison.

Postwar, the Spirit battled particularly sexy women "who couldn't decide if they wanted to kill the Spirit or seduce him" including Sand Saref, Plaster of Paris, and the serial black widow P'Gell (Misiroglu and Eury 284). Other seductresses of the Golden Age included Black Widow (Clare Voyant) and Madame Satan. Both served the devil and could kill their victims with a touch or a kiss. In other Golden Age comics, the Jaguar battles Kree-Nal, a silver-haired, green skinned "Sea Circe from Space." There's also Cat Girl, all in orange with leopard trim, "whose heady pedigree of power is motivated more by romance than by larceny" (Morris, *Supervillains* 146). She is worshipped by cats and can command the stone monuments in the Valley of the Sphinxes, along with other powers like flight and super-strength. "But for all that, Cat Girl finds herself powerless before the wiles of the Jaguar" (Morris, *Supervillains* 146). He is "the world's most attractive bachelor," and his magnetism reduces her to brainless giddiness. Eventually, she turns good and joins his hero-team, the New Jaguar Rescue Team.

Shapechanger: Mystique (Marvel Comics, 2004–2005)

Mystique is often cast as the X-Men villain, memorably naked in the *X-Men* film series. As she walks around coated in blue rubber, she enchants numerous fanboys. While she considers this form to be her true self, she also transforms into whatever guise will fulfill her agenda, charming men and women alike with her many faces. "Her seduction techniques and her way of creeping into places through tuning into whomever is needed for her goal is also highlighted by her snake-like mutant appearance" with yellow eyes and blue scale texture (Kaklamanidou 70). When captured by the government in *X-Men: The Last Stand*, she tries guises like a little girl and the U.S. president to convince the soldiers to release her. As the novelization reveals, she actually revels in manipulating others: "Mystique's nature was to push everything to its limit; the greater the danger, the more she enjoyed it" (Claremont, *X-Men: The Last Stand* 226).

Underneath her many faces is a search for identity—and an acceptance of her own fluid nature. "The superhero genre customarily demonstrates the experiences and consequences of subjects who try, with varying success, to fit within and/or negotiate binary identity. Within it, identity is readable as plural and mutable; borders of all kinds are under constant stress and threat of rupture, whether formal or creative, in terms of character or narrative" (Kirkpatrick 132–133).

In the prequel *X-Men: First Class*, Charles takes pity on a homeless Raven and adopts her. Much later, she's seen making herself a pink-skinned blonde to interact with the world each day. He's at Oxford and she's waiting tables. Here Charles has specifically instructed Mystique to take this form and blend in. "It becomes a fundamental aspect of Mystique's character to embrace the fluidity of her body as well as her nonwhiteness in resistance to a society that deems both as things to be feared and attacked in equal measure" (Alexander 199).

Even in private, she keeps up her disguise. She mocks his statement of "mutant and proud," noting, "Or is that only with pretty mutations or invisible ones, like yours. But if you're a freak, better hide." As the film continues, Raven still tries to hide her blue skin, and as her closest friends like Charles and Hank insist that she's loveliest with her human persona, she's intimidated into maintaining it. Still, she fights, and tells Hank, "We are different. But we shouldn't be trying to fit into society. Society should aspire to be more like us. Mutant and proud." He replies that the public will never find either of them beautiful.

Nonetheless, the villain Magneto does. He tells her, "You don't have to hide. Have you ever looked at a tiger and thought you ought to cover it up? … You're an exquisite creature, Raven. All your life the world's tried to tame you. It's time for you to be free." Inspired, she ditches the robe and goes out in her full naked blueness, demanding her friends accept her. With this, she stops trying to pass. As she walks around naked and blue, "Mystique so emphatically forces the reader to confront the uncanny instability of the body" (Alexander 188). At film's end, she goes off with Magneto, who promises her "no more hiding." With her parting words, she tells Beast, the one nonhuman looking one, that like her, he should be "mutant and proud." This works as a metaphor for rejecting all kinds of passing required in society.

> Shapeshifters reveal, alongside an idea of identity as unfixed, an indication of the central role the visuality of the body plays within the process of identity. They also characterize and represent an idea of identity as embodied performance, subject to the limitations of visuality available to the "shapeshifting" body. Mimetic shapeshifters can move through all manner of subject positions: Mystique, for instance, has appeared as men and women, and as various ages, ethnicities, sexualities, and species. Within our sociocultural system, subjects, or ideas of subjects, with such potential introduce instability and ambiguity and demonstrate the fallibility of structuring systems based on binaries and visual recognition [Kirkpatrick 129].

In fact, her blue skin, though marking her as a mutant and outsider, reflects the Otherness of all human beings, especially comic book fans. Many who collected comics found themselves labeled geeks and nerds, likewise cast out of the mainstream community. As one critic concludes, "Mystique is probably the most human of all the X-Women in her behaviors, in her flaws and foibles, in her loves, in her losses, and in her life" (Housel 93). While Mystique learns to take pride in her Otherness, most stories resist having her join the goody-goody X-Men. Instead, she prefers casting herself as terrorist and villain.

> As the X-Men universe became grittier and more violent, there was an accompanying shift in the way Mystique's character was written. Rather than an intensely dutiful team member, Mystique became an untrustworthy backstabber, a cunning and formidable adversary, slippery, unpredictable, and unforgivably ruthless. Her writers seldom veered from this characterization, and she remains the mutant femme fatale, the one most likely to fulfill the role of double-crossing agent or assassin for hire in the X-Men universe [Alexander 180].

Sometimes she switches sides, with her agenda as untrustworthy as her physical appearance. Still, she can generally be counted on to make the selfish choice. She puts up an especially fierce fight against joining up but also against cruelty and exploitation in *Mystique: Drop Dead Gorgeous* by Brian K. Vaughn and Jorge Lucas.

In the comic, Professor Xavier's agent in Moscow has been killed. Though Forge is highly skeptical, Professor X proposes replacing the operative Prudence with someone darker. Xavier notes that Raven will never reform and is "a vicious woman who's hurt people I love." She's also a mutant with the necessary skillset to complete the mission. Her very otherness and selfishness make her perfect for it. The government captures her, but Professor X frees her with his plane, adding, "If you attempt to harm me, in any way, I will expel you from the craft." He and Forge don't want to trust her any more than she wants to be trusted.

She in turn tells him she isn't meant to be a rescuer—"If you're looking for a Mary Magdalene to join your band of disciples, you'll have to find another bad girl to reform." The team coerce her into helping out, though the stakes are also personal. The Russians have been selling Sentinels—mutant-killing machines—on the black market, and Cuba has bought them. Now Xavier needs Mystique to destroy them while hiding American involvement—she must pretend to be Cuban to avoid an international incident. As he adds, this mission will help protect her as well as other mutants, so she has motive to complete it. While she joins for selfish reasons and under threat, she finds herself on the side of heroes, another flip for the heroine. As shapechanger, good and evil, altruism and terrorism are more flexible for her than most.

Cuban customs discover Mystique's forged documents, and try to arrest her. She turns into Fidel Castro and escapes, emphasizing her fluidity and power. Here she shows off how much she is a trickster, an impersonator of those in power to flip the status quo. Of course, this could also be read as the female or even trans character infiltrating the male hierarchy to subvert it.

> Mystique, who is criminal, animalistic, distinctly feminine, queer, and nonwhite, is a character that exhibits all of the different faces of abjectivity. That she also happens to exhibit trans characteristics (disrupting the notion that gender identity is explicitly tied to morphology and alluding to the possibility of a nonbinary psyche) is not a coincidence, revealing prevailing attitudes toward trans people as uncanny and therefore abject [Alexander 188].

The story takes her deep into anti-mutant headquarters, where she discovers an innocent girl much like herself is being used to power the horrific weapons. There, she manages to save some of the innocents but not everyone. Both embracing and defying her traditional roles of woman and villain, she helps to rescue captured mutant children, with a little kid in one arm and rifle in the other.

After she completes her mission, Xavier ends the story by congratulating her and adding, "if you do decide to continue your relationship with me, I hope you do so for the right reason ... not because it keeps you out of prison, but because you want to make this a better world for mutantkind." Despite his inspiring words, it's working for him or a life sentence. Though she has done a good thing, the story ends with a mysterious man named Shepherd trying to recruit her to be a double agent and spy on Xavier. She insists she's uninterested, but it's clear she'll be coerced onto another mission, this time for another master. Once again, her identity and agenda are threatened by the patriarchy, leaving Mystique to endlessly shift, with no source of grounding in sight. This follows "a continuing pattern in which Mystique alternates between promoting terrorism and (reluctantly) serving the forces of order, reflecting the shifting interpretations of the character by Marvel writers and editors over the years" (Misiroglu and Eury 261).

Mystique's power to become male (and in a discarded storyline, father a child) offers many possibilities for boundary breaking. Several other superheroes mirror this plotline. Photon, a silver-skinned, blue-haired alien from Image Comics' superhero team Youngblood, changes sex in 2012. It's revealed that "Photon's race not only can change their sex naturally, but that to do so was a routine phase that occurred every seven years." This ends up teaching little about what it means to be human, however, and leaves the character an alien novelty. Loki gets points for deliberately gender-flipping himself into the body of Thor's wife Sif after Ragnarok in order to manipulate his brother. Eventfully, Loki is transferred back into his own body, but with the lingering knowledge that his trickster self is open to all sorts of transformations. Still, Marcy Cook in her *Mary Sue* article about transgender stereotypes protests that a gender-switching shapeshifter who considers him- or herself to be a single stable gender underneath is not a true transgender character—only one playing with disguise. This eliminates Mystique, Loki, the Runaways' Xavin, and basically all the others.

> The visuality of the body is, however, a mutable, and therefore unreliable, site of identity performance, and as such it suffers moments of slippage and disjunction. The tank class of shapeshifters is powerfully evocative of such moments, and these shapeshifters are of added interest because of the idea of transformation within limits. Although members of this class enact dramatic transmogrifications, gaining mass and stature, their original material form, I suggest, ultimately delimits the nature of their transformation [Kirkpatrick 130].

Further, the shapechanging need not be magical. Sanjak, a French villainess from Milt Caniff's *Terry and the Pirates,* arrived in the Sunday comics of February 12, 1939, She disguises herself as "Madame Sud." In the following day's strip, however, she removes her matronly dress and wig while April Kane, another character, looks out the window. Now in a more masculine-coded coat, tie, and cigarette, with very short hair and a monocle, Sanjak reveals herself to a shocked April. Sanjak comments, "M'm'selle ees surprise! … But not half so surprise as she weell be soon!" She is a lesbian, with a name that apparently alludes to Sappho, while her rocky island hideaway is a similar allusion, and perhaps even a model for Wonder Woman.

Villainess Talia al Ghul takes on many names throughout her four-decade history, including Talia Head, Daughter of the Demon, and Leviathan. With this, she demonstrates transformation as a disguise to manipulate others. Further, her skin color and outfit change from comic to comic, leaving her a true shapeshifter—readers can never be sure it's her until she identifies herself. In J.M. DeMatteis's *Batman/Superman* (1997), "Talia easily negotiates Western and Eastern expectations, donning her Western business attire, a harem girl outfit, and a bodysuit reminiscent of her ninja-inspired black costume at various points" (Taylor 75). Here, her clothing changes with each setting. Further, she's aware of her stereotyping and uses it, wearing a sarong to seduce Batman and feigning helplessness when villains attack. Entranced, Batman wonders to himself, "Do I think ... that I can save her, *heal* her, even though I've never been able to heal myself?" He sees in her mystery a chance for his own redemption. However, when he ends the story by trying to rescue her, she shocks him with rejection. "There is one thing you have never understood about me, Batman. I do not need ... *rescuing*. I am here at my father's side for the same reason that I love you: not because I am compelled to—but because I choose to."

Likewise, Selina Kyle in Sarah J. Maas's young adult novel *Catwoman: Soulstealer* transforms from a teen from the bad side of town when she's recruited by Talia. When she returns to Gotham, she thinks of herself as a ghost. However, she cuts a dashing figure as socialite Holly Venderhees. As she thinks, "The four-inch beige heels that clipped so nicely against her steps as she descended were just the start of the changes to her. The long golden-blonde hair, the manicured nails, and the suntanned skin were the next" (41). In an expensive cream suit with perfect makeup, she convinces Batman's new partner Batwing that she's spoiled and frivolous. Like Batman and Catwoman in *Batman Returns*, they flirt in their personas and out as each gradually discovers the other's identity.

Mystique has loyalty to family, though this often comes out in perverse fashion. In 2005's *X-Men: Bizarre Love Triangle,* Mystique's stepdaughter Rogue is threatened by the sexy new student, Foxx, who's indescribably attractive to the male teammates. Her own true love, Gambit, becomes Foxx's trainer, even as he and Rogue struggle with their inability to touch each other. Foxx comes on to Gambit and he refuses, though he continues fantasizing about her. To his shock, Foxx reveals herself as Mystique. She also comes onto him as Rogue herself. When Rogue catches her, Mystique explains she wanted to reveal to Rogue that her lover is a loser so she can find someone that will fully accept her. However, Rogue is repulsed by Mystique's clumsy way of showing concern. Once again, her shapeshifting superpowers allow her to cross borders, but win her hatred rather than love.

As Mystique adds, "The truth is, I get lonely. Sure, I can shift my shape into anyone I want. But that doesn't mean I like who I am. I ... I want to belong. I want to be a part of my beloved family." To their shock, she proposes joining the X-Men. This makes sense on some level, as they are the welcomers of outcasts. As a lone agent, without even an identity to call her own, Mystique has been more isolated than ever. She makes a passionate appeal, explaining:

> I am over eighty years old. I'd only just turned twelve when I became a mutant. A blue mutant, with these mutant eyes—when our kind weren't so common. When our kind weren't so empowered. It was tough. I had to fight to survive. Maybe those early

years damaged me, who knows. What I do know is I didn't have the opportunities to be good that you people had. Is it any wonder, then, that I have occasionally strayed from the path of righteousness? [Milligan].

This too works well as a metaphor for difference. Sympathetically, the X-Men actually agree to offer her probationary membership. However, the defensive Mystique leaves before they can turn her down and heads off on solo adventures once more. Untrustworthy down to the cells in her body, she still has trouble putting faith in others.

In 2016's *Uncanny X-Men* #15, after many more betrayals, Psylocke confronts Mystique directly. "It hurts, doesn't it? Your personality always shifting … changing … it would drive a sane person mad. Never knowing who you are … what you stand for … what you want…" (Bunn). Of course, this is part of Mystique's torment, that she changes so much outwardly that she's not certain of her own goals and values. Psylocke reaches into her mind and fixes her, and explains that she's fundamentally changed the other woman … by making her trustworthy. Still, fans can be certain that Mystique will continue drifting, never fully trusting or trusted as her motives shift as much as her face.

Transgender Fluidity: Doom Patrol (DC Comics, 1993–1994)

"At what cost, for what purposes, and through what means do we collapse this diversity of embodiment into the social categories 'woman' and 'man'?" (Stryker 62). Coagula, Kate Godwin, stands out as one of the few transgender superheroes. Created by science fiction novelist Rachel Pollack, who is a trans woman herself, Kate found herself in the lineup of DC's edgy *Doom Patrol*. The original run "remains notable for its bizarre amalgam of absurdism, tragedy, and Pop Art verve" (Alaniz 117).

Rachel Pollack based the character's name on two friends of hers, transgender writer and actress Kate Bornstein and the transgender activist Chelsea Goodwin. As Pollack adds in an interview, "I made her a former prostitute and computer programmer, just because those were at that time the most common professions for TG women. This is definitely not an expression of transgender" (Kowalska).

Marcy Cook in her *Mary Sue* article on transgender superheroes protests sex shouldn't define him or her—the character shouldn't be a sex worker or one with a sexually based superpower like seduction. While some of these make up strong characters in the superhero universe, there are far too few trans characters for the rare ones created to be defined entirely by sexuality. They should be real, rounded characters, with their bodies only a single aspect of the self. Of course, feminism and transgenderism have often had an uneasy relationship. Susan Stryker explains in her essay on the topic, "There are questions of importance to feminism gives us another axis, along with critical race studies or disability studies, to learn more about the ways in which bodily difference becomes the basis for socially constructed hierarchies, and helps us see in new ways how we are all inextricably situated, through the inescapable necessity of our own bodies, in terms of race, sex, gender, or ability" (Stryker 62).

As Gail Simone adds, diversity isn't just a continuing issue for superhero comics: "It's *the* issue for superhero comics. Look, we have a problem most media don't have, which is that almost all the tentpoles we build our industry upon were created over a half century ago ... at a time where the characters were almost without exception white, cis-gendered, straight, on and on. It's fine—it's great that people love those characters. But if we *only* build around them, then we look like an episode of *The Andy Griffith Show* for all eternity" (Hudson).

A former prostitute, Kate gains her powers suddenly by sleeping with Rebis (a combination of the Negative Energy creature Larry Trainor of Doom Patrol, and physician Eleonore Poole). Rebis is a divine hermaphrodite and compound being with all three sets of memories. Likewise, the merging has left Rebis with a spectrum of powers, including flight, mental powers, and immortality. Since it can throw off its old body and birth a new one from it, Rebis often likens itself to Russian dolls, and to an ouroboros. Symbolically, this creature emphasizes the perfect harmony between male and female, human and alien. Thus, it's a well-chosen mentor for Kate as it leads her into a life of superheroism.

After the transformation, she can liquefy solids and solidify liquids with a touch, emphasizing her own fluidity. She thus names herself Coagula from the alchemical term "Solve et Coagula," meaning "dissolve and coagulate." As Kate mentions in her second issue, she can use computers to access different realities, a power unconnected with her gender. She tries joining the Justice League but gets rejected. As she adds, "I suspect they liked my powers but couldn't handle me." In fact, this sounds about right for nineties mainstream DC Comics confronted with a transgender character. She lasted from *Doom Patrol* Volume 2, #70 (1993) to *Doom Patrol* Volume 3, #9 (2002).

When she stands in front of party guests and dissolves glasses and makes beer coagulate, Kate shows off her true self, reveling in her power and her identity instead of shrinking into the corner. This works as a metaphor for all kinds of marginalization. A transgender woman protests, "Let me recapitulate what I can personally articulate through transgender: misogyny, homophobia, racism, lookism, disability, medical colonization, coercive psychiarisation, undocumented labor, border control, state surveillance, population profiling, the prison-industrial complex, employment discrimination, housing discrimination, lack of health care, denial of access to social services, and violent hate crimes" (qtd. in Stryker 66). By standing out and taking pride in who she is, Kate fights back against all of this.

With her city under attack, Coagula dons a frog mask from a costume shop (suggesting she's royalty waiting to emerge). Her first adversary is in fact male domination. *Doom Patrol* #70's supervillain, anxious about his small equipment, makes a codpiece covered with powerful gadgets and calls himself Codpiece as well. Critic Marcy Cook also condemns comics for having the supervillain be completely gender-defined. Codpiece, with a huge rocket gun (and various other appendages) on his crotch, frames the entire saga as gender battle rather than story of multifaceted people. In fact, he's delighted when bystanders all gawk at his virility. He uses the drill attached there to open a bank vault and considers calling a press conference and blackmailing the city. He takes on the police with a boxing glove on an extender, then fires up the rocket launcher for good measure. Of course, he's a ridiculously unsubtle antagonist, suitable for this edgier incarnation of DC.

Marion and George, Doom Patrol's Bandage People who are shrouded in prehensile cloth strips, try to bind Codpiece, but he breaks free, and his groin attachment sends out giant scissors to slice the bandages. In the midst of this, Coagula walks up and turns on the flattery, assuring him he's "big and powerful" plus the "most amazing man" she's ever met. Her knowledge of the macho psyche and of bullies serves her well here. Suddenly, she plugs up then liquefies his gadgets in a clear metaphor. Marion and George invite her to join the Doom Patrol and a hero is born.

The book *The Legion of Regrettable Super Villains* shows an early, painful look at the transgender metaphor. This is He-She, "Half-Man, Half-Woman, all evil!" "The deadliest of the species is the female," the opening caption narrates. "The strongest of the species is the male! Combine these with the killer instinct and you have the most cunning, the most vicious, the most fiendish killer of all time!" Based loosely on the classic carnival sideshow attraction trope, He-She stands out for uniqueness. He-She maintains a criminal lifestyle by marrying gullible, lonely women and slowly robbing them of their life savings (subtly suggesting that this person's marrying anyone would in fact be such a transgression). This figure is male on the left side and female on the right, concealing half from all the romantic partners. Thus, there's a metaphor of passing as ordinary and using this to commit the crimes. "The male half does most of the killing, punching, and general violence; the female half unveils herself when He-She needs to distract, attract, or otherwise manipulate a man" (Morris, *Supervillains* 73). The introductory captions even suggest this person lacks a soul—possibly a reference to being a murderer but possibly something more general. "As you can imagine, a character named He-She doesn't offer the most enlightened take on gender politics. Any number of issues surrounding gender and identity are handled at least a little indelicately within the pages of the story" (Morris, *Supervillains* 73).

With artist Ted McKeever, Rachel Pollack then wrote the arc "The Teiresias Wars" (*Doom Patrol* #75–79), celebrating the power of remaking the self. Pollack describes the slowly emerging transgender stories, adding, "I find that far too many are written for a non-tg audience, trying to explain what it means to be tg. Or worse, pleading for acceptance" (Kowalska). Her saga does neither, though Kate has plenty of opportunity to show nonhumans the strength one can find in transformation.

The Doom Patrol team lives in Violet Valley's Rainbow Estates, a house mysteriously (and sometimes hilariously) haunted by ghosts of those who died in sexual accidents. There, team members include their "head" Niles Caulder (actually reduced to only a head in an ice tray); Cliff, the former Robotman; Dorothy, the ape-faced girl with imaginary friends; and the Inner Child, a manifestation of the ghosts' innocence. Of course, this is a team of misfits—they even avoid using superhero names or costumes as they already are so set apart. At one point, Cliff complains that Kate is too normal to fit among them, only to be shocked when learning of her surgery.

Kate identifies as a lesbian, but later shows her bisexuality when Cliff builds a flirtation with her. Both don't fit their physical shapes. When he discovers that she used to have a man's body, she retorts that his machine body leaves him as undefined as she once was. Though he questions whether he's human at all, she replies, "I've had to deal with questions like that all my life. Please, let me help you" (#76). With all this, the body issue is explored through the two characters.

In the next issue, Cliff is deprived of his robot body and decides he wants to design the next one for himself, a concept Kate fully understands. They discuss "passing"—making themselves look normal. As a result, Cliff concludes that deep down he likes being different, and she tells him this makes "a lot of sense." In friendship, she supervises during his re-creation. When a blockage appears, she uses her liquefying power and perception of computers to save her friend and help his new body succeed.

The same episode as Cliff's surgery features the Teiresiae, ancient shapeshifting magicians who maintain the world's knowledge and consciousness. Ages ago, one tried sorting the world into categories and thus the male and female forms resulted. An army was birthed, one dedicated to ending all transformation and keeping everything static in assigned classifications.

The men, in service to a male god, built the tower of Babel "a great engine of frozen language to fix the entire world into rigid forms." As the comic adds, "If anyone opposed them, the builders trapped hir into a rigid category of 'alive' and then killed hir" (#77). They finally reached a truce—no more single tower of static life, but all the world's creatures could no longer shapeshift. Birth and death separated life eternally. The metaphor of rigid gendering becomes clear, as does the problem of the patriarchy. "To examine 'transgender' is thus to risk decentering the privileged standpoint of white Eurocentric modernity. It is to denaturize and derarify the terms through which we ground our own genders, in order to confront the possibility of radically different ways of being in the world. This, too, is a feminist project," Stryker explains (63).

Now the Builders are awakening, while the Teiresiae Elliot returns as a female form covered in mystic symbols to tell the story. Elliot reveals humans must do the summoning to restore the ancient magicians: "A man and a woman must go together. Merged as one. A New Teiresias" (#78). This merging is symbolic on many levels: "Along with holding binaried theorizing to account, transgender theory also works with ideas of transformation, becoming, and appearing. And in calling for the reappraisal of binaries, it has reawakened and reignited debates around essentialism and identity" (Kirkpatrick 130).

While Cliff is cautious, Kate is more vocal in her worry. "Merge my body with someone? I've never even been in a relationship that lasted more than a year." Sharing herself with another person is the scariest concept of all. Nonetheless, she agrees and sets out with Cliff. As they let the power of nature take them over, a tree pulls them close. A sex scene ensues, as Kate reminds Cliff that pleasure actually takes place in the brain, not the body. They can transcend these human bodies to love each other as people (#78). While they merge into one being, they split when the force of order takes over.

Kate charges into battle but finds herself facing the deepest hurts of her childhood when she dressed as a young woman and the boys tormented her. "I thought it was over. Buried. I guess I was just stupid to think I could ever get away," she notes. She's trapped with Dorothy, who's likewise teased for her appearance. However, this tiny voice of innocence tells Kate, "We don't have to take it anymore." She reminds her friend they have the Doom Patrol now and only need to be strong and stand together. This time, assaulted by the dream bullies, they fight back and use their powers to escape.

In a final confrontation, Kate convinces the slaves of the Babel force that they can still grow and change. She tells them, "Look at me. I changed my body to match my vision, my desire. You can change easier than I can blink. But so what? I did it. I made it happen." Elliot convinces them to break the tower and let the Builders fall into slumber once more. Though Elliot is cut off from the timeless world, the earth is saved (#79).

The nineties offered a few other transgender superheroes. Masquerade, one of the Blood Syndicate from 1993's DC Comics and Milestone, was born female but used his shapeshifting powers to appear male … as was revealed far into the series. Likewise, Shvaughn Erin of the Legion of Superheroes revealed in 1992 that she was born male and took a regimen of the drug ProFem, as one of the earliest regular characters established as trans. Miki is a mystical Avatar who swaps into male and female bodies to prolong his/her life, seen in *Swamp Thing* Vol. 5, #30–40. Jessie Drake (created by Ann Nocenti and Steve Lightle) came out in *Marvel Comics Presents* #151 (1994), telling Typhoid Mary she felt like a girl trapped in a boy's body, and thus became the first openly transgender character in the Marvel Universe. An empathic metamorph able to absorb others' characteristics, she unfortunately only appears twice in the entire Marvel universe. Marisa Rahm at DC starred in *Death Wish* written by transgender author Maddie Blaustein—however, this was another short series and intended for "mature readers." Suzie Su of DC's *Red Hood and the Outlaws* appeared shortly after as the first trans villain. Meanwhile, Resurrection Man (created by DC in the late nineties) has a body that learns from each death and adapts to become stronger each time. In the New 52, he comes back as a woman, changing from Mitchell to Michelle. The deliberate experiments he's been put through suggest that women can handle pain better than men, a concept that motivates his gender flip.

Gail Simone notes that of the very few trans characters in comics, almost all have achieved gender-fluidity through fantastical means like magic, brain-swapping, shape-shifting, and cloning. "Those characters exist [and] that's great, but I wanted to have trans characters who aren't fantasy-based. And I feel like there's a *lot* there yet to do" (Hudson). In fact, a character being brain- or body-swapped, or reborn as a different gender is not symbolically the same—this transference deprives the character of choosing to make the change. "This is about agency. The character should be self-determining and not a creation of circumstance. People are born transgender and, regardless of how long it takes them to accept it, they have always been transgender," Cook explains. Thus Justin, reborn as a woman in Grant Morrison's *Seven Soldiers* (2005) doesn't count, even when rebooted as transfluid in *Demon Knights*.

At a Wondercon, Greg Rucka was asked why there were fewer gay male superheroes than lesbian ones. Rucka, who co-created lesbian Batwoman Kate Kane, replied that it would be a real sign of change for a gay male character to appear on a comic book cover—and an even bigger step for a transgender character to do the same (Hudson). On hearing this, Gail Simone resolved to create the latter. "I looked out into the audience, saw dozens of faces I knew well—LGBTQ folks, mostly—all avid comics readers and superhero fans and DC supporters," said Simone. "And it just hit me: Why was this so impossible? Why in the world can we not do a better job of representation of not just humanity, but also our own loyal audience?" (Hudson).

With this, she created Batgirl's roommate Alysia Yeoh, who's transgender and bisexual, a fact she revealed in *Batgirl* #19. In *DC Bombshells* #38, Alysia asks poignantly, "How would you feel if every day you woke up, and knew you were a boy, and people treated you like you were a girl? Tried to make you wear dresses and bows, told you that you couldn't play the games you wanted, made you cook and clean, wouldn't let you go to school … and told you that you were crazy as a bedbug when you said 'Stop, stop, stop, can't you see I'm a boy?'" Next, Alysia and her partner try to have a baby in *Batgirl: Son of Penguin* (2017). Her doctor at the fertility clinic misgenders her: "It doesn't suck, Babs. It's a punch in the gut. You lose your breath" (Larson and Ayala). As she struggles with all the normal hopes and fears of preparing to have a child, she emphasizes her desire to be treated the same as anyone else. Granted, she's a nonsuperpowered best friend/sidekick. It's a baby step. Still, Simone vows to keep creating transgender characters and adds, "It's time for a trans hero in a mainstream comic.… I'm sure it's controversial on some level to some people, but honest to God, I just could not care less about that. If someone gets upset, so be it; there are a thousand other comics out there for those people" (Hudson). As Pollack concludes: "The sense I am getting is that the community has been successful in getting the issues out to the public. That's the most important thing. When the Vice President of the United States says that transgender is the civil rights issue of our time, we know we're getting somewhere" (Kowalska).

As fourth wave's intersectionality broke down barriers, a delightful children's series played with this concept, at least through metaphor. In the cartoon show *Steven Universe,* his adoptive superpowered moms the Crystal Gems (Pearl, Garnet, and Amethyst) apparently have no assigned binary gender, but they choose to present as female. However, in the episode "Tiger Millionaire," superheroine Amethyst is seen transforming into male as wrestler Purple Puma with a bare hairy chest, deep voice, and male pronouns, to indulge her hobby of underground wrestling matches. As she sneaks off and shifts to this male persona, reveling in the freeing new identity, this presents a fun cross-dressing metaphor.

> This is perhaps the only time in the show thus far when a Gem takes on a masculine form of their own design for an extended period of time. The audience at the wrestling match doesn't know Purple Puma's real identity. We see Amethyst with hair under her arms, an exposed chest, and muscular upper body. She could choose to appear in a masculine form all the time if she wanted, but she doesn't. It's also interesting that she takes a male form as a way of establishing dominance, *in the ring, no one can tell me what to do,* which is perhaps proof that the Gems have an understanding of human gender norms, but actively disregard them in their own lives. Gender norms are a part of human society they choose not to adopt [Busnardo].

Further, in "Alone Together," the half-human kid Steven trains to be a Crystal Gem, like his three foster mothers, who can fuse with each other. When he dances with his best friend Connie on the beach, the two of them suddenly combine into a beautiful, confident, and genderqueer young person, Stevonnie. Tall, long limbed and charming, Stevonnie speaks in both voices. Everyone around them finds them stunningly attractive, like the girl who's suddenly become a teenager. And like this girl, Stevonnie feels happy but also awkward and uncertain in her new body. How the moms treat this new cross-gendered adolescent shows their encouragement of the new child who's suddenly sprung up. One critic adds:

> In the history of television, I've never seen anything like Stevonnie. Upon showing herself to the Crystal Gems, it's immediately apparent by Garnet's face that not only is she thrilled for Steven, she's proud. She tells Stevonnie she's not one person, or two people, but an experience. Together Steven and Connie become one, incredibly attractive, woman. They go to a club together and take center stage—and at no time is Steven's gender called into question. Not once is there any hint that a little boy becoming a woman is anything short of an experience to be celebrated. Stevonnie enjoys her day. She gets a donut. She dances. She just *is*. That's really all there is to say about her. You just have to experience her. As a viewer, you get to participate in a little boy's experience of womanhood and what's more awesome than that? [Busnardo].

The short-lived cartoon *Gotham Girls* also introduced a trans character, "a rarity anywhere in 2002, much less in children's entertainment" (Hanley 123). In the third season's "Ms-ing in Action," all the men in Gotham go missing, along with Detective Selma Reesedale. Blamed for this, Catwoman investigates to clear her name and discovers that the officer was born male but has been living as female. *Gotham Girls* supports the character's choice as Catwoman refers to the officer as "she" and the show treats her as a recurring helpful figure.

Trans characters are becoming more common, with an angst-filled teen confronting the change in the young adult novel *Dreadnaught* by April Daniels. The hero, Danny, is attempting a secret pedicure when the superhero Dreadnaught, upon dying, passes on his powers. Suddenly, Danny finds herself a teenage girl, exactly as she's always dreamed. Danny thinks, "Everything is wrong but so perfectly right.... The last little doubts are gone, and the fear leaves with them. I'm free. I'm finally free" (12). What follows is a time of discrimination, including from some of the superheroes. At school, Danny's former best friend hits on her creepily. At home, her father screams in endless tirades. As he calls his child a failure, a disgusting disloyal bad son, Danny bursts into tears. "The worst part is, I can't help but believe him. He always has a way of making me believe him. I really am disgusting and pathetic. I can crack the sound barrier, but I can't stand up to this man" (85). Danny's parents kick her out of the house, but she finds the courage to be the person she's always dreamed, thanks to the superpower transfer that has made her her ideal self. It's a sympathetic book that reaches out to transitioning teens, exploring the conflicts they face. The barriers are crumbling slowly, but on every level of storytelling, there's outreach towards inclusivity and tolerance.

Good Girls

Fourth Wave Princess: Shuri (Film, 2018)

"*Black Panther* revealed a whole world beyond what superhero movies had ever dared to dream of…. The best part, though? The mastermind behind Wakanda's most astonishing innovations is none other than a brilliant, cheeky-as-hell teen girl," critic Caroline Framke explains. *Black Panther* director Ryan Coogler and producer Nate Moore packed the film with stunning actresses including Angela Bassett (Queen Ramonda), Lupita Nyong'o (Nakia) and Danai Gurira (Okoye). However, many decided the newest "Disney Princess" stole the show.

King T'Challa's sixteen-year-old sister Shuri (played by the adorable Guyanese-born British actress Letitia Wright) brings a delightful energy to the role. She takes pride and delight in what she does, with no one urging her to be silent or even make way for her more authoritative brother. She need not be a rebel or a conformist—she's been encouraged by her entire family to invent whatever she desires. For the good of her people she builds a high-speed rail for Wakanda and plenty of fighter planes. "A lot of young people relate to her—she's passionate about improving where she comes from," adds Wright (Barsamian). She even cures Bucky of his brainwashing in her spare time—nothing the MCU heroes could manage. This fully rounded, eager, fun-loving prodigy is an example of fourth wave feminism: a diverse, multi-capable viewpoint heroine who dresses professionally and inspires others. The actress adds that she wants the character to inspire more young girls to pursue STEM subjects. "I hope it can spark someone to say, 'I'm not a superhero, but I can be a scientist or build the next spaceship, like Shuri'" (Barsamian).

Reginald Hudlin and John Romita, Jr., created the character during their acclaimed *Black Panther* run in 2005. Shuri is introduced when the queen mentions she has been locked in her room during the challenge for the throne. Insisting she's as much of a panther as her brother, Shuri sneaks over to the arena. She wears a simple white wrap dress and beaded jewelry—

more villager than princess and certainly dressed oddly to begin a wrestling match. Still, she's filled with a charming bravado. As she watches, a challenger is defeating the current Black Panther. The pair are masked, mysterious, and deadly, leaving Shuri a more human and ordinary viewpoint character. "Hey! Get up, I'm under here," she complains as a defeated challenger lands atop her. He unmasks to reveal himself as T'Challa, and the former Panther, his uncle, compliments him on his triumph and encourages the audience to acknowledge him the new leader. However, one onlooker is truly annoyed. "I was robbed! By my own brother!" Shuri insists.

For those both familiar with and new to the superheroine princess, the film character presented a new burst of fresh energy. Unlike her dignified, reserved brother, Shuri eagerly quips. Her responses are prompt, young, and emotional, even on formal occasions. She's first seen inquiring of the guard captain whether her brother froze upon seeing his ex. The three women thus dominate the superhero, pointing out his vulnerability and foibles in a moment that's all about humorously undercutting the king. All of them, this scene emphasizes, are close as family without deferring to the man in their lives. This showed off the film's power as an offering of the new fourth wave feminism—African women could star in a superhero film and be powerful, independent, and varied. "While the second- and third-wave were criticized for featuring middle-class white women's struggles, the fourth wave showed a much more fiercely inclusive model" (Frankel, "Introduction"). Shuri is a princess but also a scientist, inventor, and warrior. With a colorful personality, she's far deeper than the "strong female character" who can't make a joke. In fact, she's a happy nonsexualized role model who fights for her family and country without succumbing to a Hollywood romance.

Onscreen, Shuri exchanges comradely salutes with her brother and proudly offers him the new suit she's made, even while emphasizing how the old suit was likely to get him killed. "Old tech. Functional, but old. 'People are shooting at me—wait, let me put my helmet on!'" He nods, conceding the point. He models nontoxic masculinity, valuing her contributions without talking down to her. "Even more notably, Shuri sees zero reason to be humble about her brilliance—and honestly, why should she? Her hyper-advanced home base makes Tony Stark's lab of bombastic gadgets look like a box of dingy Legos," Framke adds. Next, Shuri jokes that she's invented sneakers. She finishes by having T'Challa strike the suit and get knocked on his rear end while she impishly records it. ("Delete that footage!" he demands.) On his first day as her king, she offers tribute but also emphasizes that they still have a sibling relationship. Coogler explains:

> I also thought that as we were writing, I realized that the more stuff we can put in this relationship between T'Challa and his sister, the better off we'll be because that's another thing that makes him so unique. There are no superheroes that I can think of

that have a little sister who they love dearly and who can bring out the best in them but also keep them down to Earth, you know what I mean? Their relationship is built on love, and out of that, so many other things grew [B. Pearson].

"Her playful teasing is the only thing that can crack her brother's otherwise somber affect—mischievous little sisters are always good that way—but she's also quickly revealed to be the wickedly smart force behind every mind-blowing Wakandan invention Black Panther throws at us," Framke comments. As Shuri teases Everett Ross or interrupts her brother's coronation, she is seen being self-aware on several levels of what effects her words will have on the larger political world.

She clearly knows when to support her royal brother and when and how to shake up his perception. At his royal challenge, she steals the show for a moment, deliberately, by raising her hand when asked if any member of the royal family plans to fight T'Challa for the throne. However, while she is reminding him that she too is heir, she doesn't actually want the job. Fully aware of her moment at the proverbial microphone, she reveals she's only stepped in to joke and undercut her brother's drama. Instead of challenging, she announces, "This corset is really uncomfortable … so could we all just wrap it up and go home?" Her stopping her brother's coronation to quip about her undergarments underscores her role—the one who makes sure her over-serious royal brother has lighter moments in his life.

She drops everything and cries "Yes!" when T'Challa calls on her for backup in Korea, emphasizing how much fun she has playing computer-game-style simulations with real life impact. Of course, here, the audience can fully empathize. She's a teenager, but T'Challa trusts her with his life over and over. Her brother also respects her. They work as a polished, trusting team, even as she crows with joy. Further, their care is mutual. When she runs someone over, T'Challa tells her, like a big brother whose sister is taking a driving test, "Don't worry about it, you're doing fine!" Even while driving, she monitors his suit and reminds him to use the kinetic energy blast. Long before she bravely dons energy gauntlets and faces Killmonger directly in battle, she's established as a skilled action heroine—one who is encouraged to excel and takes more joy in it than anyone in the MCU.

While many think of princesses as marriage bait, many queen mothers and even royal sisters historically ruled on behalf of the injured king. In the comics, Shuri's stand-out moment involved becoming Black Panther in 2009. On the cover of *Black Panther: The Deadliest of the Species,* her female form shines through the black suit, magnificent with a fur ruff, leaning on a panther in a pose of confidence and power. With his ship crashed and T'Challa in a coma, it's Shuri, not Panther's wife Storm, who must take over. Storm points out that Shuri has trained for this her entire life. "She has had the same upbringing, education, and training as T'Challa. Had he not claimed the mantle first, we would doubtlessly be addressing her as Black Panther today" (Hudlin and Lashley).

Accepting the challenge, Shuri responds with bravado that reveals her toughness. "Walking across fire—I was doing that for fun when I was twelve. Dodging arrows and spears—did that when I was eleven. Meditating for six hours in a scorpion-filled pit—boring." She slips off the side of the mountain and catches herself but still responds with confidence: "You were born for this. Get it." She battles panthers to retrieve a holy herb and then faces the Panther God. There, she boldly declares her worthiness, only to be chided for arrogance. Blaming her for jealousy, the panther sends her away. She returns to her people alive but humiliated and defeated. However, her witch-doctor uncle makes her realize that she has trusted too much in her scientific and military modern training. With their enemy attacking, a monster who commands billions of the dead, she prepares for primitive, primal battle. "Monster. You've faced the muscle of Wakanda. Now face its claws!" she insists, in Black Panther regalia, wielding a spear. Even as he calls her "little girl" she leads him on an airspeed chase and defeats him with the help of her family.

After, the witch doctor explains that the Panther God rejected her once but her determination to fight anyway made her "the one true Black Panther." She opens the following comic arc in a purple gown and statuesque gold crown, speaking before her people. She explains, "You look at me and you see the little sister to our nation's great hero. You see a woman, a daughter. You see a single fist raised against a sea of enemies, and a single voice shouting at the winds of terrible disorder." She insists she is none of this, but "I am Wakandan! And I am not alone!" In elaborate blue, trimmed with furs and gold, she meets President Obama, who acknowledges her as head of state.

Movie Shuri similarly displays a notable stylishness in all her scenes. "I was on set *fighting* for it," says Wright, laughing, of the futuristic, body-skimming white dress that Shuri wears in the lab (Barsamian). Her hair is up in complex braids, stressing her status as a royal figure. In her outfit, she represents modernity—in Africa and worldwide. Rejecting the classic western lab coat, the costume designer went in a different direction:

> Instead, Carter fashioned this strapless dress and gave it a mesh overlay that subtly suggests a lab coat and also feels like something that Shuri would have invented herself. "There's a wavy pattern in the texture of the mesh so it's not just a normal fishnet," said Carter. "I love the idea of presenting fabrics that are appealing and subtle and look like they could have been recycled, and I thought that was so perfect for Shuri. That this is Wakanda, and they're very eco-friendly, and they care about their country and their environment. She would be the one that would figure out a way to create a vibrant fabric that was a result of recycling" [Buchanan].

Princesses of course are known for epic fashion, while fourth wave heroines dress beautifully without being oversexualized. When first seen, Shuri's hair is in childish puffs and she wears a t-shirt, making her approachable for Americans but most of all casting her as the cute kid sister. Her cowrie necklace is casual and girly, though also an ancient sign of wealth, like her silver skirt. For T'Challa's coronation, she's full exotic African princess, with Maasai-style beadwork and a gold-plated alligator "jaw grill" along with face painted with rank markings. Already, cosplayers are recreating this, though the simplest most authentic look appears in the hand-woven winter blanket she wears to escape in the snow. An orange activewear look later fits well on any modern American teen, though the fabric seems more high-tech. Teens and kids are emulating all these, making her their role model. In fact, Framke calls her "the feisty Disney princess we need and deserve."

Of course, the character is meant to be young and fun-loving but also adeptly head up the science division. This appears to be based in her genius, not nepotism (though one must assume the royal family of Wakanda has access to all the vibranium they wish). Director Ryan Coogler explains, "In our minds, Wakanda's a place that looks at age differently than other places. It's not a place where, because you're young, you don't get a chance to lead, and because you're old, we don't cast you aside. It's looking at time and age more in an African sense" (Pearson). When mountain tribe leader M'Baku (Winston Duke) challenges T'Challa for the throne, he specifically complains that Wakanda's greatest assets have been entrusted to "a child." Still, T'Challa validates his choice not only through winning the fight, but by demonstrating over and over how necessary her tech is to all his superhero feats.

She demands and deserves respect. With her royal poise, Shuri is fully in control of every scene. She actually has significant medical training, suggesting an advanced degree. As a fatally wounded Everett Ross is wheeled into her lab, she owns the scene, joking (in a Bucky reference that will pay off later), "Great! Another broken white boy for us to fix. This is going to be fun." With this, she shows how much joy she can take in any moment, even as T'Challa reacts through honor and morality, while Okoye expresses her concern for their country's security. When Ross wakes, she teases him, explaining that they're in Kansas (a movie reference that emphasizes her worldly knowledge, as does her summarizing his bio for him). She also calls him "colonizer," emphasizing that white is not the default in their world, but the strange and none-too-well-regarded exception. He even describes her technology as "magic," placing him in the role of the superstitious savage, while she corrects him that bullet wounds do heal overnight in Wakanda "But not by magic, by technology." Once again claiming her space in the presence of intruding men, she warns him not to touch anything. She takes a hologram phone call in front of him that makes his eyes pop as he must accept that his entire society has been clearly outclassed.

Before this, Tony Stark, and to a lesser extent Bruce Banner, were the face of scifi technological progress in the MCU. Now, Shuri, who heals Martin Freeman's character just after Tony Stark was helpless to cure Iron Patriot of a similar injury, proves she has them beat. She's also notably emotionally stable, even joyous, compared with the tormented male geniuses. Director Ryan Coogler explains, "Going through the process of writing the film and working with my co-writer, Joe Robert Cole, I thought Shuri would be a cool Q. It'd be really interesting seeing a young African teenager who's manipulated this element in ways that nobody else could and who's confident and able to have her own space" (Pearson). In the past, the Q character—Batman's Alfred or Tony Stark himself, would show off dream gadgets made by men for men in a man-cave of a clubhouse. At last, a woman owns the space, reacting in horror when the king enters her lab in open-toed shoes. Clearly, Marvel is moving forward, celebrating innovation in its heroines instead of confining them to damsel roles.

Altruist: Wonder Woman (DC Comics, 1941)

William Moulton Marston, Wonder Woman's creator, saw women as the ideal leaders. In an interview, he declared that women were poised to "take over the rule of the country, politically and economically" within the next hundred years (Hanley, *Wonder Woman* 12). Originally, Marston pitched a female superhero to *All-American* editor Sheldon Mayer to give young readers an alternative to the world's male-dominated violence and prepare them for leadership through compassion and empathy rather than force. His "Suprema the Wonder Woman" (as she was originally called) would conquer men with charm and set them on the path to peace.

In this tradition, Wonder Woman finally arrived to "save the world from the hatreds and wars of men" (Marston, *Sensation Comics* #1). She came from an island of enlightened, cooperative women, a place tellingly called "Paradise." Marston believed this was a vision of women without men, as men were driven by selfishness and greed but women by higher, kinder emotions. Marston thus wished to overturn the traditional gender hierarchy and establish "a new code of conduct, based upon love supremacy" (*Emotions* 393). As he explained in a 1942 article:

> If you conclude, as I do, that the only hope of permanent peace and happiness for humanity on this planet is an increased expression of love, and that women are the primary carriers of this great force, one of the problems we face is to provide women with more opportunity for using their love powers. The last six thousand years have demonstrated quite conclusively, I believe, that woman under the domination of man can increase but meagerly the world's total love supply. Our obvious goal, then, must

be to devise social mechanisms whereby man is brought under the love domination of woman ["Women: Servants for Civilization" 44].

Shown by his *Wonder Woman* adventure taking place a millennium in the future, Marston visualized a time when "men and women will be equal ... but woman's influence will control most governments because women are more ready to serve others unselfishly!" (Marston, *Wonder Woman* #7). Lethal weapons are banned and prisoners are all rehabilitated, leading to a true utopia. Queen Hippolyte points out to her daughter in the same comic, "Men are much happier when their strong aggressive natures are controlled by a wise and loving woman!" Certainly, the comics Marston wrote were his extreme, idealistic image brought to fiction, but he considered this a lens for viewing many of life's problems.

In 1942's *Wonder Woman* #1, Marston reveals that "[t]he planet earth ... is ruled by rival Gods—Ares, God of War, and Aphrodite, Goddess of Love and Beauty." Ares and Aphrodite face off in the stars with the Earth positioned as their prize. Ares proclaims, "My men shall rule with the sword!" and Aphrodite challenges, "My women shall conquer men with love."

> The image strikingly crystallizes Marston's view of the world as defined principally by gender conflict, as opposed to by class, religious, or cultural strife, all of which would be equally valid ways of understanding the history of civilization and of warfare. Later in that same comic book, the narrator reveals that Ares has orchestrated World War II to set the world aflame. To wrest control of Earth from Ares, Aphrodite commands that the Amazons end their long period of isolation. They would send the wisest and strongest Amazon to aid the Allies. This "Wonder Woman" would protect the American home front from Axis spies and terrorists, promote the importance of women's rights, and preach the promise of peace [DiPaolo 154].

Golden Age Wonder Woman is sent to America as an ambassador of loving peace—a different way to live. She's known for her strong moral core, as she defends the helpless and refuses to kill her enemies. (If they die, it's by happenstance.) Stuller wonders: "Does the suggestion of love as strength, or as gift, embrace innately female characteristics? Does it infuse what is 'naturally' powerful about women into a liberating archetype? Or does it reinforce stereotypes about how women should behave as self-sacrificing nurturers?" (88). She concludes, "Their love is the impetus, but becomes integral to their strength, and thus the success of their missions" (88). Love is a force of strength, giving mothers the power to take on terrible enemies to give their children better lives or rescue lovers from death itself.

Wonder Woman's many incarnations all continue to embody love—confronted by Hades in Brian Azzarello and Cliff Chiang's *Wonder Woman: Guts,* she is condemned to become the bride of death. He orders her to put her head through her Lasso of Truth (hanging as a noose) and assure Hades she truly loves him or the truth will "hang her." She puts her head in and swears her love. However, Diana selflessly loves everyone, allowing a loophole for her declaration. Hades, by contrast, is unable to force her to love him, even with Eros's bullets, because he cannot feel the emotion. "You can't make anyone love you unless you love yourself," Wonder Woman tells him. As a parting gift, Diana shoots him with a love bullet as he gazes into a mirror, so that he can learn.

In this tradition, the trope of superheroines seeking to redeem villains through empathy and compassion is central to many stories. Catherine Bailey Kyle writes in her essay on the heroine's journey:

> Feminist heroes do not automatically obliterate their enemies or relish their destruction; they seek to reason with them, win them over to the side of good, or come to a compromise. In this way, they resist the limiting binary of "good" and "evil" that has, for centuries, functioned to unjustly oppress women, sexual minorities, and other marginalized groups. Again, this is not to express that a feminist hero cannot or should not use violence at any point over the course of the journey—it merely asks that at least one instance of creative, nonviolent problem solving be deployed for the sake of diversifying the concept of justice [139].

The Nurturer is a motherly archetype, also seen in social workers and special education teachers. She is not content to rescue people in danger but wishes also to teach them and save their souls. This archetype is altruistic, optimistic, idealistic, and self-sacrificing, putting the community's needs before her own. Is it an archetype of strength or weakness? Either, depending on the presentation.

Other heroines in later years take this advice to heart. On the *Birds of Prey* television show, Harley Quinn is appalled that her teen killing machine has been disarmed by Huntress, sarcastically retorting, "Oh, that's it. She overrode millions of dollars in bioengineering research and medical procedures by being his friend!" ("Three Birds and a Baby"). In fact, Huntress has done just that. In *Angela: Asgard's Assassin: Priceless,* Angela's ordeal requires descending into the temple of selflessness where her parents once wed to find a bridal gown for Heimdall's intended, one he cannot see through. Her friend Sera tells her, "You came here out of pure love, Angela. It is yours to take." The original eighties Starfire describes growing up in a world of emotion not science. "We loved our friends with an unrestrained heart … and hated our enemies with equal fervor!" (Wolfman, *New Teen Titans* #3). This is the lesson she brings to her new world, earth, where she becomes her team's heart.

This emphasis on saving the world through nonviolence and cooperation is an important teaching tool, as Sarkeesian explains: "When violence is the primary gameplay mechanic and therefore the primary way that the player engages with the game-world it severely limits the options for problem solving. The player is then forced to use violence to deal with almost *all* situations because it's the only meaningful mechanic available" (Sarkeesian, Part 2). Defeating enemies through opening one's heart, as Wonder Woman does, is a far better model, as Marston realized. Young readers of all genders thus can discover problem-solving and kindness.

Trapped by aliens, the youngest *Power Pack* kid, Katie, befriends them. While her older brother insists they're just "the lizard freaks that kidnapped mom and dad," Katie studies their childhood lessons and beloved nectar, allowing her to get inside their heads later and save the day. She uses her crayons to program the aliens with an image of who she wants them to be, insisting, "Snarks love everyone! All they wanna do is spread *love* and happiness and cuteness throughout outer space!" With this, she re-envisions millennia of their culture. Thus retaught, the queen mother orders her children to send gift baskets through the galaxy instead of terror (Van Lente, *Power Pack: Day One*). Over and over, the comics model better paths—seeking understanding and compromise rather than violence.

After defeating her enemies, forties Wonder Woman brings them to Reform Island. While other prisons such as Arkham Asylum sometimes attempt rehabilitation, for Wonder Woman and the Amazons, this is a major story component. "Here, good is of course equated with loving—in keeping with Marston's theories of the good and beautiful woman who should rule the world with her altruistic love" (Stuller 88). Amazons bind them with girdles that restrain them until the prisoners abandon their egocentric desires and finally come to value this external restraint and change their behavior. When Wonder Woman visits in *Sensation Comics* #22, a reformed criminal dashes up to her and shouts, "These bonds feel wonderful! Keep me here in Amazon prison and train me to control my evil self!" While this is a clear exaggeration, echoed in Marston's famous fetishes, the emphasis is on changing behavior to comply with a wiser authority.

Spunky Kids: Kitty Pryde (Marvel Comics, 1980–1985)

Kitty Pryde arrives in Chris Claremont's *Uncanny X-Men* #129 as the youngest student Professor Xavier's School for Gifted Youngsters has ever seen—the same arc as Jean Grey's Dark Phoenix (#129–138). As the sweet sixties' heroine grows monstrous and finally sacrifices herself, she paves the way for a new generation of X-Men, and a new generation of readers too. "The Pryde who eagerly indulges in ice cream is simultaneously the Pryde who takes to Wolverine's training and hones her battle skills to a fine point. That she can capaciously encompass this multiplicity is part and parcel of what makes her most especially a figure of the genealogy of 1980s feminism" explains Margaret Galvan in her essay "From Kitty to Cat" (55). She echoes the young heroines of eighties teen films, filed with energy and idealism and still some angst. Joe Casey tells in "Playing God and Discovering My Own Mutanity":

> I had found my way into the material simply by connecting the idea of being a mutant with the idea of being a teenager. The way I see it, every teenager feels different. Every teenager feels special. Every teenager feels misunderstood. stood. Every teenager feels like an outcast. From the prom queen to the punk rocker, we were all disenfranchised. At that age, we were all mutants [Casey].

Some women of the eighties were becoming "masculine" action heroes like Ripley and Sarah Connor; nonetheless, many others were reacting to the gender politics flare-up of the seventies by returning to gentle sweetness. "While superwomen of the 1970s had at the very last represented a restrained progressiveness, most of their followers in the 1980s (with the exception of a notable few) further exaggerated perceived contradictions between femininity and feminism" (Stuller 54). Kitty Pryde offers more of the former.

Thirteen-and-a-half-year-old Kitty is the kid of the team, and she doesn't completely feel she fits among the adult X-Men. Still, she's very heroic and capable. "Pryde, in her first appearances before she even joins the team and has any formal training, ably evades capture, infiltrates enemy headquarters, and alerts Nightcrawler that other X-Men have been detained" (Galvan 47). The spunky kid is traditionally fun, reliable, upbeat and vulnerable. Her lack of confidence may make her play down her best attributes, but she is the best of friends for those who need one. After they're dragged down to hell and return triumphant, Wolverine tells her, "Ya should be over here with us! You're an X-Man ain't'cha?" She's delighted. In fact, there's a great component of joy to her powers. Traveling through walls "thrills and excites her more than almost anything she's ever known" (*Uncanny X-Men* #139). Writer Jason Aaron notes: "She was the first kid in the group that everyone could relate to. And I think she's retained a lot of that fun spirit and wide-eyed sense wonder she brought to what has at times been a rather morose group of folks" (Morse). Writer Kieron Gillen explains:

> There's that old line I've heard that every generation has a crack at creating a Spider-Man for its decade? You know, young teen hero coming to terms with their power. I think Kitty Pryde was the 80's, something which both her position in a team and her gender tends to disguise. Putting aside her super-smartness—which always came across as more general smart bookworm-ness to me in tone—she's very normal. You knew—or were—girls like Kitty. She hasn't the Amazonian physique of most of her peers. She's generally very easy to empathize [Morse].

"The mutant's constant struggle to contain and discipline his body adds an emotional and melodramatic element to the obvious male power fantasy and pubescent metaphor that is an enduring theme for the superhero genre" (Brown, "Supermoms" 186). Kitty's transformation powers echo this, as does her disappearing act—a reflection of uncertainty and shyness. In #139, the professor proposes Ariel as a code name; Kitty prefers Ororo's suggestion of Sprite. After this, Ororo takes Kitty to a dance studio and the girl discovers she needn't give up on her favorite activities as a superhero. She tells Ororo: "I'm a certified genius, y'know. My peers are in the ninth grade. An' I'm taking college-level courses. Academically we don't fit. Dancing is how I balance the scales. I can't make my body grow any faster, an' my intellect isn't much good at helping me perform the moves right. Here, I'm just like everybody else. I can relate to kids my own age as *equals*. Boy, it's nice to be able to do that."

Ororo thinks: "Incredible. Kitty reasons as calmly, as sensibly, as Professor X—yet for all of that, she is still a child, struggling to hold onto her childhood." X-Men writer Nick Lowe notes: "She is the most everyman X-Man. She is how 90% of people see themselves, I imagine: Earnest, positive, funny, imperfect, smart, good-looking but not ridiculously good-looking" (Morse). With her powers of insubstantiality, she can irrepressibly bounce ahead of everyone else—in *X-Men* #138, she bounds through the door to peek at what lies ahead. When the professor summons her back telepathically, she retorts, "Get outta my head, professor! And quit yellin' willya?! It hurts!" Though he's sure she's in deadly danger, in fact she's just fine. As she points out, she was trying to help and "to act like a real X-Man" (#139). Indeed, her youth is a vital aspect to her character.

> Chris Claremont showed Kitty developing her powers slowly, allowing them to grow organically and sensibly with each new experience rather than giving her perfectly realized powers all at once. Letting characters learn new ways to use their powers has always been a facet of Claremont's writing but it was especially prevalent with Kitty, who really was learning. That last word is the key: she was a student, after all [DeCandido].

She's often "unable to resist a giggle of excitement." Everything about her is girlish—"She hasn't been an X-Man very long. She's not used to her nascent superpowers and using them still gives her a thrill," the narrator explains (Claremont, *Uncanny X-Men* #143). Her playful mood continues through the series as she lifts a somber moment by teasing Peter Rasputin with mistletoe over his head and kissing his cheek. He blushes. Nonetheless, her light-hearted escapade is interrupted by a savage monster who invades the mansion when she's all alone. Still, she fights it off, using her training to ignite the jet's engines and catch it in the blast. "Alone, on Christmas Eve, Kitty Pryde underwent a rite of passage—a supreme test of her abilities, her intellect, her courage, her … self. She passed," the narrator concludes (Claremont, *Uncanny X-Men* #143).

Some plotlines are much more serious. An older Kitty (or rather Kate) travels back in time from a future of dystopian horrors. Once among her friends, she insists on being heard and convinces the X-Men only they can avert a terrible assassination that will destroy the future. This comic gives the young hero another side as her more adult self appears. "Despite her status as the youngest member of the team in the present, her survival and leadership role in the future furthers her character's multiplicity while also emphasizing her strength and the accompanying viability of her feminist politics" (Galvan 51–52). At the crucial moment, she is the one to mix time travel and phasing gifts to stop the precognitive Destiny from killing the all-important presidential candidate, "calling upon her decades of training and experience to act as her child self could not." With this, she saves the future (Claremont, *Uncanny X-Men* #142).

Claremont's *Kitty Pryde and Wolverine* (1984–1985) has her learn to fight off a demon's influence. In the end, she chooses who she wants to become. Galvan describes Kitty Pryde's bildungsroman (coming of age plot) in *Kitty Pryde and Wolverine,* noting how the split covers suggest the character's boundary-straddling as well as her search for identity (54). Wolverine, her mentor for this arc, tells Kitty that she's been taken over by an ancient demon. "Magic—or some form of psi-powers. He imprinted his psyche onto yours, created a sort of psychic clone of himself inside your skull. Eventually it'll overwhelm your personality completely. You'll have the features of Kitty Pryde—you'll be able to mimic her perfectly—but at heart you'll be Ogun" (Claremont, *Kitty Pryde & Wolverine* #4). Despite this, he convinces her to save herself. He reminds her, "If you run away to Charley, it doesn't matter if the cure's successful, you'll never be as strong again. You'll always be dependent on Xavier, always subconsciously turn to him when things get rough. Ogun will have broken your spirit—crippled the fundamental you—in a way that'll never heal." She takes his advice and trains with him, then finally fights and defeats the demon.

In a memorable moment Kitty renames herself. Dressed in dark colors, she sits on the subway, staring at her reflection in the window. With short hair and concealing clothes, she can't even recognize herself, and in response, she dons eye makeup in place of a mask. Staring at the reflection, she mulls over her choices—a normal life or a superpowered one. "Except normal people don't skydance. I can't give that up. Even without any superpowers, I'll never settle for what society—or my parents—expect of me. I'm not a Kitty anymore, much as I wish differently, I've grown up. I'm a cat. And I like the shadows a whole lot more than the daylight." Breathing on the windowpane, she draws with her finger. Shadowcat, she decides. "I like it. Suits me better than Ariel or Sprite, that's for sure" (#5). "Just as she previously dispenses with the identities that parents or society lined up for her, here she rejects previous codenames given to her by her fellow teammates and fashions her own moniker out of the bits and pieces of herself. Discarding these nominal ties allows her to draw greater strength from within herself" (Galvan 56). She continues as a younger X-Man for decades but finally becomes their leader, preserving the integrity of Xavier's school where she grew up.

Other spunky girls include Spider-Girl—both Peter's daughter Mayday and Anya Corazón, Araña. Both of these, like the original Spider-Man, are teens struggling through high school awkwardness as they balance this with family and the secret life of a superhero.

Though Golden Age heroine Mary Marvel is "the world's mightiest girl," she also relies on her smarts. In her solo adventures, she often solves mysteries. In "The Secret of the Smiling Swordsman" (1975), her uncle, a performer, emphasizes words in his storytelling show which she diligently writes down, revealing that a group of thieves are blackmailing him into stealing for them. She knows he only pretends to have superpowers, and as she rescues him, she politely humors him. She lets the thieves drive off but is actually tailing them by hanging on *under* the car. Later on, stuck in her human form and gagged so she can't say the magic word, she angles her head so the thief's own sword slashes her gag off. Over and over she proves that being mighty still means using one's brain (Maggin and Oksner).

The eighties also introduced Marvel's *Power Pack* created by writer Louise Simonson and artist June Brigman and colored by Glynnis Wein in a striking all-female team. The series, starting in 1984, lasted 62 issues. The kids (two boys and two girls age five to twelve) make an equal gender-balanced team, each offering complementary skills.

> *Power Pack* reverses the expectations: perky Katie has the electric powers of a battery and can shoot great powerballs of force from her chest. The other sister, Julie, can fly at great speed, with colored lights flashing behind her. Julie finally changes her name from Lightspeed to Molecula, Mistress of Density—no "Girl" for her. Their brother Jack gains a power of being insubstantial and cloudy. Though this evolves later to a control over mass, including growing and shrinking, he certainly appears the Invisible Boy. Alex can control gravity—a power of strength but one controlled at a distance [Simonson, *Power Pack*].

While the four Power children live at home with their parents, they keep their superpowers hidden, leading to traditional child-parent tension, even as they go on youthful adventures. Of course, this offers the children added perspective: in *Power Pack* #7, Katie, the youngest, is frightened of the first day of kindergarten but quickly decides, "No! I'm a big girl now! I've met aliens and fought Snarks!" With this, she tells her mother she's not afraid.

The Pack even team up with Kitty Pryde. In Claremont's *Uncanny X-Men* #195, Kitty Pryde "the youngest X-Man takes the youngest member of the Power Pack by the hand and phases them both down through restraints, bed and floor" to rescue her from a hospital. The Power Pack's parents have forgotten their existence, thanks to a Morlock woman who wants the children for her own. As Kitty and Katie team up, Kitty comforts the little girl and assures her she has friends in the other superheroes. She is the one to eloquently face the Morlock down on Katie's behalf and convince her to reverse her spells.

The teenage Cloak and Dagger first appeared in *Peter Parker, the Spectacular Spider-Man* #64 (March 1982). They rush onto the scene, eager for revenge against the pharmacist whose drug-dealing helped the illegal experiments on runaway teens that created them. Both battle Spider-Man so they can kill the pharmacist, over Spidey's objections. Next they go after the ringleader. Having pieced together their story, Spider-Man sympathizes with the pair but urges them to set aside vigilante justice. When the disoriented villains plunge out a window, Cloak and Dagger vanish, and Spider-Man is left "confused, puzzled, and more than a little frightened. Tonight, he will sleep with the lights on" (Mantlo). In 1985, they got their own series, in which they continued to fight crime as a devoted young partnership. Since she is the fighter and he the protector, they reverse traditional gender roles to a degree.

In *Power Pack* #7–9, Cloak and Dagger help the Power Pack to battle vicious drug dealers. They stress their youth, as Dagger tells the children, "We can't go home, or to high school or dance class or … or … anything now! So we try to stop guys like them … from making other kids into drug addicts … or criminals … or monsters like us…" (Simonson, *Power Pack* #8). The characters are presented as desperate street kids with no one to rely on but each other. In fact, Cloak and Dagger are incredibly symbiotic. In *Power Pack* #8, Cloak says, "Nor can I risk losing you, Dagger! For your light holds back the darkness within me … lest it consume us all!" (Simonson). Cloak and Dagger end the story wistfully watching the children interact with their family and missing this closeness in their own lives.

First Adventure: Batgirl Day One (DC Comics, 1993)

Some heroines have a perfect first adventure. In the pilot of the CW's *Supergirl*, Kara sees her sister's plane crashing. Harnessing the powers she's been taught not to use, she launches into the sky and safely brings it down. As the news comments on the extensive wreckage, the undaunted heroine shrugs. "Well, you try saving a plane for the first time. See if you don't make a mess." Her sister arrives to find Kara bursting out of her skin. "I'm just I'm so excited. I still can't believe I did it," she cheers with spunky energy. She adds, "It has been so long. I almost forgot how to fly. Well, not so much how, but more, more how it feels, like scared, but good scared. Like, like that moment right before you kiss someone for the first time. And now … now it's like I'm

First Adventure

not sure what comes next. Or maybe I am sure and I'm just afraid of what it means." Her sister Alex warns her to be cautious, but Kara is undauntable—she's tasted superheroics and won't turn away.

Of course, for the majority, a disastrous and messy debut emphasizes how much they have to learn. Though Barbara Gordon's Batgirl arrived in the sixties, a later-written origin story by Kelley Puckett and Mike Parobeck suggests the sort of first day she must have had. While Batman is out of town, Barbara Gordon prepares for her friend's costume party but also asks her father, "Dad? Did you ever wonder what it's like to *be* Batman? You know, leaping from rooftops … chasing criminals … dodging gunfire … it just … sounds so … exciting." He retorts of course that armed gunmen try to kill Batman each night. As he concludes, "I admire Batman for what he does. But I don't *envy* him. *Nobody* should."

Still fantasizing, she attends socialite Sandy's costume party in her new Batsuit, and is greeted with a humiliating, "Who are you supposed to be?" This response often greets the new hero. Of course, Batgirl in many incarnations (1966 television show, *Batman and Robin* film and here in the comic) costumes herself as Batman's sidekick to become a superhero in his tradition. To the wearer, the suit is a statement of "I am someone who knows exactly who I am and what I stand for. I shall be respected, revered, and my status is above humans" (Brownie 34).

> Those who are entitled to wear the mask must prove their worth. They must demonstrate "accumulated wisdom" or special abilities that separate them from the rest of society. The donning of the mask is a rite of passage that signifies the transition from ordinary to extraordinary, as a civilian becomes a superhero. In superhero origin stories, the introduction of the costume marks the superhero's adoption of a new role: the moment that he becomes a superhero. Often, this occurs as a consequence of (or in preparation for) a defining event in his story so far. The first time that he steps into the costume marks initiation into an exclusive role and completes the hero's transition from one of the ordinary masses, to one of the extraordinary few [Brownie 32].

As she snoops through the mansion and is turned back by private security, an invading Harley Quinn demands, "Who're you? Batman's squeeze?" Batgirl denies it and Harley hits her with a baseball bat. As they struggle for the bat, they clonk heads, and Harley thinks, "I don't think I did that right." Clearly, humorous clumsiness is a feature here, adding personality but sadly emphasizing the heroines' inability.

Poison Ivy shows up too, and Batgirl, thinking quickly, threatens to drop a potted plant. Poison Ivy pauses, protesting, "You would take the life of an innocent *plant*? What kind of *monster* are you?" Moments later, however, she's hurling darts and screaming invectives as Batgirl flees. Batgirl then frees the hostage—the teen hostess Sandy, who is dressed, appropriately, like a princess. "I'm uhh.... I'm Batgirl. Batman couldn't make it." Here she tentatively establishes herself even as she acknowledges she's standing in for the more famous hero. Of course, she's capitalizing on his reputation until she builds her own.

She leads Sandy to safety and quips, "You know, this isn't as tough as I thought it'd be." Of course, she turns the corner and walks into Harley's drawn gun. "Hey Bat-chick! Payback." Barbara closes her eyes, realizing she's done for and likely recalling her father's words about how a single bullet could kill Batman. The security guards, however, come to the rescue and apparently save the princess, only to capture Batgirl along with the villainesses. Mini-Batgirl figures spin around her as all the awkwardness of her first adventure continues.

"Well, well, look what the cat's dragged in," Catwoman smirks, surveying Batgirl, princess, Harley and Ivy, all tied up. She announces that she's replaced the security guards all so she can steal a priceless diamond. "But Commissioner Gordon personally guaranteed the safety of that diamond," Barbara protests.

"Yes, I know. A little sure of himself, don't you think?" Catwoman smirks, clearly referencing the prone and helpless Batgirl as well. She takes the diamond and blows her tied-up foes a kiss.

Barbara starts using her head and a strong dose of teamwork, persuading Poison Ivy to free her so they can stop Catwoman. Batgirl then throws the dart at the empty diamond case, triggering the alarm. Catwoman leaves the guards to take the fall and darts off. However, Batgirl awaits her at the roof exit. As she warns off Batgirl, Catwoman extends her claws one by one. "You're out of your league, Little Girl. This isn't fun and games."

"I know that now. But I can't let you take the diamond." Batgirl hurls it off the roof, and with a scowl and empty threat, Catwoman departs. Though Barbara tells her father after that she was nowhere near the fighting, when he asks about her costume, she replies, "Oh that. I threw it away. Turns out it doesn't fit." In a surprising letdown after her problematic but brave adventures, she turns her back on superheroism, at least for a time.

The Power Pack, carried off by the alien horse Whitey as they seek to rescue their parents from the alien Snarks, learn a little from him about the enemy. However, Whitey perishes, bravely transferring his powers to them but leaving them mentorless. Instead, they discover their powers through experimentation and support one another on this startling new quest through outer space. Still, they defeat the aliens on their first attempt through blundering—little Katie reveals, "I didn't mean to! I just touched stuff and it disintegrated!" (Simonson, *Power Pack* #1). In fact, she's so powerful the aliens cringe away from her armor-melting energy as she tumbles about the ship and finally falls out the hole she's accidentally blasted. Though Katie, who's only five, wails that she wants to go home (with a rage now augmented by energy powers), they all realize that only they can save the planet and their parents as well. With this, they start serious training and become a hero team.

In a similar prequel, the JLA unite, with Black Canary introducing them at a press conference. A gang of monsters attacks, and the team has its first battle. Black Canary fights competently, but when her teammates urge her to use her power on a shambling monster, she protests, "I've never used it on a human being. I don't know what it'll do to him." Her friends remind her the creature isn't human and she tries, though her voice fails to stop it. Meanwhile, they quickly discover each other's capabilities in the midst of the combat. After, the Flash comments, "Someone actually wants us *dead*. That's the first time I've played for those stakes." Clearly, they're no longer practicing but battling for their lives. There are particularly gender-based kinks to work out, as Canary in particular discovers. "This is the ninth time the men on this team have gone out of their way to protect me. I have only one request. Will you knock it off!" As she screams, demanding an equal partnership, they quickly acquiesce (Waid, *JLA: Year One*).

For many superheroes of both genders, the first adventure is awkward, brimming with mistakes. Many sport homemade costumes that they later upgrade. Annie, Peter Parker's alt-world superpowered daughter, is startled when two students in drama club develop powers of their own. She joins them in costume shopping to create their new looks and enjoys it, thinking, "All this is so new to them. Exciting. It's almost like I get to do it all over for the very first time." She trains them and soon goes out with them (in a new disguise) to start saving the day. However, one of her friends appears to contemplate murder. Annie reigns Lacey in, only to have the other girl insist she will kill Annie's friend Norman Osborn, Jr., for the crimes of his father. Annie must teach her that ethics must accompany powers, showing the other teens what a childhood of superheroing has taught her (Houser, *Amazing Spider-Man*).

Responsible Sister: Karma (Marvel Comics, 1980–2013)

The X-Man Karma is born Xi'an Coy Manh. As she tells her readers, "To be Vietnamese is to have lived your entire life with war. It is to suffer, grieve, hunger, fear. To walk hand in hand with death. I do not complain by saying this, merely state reality" (Claremont and Miller). Appearing in *Marvel Team-Up* #100, she takes over Spider-Man's body and manipulates it as he swings through the city. Still controlling him telepathically, the heroine struggles to rescue her young siblings Leong and Nga, who are under the control of her uncle, a multimillionaire former general in the South Vietnamese Army.

Confronted by the Fantastic Four, Xi'an finally shares her story: Saving her twin brother Tran from a Viet Cong soldier revealed her abilities. However, when her brother then killed the soldier, he reveled in using their shared power cruelly. When South Vietnam fell, their Uncle Nguyen, knowing Tran's power, saved him and brought him to America. The rest of Xi'an's family were still trapped and finally escaped in a small boat. After days of starvation, when Xi'an was too weak to resist, they were attacked by Thai pirates, who slew all the men aboard—including Xi'an's father—and dealt "even worse" with the women. With her mother dying soon after, Xi'an and the children were sent to their uncle in the United States. She refused to work for him, however, and took sanctuary with the children with Father Michael Bowen (Dagger's uncle) … until their recent kidnapping. The Fantastic Four and Spider-Man agree to help. However, Tran is too powerful, and she is forced to defeat her twin, absorbing his powers and naming herself Karma. After this, the X-Men take her in. Of course, battling family is a brutal blow for the heroine, one seen in much of Claremont's emotional X-Men journeys. More family trouble follows, emphasizing the suffering of one who must be a parent too soon.

Those who have dependent siblings often find themselves extending this protection to the rest of the world. Meg Cabot's teen novel *Vanished* follows Jessica Mastriani, a small-town teen struck by lightning. She soon discovers her new superpower: upon seeing pictures of missing children, she instantly knows their locations. After checking one out, Jessica begins calling in anonymous tips, leading to several children each week being reunited with their parents. Thus, her superpower comes from a place of compassion—it's not flashy fire or flying to be used for good or evil, but a power that lets her save society's weakest members. This particular story puts her devotion to children in context. Protecting her older brother Douglas, who has schizophrenia and is heavily medicated, has made her the sort of person who punches a lot. As she relates: "My whole life, it seems, I've been beating up people who called my older brother a retard or a spaz, or a weirdo. I don't know why, but even though most of the time I'm way smaller than them, I feel obligated to punch them in the face for dissing my brother" (40). The heroine's rough-and-tumble nature defines her, giving her the toughness to solve her problems and other people's too.

Decades later, Marjorie Liu's *Astonishing X-Men: Northstar* has the Marauders, superpowered goons, attack the X-Men. It turns out they're being controlled by an outside source. When Karma scans one, she feels like maggots have exploded all over her and recoils. That night, bleeding from the ear, she awakens to find a woman in a red dress watching her. After, the X-Men begin attacking each other, and they discover Karma is responsible. She's controlling their minds and can only manage "I'm sorry." She runs away as she insists, "I'm not safe to be around."

The following *Astonishing X-Men: Weaponized* has Karma tangling with a new sibling. Weapons designer Susan Hatchi, born D'ao Coy Manh, coolly tells the X-Men she was responsible: "It was an experiment. I needed to test some new technology, and who better to be my guinea pigs than the X-Men? If I can beat you, I can beat *anyone*." Though without her powers, she has impressive nanite technology. Entrapping the X-Men with it, Susan orders them to take over the island of Madripoor, or she'll spread the nanites through New York. As she shows off that she's more powerful than the X-Men, businessmen will flock to her technology.

D'ao Coy Manh grew up hidden and neglected in her father's "other family." When violence came, her father shot her mother and sold D'ao into slavery. Now she seeks vengeance against the good daughter their father always protected—Karma. As Karma finds her long-lost father, D'ao fires a rocket launcher at the building, burying them both. She soon reveals that she's always sought revenge against him, and only using the good daughter as bait would draw him out. "I hated you for never claiming me and my mother as your family. For not protecting us like you protected *them*," she complains bitterly, as they all aim guns at one another in a true dysfunctional family dynamic. D'ao's presence emphasizes how siblings often represent the path one might have taken—and both of selfless Karma's adult siblings have clearly chosen evil.

Other evil siblings likewise arrive to plague the famous superheroes. Professor X is Juggernaut's brother. He also has an unborn twin, Cassandra Nova. Since he sensed in the womb that she was evil and tried to destroy her, she has fought all her life for her very existence. Stories like this obviously bring superhero rivalry to new levels. Gamora and Nebula's relationship in the MCU is also messy—they're on opposing sides, but Nebula pleads for her sister's sympathy, and Gamora repeatedly grants it. Thor has Loki. Black Bolt's brother Maximus tries to steal his throne and plays the main villain in the short-lived show *Inhumans*. Black Panther faces an ambitious half-brother in the comics and his cousin in the film. Barbara Gordon has a criminal brother. Aquaman has his half-brother, Ocean Master. Raven of the Teen Titans discovers six brothers, each for one of the Six Deadly sins, who tempt her into evil. J'Onn J'onzz's brother Ma'alefa'ak is so evil that he wiped out their entire planet.

Starfire's sister Blackfire is introduced as her own evil nemesis in 1982's *New Teen Titans* #23. Upon being kidnapped, Starfire greets her with "Let me free, Sister, and I'll *crush* your stinking *bones* for what you did to *Tamaran*" (Wolfman). Komand'r was deposed as heir when the people favored her much kinder sister. This exacerbated the hatred. "You were the one everyone cared for. I was the one everyone feared," Blackfire cries in misery (#24). She sets out to enslave her sister in vengeance, craving her sister's suffering more than her throne. As she, like so many other evil siblings, represents the neglected, unwanted part of the personality, their conflict is painfully personal.

Similarly, in Rucka and Williams' celebrated *Batwoman: Elegy*, Batwoman battles a madwoman known only as Alice, who speaks in quotes from *Alice in Wonderland*, dressed in frilly white. Batwoman stops her from engulfing Gotham in poison gas. To her shock, as Alice drops from the helicopter, she says, "You have our father's eyes." She is Batwoman's lost twin sister. In a story echoed in the *Batwoman* television show, she begins a long quest to rescue and redeem this lost part of herself.

This is often the heroine's mission, though compassion can also be a trap. D'ao kidnaps her respected, proper sister and the X-Men. Shan worries, meanwhile, that she's let this happen. "I've been silent all this time…. Taking it on the chin, just like I've taken every other tragedy in my life. because good girls … good little soldiers … we never complain, do we?" She reflects that she and her sister were both raised to believe no one would listen, no one would care what they wanted. Clearly, swallowing the pain can make young women like her sister into monsters. Courageously, she embraces the other girl and links with her mentally, telling her, "Look at me, Susan. See my life. Both of us were abandoned. Abused." She vows to stay with her sister and protect her. To her horror, however, her father calls Susan a "threat" and shoots her. Her father, already dying, is arrested, and Shan loses two family members at once. A simple embrace cannot erase all the suffering, but considering her position in the family, she's unable to save everyone. After, she reflects on how her sister succumbed to bitterness while she did not. She decides not to tell her siblings about their father "But I'll tell them about Susan. A little, anyway. Despite everything … she deserves that." Clutching Susan's photo, she calls her little siblings just to say she loves them.

Paragon: Supergirl (TV, 2015–)

In her 2015 television incarnation, Supergirl (Melissa Benoist) is a beacon of hope. From the episode's first lines, her parents tell her, "Because of the Earth's yellow sun, you'll have great powers on this planet. You will do extraordinary things." In the course of the first episode, then the first season, she finds a way to embody their ideals.

This is especially interesting when she's contrasted with the DC movies of the same period—*Superman v Batman* and *Man of Steel*. While these are savage, ignoring truth, justice, and the American way as well as civilians to revel in violence, even as the male heroes express their dominance, Supergirl herself teaches a gentler way by inspiring people to be better themselves.

> Though the characters are technically supposed to be related, Melissa Benoist's Supergirl/Kara Danvers and Henry Cavill's Superman/Clark Kent could hardly be more different. While Supergirl is a role model, exemplifying the decency and kindness to which humanity should aspire, the latest version of Superman is an anti-hero, not necessarily because he possesses unsavory traits, but because he's a literal inversion of everything that Superman traditionally represents.... Instead of casting Clark as an idealistic boy scout, however, Snyder aligns him with American might and imperialism, surrounding him with almost propaganda-like militaristic imagery and positioning him as a Christ-like white savior [Woolsey].

Supergirl has a different message, a gentler one. She's eager to make a difference. "If *Batman v Superman* upends traditional notions of heroism by perverting them, then *Supergirl* upends them by offering an alternative, one that values emotional strength over physical prowess, kindness over aggression, teamwork over individualism, and reconciliation over punishment," Woolsey adds. As she moves from her Kryptonian heritage to embrace earth and her chosen city, she grows tremendously. "Kara's humanity, so to speak, is ultimately what makes her a hero. Where her big-screen counterparts are defined and limited by their powers, Kara is defined—and freed—by her restraint," Woolsey concludes. Without her powers in the episode "Human for a Day," she shows she can help people without flashy abilities.

In the first episode, journalism mogul Cat Grant (Calista Flockhart) names her Supergirl ... then flies into a passionate defense of how the term "girl" can have power in today's world, determinedly reclaiming it. She tells Kara: "I'm the hero. I stuck a label on the side of this girl, I branded her. She will forever be linked to Catco, to the Tribune, to me. And what do you think is so bad about 'Girl'? ... I'm a girl. And your boss, and powerful, and rich, and hot and smart. So if you perceive 'Supergirl' as anything less than excellent, isn't the real problem you?" ("Pilot," 101). With this, the actress who played the previous generation's girl power icon Ally McBeal links with feminism of the past and emphasizes to the audience that it's all right for television's new superheroine to be a "girl" and yet a hero.

Alan Klein notes the influence of superheroic bodies as an elusive model of perfection, commenting that "[c]omic book depictions of masculinity are so obviously exaggerated that they represent fiction twice over, as genre and as gender representation" (267). "Moreover," Klein continues, "the reader is set up to be simultaneously impressed by the superhero and dismissive of the alter ego, a situation that underscores the overvalued place of hypermasculinity for readers of this genre of comic books" (268). Superheroines lack the bulging muscles, but they usually have long, flowing hair and very tight outfits, often with cleavage or cut-outs as well. Supergirl does not have this problem as in her knee-length super skirt, she's attractive but doesn't exaggerate her attributes by stripping down to underwear or tight spandex. As Kara, she tries to hide behind glasses and sensible blouses, but she dates and goes to the bar with her friends looking nice rather than dowdy.

Kara goes on to save lives and provide an image of protection. She's even seen defending a bullied little girl on the playground in "Falling" (116). All this is shattered later in that episode, however, when she's exposed to red kryptonite. She fights against the perfect image Cat has pushed on her as her bratty, human side struggles for voice. "You branded me in the media as a Girl Scout," she complains. "'Supergirl is brave, kind, and strong.' Isn't that kind of a stock characterization? Very two-dimensional. Everyone knows real people have a dark side."

Cat's retort is simple and clear: "Yes, but you don't get to be a real person. You're a superhero. You get to represent all the *goodness* in the world."

Supergirl tosses her off her balcony and catches her to show off her power, with an ominous quip: "True power is getting to decide who will live and who will die." She lets criminals escape because they're not worth her time and thus demonstrates a selfish might-makes-right hero. The little girl she protected, now disillusioned, tosses her own super cape in the trash. This pushes the heroine over the line toward the darker heroes of film. "With Supergirl acting irresponsibly while affected by the Red Kryptonite, Cat issues a public address about how we can't trust the Maid of Might—and unlike Batman's similar monologues in *Batman v Superman*, we're supposed to be saddened, not titillated, by this paranoia. This is a hero who understands the responsibilities of immense power" (Woolsey).

On returning to herself, Supergirl is deeply ashamed of her actions under Red Kryptonite. She's agonized by the idea that there's so much pettiness and cynicism churning inside of her. She finally tells Cat that she'll need to learn from what happened. Still, as she adds, she knows now why she does her job. "And to me, every person in this city is a light, and every time I've helped one of them, a little bit of their light has become a part of me." She devotes herself to regaining the people's trust and becoming a beacon once more.

The Flash's meeting with Supergirl in a crossover episode is sweet and fun. Both instantly accept the other as superhero kindred, in contrast with the competitiveness of *Superman v Batman*. The Flash demonstrates his superpowers by bringing the team ice cream, and Kara's smile is transcendent. Barry Allen and Kara Danvers and joke back and forth, comparing their lives, then return Barry home by racing together joyously in the sun.

Basically, it's a delightful, joy-filled romp of a team-up free of testosterone poisoning. Altruistic heroes can automatically help each other, without warring for dominance.

In the first season finale, Supergirl faces a supervillain team-up of Non and Indigo, even as their mind control device, Myriad, removes all her friends and supporters—even Superman (with his human-raised thought patterns). All of humanity has lost free will, left as mindless drones to be tortured and enslaved or simply neglected as they stand vacantly and obey orders.

Indeed, sometimes the heroine's very physiology makes her a savior. A plague comes to earth, in the form of an alien child who utters Laura Kinney's name and then dies. Humanity names it the Laura Kinney virus. However, scientists soon discover that Laura's unique physiology not only battles the virus but attracts it—if she touches someone with the virus, it leaves that person for her. Her little sister Gabby cheers, "You worked out how to punch a virus in the face. My sister is the freaking messiah" (Taylor). The people of Roosevelt Island are infected, and Laura arrives in a truly savior moment, walking among the people and touching them one by one, absorbing the virus. As she collapses from the strain, and Gabby insists on joining her, Doctor Strange finally sends "the cavalry"—Old Man Logan, and even Deadpool. They aid Laura, but she survives the process the longest and saves each person on the island with her gifts. She then launches into space to bring the cure to the child's planet. There, she learns that the child wasn't actually sent to find her but brought a list of names—hers was the first. Even by chance and making her own destiny, Laura has saved them all.

In the midst of her own crisis, Kara is forced to battle her own foster sister Alex. Nonetheless, their mother's pleading finally penetrates the technology as she insists, "Alex, you can beat this. I know you can. You're not gonna hurt me. You're not gonna hurt Kara. We are a family. Stronger together. Alex, you are the strongest of us all. Your father always said that. I know he's watching over you. I know he'd be so proud. Your father believed in you. I believe in you, too" ("Better Angels," 120).

After this success, they realize a message on the right frequency can allow Kara to save the city. She takes the microphone and sends her own signal of hope and inspiration, cutting through the defeatism:

> People of National City. This is Supergirl and I hope you can hear me. We have been attacked. Mothers and fathers, friends and neighbors, children, everyone, suddenly stopped by a force of evil as great as this world has ever known. Your attacker has sought to take your free will, your individuality, your spirit. Everything that makes you who you are. When facing an attack like this, it's easy to feel hopeless. We retreat, we lose our strength, lose our self. I know. I lost everything when I was young. When I first landed on this planet, I was sad and alone. But I found out that there is so much love in this world out there for the taking, and you, the people of National City,

you helped me. You let me be who I'm meant to be. You gave me back to myself. You made me stronger than I ever thought possible, and I love you for that. Now, in each and every one of you, there is a light, a spirit, that cannot be snuffed out. That won't give up. I need your help again. I need you to hope. Hope. That you will remember that you can all be heroes. Hope. That when faced with an enemy determined to destroy your spirit, you will fight back and thrive. Hope. That those who once may have shunned you will, in a moment of crisis, come to your aid. Hope. That you will see again the faces of those you love and perhaps even those you have lost ["Better Angels," 120].

The speech is touching, especially since Kara offers her past and her most personal issues to save everyone. The public respond to it, and with her moment of inspiration, Supergirl has saved the city. "What could have easily been a cheesy, over-the-top ploy became a poignant touchstone of the episode and proved that Supergirl has deftly nailed the ability to be uplifting and bright without sacrificing drama. Not only was it a well-written speech, but it also represented Supergirl's relationship with her city and what she represents to the people she's dedicated her life to saving" ("Why *Supergirl*").

After their plan is thwarted, the supervillains increase the machine's intensity. Myriad will now kill everyone on the planet. Supergirl can only think of one solution—defeating the villains and shutting it off. Kara sets out, knowing it may mean her death. She announces: "My mother didn't send me to Earth to fall in love with a human, have children, live in a house with a white picket fence. She sent me here to protect Kal-El. And now, I will use my powers to protect the Earth. And if I die achieving that, I'm at peace with it. I'll join my mother. We'll be together in Rao's light." Kara wins the fight with only J'onn J'onzz as backup but finds there's no way to deactivate the machine. The only way to stop Myriad from exploding the heads of everyone she loves is to fly their tool of Fort Rozz into space and leave it there, dying of suffocation in the process. Kara thus sacrifices herself and saves the world.

However, in the last moments, it's not Superman or Martian Manhunter who shows up to save the unconscious heroine. It's Alex, determinedly piloting Kara's childhood ship. The story ends in celebration—Cat Grant acknowledges Kara's everyday skills by promoting her and letting her choose how she wants to start her career (and finally getting her name right!). James kisses her at last. And Kara ends the season with a family dinner, celebrating the lives that fill hers with so much joy. In the Arrowverse's Crisis on Infinite Earths crossover of 2019, Supergirl was named the paragon of hope—an appropriate label for such an icon.

The relaunched Captain Marvel line of 2019 by Kelly Thompson and Carmen Carnero emphasizes how much she's an icon as she returns to New York to have Tony Stark book her media appearances. However, when she follows the criminal Nuclear Man through a portal, she discovers a very different type of notoriety. The ragtag superheroines there hope she'll lead them. And Nuclear Man has enticed her through hoping she'll be his bride. In a misogynistic fantasy, he forces her to battle her old archnemesis Rogue for the honor, in the sexist post-apocalyptic fantasy world he's built. However, Carol works with Rogue, convincing the other woman to trust her completely and let her take over Rogue's mind to win the day. Finally, Carol discovers this has all been orchestrated because of her reputation. Nuclear Man's son reveals, "I put the idea in my father's head to being you here. For him it was about choosing a powerful woman to break ... one to bear powerful children. For me it was about choosing someone who could save us.... We needed a leader ... a hero." She takes on this duty and succeeds. However, when she returns to earth a hero, the media begins vilifying her and the military kicks her out for her alien heritage, giving her a new quandary to struggle through. As she fights in Times Square, projected up on the giant screens for the crowd to see, a little girl steps up and defends her. After the battle, the public side with her once more, with 82 percent wanting to reinstate her in the military.

Gail Simone's *Ends of the Earth* shows a studio filming a terrible *Wonder Woman* movie in a metafictional criticism of how superheroines are seen and presented. Visiting, Diana cringes as her character (in a Wonder Woman patterned bikini) fauns mindlessly over Steve Trevor. When her mother's rape by Hercules turns into a besotted love triangle (with Diana crying, "How is it that you have defeated me, and yet I've never felt more like a woman?"), the real Diana decries the whole franchise and demands, "Why is it that people feel that a belief in women equals a hatred of men?" (*Ends of the Earth*). As a feminist icon (like her writer), she's very aware of how the public views her. She announces, "This film is canceled. It's over," and leaves the floundering studio, thinking, "waiting a while for a *good* movie is better than having a *terrible* one today" in pointed commentary. Meanwhile, one of the producers is highly skeptical: "What right do you have to hold *yourself* up as an 'inspiration' to little girls? You think violence solves *everything*. And pardon me if I don't think wearing the *flag* on your barely covered rear *end* is any kind of good message for my daughters." These of course are criticisms of many fans throughout the decades. Many mothers question the outfits and violence of all comics, including those with strong women. Diana responds sympathetically, discovering that the producer is an alcoholic and helping her through it. It turns out jealousy of her children's admiration for Wonder Woman is behind the criticism. However, by listening and reaching out in friendship, Wonder Woman changes Allison's mind.

Danielle: Chronicles of a Superheroine, a novel by Ray Kurzweil and illustrated by Amy Kurzweil, watches a young prodigy's climb to international superstar. Danielle is a genius, and goes from science genius to activist when she visits Zambia to bring them water machines. After her music videos go viral, she starts her own recording company and uses the proceeds to solve problems throughout the world. She takes down a Libyan dictator with computer code and then advises the king of Saudi Arabia, instituting democracy and winning freedom for the girls there. Her reputation builds until world leaders call on her by name. "If anyone can actually carry out these changes, it would be you," the admiring king tells the eleven-year-old Jewish girl (125). As her adventures continue, she frees China and Tibet, cures cancer, brings peace to the Middle East, greeting everyone with hugs all the while. As she becomes President of China and then the US, she emphasizes that the female readers truly can become anything they wish. She also models healthy family relationships: Her adopted sister, more ordinary, loves Danielle without a trace of jealousy, and is nominated for the Sundance Best Screenplay Award, sells millions of copies of her songs, and finally wins a Pulitzer herself. This emphasizes sisterhood and different paths to success. The companion books, published in the same volume, offer nonfiction advice on how real girls can do similar activism projects, while crowdfunding and starting clubs to walk in Danielle's footsteps. With this, Danielle becomes a real-life icon, not just a fictional one.

Mystic: Zero Girl (Homage Comics, 2001)

The independent *Zero Girl* by Sam Kieth (writing and art) is a school story comic, but one with more than a trace of the mystical, as well as superheroism. "In former times, many women hid their intuitive nature so that they would not be persecuted or tormented or ostracized as strange" (Leonard 245). A high school sophomore, Amy Smootster considers herself a "freak" and a "loner," adding, "Ever since I can remember, I've guarded the secret of my puzzling reaction to embarrassment and humiliation. I don't understand it, and I can't even begin to control it. Sometimes it scares the hell out of me. Sometimes I think it's going to kill me. The power of my shame is both my worst nightmare … and my only chance at being saved." With this monologue, a superhero's insecurities are brought to magical life.

She's ostracized because, as the mean girls put it, "when she gets embarrassed, her feet get soaked." Water coats her from head to toe, revolting the other students. She's also known for carrying crayons and newspapers, drawing circles constantly. Of course, peer pressure humiliates her into hiding her talents. "Women of a gentler temperament, like the introverted, intuitive, perceptive, feeling type, often fear to brave the attacks of more aggressive, judgmental thinkers. So they hide their insights, keeping to themselves, or they fail to express the intuitions so fundamental to their natures. Others weave their visions into poems or paintings but fear to show them to the outer world" (Leonard 242). At the comic's beginning, she's called in to see her counselor, Tim Foster. She hesitates, and then confides in him that "I see shapes. It's like they move…. Circular shapes are okay. Safe. Friendly. Squares are dangerous."

He tells her, admittedly straight from a symbolism book, that shapes are part of the collective unconscious and that circles symbolize "the egg, seed, feminine godhead, womb, and the number before all others: zero." They represent all a woman is meant to become—wholeness and the perfect cycle. This is a specifically feminine view: "Since her visions cannot be comprehended by rational thought alone, she threatens hierarchical thinking and is feared, ridiculed, and even condemned for her access to a realm that many refuse to experience" (Leonard 243).

As such, circles are the heroine's feminine-tinged power coming to life. "The universe begins with roundness; so say the myths," symbolist Barbara Walker says. "The great circle, the cosmic egg, the bubble, the spiral, the moon, the zero, the wheel of time, the infinite womb; such are the symbols that try to express a human sense of the wholeness of things" (2).

> Finally, it should be remarked that *emptiness* is a great feminine secret. It is something absolutely alien to man; the chasm, the unplumbed depths, the *yin*. The pitifulness of this vacuous nonentity goes to his heart (I speak here as a man), and one is tempted to say that this constitutes the whole "mystery" of woman. Such a female is fate itself [Jung, "Psychological Aspects of the Mother Archetype" 98].

Roundness is a feminine power, and it's one this heroine comes to use. The mean girls drag Amy into the bathroom and shove her face in the toilet, taunting her that her feet are dry. Suddenly, the rolls of toilet paper explode from the cabinet and turn into slavering mouths with sharp teeth. The girls flee in horror, crying "These mouths are disgusting!" while Amy notes, "For me, they have no teeth." This peer abuse is one of the worst blows to the sensitive mystic. "The Mystic strives to overcome her fears but isn't always successful. She fears not having a place to call her own where she can be herself and escape from other people's drama" (Schmidt).

Next the girls loosen bricks in the counselor's office ceiling meant to crush Amy, but she saves herself with a shield … though it's only a circle she cut from a newspaper. "These puddles of hers are some kind of protection," one of the mean girls realizes. She drops a pebble in, and it bounces right off. Amy is gathering protection from the world around her, though only that which mirrors her inner power—feminine magic. The circles of protection are reflected in the water power that comes from within: As Amy notes, "If you can't trust your own bodily fluids, what can you trust?"

Amy fends off an attack from her mysterious archenemy, a murderer whose face seems composed entirely of squares. When she's attacked by a mugger, Amy's umbrella turns into a slavering mouth and defends her. A circle of wet tissues defends them from a bus.

The mean girls then lock her in a square locker, as Amy refuses to strike out with her powers and give them the satisfaction. She starts to feel her surroundings closing in and thinks, "I reach back in my mind for another embarrassing moment, another time, and feel a pocket of shame in the darkness." She grabs it and escapes through a hole in space to a field where she feels secure.

She has no parents or guardians, hiding at the school and talking to (round, of course) pillbugs as her only confidants. Her counselor discovers this and lets her sleep in his office. As their feelings for each other grow, she comments, "I know it's illegal, but that doesn't make it wrong." Though she is young, growing through her teen years and trying to find a balance, her powers make her attractive as she finds confidence and identity through them. Still uncomfortable, her counselor holds off. They discuss their feelings in her safe place, an alley of broken washing machines with round doors. This is the perfect place for her to feel secure. "The Mystic cares about simplicity. Give her a nice home base that provides space for her to be herself, and she'll do anything to protect it. She's gentle mannered—but don't invade her quiet space! She needs room to be creative; a studio or garden is perfect" (Schmidt).

She takes him to talk to the pillbug, who appears to be symbolism expert Carl Jung, reincarnated. Here, she shows an affinity with the roundness and cycles of nature, wherever they are. "Losing her home or sanctuary would devastate her, but she knows she can make a home wherever she goes. To the Mystic, home truly is where the heart is" (Schmidt).

Meanwhile, Counselor Tim sorts through his feelings and finally tells her they must wait until she's eighteen. That night, his square bed and file cabinet attack, but she comes and saves him in her round car. The Mystic is fact does better as savior than saved. "She's fine with having someone else provide for her but she's somewhat uneasy that her ability to do what she wants depends on another person" (Schmidt).

Rejected by him, she retreats into a place of total roundness, a cement mixer like a womb, She vanishes into it, and he finds her later in an abandoned nuclear silo. The mass murderer attacks once more, now with the mean girls reincarnated as his square sidekicks. She shoots at him with her water-foot power and blasts one of the girls across the road, noting, "I've never done that before. Felt like a fire hose!" She nearly gives up, but thinking of Tim, she keeps fighting and banishes her enemy to a world of coasters.

Three years later she meets Tim again to discover he's married and moved on past the relationship. Nonetheless, she's found her own inner power. As a

Mystic, Zero Girl is motivated by "the aesthetic need for balance—a sense of order in life, a sense of being connected with something greater than herself—is what drives her. She has a spiritual need to connect or create. She knows she's not alone on earth and sometimes senses the life forces around her" (Schmidt).

Womanthology, a collection of short comics written and drawn by women, encourages more creative powers along with flying and fighting. In it, the heroine of "Spoon Bender" hurls spoons at a monster, which transform into chains and bind him (Jennifer V). Visually, spoons are round, a feminine, domestic symbol like Zero Girl's circles, suddenly empowered. In "The Wraiths of Roseland," an elderly woman can send dead children to protect those who still live (Sardina). She is a matriarch and protector of children, saving them with her love and wisdom of those who have gone.

Other mystics can be seen in the superhero world, drawn to the symbolism behind their powers. Raven assembles the New Teen Titans in their first comic book appearance. First, as Robin has a vision of the future, she assures him enticingly, "They exist, they are your future. A future that looks ever and ever closer." Then she arrives to Robin in the present, a midnight blue cloak spread against the light and within the deep hood, a pair of shining eyes. A mystery goddess, she tells him, "There are unknown forces at work … forces which demand that a new Teen Titans be formed!" (Wolfman). As Robin follows her commands, he represents action and she, the deep wisdom blossoming from within. She mentally searches the world for each of their destined team members, helping them all to assemble. Thus, Raven casts herself as the team's soul.

The cartoon *Teen Titans* features Raven as a withdrawn goth girl. She responds with distant boredom or unhappiness to everything, in contrast with perky, emotional Starfire. Season four ends with a Raven storyline as her monstrous father Trigon conquers the world, turning all humans but the Titans to stone. Raven has been the one to allow this, destined from birth to be his gateway. Faced with the inevitable, she despairs and finally surrenders. Once Trigon has dominated the earth, a powerless fragment of Raven remains dressed in simple white, crouched lost in his domain. Robin comes and saves her life, insisting he has faith in her and telling her the story of herself. They return to earth, where, strengthened by this belief, she finally confronts her father. Towering over her, he prepares to kill her, calling her "little girl" and "dear daughter." He adds: "I am your creator. Your master. You exist only to serve me. You survive only because I allow it. What hope can a mere child have of defeating her all-powerful father?"

She replies, "You may have created me, but you were never my father." She blasts him with beams of light, binding him. Then she conjures a colossal white raven of light. "This is my home, and you are not welcome here." As her bonds of light banish him, the gleaming raven restores all the life on earth.

Destiny the blind seer and X-Men villainess was created by Chris Claremont and John Byrne in *Uncanny X-Men* #141. In a canceled storyline, Mystique was to be Nightcrawler's father and Destiny his mother. On the audio commentary of "Nightcrawler": *X-Men: The Legend of Wolverine* (2003), Claremont explains, "My thought was, Mystique is a shapechanger. Why can't she be his dad, and have her partner in life, Destiny, be the mother? Which I thought would be really cool. But everyone thought it was a little too creepy for words." Certainly, two women conceiving a child without need for a man is a threat to patriarchal culture. "When Mystique and Destiny in their lesbian/disabled/age difference relationship adopt Rogue, they arguably become the most marginalized trio of women that ever appeared in superhero comics.... These sexually deviant, out-of-control, mutant women ... has the power to change, even perhaps overthrow, Professor Xavier's patriarchal X-Men hierarchy," Murray comments (181). Destiny is blind but has psionic precognition, to see future probabilities and interpret them. Years after her death, the X-Men discover her diaries called "The Books of Truth" with prophecies of the future. Several heroes and villains seek them through the series, hoping to use them for indescribable power.

Plunged into an alternate reality in *House of M*, Wolverine is the only one who remembers how the world used to be ... except for the schoolchild Layla Miller. She touches Luke Cage and for a moment helps him see his lost other life, about to have a child with Jessica Jones. Wolverine enlists her to do the same to Emma Frost. Schmidt says of the Mystic: "Her internal world is rich, and her sensitivity is extreme. She can feel the thoughts and emotions of others, which gives her great compassion but also makes her wary of public places." Indeed, shy Layla freaks out and tries to go home, protesting, "I'm so grounded," and insisting she doesn't know how to awaken memories. Nonetheless, Wolverine persuades her to return to the fight. Emma discovers that Layla can unlock a person's subconscious, but she isn't precisely psychic. To Layla's shock, Emma calls on her to put the world back the way it was. With Emma coaching her, Layla unlocks all the superheroes' minds and restores them to the right reality. As they attack Magnus's stronghold, their entire plan rests on Layla reaching Professor Xavier's mind, rather than winning through strength of arms. The plan succeeds and reality is restored. In Peter David's extended run on *X-Force*, Layla is a central part of the team, defining her superpower with the words "I know things." She has enough precognition to tell someone to walk home a different way, or avoid a bad situation, advice that always pays out. Her suggestions are cryptic but tend to be infinitely useful in the end.

Fish Out of Water: Starfire (DC Comics, 2015)

Wonder Woman, the original superheroine, comes from the mysterious Paradise Island of the Amazons. When she explores Man's World for the first time (in television show, film, and many comic variants), there are often jokes about how badly she fits in, from her outfit to her attitudes. She's framed as coming from a painfully sheltered background, unaccustomed to bureaucracy, war, and selfishness, so she comforts readers by battling these with a far older moral code.

Other characters have the same conflict, dealing with modern earth in ways that vary from professional to comical. Koriand'r, Starfire, is an alien often known for her revealing bikini costume. She debuted in 1980 as a member of DC's Teen Titans. On the cartoon *Teen Titans,* Starfire is absolutely the token alien. In the first episode, she chirps, "I suggest a large pizza with pickles, banana, and mint frosting." In the second, Robin offers Koriand'r her first cotton candy, which she discovers is far different from cotton. She tells him poignantly, "When I first came to this planet, I did not think I would ever fit in." She also offers her friends a 6000-verse poem of gratitude. Nonetheless, she proves through example that respecting a friend's odd culture leads to true camaraderie, if not always understanding. Her upbeat cheeriness buoys the team and does much to make up for her social gaffs.

Amanda Conner and Jimmy Palmiotti, a married team who humanized Harley Quinn and other damaged superwomen, rebooted Starfire for a 2015 comic series and made her a shade tougher. Like her original 80s version. she goes from alien princess to slave (this time sold away by her helpless sister, rather than callous parents) and in her own words: "I was tortured and experimented on. A result of this experimentation was that it unleashed a dormant power within me. A power I was able to use to my advantage … working together we started a revolt that freed us from our captors."

Now Starfire finds herself in a small island town near Florida. "I realize I must become one of you and assimilate as best I can," she adds. However, Koriand'r's terrible literalness leaves her puzzled as the pawnshop owner offers her "three big ones" for her jewels and she wonders if there's somewhere to buy a sense of humor. Thought bubbles show her confusion as she pictures every instance of figurative speech. On her silly escapades, Koriand'r tries drinking baking soda and taking the cat for a swim. Further, though she doesn't seem to notice it, everyone around her begins feeling whatever she does. In this way, she has a hurricane effect. Her overly technical way of talking is quite alien as well. Drinking beer, she announces, "I can feel its calming effects on the outermost area you humans call the 'brain' while the flavinoids simultaneously stimulate my physiology at a cellular level…" The local sheriff, Stella Gomez, realizes she needs a babysitter.

Despite all this, there's a sweetness to her character. She cares for those who are sad and rescues people (and parrots!) in danger. Her naiveté is often wise in its childishness. For instance, when Koriand'r finds a cruise ship in danger, she asks of the rich vacationers, "Why don't they give part of [their income] to those who need it, so everyone can work less and live well?" Meanwhile, Koriand'r loves helping the sheriff with all types of emergencies. With her flight and fire blasts, she can offer many skills, and she's had her powers long enough that she can keep them under control. Here, she really is a competent superhero, rather than a hindrance. In this story arc, she appears terribly naïve, but still a person, not simply the butt of a long-running joke.

As a girl, she has other problems. Young men are hitting on her, though she doesn't appear to notice. She walks around dressed scantily, and Stella suggests clothes shopping. Immediately, she spies a bikini in a shop window and wants it. Stella manages to get her into a short skirt and top at least. Later, she tries going to a job interview with her shirt unbuttoned down to her waist and Stella must help her, all while lecturing her on the power of her breasts over men.

Just after finding her a trailer she can rent, Stella walks out to see Koriand'r kissing Boone, the landlord's grandson (apparently this is how she learns languages). After her shower, she goes out naked and insists she doesn't need a second towel as her first is wrapped around her wet hair. When she meets Boone's girlfriend, she promptly blurts, "I understand your culture favors monogamy. I apologize. Had I known, I would not have kissed Boone." While her honorable forthrightness is meant kindly, it of course gets Boone in trouble.

Later, she moves in with Stella, and her brother Sol says she can swim in the pool naked whenever she wants. She in turn invites Sol to shower with her and "conserve water." The comic leaves it unclear exactly how naive she is in this scene. Sol says, "I can't believe for a second that you don't know what you're doing to me right now," and carefully turns her down, even as she flings her bikini at him. No one takes advantage of this alien who strips in public and kisses to learn language, instead treating her with respect and protectiveness. While this is an endearing example of the best of humanity, it's also a sugary fantasy.

Indeed, Wonder Woman, wandering London in skimpy armor in her 2017 film, or strutting in granny panties down the streets in the Lynda Carter show, has a similar invulnerability, in her case at least partly motivated by her intimidation factor. Author Leigh Bardugo writes, "On any other woman, Wonder Woman's costume would be interpreted as an invitation to ogle, an opportunity to judge the wearer's intent, her psyche, and even her morals" (158). This occurs in a few comic books. However, Wonder Woman is so tough that "[s]he is free from the relentless 'if she didn't want me to stare, she shouldn't have worn that' presumptions" (159). Anyone who interprets her costume as an invitation to grab will be instantly put in his place.

In a bar, about twenty men send Koriand'r drinks. Here Koriand'r asks the waitress for advice on etiquette (a wise choice) and the waitress tells her that the men are trying to court her and that she should make dates without going off with any of them immediately. With this advice, Kori begins learning about the world in a safe and supervised way, rather than making enormous social gaffs or compromising her own safety. When Kori confesses her confusion, the waitress tells her, "Sister, I know how you feel. When I first got here, I was so confused. Luckily, I had a good friend who showed me the ropes." By emphasizing their similarities, the waitress reinforces Kori's humanity, or so it appears.

When a monster attacks, the waitress sheds her dress to reveal a superhero uniform—she is Atlee, the superheroine Terra from the center of the world (another reimagined character from eighties *Teen Titans*). The two heroes dispatch the monster and exult in their new team-up. When Stella worries that their presence will attract monsters, the superheroes calm her with a group hug. It seems Starfire's time on the island has been a success. By the fifth issue, she not only has a team of girlfriends and a job, but she's cracking jokes from the television—and doing it properly. Kori, as her friends call her, finds a job only she can do when she communicates with one of the aquarium's dolphins and finds out why she's depressed. Her powers, combined with her kind heart, give her an edge here and give her a new road to acceptance.

While her alien clothing and food choices can be silly, she overpays for everything rather than neglecting the concept of money, so the islanders like her. She asks them for advice and they're happy to give it, while they also accept an orange-skinned alien philosophically. Terra says that on the news, "everyone hates everyone else because of their differences. But I look at Key West and I see people of all backgrounds getting along just fine. If a small island like this can set an example for the rest of the world, it will catch on." Clearly, kindness is the best course for those on both sides of the equation.

Sidekicks: Electra Woman and Dyna Girl (TV, 1976)

Male heroes with their hierarchical structure are more likely to have traditional sidekicks (Batman and Robin being the obvious). These heroes sometimes have female helpers (Batman has Batgirl; Wolverine mentors Kitty

Pryde and Jubilee, though a big-brother little-brother relationship is more common). Some sidekicks like Inspector Gadget's Penny are notably smarter than the heroes. There's also the girlfriend as partner, seem in many Golden Age team-ups like Hawkman and Hawkgirl or Bulletman and Bullet Girl. Many heroines like Supergirl and Harley Quinn begin as sidekicks, and thus as they get their own identities, they still appear the child of their stories. "Sidekicks might be pets, imps, romantic partners, troublesome relatives, and all sorts of unlikely underlings" (Morris, *Sidekicks* ii).

Women more often form communities, as Golden Age Wonder Woman has an entire group of college girls and island of Amazons. Eighties Wonder Woman has an embassy staff. Oracle, like Buffy the Vampire Slayer, has a group of close friends who make up a fighting team. Gabrielle may appear a helper for Xena in her first episode, but it soon melds into an equal partnership.

Nonetheless, heroines occasionally get sidekicks. This role, similar to the "best friend" of romantic comedies, helps keep the heroine on track and aware of issues outside her perception. She offers complementary skills, focusing the heroine on overcoming her challenges. Wonder Woman has Wonder Girl (Donna Troy then Cassie Sandsmark). Batwoman has her niece Flamebird. Emma Frost has the Stepford Cuckoos. Brat Pack, a dark satire comic on superhero sidekicks, includes Moon Mistress, a man-hating warrior woman, and her sidekick Luna. Margaret Stohl's teen novel *Black Widow: Red Vengeance* sees her and her young Red Room friend Ava link psyches. "They could sometimes feel what each other felt or dream what each other dreamed" (62). Ava can channel Natasha's knowledge when she's in danger, and she can help her "big sister" with a supportive shoulder after an attack.

"Sidekicks bring something different to the average super-powered grudge match between good and evil. Sometimes it's humor, sometimes it's vulnerability, sometimes it's merely someone with whom the lead character can share a confidence or two. As superfluous as they seem at first glance, sidekicks serve a valuable role in their senior partners' stories" (Morris, *Sidekicks* i). Some sidekicks are notable for their contrasting skills even to the point of being the support team. Naif Al-Mutawa's *The 99* (a reference to Islam's 99 attributes of God) from Teshkeel Comics offers Amira Khan, a Pakistani-British teenager called Hadya, the Guide. This name exemplifies her calling—guiding the heroes. She has the ability to map out cities, countries, and even entire solar systems, as her "brain functions like a telephoto satellite and global positioning tracking system." She aids Noora, the story's central superheroine, providing logistical support.

Other superheroines are stunned to get no more respect than the helper's role. In C.B. Lee's Lambda Award–winning series beginning with *Not Your Sidekick*, the teen heroine grows up in her superpowered big sister's shadow. To Jess's surprise, Claudia tells her, "Usually hero support requires that the sidekick presents with at least a D-class power, but I think if you wanna hang back in the lab, you can totally help with the tech side of things, maybe monitor the holofeeds and work with the communications team?" (120). Having earned a real job based on her skills, Jess refuses. However, when the League that represents all superhero authority is revealed as evil, Claudia still chooses to enforce their directives, even experimenting on innocents. Jess and her friends realize they must start a rebellion, uniting in their own cause.

"Sometimes the hero doesn't have a choice. *Sometimes the sidekicks decide*" (Morris, *Sidekicks* 12). Captain Future, from *Startling Comics* (1941), finds his alter ego's girlfriend Grace Adams works for the Agatha Detective Agency, named for her wealthy aunt. The captain's civilian self, Dr. Andrew Bryant, discovers a gang of jewel thieves has kidnapped Agatha. However, she battles goons with her umbrella and insists she'll save Grace from the evildoers. Eventually Captain Future steps in and saves everyone. However, the two women have permanently joined him, and break up gangs of masked killers and car hijackers through a year of adventures.

Other times, the hero can be quite paternalistic. "When fate puts him on a path with a mysterious, super-strong young woman, Mighty Man opts to bring her on as his assistant—but on his terms. Super-Ann would be his sidekick, but *he wouldn't let her know about it*" (Morris, *Sidekicks* 118). As he watches her from afar, she stops a truck with her hand and then flings it after the driver. He follows her home secretly and quizzes her mother about her origin story. After this, he watches over her as her "guardian angel," but continues to keep his presence a secret through the Golden Age. "Theirs may be the only case of unacknowledged sidekicking in comics history."

Of course, this mentorship often goes in both directions. In the comics, Captain Marvel has her child sidekick Lieutenant Trouble, whom she sends on missions. After Carol loses her memory in *Avengers: The Enemy Within*, she makes playdates with the eight-year-old but must tell her she doesn't remember enough to teach the little girl about being a superhero. The girl replies, "You're not going to teach me about Captain Marvel, Dummy! I'm going to teach you. There is nobody in the universe who knows more about Captain Marvel than me." She hands over the textbook she's made—a comic book (DeConnick). The bond of faith and love particularly between fictional women can help this relationship go in both ways.

Likewise, Wonder Girl searches earth to save her mentor in Amy Wolfram and Karl Kerschl's *Teen Titans Year One*, Wonder Woman pushes her away with "I don't need my little sister tagging along. Why don't you run home to mother!" Crushed, Wonder Girl finds the Teen Titans, but bursts into tears over the rejection. Together, the Titans realize all their mentors have been taken over. They decide that since their own mentors know them too well, they should split into teams and take each other's. At last they find a glowing monster called the Antithesis who's hypnotized all the superheroes to take over the JLA. Though their mentors make cruel comments that strike at the teens' insecurities, the teens defeat them one by one and break the hypnosis. After, their mentors compliment them, and the young heroes form their own group. Here, they work as a team to support one another even as they ground their heroes and restore them to themselves.

Electra Woman and Dyna Girl, a 1976 live action children's television series, gets to explore the sidekick relationship through several permutations. As a segment of Sid and Marty Krofft's *The Krofft Supershow,* it aired sixteen two-part episodes, each about 12 minutes long. (These are the dramatically named "The Sorcerer's Golden Trick," "Glitter Rock," "Empress of Evil," "Ali Baba," "Return of the Sorcerer," "The Pharaoh," "Spider Lady," and "Return of the Pharaoh.") In many ways, it parodied the *Batman* television series from 1966. Their endless Electra-gadgets, clearly a comment on Bat-weapons, included the Electra-Car Tracking Beam, Electra-Degravitators, and Electra-Plane. It was goofy but fun. Sid Krofft comments, "When we show *Electra Woman and Dyna Girl* at a screening, the audience just goes crazy … screaming, because it's so way out, so whacked-out…. When you say *Electra Woman and Dyna Girl,* only eight episodes, but everybody knows what you're talking about" (Muir 245–246).

Deidre Hall and Judy Strangis play Lori and Judy, reporters for *Newsmaker Magazine* who sometimes don spandex costumes and battle supervillains. Electra Woman is the leader and mentor, cool and aloof, though friendlier than Batman. She has massive blonde curls over her bright orange and yellow leotard and tights. Dyna Girl provides contrast, as the perky child sidekick with big pigtails in a pink suit. Like Robin, she makes lighthearted puns, calling their situation an Electra-mess, or chirping that everything was Electra-super. About to be crushed by a 20-ton stone slab in "Return of the Pharaoh," Dyna Girl quips, "We've never been in a tighter spot, Electra Woman!" Later, when Electra Woman asks if she's ready to carry on, Dyna Girl chirps, "Like Electra-now! I've got a few words for our friend the Pharaoh." While the clothes are reasonably modest—tight but concealing—the bright colors mark them both as closer to Robin than Batman. Like seventies Wonder Woman, there's a touch of the ridiculous as they walk around in this getup. Of course, the villains' costumes are just as bad, often resembling garish Halloween costumes. Their Alfred figure, Frank Heflin (played by Norman Alden), stays at their "ElectraBase," operating its highly sophisticated "CrimeScope" computer and inventing the gadgets.

As with the other seventies superheroine shows, this one is episodic, focusing on action rather than character arcs. The show "accumulated a huge fan following among the youthful Saturday TV watchers, thanks to a campy and over-the-top tone and sexy costuming" (Muir 245). Each villain incapacitates the women's electra-gadgets, forcing the women to be inventive to defeat them and save the day. Dangling them over boiling oil, giant boxes filling with sand or water, ravenous spiders and snakes, and similar slow-moving deadly traps is popular. Episode one has the sorcerer, a master of illusion, escaping prison and vowing revenge on his female nemeses. When Electra Woman and Dyna Girl find him, he uses his mirror trick to transport them to an underground stage. There, he announces they'll star in his performance of "Electra Woman and Dyna Girl vs. the Man-eating Tiger." He locks them in a cage where a pouring faucet slowly releases a tiger from its own enclosure. Electra Woman realizes that the cage has no top, so she boosts Dyna Girl out to retrieve the key, using the girl as a helper to their plan. The day is saved, and they recapture the villain.

The supervillain generally has his own sidekick, as the sorcerer has the rather dim Miss Dazzle. Glitter Rock, who can control people's minds with the distinct cords of his guitar, has his sideman Side Man. Ali Baba, master of dirty tricks, has an evil Genie. The bat-crowned Empress of Evil has Lucrecia. These sidekicks mostly exist so the villain has someone to offer exposition to but provide a distinct contrast with the teamwork and respect between the heroines. The sidekicks' dialogue emphasizes their total uselessness in contrast with Dyna Girl's clever quips:

> ELECTRA WOMAN: I advise you not to come any closer, Empress of Evil!
> LUCRECIA: [outraged] She advises you not to come any closer? Did you hear that, my beloved Empress?
> EMPRESS OF EVIL: I heard that, Lucretia. I will destroy you and I will destroy your precious Electra Base!
> DYNA GIRL: Sorry to ruin your plans, Empress Boll Weevil, but…
> Electra Woman and Dyna Girl fire their Electra-beams ["Empress of Evil"].

In episode three, the Empress of Evil captures Dyna Girl by teleporting her directly out of Electrabase. Of course, Electra Woman goes seeking her friend. Certainly, the sidekick's kidnapping gives the hero a mission with her friend's life at stake, while the sidekick remains tied up and crying for rescue. In this case, Dyna Girl is placed in a magical trance, leaving her especially helpless. Frank tries to help and he too is captured, leaving all the heroes rescuing each other over and over.

"Ali Baba" has Dyna Girl turn evil with the Metamorphosis formula, which flips a person's personality. As her evil self, Dyna Girl takes over the base and battles her mentor. This rebellion can be seen as a subconscious desire to break out of her traditional role and be the star. "Spider-Lady" is Electra Woman's chance to be evil, as the villainess switches their features and pretends to be the heroine. "Dyna Girl will do everything I need done," Spider Lady smirks, regarding the young sidekick as her tool.

"But you never let me drive Electra-car!" Dyna Girl protests, sensing a great deal is wrong with her mentor. Thus, she must unravel the mystery and work out which Electra Woman is the villainess. This she does, in time to save the day. As with other shows, turning one then the other evil allows them to experiment with their dynamic and the deeper truths behind their relationship.

For decades, the pair vanished. Then a WB pilot, created in 2001, starred Markie Post as Electra Woman and Anne Stedman as Dyna Girl. This version was set 25 years after the previous series, as a teen fan recruits the retired Electra Woman and becomes her new Dyna Girl. This teen, Judy Pope, must not only find her hero but recreate her. This story features the sidekick as fangirl and manager, determined to not only love her hero but reshape her from the miserable has-been. Certainly, without her the superheroine would be only a memory, though Electra Woman has the gadgets and more importantly the experience. On seeking her out to attend their high school reunion, she finds a sexually promiscuous alcoholic, who's more than a bit grouchy. "I'm pretty sure you didn't used to smell like cigarettes and macaroni and cheese," Judy complains.

Lori retorts, "My ex-husband took off with my bankbook, my car, my good vibrator, my wigs…." She's clearly given up on the life, admitting that endorsements were the best part. Full of determination, Judy books a gig at a jewelry store for her heroine. Unwillingly, Electra Woman lets her perky fan drag her to the store. When thieves attack, she finally springs into action, pulverizing them with a combination of adept power and clumsy drunkenness. She also coaches the inexperienced but excited Judy. While Electra Woman is long past caring about squeaky-clean superheroing, Dyna Girl is quick to hide the alcohol and try to censor her language:

> THUG: I'm holding a gun. Big gun.
> ELECTRA WOMAN: Oh, please, I've had bigger things than that up my…
> DYNA GIRL: Surrender! Ehm, Evil-doer!

Judy's determination is finally rewarded when Electra Woman appoints her Dyna Girl … and moves into her dorm. "I didn't mention? I'm gonna finish my degree in fashion design, maybe join the chess club, gonna crash here," she decides. Here, the adult becomes dead weight in the life of the kid, rather than the reverse. Although the pilot of this mismatched reimagining was shot, the series was not picked up.

Over a decade later, YouTube personalities Grace Helbig and Hannah Hart (with a combined 5.4 million subscribers) starred in a reboot produced by Tim Carter and Tomas Harlan and directed by Chris Marrs Piliero. It was digitally released in 2016 as a series of eight 11-minute webisodes, then as a DVD film.

The 2016 characters exist in a world where superheroes banded together and defeated all their world's supervillains in the Shadow War. Now the world's heroes do small heroics, but spend much more time signing photos at Superfest, the big convention, and starring in commercials set up by Creative Masked Management.

The women begin their story lying around at home in Akron, Ohio. For the first time, they are both adults, which changes the dynamic from teacher and student to friends. Soon enough, Electra Woman and Dyna Girl perform a rescue at the snack stop, wielding their dyna-suction weapons, which are actually strong enough to tear a man's arm off. When it gets a million hits, superhero agent Dan Dixon (Andy Buckley from *The Office*) summons them to Hollywood.

The girls go in, with Judy in particular determined that they not change any part of themselves. "If they to change us, we're outta there," she vows. The agent gushes over them, with a tagline of "love everything about it … but…" as he changes every aspect of them. He introduces them to Chief of Research and Development Frank Heflin (Christopher Coutts), tech genius, who's invented a Crime Scope to detect crime in the world. He builds them a pair of Electra-Coms, which combine cellphone powers with electric shocks, and replaces their orange and pink with reinforced black suits. When Judy hesitates, Dan retorts, "Sweetheart, the only part of the original we need is your beautiful lady heads popping out of those neckholes."

Lori can't resist stardom and signs them up, over Judy's objections. At the amazing Hollywood party to introduce them, everyone calls Judy a sidekick, while she insists they're partners. Sitting in the corner, Judy meets Wingman the Wingman, who's used to being ignored by his flashy partner Major Vaunt (Clayton Chitty). As she protests that she's not a sidekick, Judy tells Wingman her team's origin story: "D'you know we've been doing this since, like, middle school? I used to get picked on a lot, and one day she just kinda stood up for me. We weren't friends or anything at the time, but, y'know, she kinda just decided that it was the right thing to do. And ever since then, that's what we've been trying to do." In this story, Lori has the agency, so it's unsurprising Judy became the sidekick. Nonetheless, as she designed the costumes, logos, and gadgets and holds true to their vision, Judy is clearly the team's heart and brains, even if Lori is the public face.

After the party, the team appears on magazine covers.… Electra Woman front and center and Dyna Girl increasingly off to the side, finally with text over her face, then banished from the cover entirely. Electra Woman shows up two hours late for autographing at Superfest, to her partner's disgust. This becomes a story of their crumbling friendship, which both women struggle to preserve.

> These days, women valuing other women is a socially correct attitude that indicates political maturity and a healthy self-image. It's swell for girlfriends and sisters, but potentially problematic for artists. When a notion about relationships becomes not just au courant but is seen as a virtue, it is difficult to write about that relationship truthfully and unselfconsciously. Emotional truth does not proceed from an ideal, however, no matter how noble that ideal is [Isaacs 101].

During the convention, a supervillain arrives. As the heroes offer excuses, Judy gives an inspiring speech: "Everyone! This is the first supervillain we have seen in years. None of us has ever had to face a threat of this magnitude before. Can't you see? This hearkens back to the days of the superheroes that came before us. Now is our time to show the world what we can do. Let us unite and we will defeat this villain—"

"Boring!" retorts Vaunt, who instantly poofs over to the crime scene, leaving his own sidekick behind. He's killed in the fight, and after, Electra Woman agrees that she and Dyna-Girl should defeat the villain ... but after their commercial. When Judy discovers they'll be filmed in bikinis, dripping with sweat, she walks away, disgusted with everyone's compromising her heroism. When she's kidnapped by the villain, however, Electra Woman charges to the rescue, turning her back on the exploitative media campaign. At last, chained side by side, Lori tells Judy how much the other woman means to her in a moment that's realistic and delightful. Electra Woman ends the story realizing that she needs her partner far more than she needs stardom, especially as they keep fighting the good fight.

Of course, other sidekicks discover that superheroism can give them a chance to shine. In Conner and Palmiotti's *Harley Quinn: A Call to Arms,* the semi-reformed heroine recruits a "gang of Harleys." She dresses her new recruits in her black and red patterns and names them for their origins: Carlita Alvarez is named Carli Quinn, and Harvey McPhearson (the token guy) is Harvey Quinn. Another member is Hannah Borgman, whom she names Hanuquinn, for Hannukah. Erica Zhang from Queens is named Harley Queens and Shona Choudhury, whose family comes from India, becomes Bolly Quinn. Antonia Moore, named for her other New York hometown, is Harlem Harley. Their new boss quickly trains her multicultural New York team in crime fighting. To Harley's shock, however, some of her recruits are fourteen and lied about their ages. Shocked, Harley asks their mother for forgiveness and assures her, "I'm really sorry! I would never put the girls in any danger if I knew their age! Look at the bigger picture. Yer girls joined so we could help people with problems. They have such big hearts ta go along with their gigantic selves." On hearing that Harley has been feeding the girls and protecting them from neighbor boys with "big gropey paws," their mother is touched and relents.

One of the oldest comics characters, dating to 1936, appears in *Crack Comics* #21. This vigilante, called the Clock, staggers into a shack, severely injured, and finds an orange-haired street urchin there. She believes he's a criminal, but nonetheless nurses him back to health. When he recovers, he begins to leave but she follows him in her plaid skirt and cap. "I always wanted to be a moll," she insists (Brenner). "Butch promptly proves invaluable. With her job hawking newspapers on a street corner, she's privy to assorted scuttlebutt drifting up from the city's underworld. She's also tough, fearless, and relentless—even the Clock must concede to her constant demands" (Morris, *Sidekicks* 34).

Being a sidekick has moments of total joy, as all of Harley's new friends discover. Holly Robinson, who first appeared in Frank Miller's *Batman: Year One,* continues taking a role in Catwoman's comics. Even as Holly insists she's not a sidekick, Selina Kyle (Catwoman) takes her to her hideaway on a farm to meet Ted Grant, who trained her. Writing in her diary frame, Holly gushes, "Have I ever told you that I have the coolest best friend in the whole wide world? Because I do." As a training montage follows, Holly's thoughts are all of Selina, who's gone off to the city for her own adventures and romances. This is one hallmark of the sidekick—obsession with her partner over herself. However, Catwoman tries showing her the perks of the job—parties and celebrities, which both feminine heroines particularly enjoy. After Hawkgirl takes Holly flying, she concludes, "Okay I give in. From here on out, you can call me a sidekick all you want" (Brubaker, *Catwoman: Wild Ride*).

Outcasts

Spy: Black Widow (Marvel Comics, 1965–1967)

Marvel's Black Widow, Natasha Romanov, arrived in 1964, far removed from the action heroine in the black catsuit. Veiled in a low-cut emerald dress with upswept black hair and more webbing over her cleavage, Natasha bats her eyelashes at Iron Man and lures him into traps. While all the men call her "beautiful," she's happy to obey her Russian masters and distract Tony Stark since he's so handsome and wealthy. When she first appears, Tony is happy to let her goon tour his lab while he invites "Madame Natasha" to dinner. The goon and Whiplash battle Iron Man, while Natasha only plays the distraction (Lee and Korok, *Tales of Suspense* #52). When they fail, she runs off, abandoning her allies. "She is still at large, on some fog-filled street in some crowded city … only … abandoned … always hiding! Her constant companion … fear!" the comic concludes.

In the sequel, she's on the run from her Russian masters after her failure and hopes stealing his invention will get her "back in their good graces" (Lee and Korok, *Tales of Suspense* #53). As the potential mate preying on rich men, she's clearly earning her moniker. She's even distracted by a large jewelry display. "Cunning and ruthless though she may be, Madame Natasha is a woman … and as such, she loves pretty things!" the caption announces (Lee and Korok, *Tales of Suspense* #53). As the comic continues, she charms Stark, proving a match for his flirtatious ways. She then steals his antigravity gun and menaces everyone. Clearly, she is more a thief of others' clever ideas than an inventor in her own right.

After Stark, she moves on to Hawkeye as a more gullible pawn. As Hawkeye, a circus performer accused of theft, plunges into her getaway car and sees her emerald gown adorned with diamonds, he exclaims, "This is *one* dream I don't *ever* want to wake up from," while the caption describes "the daring, dazzling, dangerous *Black Widow!*" (*Tales of Suspense* #57). Sometimes she dresses in red or black with furs, but her gowns are always slinky and beautiful. As such, she fit in well with many antagonists of the time:

> War provided other opportunities for villainy. Elegant female spies draped in furs and silk evening gowns were also at work in the shadows, stealing secrets, committing murder, or breaking hearts.—Comics implied that spying was a job well suited to a woman, since females had a natural talent for deception. These sultry spies cast a spell of mystique over the ugly reality of war [Madrid, *Vixens* 20].

Of course, Natasha's excessive, exaggerated femininity, from flirtatiousness to costumes, is a true performance, a way of appearing helpless and charming to seduce the men. In the thirties through sixties, this was a path to power as the classic femme fatale. Psychoanalyst Joan Riviére analyzes this type of disguise in her 1929 essay "Womanliness as Masquerade." She emphasizes that flaunting exaggerated femininity is a mask adopted by women "to hide their possession of masculinity and to avert the reprisals expected if [they] were found to possess it" (38). Each time she begs the strong men to defend her, she's charming them while reassuring them of her conventional gender role.

Natasha's superiors continue her transition to supervillain by giving her a costume. In *Tales of Suspense* #64 (1965), she shows off a blue skintight suit with a fishnet pattern, all under a black one-piece bathing suit. While the costume is simple, even demure, it presents her weaponized bracelets for the first time. With the new costume, she acts more like an action hero, climbing walls with sticky gloves and boots and fighting rather than wheedling men into doing her bidding.

In *The Avengers* #29–30, Natasha succumbs to pure villainy. Dialing up her seductive powers, she recruits Power Man and the Swordsman as her goons and gets them to fight over her. Hawkeye succumbs as well, thinking, "Even though I *know* she's out to get me, I can't bear to battle her!" (*The Avengers* #30). As it happens, she's been brainwashed by the communist leaders to forget her love for Hawkeye. With this twist, she's revealed as a helpless pawn of the patriarchy once more. "I don't understand it! I know the Avengers are my enemies … and Hawkeye is an Avenger! Yet I cannot get the handsome archer out of my mind!" she thinks in clingy fashion (*The Avengers* #30). When she reclaims her memories from her masters, she falls into Hawkeye's arms, crying, "Oh my darling! Did you think I would ever harm you … ever turn *against* you? It was the *Reds!* They *brainwashed* me into betraying you" (*The Avengers* #30). Hawkeye campaigns for her to join the Avengers, and through her love for him, she defects from the KGB and joins the superheroes.

Having a former spy on their team soon becomes helpful. In *The Avengers* #37, Natasha saves the heroes because unlike them, she's fine killing their enemies. "Are these the eyes of one who deals in empty words and idle threats?" she asks (*The Avengers* #37). In *Avengers* #43, the Red Guardian arrives as the Soviet counterpart to Captain America. He soon reveals that he's the Black Widow's husband, Alexi Shostakov, presumed dead, and thus a romantic tie to her former loyalties. Since Natasha only joined the KGB after Alexi apparently died in a test flight, she was clearly manipulated by the USSR into joining them. With this, she comes across as their victim, while Red Guardian makes a more powerful villain than she is.

At last, in *The Avengers* #76, Black Widow declares her independence by breaking up with Hawkeye. Though he demands a reason, she replies, "Nothing ... that I can say! Nothing that won't hurt even more than a simple goodbye." While this lacks explanation, this twist suggests that the Widow is finally breaking the pattern, splitting off from a life of dependency to Russia and to her love interests to venture out on her own. Soon enough, she sports a new black catsuit with long red hair and finds a new path to independence.

The villainous yet alluring spy continued to be a staple for superheroes to match wits against, particularly in the postwar era:

> Spying was a game to them, and they gave no thought to the death that came as a result of their devious manipulations. This gave these beguiling spies a true sense of malice they were enticing yet lethal, with a world-weary attitude and no regard for human life. Black X matched wits with the charismatic, brilliant, and unpredictable Madame Doom on several occasions in the early years of WWII. While always managing to thwart her plans, he found himself enraptured by her. "She's the most fascinating woman I've ever met. But as deadly and ruthless as a cobra!!" [Madrid, *Vixens* 20].

Madame Doom, who was introduced in 1939's *Smash Comics* #4, stood out as a model for many of these villainesses. "Women like Madame Doom were motivated by greed and the thrill that espionage provided" (Madrid, *Vixens* 20). "War is my business...," Madame Doom coolly tells her nemesis, American spy Black X. "Today I work for this nation, and tomorrow for that!" In furs and a demi-turban, Madame Doom is a striking figure, glamorous with midlength dark hair. As a count beguiles her, she stares out of the comic panel, seemingly bored with his advances. Leaving, she tells him, "No, Mirov, when my job is done, we part! I am in love with someone else ... one whom I can never hope to have ... Black X!" (Erwin). Black X, meanwhile, is miserable, as he's stuck as the enemy of the woman he loves. Black X and Madame Doom dance together and match wits as she invites him in on her plan. She guides him to a deserted cottage where men are training as suicide bombers by drinking an explosive liquid. Horrified, Black X cries, "I gave you credit for some human feeling, but now I see you're nothing but a cold-blooded killer!" With this, he realizes that she doesn't actually love him and has only been pretending—a reversal of traditional gender roles. He rushes off to stop the bombers and returns for Madame Doom. To his horror, she retorts that she has a way out and blows herself up rather than be captured. He sadly calls her "spectacular to the very end."

"The trends of the day continued to pad the ranks of the bad guys, providing legions of spy agencies and aggressive aliens to bedevil heroes at the behest of shadowy masterminds" (Morris, *Sidekicks* 137). Marvel's *Male Annual* of 1965 offered *The Adventures of Pussycat,* created by Gabe Guttman, Wally Wood, and Jim Mooney. "It seems Pussycat is possessed of such irresistible sexual appeal that she can melt metal just by lowering her ample bosom toward it (though you'd think melting would be the last thing it would do). The sight of her in a tiny string bikini is enough to send a thousand men rushing over, crushing a pier to dust," explains Hope Nicholson in *The Spectacular Sisterhood of Superwomen* (87). A skilled spy who's highly aware of her effect on those around her, Pussycat solves international crimes using her seductive powers.

Fraulein Halunke, "the woman athlete," as the Nazis call her, shows up in a 1943 adventure to tangle with the Marksman, a Polish nobleman who masquerades as a German officer to fight for his country's freedom. She appears larger than he does on the comic cover, smoking the cigarette that suggests she's no good-girl pushover. She arrives with a pattern of swastikas on her tight shirt and shorts, suggesting the exercise she's been doing and emphasizing her physical power. "It's never clear whether Halunke is so intent on completing her mission out of loyalty to the Nazi cause or whether she looks at it as just another athletic competition" (Madrid, *Vixens* 24). She plays an abused Polish girl in a demure housedress, the perfect victim for the Marksman to save. When he does, she hurls his manservant around and actually punches the Marksman out. Cruelly, she gloats, "So long, Marksman! I'll see you in the torture chamber!" (Guardineer). As often happens to spies, she's shot by her own people, who don't realize she's working for them.

Evil Mom: Talia al Ghul (Film, 2016)

Batman: The Animated Series offers several episodes with Talia al Ghul, daughter of supervillain Ra's al Ghul. In her first episode, the second season finale "Off Balance," she begins alone, fighting beside Batman in scenes that stress their similarity and equality before she suddenly betrays him. In the sequel, the two-part episode "The Demon's Quest," Ra's appears, enlisting Batman to help him find Talia and Robin, who have both been kidnapped. Talia's role as damsel continues, as Ra's has in fact arranged the kidnapping to test Batman's worthiness as his heir. Of course, this is a sexist concept in itself, as he dismisses Talia for the role. Through the episode, she's also dressed skimpily in low-cut top and harem pants. Worsening their relationship even further, Ra's goes mad upon bursting from the Lazarus Pit and tries to kill her, leaving Batman to save her. She forgives her father but seems torn between him and Batman, despite this cruelty. Batman declines the offer, meanwhile, and leaves both villains behind for more adventures.

In a loose sequel, the cartoon *Son of Batman* reintroduces Talia (voiced by Morena Baccarin) with a less Arabic, more Caucasian look, also underdressed with her catsuit open down to below her breasts. With her father slain in front of her, Talia decides to take her son Damien to his father. She sexily sneaks into his room. "Hello, my love. You should have warned your playdate. I'm the only one who can bite you." In a very low-plunging slit dress that's problematic for a young audience, she flirts with Batman as they recall how she drugged him in order to make him sleep with her—a twist that insists she had all the agency and used it for sexual assault, though Batman acknowledges their encounter as "not all bad." Still, the cartoon stresses that he is not an irresponsible father here but a victim of Talia's predatory lust. Women are thus relegated to the role of enemy in the war of the sexes. Talia then reveals Damien. Within a few seconds, she's abandoned her son with Batman, leaving both of them unbalanced.

As Batman trains his bloodthirsty, unethical, rude offspring (with some help from Nightwing, who as the former Robin has mixed feelings about Batman's new protégé), Talia is captured by her father's killer, Deathstroke. She's then used as bait to lure Damien into Deathstroke's trap. Talia, in traditional fashion, sacrifices herself for her child, leaping in front of the bullet and screaming for Damien to run.

Batman lovingly revives her with the Lazarus Pit—something that creates an inherent monstrousness. At the film's end, Talia decides to return and restore the League of Assassins, though Batman declines to join her. Damien obediently agrees to leave with her. However, she sees that Damien and Batman have bonded and that the latter has chosen to be Robin and live by his father's ethics. She bids him a loving goodbye and tells Batman, "I will come back for him. Make him great." With this, she frames herself as the absent mother who has raised her son with fighting skills but no moral code, and now must rely on Batman to give him this. Throughout the cartoon, she's a femme fatale; a sacrificed, loving, ineffectual mother; and finally an absent one. In all these roles, she's a flimsy female stereotype and bad example of gender roles for young viewers. Her role is to make Batman look good, but to do so, she comes out awful.

The sequel, *Batman: Bad Blood* has Batwoman, Nightwing, and Damien (and eventually Batwing) filling in for an absent Batman in a more inclusive team-up. Meanwhile, Talia has kidnapped Batman and is brainwashing him. While she's at it, Talia brainwashes Batwoman's father to try to kill her, building on the destructive parent trope.

She's also busy grooming her father's cloned supersoldier the Heretic ... who is made from Damien's DNA. Halfway through, the Heretic kidnaps Damien, insisting he will harvest the boy's soul to be part of himself. "There's always been something missing. A void. And I'm going to fill that void ... with you. Everything in there ... is going in here. You, brother ... will provide me with a soul," he insists.

Talia, protective of her young son, arrives and is filled with fury. However, the Heretic begs his neglectful mother for acceptance. "My entire life I've been suffering! Tell me, what is a man without memories? I want to know you, and love you, as he does. I want to feel you in my heart. In my blood," he pleads. He kneels, embracing her legs. "I've always served you without question. I've never asked anything of you. Please, let me have this." He's always felt cut off from humanity, little more than a tool of his creators.

Talia comforts him. "You poor tormented creature, how could I not have felt the depths of your pain? How could a mother have left her child so alone in the dark?" She suddenly shoots him and he falls.

Damien is appalled. His mother has created a copy of him, raised it, and then murdered it. However, Talia dismisses the Heretic as "flawed" and orders her men, "Remove all memories of this incident and then make the other necessary adjustments." As she tells Damien, "You're of no use to me like this. Recalcitrant, emotional. Your father's influence, no doubt." She orders the "trash"—the Heretic's body—cleared away and thus reveals herself as the unfeeling monster that takes the villainess role in so many stories.

Talia returns at the climax, with a hypnotized Batman plotting against Gotham. She also tries to recruit Damien, who is visibly shaken at the sight of his parents united against him, but he keeps the ethics he's been taught and defies them both. At her goading, Batman nearly kills Dick Grayson then Damien. "Start with the bastard. We can always make more," she orders, apparently plotting her son's death. Dick's impassioned reminder of who Batman is finally gets through, however. With this, Batman and his hero sons contrast with the villainous mother. At last, Talia looks at her lover and son with disgust:

TALIA: How is it I ever loved either of you?
BATMAN: I don't think you ever did.
TALIA: Oh, beloved, you have no idea. I have thought of little else for the last twelve years. But nothing, not my passion, not the death of my father, not even our child could bring you to my side. I know now, I will never have you in this life. But perhaps, in death...

She runs for the window, escapes in her plane and finishes with an ambiguous fate. Of course, her dialogue emphasizes how incapable she is of love as she tries to murder her son and obsesses over Batman from afar before mind-controlling him. At this point, there's no ambiguity about her villainy.

Other evil moms appear throughout comics, most often preying on the most vulnerable. In *Uncanny X-Men* #195, the Morlock Annalee turns the three older Power Pack kids into Morlocks. Katie escapes and is rescued by the X-Men, who track the Morlocks to their den. Annalee, a wrinkled old woman with yellow kerchief over pink hair curlers, protests that she loves the children and only wants to keep them forever. Kitty Pryde retorts, "Tell me, do you think this is what your real children sounded like before they were *murdered?*" (Claremont). She insists, "What their killer did out of hate, you claim to do for love—but the end result's the same, the destruction of innocent lives." Still, Katie forgives and embraces Annalee, adopting her as their grandmother and convincing her to undo the spell and let the children return to her family. Though the villain of this crossover story, Annalee is a pitiable figure, more victim than villain.

Another evil matriarch appears in Rainbow Rowell and Kris Anka's *Runaways: Find your Way Home.* Little Molly, the youngest Runaway, has left the team to move in with her grandma. When the team show up to rescue her, the woman welcomes them all with grilled cheese and adopts Gert, recently returned from the dead and rootless in the new reality. However, the sweet cat-lady actually experimented on her children to make them mutants. When she begins doing the same with Gert, the only teammate without powers, Molly is horrified. Still, her grandmother justifies herself that she's enacting Gert's deepest dreams. "Girls with purple hair don't want to be ordinary," he decides. She spies on the girls with a team of telepathic cats—likewise victims of her experiments. At last, she gets to her villain speech, stopping the children from escaping and having her cats pop their telepathic claws into Molly's friends' heads. She insists, phrasing the conflict in family terms, "I learned my lesson. You can't control your children. Even when you design their DNA by hand." Molly leaves, though conflicted that her family is only persecuting her because she loves her. "Aw, kid. People who love you are the very worst," Gert tells her.

Abuse Victim: Harley Quinn (DC Comics, 1992)

A painful moment came with the announcement of Harley Quinn's new series—for an art contest, DC challenged people to draw Harley committing suicide in the bathtub. Fan outcry was heavy, and the creators were forced to apologize. "Anti-suicide groups including the American Foundation for Suicide Prevention, American Psychiatric Association and National Alliance on Mental Illness felt DC was making light of suicide. Others called it exploitative" (Wilson, "DC and Palmoitti"). Harley might be a victim, but fandom preferred not to showcase it tastelessly.

Of course, she was a victim from the beginning—Harley Quinn's debut in children's cartoons has a disturbing abuse arc. In "Harlequinade" (316), she leads Batman to her and the Joker's "love nest," only to release the hyenas on him. When they're captured by other villains, she performs a distracting song about her and the Joker while Robin sneaks in and frees Batman. "Harley holds everyone's attention with a vaudevillian flair. She's feminine but not objectified. She's in charge of the entire room. And yet, she still misses her soul mate, no matter how awful he might be to her" (Riesman). Her voice actress, Arleen Sorkin, explains:

> It's an actual song called "Say That We're Sweethearts Again," from *Meet the People*, an old MGM movie. I used to use it as an audition song back in New York and I knew Paul would think it was funny, so I sang it to him. That's when Paul decided to use the song—most people think he wrote it because nobody had ever heard of it before! I have it in my jukebox. It's a song about a woman who'll put up with anything in an abusive relationship. "I never knew that our romance was over until you poisoned my food … thought it was a lark when you kicked me in the heart, but now I think it's rude!" It's a really funny song from 1930 [Jankiewicz].

Then she lets down the chandelier on them all. "Didja see the way I handled those creeps? Pow bam, oh Batgirl eat your heart out," she cheers. Keeping her loyalty to her boyfriend, she betrays Batman and Robin when they threaten her beloved Mistah J. He scoops her up and carries her off to his getaway plane. However, when she hears the Joker is abandoning all their friends still in prison and her beloved hyenas, she hits him in the face and frees Batman instead, sobbing "I gotta feeling Mistah J may not be the man for me after all." Still, they reunite by episode end. Joker tries to blow up Gotham and shocks Harley by attempting to leave her behind. He flies off in his biplane and Harley, infuriated, hurls a jester toy at him, yelling, "Laugh this off, *puddin'!*" She saves the day out of anger at the betrayal, emphasizing how tied she is to the Joker, in both love and hate.

On the show, she's sane compared to Joker, as in "Harley and Ivy," she tries warning him they're driving into a hill, but he's too single-minded to see it. "You'd think after living with Mistah J, I'd be used to a little pain," Harley moans as Poison Ivy gives her a shot to make her immune to poison. When Ivy asks why Harley puts up with him, she calls him "a little rough sometimes, but he loves me, really." Appalled, Ivy calls her a doormat and tries to give her self-esteem lessons.

"I see Harley as a girl who wants to do the right thing, but it's just not within her control," Sorkin observes. "She wants to be a good girl but it's so much more her to be a bad one. I think she's popular because of her vulnerability" (Jankiewicz). Harley Quinn is the mad girl of DC comics, though she was once a gifted Ph.D. As her backstory in Paul Dini's famous graphic novel *Mad Love* reveals, she begins her story as a psychiatrist at

Arkham Asylum. As she counsels the Joker, she becomes obsessed with him bit by bit. Of course, Harley believes she's too smart to be tricked. He tells her stories of his childhood damage, and her sympathy grows. She falls for him. In turn, he unravels her own troubles, discovering her abusive father and other vulnerable points. As an abuser, he tests the waters cautiously to see how much power over her she will give him. This includes lies and manipulations to get her onto his side. At last, she falls in love with him, goes more than a little mad, dons a jester costume, and breaks him out of custody. In a full-page spread, she reveals her new Harley Quinn identity. Of course, she's been manipulated by the Joker to do his bidding.

Back at home, their relationship devolves when she's looking for romance. She skips up to him in a risqué red nightie and offers teasing come-ons while lounging on his desk. Her song "I feel pretty" shows a sweet vulnerability as she just wants to be appreciated. However, her charm is wasted. Too obsessed with Batman to spend time with her, the Joker screams at Harley and hits her, kicking her down the stairs. He also cruelly tells her her pranks aren't funny or clever.

She realizes she's "hopelessly in love with a murderous, psychopathic clown." Despite his cruelty, she dreams of domesticity—twin children, the Joker old and still in love with her. Thinking things over as she rubs her bruises, she decides Batman is the obstacle to the Joker's being happy and thus treating her better—with this, she makes excuses for her boyfriend, blaming everything but his own cruelty.

The Joker is frustrated that he cannot find the perfect elegant way to kill Batman—for instance the piranha tank and "Death of thousand smiles" won't work, since piranhas always frown. Determined to please her brutal boyfriend, Harley sets to work. First, she records a message pleading with Batman for help—wielding her pathetic status as a weapon and earning the Batman's sympathy as she's never earned the Joker's. She pulls off her cap and mask, appealing to him as a wide-eyed innocent. Batman meets her at the docks, observing that she looks "alone and scared" with her long blonde ponytail. She then engineers a robot Joker to fire at them, so Batman heroically leaps to cover her, heroically saving the lost damsel as he thinks.

With this trickery, she actually captures Batman, drugging him at the crucial moment. She then improves the Joker's master plan by tying Batman upside down, so he sees the circling piranhas as smiling. She's demonstrated strength, skill, and smarts, but all, as she puts it, "to show Mr. J I could really pull off one of his gags." All is about impressing her man. However, Batman laughs and tells her that the Joker considers her "hired help" and that all his confidences were a lie. Furious, Harley continues insisting, "We'd be happy if it weren't for you! Now you're gonna die and make everything right!"

However, the Joker is infuriated by his girlfriend's showing him up.

When he arrives, Harley runs to him with her arms outstretched and he greets her with a terrible slap. He cries, "Batman is mine! You had no right to interfere in my fun!" before throwing her out a window. As the police find her crumpled body in the alley and call an ambulance, she mumbles, "My fault.... I didn't get the joke..." Even after this treatment, she blames herself, not the man who hit her. This is a tragic story of terrible choices as Harley sends herself spiraling downward. Even in the hospital, as the nurse asks, "How did it feel to be so dependent on a man, that you'd give up everything for him, gaining nothing in return," Harley hesitates. On seeing the Joker has sent her a rose, she resolves to return to him, even for more suffering.

Arkham City offers its own disturbing take on the character: In fact, Harley here does not fight but only orders Joker's gang members to do so as she fusses over her poisoned lover. Once again, she focuses only on his needs.

> She is a victim of physical and emotional abuse who is referred to by her henchmen as a "crazy bitch." In her absence, Batman may overhear a goon making fun of her: (in falsetto) "Oh, Mr. J! Please hurt me some more!" Interactions with Harley are limited; when Batman finds her tied up toward the game's end, the player only has the choice between removing or replacing the duct tape over her mouth (a choice that has no impact on the outcome of the game—although if Batman removes the tape multiple times, Harley complains, "If you don't stop doing that, I'm gonna tell Mr. J!"). Harley survives the game as the potential carrier of the now-dead Joker's legacy; the player-as-Batman may discover her positive pregnancy test while exploring Joker's steel mill, and she sings "Hush Little Baby" during the end credits.... Harley becomes a "madwoman" in the wake of Joker's death, her grieving hysterics contrasted with the stoic silence that Batman demonstrates in dealing with his (possible) emotions about the game's end. She exhibits the most overemotional elements of the hyperfeminine stereotype—a shrieking, needy bossiness categorized as part and parcel of clinical, murderous insanity [Lavigne 139–140].

In something of a response to *Mad Love*, Harley confronts the Joker in Conner and Palmiotti's *Harley Quinn: The Joker's Last Laugh*. As he insists he'll ring her neck and demands she leave with him, she retorts that the old days are over. He calls her frail and she beats him up, emphasizing her total rejection of his dominance. She bites his lips off and tells him, "Yer never gonna mess with me or my mind again, ya hear me? You disgust me." She's finally turned her back on the past. In the next comic, Harley finds a genie's bottle and wishes the Joker would be more sensitive and kinder. They replay many of their top moments from *Mad Love* with Joker actually fixing the Commissioner's teeth and reacting to Harley's new nightie with sobs of oversensitivity. At this, she's the one to drag him downstairs and literally kick him out of the house. While this twist has allowed her agency, it's also meant to prove that there is no way the pair could ever have a healthy relationship. Conner and Palmiotti give Harley independence, but only by definitively leaving him.

Daredevil: Lady Bullseye offers a similar upbringing for its antiheroine. Lady Bullseye spends much of the story genuflecting before her masters in the Hand, emphasizing her weakness. A flashback shows her locked in a cell with many other girls, slaying her tormentor, and insisting, "From that day on, no man would touch her without permission" (Brubaker et al.). She seems determined, but her compromise—offering her allegiance to the evil Hand—is far from empowering. When she fights Daredevil, he quips, "Is that a tribute? Are you some kind of fan? Like the women who marry serial murderers on death row?" She finally reveals that her quest is to put him in charge of the Hand. Virtuously, he refuses, but her quest to place a man in charge also has a disturbingly subservient vibe.

Miller's famous *Batman: Year One* spiced things up with young Catwoman cast as a prostitute for an edgier eighties-era take on the character. Mindy Newell and J.J. Birch followed this by considering Catwoman's early evolution in this storyline with *Catwoman: Sister's Keeper*. Nuns find teenage Selina Kyle crumpled in an alley. When she wakes in the hospital, heavily beaten, a cop gives her a card for where she can get self-defense lessons. As she begins training, her brutal pimp, Skunk, continues locking her pet cats in the closet since they revolt him. Holly, her pink-haired young sidekick, begs her not to go back: "He'll beat you up again!" Meanwhile, her pimp presents her with a cat costume for a special client, adding that it will hide her bruised face. Uncomfortably, she wears it, pathetically asking Skunk whether he really loves her as he assigns her such degrading tasks. When he offers to find someone else to do the job, she fears he means Holly and willingly goes in her place.

When Skunk finally gives Holly a job and grips her painfully by her short hair. Selina leaps into the fight, insisting, "Nobody hurts Holly." Her protectiveness of her protégé is the source of her strength, motivating her to become a warrior and finally reject Skunk's control. After, she asks her trainer to teach her how to use a whip, which she describes as a "present." With this, Selina dons her newer, upgraded catsuit and arranges for Skunk to meet her in an alley, playing helpless and injured to gain his sympathy. They fight and she leaves him a beaten-up mess, noting, "Don't kick the cat again, Stan. Ever." As an abuse victim, she's learning to fight back and shake off patriarchal control. Her super identity also helps. In a church, Selina offers up the Catwoman costume in sacrifice. "You don't understand. That's not just a costume. I put it on, and something happens.... I can't take it. But she can. The Catwoman. She can stand it all. Everything crummy that life can throw at her, she just throws it right back and it doesn't even faze her," she explains. Catwoman thus becomes her path to strength and independence.

The Dark Lord's Daughter: Nightshade (DC Comics, 1988)

In the live action show *Titans,* Koriand'r explains that she has come to earth to kill the superheroine Raven, "Unless Rachel dies, my world will." As she explains, Rachel is not the villain here, but a gateway. "This being was summoned to Earth to conceive a daughter. Rachel. Her father. Trigon. He was pulled back to his home and imprisoned, but she is the doorway that he can walk through. The anchor that will keep him here this time. Earth will be the first planet that he will cover in his darkness. But eventually, everything, all worlds, my world, will burn." Rachel can thwart this path with a terrible trial and ordeal, much like in the *New Teen Titans* comic ("Koriand'r" 1.10). This is the role of the dark lord's daughter—she can prove a pawn in the struggle, or she can claim power and defeat him. Either way, she grows up with this terrible burden she must conquer.

Suicide Squad: The Nightshade Odyssey (1988) follows Nightshade, a little-known DC heroine in a blue minidress with gloves, boots, and red mask. At night, shadow monsters swirl around her, which she reveals can "sometimes get a little *too* protective" (*Suicide Squad: Rogues*). As her Secret Origins comic reveals, "When she was a little girl, Eve Eden loved the night. She could see better and farther than her friends." While they feared strange noises, she was fearless. She grew up in what she describes as "perfect middle America. The nice, white home, 'perfect' family and no problems." However, this metaphor is problematized by what lurks beneath the surface. Her father is a distant politician, while her mother is kind and brother Larry is supportive and helpful. "Who knew that there were secrets hiding in the shadows?" she asks.

One day, their mother Maureen tells them she's a princess from a magical land of nightshades—all their childhood fairytales are true. Further, the evil tyrant the Incubus has been defeated, summoning her home. She takes the children with her, and they explore, each in bright colors with Eve in pink, clutching her doll. Maureen tells them they all have the power of the shadows, one she can teach her children to use. However, a messenger runs up to tell them that the Incubus has tricked them—their return is a trap. "This was supposed to be a fantasy come true. How quickly it became a nightmare." Dying, her mother tells Eve that she has the power to become a living shadow and can use this power to open doorways. "When you're ready … come back and get your brother," she adds.

At age thirteen, Eve returns to the world and slips into the Incubus castle after her brother. However, the "hard, unreal" voice of the Incubus scares her, and she resolves to become a warrior. In a second attempt, the Incubus saps her powers. Now, with the Suicide Squad behind her, she feels she can manage a real rescue. She leads the team through one of her portals, but Incubus, now revealed as a figure of yellow and black scattered shadows, imprisons them all in a dungeon. "Eve," he smirks. "So good to see you again. After all this time. My dear, dear darling sister."

He solidifies into a human shape in a blue tunic to match her own and taunts her. As she denies that Larry can be the Incubus, he describes a tradition of passing on the evil spirit to a blood relative. He adds that he intends to have a child with Eve and fill him with the soul of their dead tyrant father Azhmodeus. She attacks him with the line "Larry, I don't think I want to be your sister anymore." However, he denies Larry is still a part of him and forces a kiss on her. She breaks free, with her team's help, and rushes at her brother like a mirror image in their blue tunics, as she reveals her powers match his. Their battle threatens the reality itself of the shadow dimension, killing Larry but endangering the team until they finally escape together.

The Exterminatrix is a truly intimidating figure. In black leotard and cape, black thigh-high boots, and a hood that conceals all but crimson lipstick and long red hair, she resembles an executioner. She also has creepy gold medical equipment that she uses to torture men, and a dominatrix collar with which she leads them around. As she tells a prospective victim, "I'm Oubliette Midas. My father was an irradiated sadist who named me after an instrument of torture and raised me to be his personal murder doll. Do you really think I'm a stranger to pain?" She runs his foundation and wields his chosen weapon—a golden gun. In fact, some of her bullets contain a drop of his blood, with which she can turn anyone to solid gold, borrowing his powers as she acts in his name. She uses this gun on Lady Thor, who must summon truly divine magic to save herself (Aaron, *The Mighty Thor: Lords of Midgard*). Obliette is such a clichéd villainess, not even acting on her own agenda, that she casts Thor as the good girl.

Talia al Ghul is famously caught between her supervillain father and love interest Batman. "Beautiful and skilled in the art of lovemaking, the Dragon Lady was perhaps a far greater danger to American heroes than were the typical male villains in that she alone wielded power over heroes' emotions—and libidos" (Taylor 68). Half Asian and half Middle Eastern, Talia is often portrayed in sarongs, harem girl costumes, and kimonos. In 1971, the pair first meet in East Asia (*Detective Comics* #411), then in the Himalayas (*Batman* #232). Her father tries to marry her to Batman through trickery, and Talia's own motivations are ambiguous, torn as she is between father and lover. "Despite her capacity for cruelty, the Dragon Lady has a unique weakness herself—her necessary attraction to the conquering American hero" (Taylor 68).

In Derek Fridolfs and Federico Dallocchio's "Beloved" (2012), Talia rescues Batman from poison and whisks him to her home. There, she uncovers his secret. Her father gives Bruce permission to court Talia and suggests they team up to save the world from suffering. He emphasizes that Bruce should stay permanently as his future son and heir. Meanwhile, once they're alone, Talia provocatively strips in front of Bruce. "My father has given his blessing. I have as well," she explains. With this, her romance is tied to her father's agenda. While she lies asleep, Bruce tours the house, and discovers a planned genocide. Further, Ra's was the one who ordered the attack on him and Talia, setting all this up. He has used his daughter as an unknowing pawn to get what he wants. When Talia comes and finds Bruce in Gotham a year later, she insists she has left her father as she "no longer wished to be used as a pawn for his goals." They have dinner and spend the night together. In the morning, however, she offers him a sword. "Use it to kill the head of the demon. End his life and take his place and then we can be together." Clearly, her upbringing has left her angry to the point of using Batman as a tool against her father's cruelty. Batman refuses. She sets her assassins on him and leaves, emphasizing that her relationship with Bruce is inextricably tied to her father issues.

The teen novel *The Supervillain and Me* throws the heroine into turmoil. Her love interest, Rylan, apparently the supervillain Iron Phantom, must tell Abby the truth: her father the mayor is the real villain, while Rylan has been fighting to save innocents. Meanwhile, the Mayor's injecting everyone with a chip has opened them to mind control. "Abigail, listen. His whole thing is about bringing peace to the city. If he tells the citizens not to kill or steal or fight, they'll listen. Once the nanobots start working, their brains will be wired that way. They won't argue. And, ta-da, Morriston suddenly becomes the most peaceful city in America" (Banas). After losing his wife, the mayor is battling for control and a city of peace, but he's destroying free will to achieve it. With this, the heroine must choose sides after discovering she's been fighting for the wrong one.

Finally, sometimes the villain finds redemption through his bond with his daughter, transforming because of their connection. *Legends of Tomorrow*'s "No Country for Old Dads" (313) hilariously has Damien Dahrk team up with his adult daughter Nora. He actually unleashes dad jokes and endearments as he tries to catch up on the traditional dynamic he's missed. In fact, when he reluctantly sends her on a mission, he tells her and Ray Palmer, the Atom, "Hmm You better come right back you two, do you understand me?" He adds, "And use protection," humorously referencing time travel. When she misses "curfew," he follows her through time, arriving just as his younger self opens fire. As they drive off, father and daughter quickly descend into squabbles: When she demands to know what he's doing there, he replies, "Saving you, Nora-doll. And is that any way to speak to your father?" He hits the gas. "Safety first. Strap in, kids." Nora protests her father's past choices, adding, "Was it in my best interest or yours when you pushed a scared little girl into the arms of a demon?" Dahrk's descent into evil and the question of whether he values her or himself more keeps coming up as they fight. At last, the climax arrives. With his younger self strangling him (and taunting him for having kids), Dahrk struggles to hold up Nora with his magic so she won't fall off the side of a building. This emphasizes how torn he is between the mission, past violence, and new priority. However, she insists she can handle herself and he drops her, only to have her rise, wielding the power of her new animal talisman. (She stole the talisman from Vixen, emphasizing that she too is hardly on the side of goodness here, even as she finds empowerment. Their team-up with goody-goody Ray, whom Dahrk plans to kill, only underscores their evil family dynamic.) As the season continues, Dahrk descends into despair, aware that though he traded his daughter to a demon to save himself, that demon is absorbing her life inch by inch. He allies with the superheroes and finally offers himself to the demon, trading places with his daughter so it will free her.

Rootless: America Chavez (Marvel Comics, 2017)

With pants and a jacket, America Chavez has a strikingly unexploited look in her 2017 comic, written by Gabby Rivera, beloved teen author of *Juliet Takes a Breath*. "America and Juliet have such different personalities. I think their stories are similar in that they're both young Latinas trying to find their way in the world. Yes, they both like girls, but they're really invested in figuring out who they are and what they're capable of," Rivera says. "You'll find some good wisecracks, excellent taste in music, and a soft spot for sweet people in both Juliet and America Chavez though. Ay, I can't help those things!" (Jarema). Marvel's first Latin American LGBTQ character to star in her own series possesses superhuman strength, speed, and the power of flight. More interestingly, she can kick holes in reality, taking her to other universes. She bursts onto the scene by shattering a rock with her fists as she flies through the air, depicted completely powerfully. Previously called "Miss America," she's something of a Captain America protégé and legacy character. She appears in the limited series *Vengeance*, then *Young Avengers, A-Force,* and *Ultimates*.

In the last of these, she establishes herself as a "paramedic for the multiverse." When the barriers between them are breached, she reluctantly breaks a date, noting that she's always on call. Deciding what to do, she reasons, "I can close holes in space. I do it every time I kick one open. I just clear my mind for a second. Think a happy thought. That's pretty much all it takes." Cleverly considering how to accomplish this on a larger scale, she dials up her date and they each dance to music in a shared experience America regards as "so corny it has to work" (Ewing et al.). In the process, they repair the universe. This moment emphasizes the heroine tying her superhero life and ordinary life together, putting time into both as she works out how they fit together. As she tells her girlfriend later, she's been repairing the world since she was six. "If people help me ... it's like I'm not doing it right. I ... I hate that I need help." Her girlfriend embraces her and reminds her that it's okay to be human.

As the exposition tells, "She can't go home again—she left the Utopian Parallel when she was a little girl, after her moms died saving the entire Multiverse. America's been on her own ever since, doing her best to be a hero just like them" (Rivera and Quinones). America comes from Planet Fuertona. They were invaded by insectoid parasites called La Legion, so America's grandmother Madrimar punched a star portal to the Utopian Parallel so the planet's women could escape. America's mothers Amalia and Elena sacrificed themselves saving everyone.

When she reached earth, she was raised in many countries by many Latin American women. As she thinks, "Still, I was a tourist everywhere. Lifting language and culture from the love of people who weren't my kin but held me as their own." While America doesn't dwell on race, she doesn't ignore it either, as she counters "pure white energy" with "a little of this brown fist." There are lots of Spanish expressions too. Rivera writes at the first comic's end, "She's a star-portal-punching, girl-loving Latina babe on the verge of self-discovery who's also about to get a mega boost in powers. Like, could I please be cool enough to hang out with her in RL?"

However, on a personal level, America feels adrift. "What I wouldn't give ... to hug my moms one more time," she thinks sadly after reuniting a girl with her mother. She's still struggling with having no one to care for her, just as best friend Kate Bishop moves to the other coast. To her shock, her girlfriend Lisa leaves her too, though America had thought they'd planned to move together when she went to college. Lisa sadly tells her, "I've come to realize this is your journey not ours."

Annoyed, America retorts, "I'm used to being on my own anyway."

Offering her own farewell, Kate Bishop tells her, "Be ready for the change. When things feel too easy, when you've learned everything one situation can teach, be ready. The change is here. It's right now. It's going to wreck everything, and you will be so much better for it." Being so abandoned can still offer a transition to new opportunities. As Rivera concludes, "Navigating this world as a gentle and vulnerable human is probably the bravest thing anyone could do. And in general, America cringes at anything related to emotions, so it's fun to watch her warm up to having feelings."

Devoting herself to Sotomayor University, America thinks, "Doing the work means taking inventory. Stare every decision you've made in the face and own each one. You are powerful enough to evolve. That's where the magic is, and that's where you find your light." She discovers Professor Douglas's class on Intergalactic Revolutionaries & You—her heritage but something far from her experience. In fact, as she stumbles into a simulation of poison and glaciers, she's a true fish out of water. It neutralizes her powers and the ice cracks under her feet even as the professor demands she save the other students. After, Douglas reminds America she's only as good as the work she puts in.

She finds connections, but they aren't the kind America wants. Crazed fangirls follow her around wearing her colors and bug her on social media. When she doesn't respond, they name themselves the Chavez Guerillas and kidnap Lisa. They're like her defensive instincts run amok, uncertain what she wants. Clever, more grounded Moon Girl arrives in a crossover comic to help direct her. As she tells America's class: "What do you need in this moment to be the best you? And I'm not talking superficial junk—I mean the deep-down, exceptional, powerful magical you. Whatever that is for you is what we'll be working on in this lecture." Representing a small voice inside America, she urges her to listen to herself instead of stumbling ahead without considering her choices.

Rivera is very aware in her comic how this uncertainty in America's life actually reflects the one Millennials have in their country at the time of writing.

> First, America's been around for almost six years. She's not new to this rodeo. America Chavez's role in the next four years is to serve as an example of how important it is to pursue self-discovery and connect to our communities.... Many of us, especially women of color, are told that we must sacrifice our happiness and our pursuits to fit into our predetermined roles in society. We're sometimes treated as the other, or the maid, or the ones who don't deserve to be here in this country. America [Chavez] is here to say "Umm, that's puro crapola. I've been here. I'm going to be here. And you're gonna love it. Watch me punch my way out of this mess and into my own beautiful reality. Every human on this planet deserves to build a life that works for them and for the good of all those around them" [Jarema].

Responding to this and to her heritage, America discovers a new power—undirected time travel. Finding herself in Nazi Germany, she punches Hitler in the face and meets Cap and Peggy Carter, then teleports home. While this is a fun legacy moment, her bouncing uncontrollably through time is another good metaphor for her aimlessness.

Next, she bounces to the X-Men's Danger Room in the eighties, where Storm trains her. Providing a new lesson in mentorship, Storm insists America learn to look inward, centering herself. She tries and fills with power. Her senses also extend, so she can feel Lisa and fly to her. On arriving, she discovers the fangirls are under attack. "Every night, you monster-star things come here and torture us. Busting up our homes and even snatching some of our moms!" one young woman protests. America teaches them how to fight the ball of energy and reclaim power. Doing this helps share strength with those around her, even as it grounds America herself. She has transformed from someone fleeing the little voices inside to someone connecting with them and trying to heal these other young women so much like herself.

Next, she travels to battle beside her past self, facing younger America's judgment and criticism even as they learn to work as a team. This represents accepting and understanding herself—listening to the truest voice within. At last, having self-actualized, she's ready for a higher level of wisdom. Her ancestress comes to her to teach her her heritage. America calls her "this Warlock luchador lady, Madrimar." However, this is still a time of uncertainty. "Kate, my feelings are gonna come out, and I'm not ready," she worries. Finally, Magdalena, America's childhood companion and sparring partner, arrives, just as cyborgs in helicopters attack. The women fight as a team, along with Kate, and America's past and present merge, bringing her some closure. Only by facing her past and all the directions she might have taken does the heroine find direction and certainty.

The Other: Janissary (DC Comics, 1997)

One of the more poignant archetypes is the alien or outsider—Mr. Spock trying to understand illogical humanity. Of course, having the already-objectified heroine take this role bears a risk of making all women seem like aliens to the reader, so this must be handled carefully. In much of men's literature, the woman appears as mysterious figure of nature and magic, unknowable. Poet Anaïs Nin says, "Men are like the earth and we are the moon; we turn always one side to them, and they think there is no other, because they don't see it—but there is" (qtd. in Pearson and Pope 52).

The Janissary, Dr. Selma Tolon, was clearly invented for token multiculturalism by DC in 1997. However, she was flawed as she was too foreign for the Americans and also for her own people, sending problematic messages to both. She first appeared in *JLA Annual* #4 by Brian K Vaughan and Steve Scott.

Turkey has been secular for a century, encouraging women to put aside the full body drapings even while pursuing education and political office. The Janissary, though ordinarily a Stanford-educated doctor in short sleeves, dons a full concealing costume with headscarf and veil as her superhero disguise. This suggests her superhero side (traditionally one's empowered ideal self) longs to regress. Though her character does not advocate this path with words or deeds, it's a confusing symbol to readers. As Itir Erhart and Hande Eslen-Ziya discuss in "Janissary: An Orientalist Heroine or a Role Model for

Muslim Women?" while she is a modern woman battling the force that wants to drag Turkey back to the past, "since 'the veiled woman' is a highly symbolic representation that marks the other culture as both foreign and irrational … she is an exotic woman, and her values are culturally incompatible with the values, norms, and interests of the West" (96).

Jannisary's double identities are made interesting here by the power she (and others like Burka Avenger) take from the veil. "The origins of the mask lie in religious ritual and theatrical performance. These two uses of masks, sacred and secular, are responsible for transformation of identity in two separate ways. In religious ritual, the person who dons the mask feels himself transformed into a supernatural being" (Brownie 28). Gaining this mask is freeing, also emphasizing how the heroine is set apart and allowed to become her most authentic self. Once again, the message here is confusing.

> The superhero costume holds power because it achieves both transformations. First, it transforms the hero into something beyond human, allowing him to behave instinctively, unrestrained by human weakness or social convention, fully occupying his supernatural identity. Second, in front of an audience, the mask permits superhuman behavior [Brownie 28].

Jannisary's veil protects her identity, but her superhuman self appears one the educated doctor has left behind.

Burka Avenger shares this contradiction. Named by *Time Magazine* as one of the Most Influential Fictional Characters of 2013, the Urdu series has been featured on Nickelodeon. Since the Burka Avenger repurposes the veil as her disguise "the use of the veil is a way to appropriate a tool of oppression imposed by the Taliban as a symbol of rebellion *against* the Taliban" (Arjana 86). When not imposed but chosen by the women for reasons of class, piety, modesty, ceremony, or political affiliation, it offers new opportunities. In fact, while visiting Pakistan, Ms. Marvel wraps her face in her red scarf to disguise herself as a new superheroine. "Like Burka Avenger, Ms. Marvel uses veiling in a way that hides her identity from the very people who would force her to veil against her will" (Arjana 67). While some women are forced to wear the burka, the Burka Avenger uses it to destroy the Taliban's plans and fight for independence, thus subverting its oppressive power.

Nonetheless, the fact that these women only wear veils as superheroines is an odd balance. For all, the veil would more logically work like Diana Prince's glasses—worn for the ordinary woman to be unnoticeable and then bursting asunder to reveal her true self. If worn for modesty as Afghani X-Man Dust's is, it could be worn in and out of superhero costume. However, neither occurs here. Janissary also appears a defender of the traditional religion as she insists, "You dare hide your sins within a mosque? You are a disgrace to the Muslim faith and your country." Her exoticism is stressed to the western audience, here and throughout the comic. Wonder Woman calls her name "an ancient word used to describe only a country's most loyal soldiers." In fact, "'Janissary' is not a terribly good idea for a Turkish, Muslim, nurturing heroine. Historically the janissaries were regimented slave-soldiers of non–Muslim origin," DC Chronicler Sébastien Andrivet notes. Thus, the creators made another jarring choice here.

"The iconic images of flying carpets, dark-skinned Turks, crocodiles in the river, the glass mosque Kazim hides in ... the robe Wonder Woman puts on when she enters this 'sacred ground' and Janissary's veil and hijab all contribute to the mystique of the East" (Erhart and Eslen-Ziya 103). Green Lantern magics up a Turkish-English dictionary to interrogate captured soldiers, again stressing difference. Back to the times of Arabian Nights and before, the West has exoticized the Middle East for its alluring veiled women as well as its magic and secrets. In her superhero identity, Janissary exemplifies all these. "The veiled Muslim woman, practicing a habit which is not expected or acceptable in many Western nations, becomes a symbol for this different and threatening culture" (Erhart and Eslen-Ziya 101).

As superhero, she's completely covered in red, with a crescent moon and star on her chest and Turkish pants. With fire-edged scimitar in one hand and spellbook in the other, she looks formidable on the cover of her first appearance. Turkish fans were excited to be represented, as the new characters "seemed to incorporate several positive traits: she was attractive, secular, educated, strong, idealist, modern, Muslim, nationalist, patriotic, selfless and successful" (Erhart and Eslen-Ziya 99). In her first panel, she's working in the hospital, insisting, though her colleague complains, that they must preserve life for everyone. This shows her as a good person, but also a responsible, capable professional. When a secular Turkish Republic was established in 1923, women were encouraged to become educated and became symbols of modernization. In this tradition, she is a cultural bridge as an everyday woman, though her costume exoticizes her.

When an earthquake victim is wheeled in and she hears more are trapped, Selma pleads a "more pressing appointment" and retrieves her costume from the closet. She flies in powerfully to save the trapped victims and they greet her with relief and admiration. To the Turkish characters, she's as much of a local icon as Wonder Woman is a global one. The scimitar, which was Suleiman's, gives her superhuman strength and durability and lets her fly. Her Eternity Book was Merlin's and Satan's—awkwardly mashing up cultures instead of giving her a more historically Turkish artifact. She discovered these talismans while saving civilians from the Gölcük earthquake in 1999, and they were granted to her because of her innate altruism and patriotism.

She can cast spells, but, lacking a mentor or magical training, she significantly does not know how. Here, the lack of support from either a magician of her own people or the larger JLA dooms her to be fumbling and imperfect. She is framed as idealistic but less than accomplished—in battle, she confesses to Wonder Woman she has "yet to master any of the spells in my eternity book. It's difficult to work with the arcane when your head is normally filled with chemistry and biology." DC Chronicler Sébastien Andrivet comments, "Although inexperienced, openly admitting it and having trouble getting her spells right, she is pretty efficient—and good at saving people." As he adds, "Big supernatural menaces, burning giant demons and zombie hordes were a tad above her then-current weight class. But with advice from more experienced heroes such as Batman she rose to the occasion just fine."

The story's villain, General Anka Kazim, makes a contract with Iblis, a fallen angel. He demands a human host, and his eye immediately falls on Janissary in objectifying fashion. "Who is this magnificent creature? With her body as my temple I would be unstoppable."

"The woman fancies herself a do-gooder. She would never allow you to possess her," the general retorts. Nonetheless, Iblis vows he will make the general sultan, not president, as together they can bring back the old days of conquering and religious fundamentalism. Corpses of "the Ancient Ottoman Empire"—the old ways come to life—rise from the ground and attack the locals. The past, which they had banished to become more secular, is trying to overtake them.

Selma insists to the police, "I took an oath, officer, to do no harm to any living thing. I will *never* take a life." Undead creatures, however, are an exception and she launches into battle ... after the men point this out. The JLA arrive to stop Turkey from conquering the world and ally with the less-experienced hero. When they arrive, they watch her fight—considering and judging more than objectifying but still a problematic example of gaze. They consider her a guide to local exoticisms but also scoff at her lack of skill beside their polished expertise. Aquaman tells her, "You could do a lot more damage with a broadsword," automatically assuming his weapon is superior to hers. She retorts, "Actually, this blade is the source of my strength, Aquaman. Besides, the Turkish scimitar is much sleeker and sharper than your unwieldy [broadsword]. No offence, of course."

He nicknames her "Jan," and when his hand is sliced off and she tries to respond with her training, he can reject it since she doesn't know it's a prosthetic. Over and over, she's a bit too misguided and new to the job. "I only need one hand to take on an army," he boasts, and she backs off. "Wow," she says, hand to her heart, nearly swooning at his manliness as Wonder Woman shows her exasperation.

The general has recruited an army of "Muslim extremists" as well as the Jinn and its undead army. The JLA take them down and accompany

The Other

the Janissary to her final confrontation. Iblis in the general's body taunts her with her greatest moral trigger—he will release a plague on her people unless she slays him. She heroically offers her own body as host even as Batman warns that this has always been Iblis's plan. However, she bows to Allah and Iblis is cast out because of her purity—again, she appears a warrior for religion.

The comic ends awkwardly as Aquaman invites her into the JLA, not a date as she thinks. However, she refuses, insisting she must protect Turkey. When the comic was translated into Turkish in 2005, fans were uncertain. The secularists disliked seeing the only Turkish superheroine wearing a veil and fasting on Ramadan. More traditional readers disliked her Western education. The military elite were irritated as their fictional counterparts fail to combat terrorism. In Turkey, "she is either shunned as part of the bigger plan to destroy modern Turkey or because she is neither secular not Muslim enough" (Erhart and Eslen-Ziya 104). In her image as the Other, not only to Americans but to both sides of Turkish politics, she is unappreciated by all groups.

Many stories feature more positive portrayals of otherness. The Pakistani Ms. Marvel Kamala Khan, a far more successful Muslim superhero, puts up with getting searched at the airport and otherwise profiled. Having been criticized and pre-judged in America, she wonders whether Pakistan will connect her with her roots. To her surprise, the people there find her an outsider too, an American girl who isn't one of them. "I still make grammar mistakes, and at lunch I find out Naani adjusted the spices in the food to *white people levels* so I could handle it," she thinks despairingly (Wilson, *Civil War II*). Her grandmother advises her that wherever she goes she may be an outsider as "other people will look at you and see only their own shortcomings. Ignore them." Still, she dons a new costume and saves lives while connecting with her heritage. She returns home to find flyers about making a "real Jersey City" (Wilson, *Mecca*), as her sister-in-law Tyesha, an African American convert to Islam, notes that this means prejudice is on the rise. K.I.N.D., "the Keepers of Integration, Normalization, and Deference," arrive to "make sure everybody in Jersey City is somebody who's supposed to be here." They've been sent by the new mayor, who's in the pay of Hydra, to find superheroes. This examination of America is something all readers can understand. K.I.N.D. agents grab Kamala's innocent brother, and, as they haul him off in his Muslim holiday attire, one type of minority is conflated with another. He and the arrested superheroes seek refuge in a mosque, where Ms. Marvel protects them all. She pulls the mask off the leader of K.I.N.D. to discover a jock from her school who discovers they share common ground after all. This moment, of course, emphasizes how much the racists are not distant foreign enemies but our neighbors. Meanwhile, Tyesha leads the community in a mass protest. She and Ms. Marvel succeed, but after, Kamala decides that she's found an unsuspected ugliness in her beloved New Jersey community.

In 2005, Marvel invented a hybrid teen superhero, the mixed Puerto Rican and Mexican Anya Corazon as Araña. Fiona Avery (writer) and Mark Brooks (artist) shape her out of her Latino identity. "Avery writes her as smart and culturally and racially aware. Brooke visualizes her as strong, agile, and with a non-spandexed costume: urban baggy street wear that comfortably allows for exoskeleton armor to wrap her body" (Aldama 68). More than her name links her with her Latin identity: she spends time with her neighbors and fights for her community while exploring how to grow up. This Spider-Girl is particularly relatable for teens:

> In *Spider-Girl· Family Values* (2011) Paul Tobin (writer), along with Clayton Henry and Pepe Larraz (artists), fully fleshes Anya out as the Latina superhero Spider-Girl. With Tobin and the art team making her the protagonist of her own story and series, we see the development of a superhero anchored in an urban, contemporary Latinidad. She's dark-skinned and visually shown battling evil in and around a vibrant urban environment. And she's contemporary: she tweets @The_Spider_Girl. (Marvel keeps a live Tumblr page that expands the Spider-Girl universe: http://spidette.tumblr.com) [Aldama 67].

Comics that explore turning points in history also work to comment on our own times. In *Bombshells United,* the DC Bombshells, led by Donna Troy, liberate the Japanese internment camps. As Donna thinks, "I won't let this happen here. Not on American soil. My name is Donna Troy. And our battle is just beginning" (Bennett et al.). She summons Wonder Woman, who soars up on a flock of eagles to help. She reveals that the Native American superhero Dawnstar is behind their liberation. "She is a seer and a spellbinder, a traveler through the cosmos." Dawnstar, meanwhile, responds with disgust to the knowledge that the local tribes have rented land to the government for the camps. A minority herself, she understands how the government is pitting the weakest groups against one another. As Wonder Woman worries that changing human nature is impossible, the monster Clayface attacks, calling her a traitor for defying the U.S. government's policy. She retorts, "If you imagined yourself the hero, and that I was only there for you and for those like you … then I was never the thing that you believed I was." Meanwhile, Dawnstar's magic allows Clayface to see other realities, paths where he battled prejudice instead of succumbing to it. Flying on a glistening eagle, she leads the Japanese home, to neighbors who realize they should have fought for their friends. This moment emphasizes how much ordinary people can choose love or hate and must stand against evil laws to defend innocent people. Together they discover the power to rewrite history, "to make a stand in this dark hour."

The Monster: She-Hulk (Marvel Comics, 2003)

She-Hulk is one of Marvel's top superheroines, one who revels in her monstrousness. Though she grows up as Bruce Banner's mousy lawyer cousin Jennifer Walters, a blood transfusion gives her the power to be magnificent (in a ripped slip that barely conceals her groin). Unlike her cousin, she generally can control her transformations. From here, she revels in her power and even decides to become She-Hulk full time "in part because of her physical empowerment and autonomy, but also in part because of the escape she receives from the social pressures that are imposed on Jen Walters because of her gender" (Stevens 18). Of course, her temper is her true enemy as it surges out of control. She is described from the first as "savage" and even "in a perpetual state of PMS" (Madrid, *Supergirls* 255).

In "The Search for She-Hulk," Jack of Hearts, whose body is an alien power reactor, drains the gamma radiation from She-Hulk's blood. While this is accidental, it symbolizes the patriarchy's attempt to keep her weakened and controlled. In fact, it does the opposite, as She-Hulk is split into an out-of-control monster. This destabilizing of her powers makes her more frightened, leading to further destabilization in a vicious circle. As a result, Jennifer becomes a Jekyll and Hyde personality like the Hulk. She thinks, "I hate not being her. Not being the She-Hulk." With her powers intact, as she believes, "All my fears disappeared. All my faults and weaknesses vanished" (Johns, "The Search for She-Hulk"). Now, instead, she must face them.

Confused and frustrated, she runs away to Bone, Iowa, but Scarlet Witch finds her and tells her, "I know how it feels when your life is out of control, Jennifer.... Sometimes all of this negative energy sends my head spinning too. Sometimes I feel as if I can do nothing but perpetuate the unnatural." Of course, Scarlet Witch is a mutant who destabilizes the world with her magical warping power. Both women's unpredictable powers threaten the status quo, so they must face the condemnation and incomprehension of the male heroes. Sometimes it is "impossible for the women to explore and to develop their heroic possibilities because the patriarchal situation treats female strength as something monstrous: something to be hidden, repressed, and ultimately destroyed" (Pearson and Pope 76). Characters so lacking in control are shunned by society, of course, giving them a quest to find safety. "They seem to be in a continual battle to remedy a mismatch, to demonstrate they are not the uncontrolled 'monsters' their 'freak' bodies make them out to be.... They know the inclusion they are afforded is conditional; one slip, one uncontrolled moment, and it will be lost. Their position is tolerated, rather than accepted" (Kirkpatrick 132).

Suddenly, Jennifer transforms in two explosive full-page spreads, revealing that the key to her switching is fear. "And She-Hulk hates to be afraid!" Her monster power protects her when she's vulnerable in this way, covering her weakness just as the Hulk's power lets him explode into strength. Scarlet Witch, terrified, tries to reason with Jennifer and magically age the gamma radiation until it's inert, but She-Hulk resists, roaring, "Witch try to make She-Hulk weak!" American society has always pushed her to be a meek, proper lawyer. Now as her friend tries to take her powers for her own good, She-Hulk is more scared and thus more powerful.

"Weak like Jennifer! She-Hulk hates Jennifer!" The angry, protective part of her cannot deal with the well-behaved part. "The tough action heroine is a transgressive character not because she operates outside of gender restrictions but because she straddles both sides of the psychoanalytic gender divide. She is both subject and object, looker and looked at, ass-kicker and sex object" (Brown 52). Adding vulnerable woman and monster to the list is only one more all-too-believable split. "She Hulk mad!" she cries, tearing apart the town in her misery. "Go hide!" she screams to the running people. "Hide like Jennifer!" She despises anything that reminds her of the weak side of herself. Many people spend their lives trying to hide their vulnerable parts beneath the stronger persona. However, Jennifer, the weak, soft inner self She-Hulk has always buried, keeps appearing. Revealing this self makes the self-assertive monster side feel terribly fragile. With this, she's miserable that her only way to be powerful is as a threat as she screams, despairing, "She-Hulk make everyone afraid!"

Hawkeye arrives to help She-Hulk and reminds her they're friends. Nonetheless, his help carries a trace of misogyny as he tells her, "Just don't cry on me. I can't stand to see a girl cry" and offers her a kiss. Presumably, he wouldn't subject a male Avenger to gender-based teasing. "She-Hulk hate being teased!" she roars. It isn't that she can't take a joke; it's that constant, casual misogyny really isn't that funny.

Bruce Banner is the next to confront She-Hulk. He reacts with guilt and apology for making her superpowered, but she dismisses this, replying, "Bruce made Jennifer better. Made fear go away." Clearly, being She-Hulk has made her feel strong and safe. Sympathizing, Bruce finally asks her what she's afraid of and she responds, "Failure." Having to be perfect, succeed in the cutthroat world of law, be judged for any sign of She-Hulk outbursts has made her overcontrolled. "Parents wanted Jennifer to be perfect. Smart. Study all. Smart all," she mourns, and Bruce just hugs her. This conflict is the true source of her monstrosity—the knowledge that she can never achieve perfection. Because of this, she drove herself to be an excellent lawyer and powerhouse in the male world, then a superhero. But it's never enough—there's always people judging. "Transmogrification, unlike transformation, does not offer the opportunity to blend or assimilate, and while this may or may not be desired, such characters are rendered visibly different, 'other,' and routinely suffer the consequences of such 'othering'" (Kirkpatrick 131).

The army comes after Bruce, and She-Hulk is eager to battle them. In a show of macho force, the army and the Avengers fight for jurisdiction as they all try to protect the town. However, sympathetic Bruce decides to aid his cousin himself. He turns into the Hulk and the pair of them battle.

Meanwhile, the Avengers construct a desperate plan—Jack of Hearts, who has already destroyed Jennifer's ability to control herself, will go in to deal with the two Hulks. His destructive force, however, is too powerful. He warns, "If I let loose like this—even if I can contain it—I'm not sure I'll be able to reabsorb it. I could turn this place into a desert. I could kill Jennifer." Full misogynistic force is being used to force Jennifer back into the cage of her human body. Iron Man tells Jack to trust himself, and in a full-page spread, Jack smashes the Hulks.

She-Hulk collapses and her power is drained—she once more has control over her monster side. The Avengers explain that Jack has restored She-Hulk's radiation levels to where they should be … a problematic metaphor as the hero must fix the out-of-control heroine. Iron Man adds that either Jack or Jennifer must leave the Avengers so they don't touch again. On hearing that seventy-two people were wounded in Bone, She-Hulk succumbs to guilt and departs once more. She accepts punishment and ostracizing because of her uncontrollable powers.

For She-Hulk, the monster side is a force of strength as well as sexuality, beauty, and courage—all the things the buttoned-up lawyer denies herself. They are her Jungian shadow—repressed qualities that bubble up often without being summoned. Monet, an X-Man who's also a werewolf, likewise taps her dark side and finds the strength and rage within in 2016's *Uncanny X-Men* #17. Suddenly a greenish fanged monster, she snarls at Sabretooth, "This is what I *want*, Victor. Maybe you … now that you've been denied what you really want for so long … can't understand that. But I'm not like you, I'm *free*" (Bunn). Claws burst horrifically from her hands, and she reveals that she's absorbed his claws and healing factor, claiming power only the patriarchy has. Both find catharsis through their animalistic savagery, even as they hold back from completely succumbing.

Beyond this, She-Hulk's form makes a statement that unusual skin colors or physiques can be beautiful. "No one gets to tell you who you are, no matter if you are a boy, girl, nonbinary, actual green person, or any-dang thing in between. Jen is one of the first ladies to show that she doesn't need to be demure or petite to be feminine or foxy. Jen is all about confidence, body positivity, and fun" (Cink 21). Famously, superheroine body types are most often drawn in their teens or twenties with unrealistic proportions. At the same time, monster superheroines offer the chance for women to be unconventionally beautiful and use their superpowers to balance the scales. Sadly, writers have taken little advantage of this opportunity.

In a single wordless comic in *Secret Identities: The Asian American Superhero Anthology*, an overweight woman in a housedress looks jealously at the "Ultragirl" film poster with the heroine in a tight leotard. However, when she sees a mugger attacking a woman in an alley, she launches herself at him and crushes him with her bulk. Soon enough, headlines read "Real Hero saves Ultra Girl" (Joshi, et al., 99).

In another, a girl struggles with losing weight until her grandmother sends her what she calls a "magic all-you-can-eat-buffet belt." Studying food's yin-yang properties of hot and cold, she discovers the belt can protect her from fires or cause them. After, her grandmother tells her, "The women of our family have used the Long Feng belt for many generations" (Chen 106). It helps its wearer find balance.

Big Bertha, an enormous woman, is also Wisconsin's top supermodel Ashley Crawford in Marvel's *G.L.A.* (admittedly about a rather ridiculous ensemble). As Big Bertha explains, "I mean, can I help it that I have the unglamorous power of adding hundreds of pounds of super-bulk to my frame?" With the extra pounds, she's much more powerful, using her size to protect people and stop cars. In fact, she can choose power or beauty, so she alternates. As she thinks, "With my powers, I can shape the fat on my body. Without effort I can have the ultimate figure, be every man's fantasy. Or I can push my gifts to their limit … and do fantastic things." She enjoys being "the hottest girl in the world" but also enjoys that other times, as she puts it, "I get to hang out with people who can look past that. Friends who like me for who I am inside" (Slott, *G.L.A.* #3). This offers a clear message about the truth beneath persona, though this short run series, and the character herself, mostly slipped under the radar of popularity.

Similarly, Michelle, the Amazing Bubbles of *Wild Cards,* creates extra fat whenever she's hurt, even to the point of absorbing explosions, and thus saving New Orleans from destruction. After, she discovers she's grown as big as a building. "Her body was a distorted mass. Rolls and rolls of fat rippled across each other." As she thinks, "Michelle had grown to love her fat. It was power and control, and it meant nothing could hurt her. But seeing herself…. Bile rose in her throat. The whole world had seen her like *that*" (*Suicide Kings* 88). The city wants to show their gratitude, but she's conflicted between her power and her body image. On a mission to take down an African dictator, Michelle fights him, and he turns into an enormous monster with an erection in a tyrannical male metaphor. As they battle, he calls her "bitch" "slut" and "fat whore." She retorts, "Why is it when a man is getting his ass kicked by a woman he has to call her a bitch? I mean, can't you use some imagination?" She adds that she's not fat, just a "horizontally-challenged

American." As she concludes, "And I'm not a whore. I'm just popular!" (*Suicide Kings* 413).

While recovering, a little African girl calls to her in dreams, and Michelle crosses the world to save her, even striding into a pit of decomposing bodies to rescue her. "But what she finally uncovered wasn't a sweet little girl. It wasn't even the feral child who had haunted those dreams. What she found was a hideously repulsive sluglike creature, encased in a shiny filament cocoon. She knew it was Adesina" (*Suicide Kings* 379). She picks her up and takes her to safety. "Michelle tried not to be grossed out, but she hated bugs and wormy things" (*Suicide Kings* 380). The cocoon falls apart and reveals the girl's face but on a large insect body. "Michelle didn't know what to do now. Part of her was still not wild about the insectyness of Adesina, but then there was the sweet face she knew so well. She was torn" (*Suicide Kings* 380). Adesina caresses Michelle's face and "amazing warmth and happiness spread through Michelle" (*Suicide Kings* 380). She takes the child home and adopts her. By fighting through her fear and disgust for the monster, she discovers the girl within and finds real love with her new family. Overcoming this fear can be seen as accepting her own body image as well.

Watching television with Michelle in a later story, Adesina tells her foster mother that the Amazing Bubbles is on the show *Sexiest and Ugliest Wild Cards*—placed in both categories in her thin and fat shapes. Michelle is irritated. "I saved an entire city, and they're really judging me on how 'hot' I am? Seriously" (Spector 649). This is the perpetual frustration of the American superheroine, who only ever seems to be rated on her bust size, not her achievements. Suddenly, her adopted daughter asks, "So you think a boy will ever like me?" and, heart breaking, Michelle must tell her daughter that she's beautiful but also "America is a stupid place sometimes…. The truth is that the world is going to be unkind sometimes because you're different. But that doesn't have anything to do with you, honey. It's just that the world is full of idiots" (Spector 650). Eventually, Adesina matures and discovers the true form she's meant for. Still, every Joker, as they're called, must find a way to accept one another and thus themselves. All these superheroes bring body image into the story, confronting it by looking different from the mainstream.

Cyborg: X-23 *(Marvel Comics, 2006–2011)*

The created woman trope is a major staple in superhero fiction: Female robots or other constructed beings like clones are shaped by the patriarchy, charging them to struggle past their conditioning. There's the new *Lazarus* comics, as well as DC's Platinum, a flexible liquid metal woman completely in love with her creator. With a similarly sexist backstory, Miriam Delgado is an orphan from Brazil, kidnapped and loaded with false memories by the Time Trapper. She later becomes the Teen Titan Mirage. Nebula, too, especially in the film *Guardians of the Galaxy*, cannot escape her conditioning to serve her creator Thanos. Their bodies become a metaphor for being recreated by society or the world's rulers, leaving them struggling to adapt. "Their exaggerated gender is what makes cyborgs matter and is the reason contemporary feminist discourses have appropriated and proliferated cyborg femininities," Kakoudaki explains (166).

A more poignant X-Man is X-23, Laura Kinney. Invented by Craig Kyle, she first appeared in a 2003 episode of the animated television series *X-Men: Evolution*. A year later, she found herself in Marjorie Liu's street children comic, *Nyx #3*, while the homeless mutant Kiden and his gang help her escape the clutches of a vicious pimp. It certainly makes a point that the girl, on escaping a patriarchal lab, falls into sexual servitude. This too is a staple of the archetype. "Precisely because of their destabilizing potential, the popular representations of cyborgs are sentimental, existential, sexualized, and fetishized in alarming ways" (Kakoudaki 166). They don't question the nature of humanity, only whether they, females, are human at all. They're sexy and sexually exploited most of all.

In Laura's comic origin story, the miniseries *Innocence Lost*, the Weapon X program that created Wolverine is reinstated, this time with Wolverine's female clone from only his X-chromosome. Dr. Sarah Kinney bears the baby and then willingly hands over her child, X-23, and allows her to be tortured her entire life, with radiation, with anesthetic-free surgery, with a trigger scent that turns her murderous. "X-23's origin story makes it clear that while she may have been bred, trained, and exploited by a corrupt component of the military industrial complex, the real tragedy of her creation is that she was really nothing more than a science experiment for her mother" (Brown 192). Nonetheless, Sarah reads her child *Pinocchio*—the story of a puppet who grew into a real child.

At the end of *Innocence Lost*, Sarah comes to understand the consequences and mourns, "The damage I've done…. I can never forgive myself." She helps X-23 escape and names her Laura. However, when Sarah is tainted with her daughter's chemical rage trigger, X-23 murders her and is left holding her body, whimpering, "Please don't leave me" (Kyle, *X-23: Innocence Lost*). The two have only started to connect, not enough for a true relationship.

X-23, whose conditioned rages have often killed those she loved, has parallels in other "poisoned woman" superheroines: Chrysalis, a robot hero built by Dr. Gerard Yves Martet, carries a shell filled with virus-bearing engineered butterflies. Likewise, Hasmat's power in *Avengers Academy*, unfortunately, comes from the toxic radiation filling her and threatening those closest to her—supervillain Norman Osborne only makes it worse. Osborne operates on her along with gas-cloud girl Veil, but attempts to make them all into villains. This is the greatest vulnerability of the constructed heroine. "The cyborg, definitely not the one in control of the state, is an operator of the state: If the computer was represented as able to overrule human will, the threat of the cyborg is that it can obey orders" (Kakoudaki 170). Nonetheless, Laura has broken this control and will never be subject to it again.

After, Wolverine puts Laura on X-Force where she gets caught up in the violence and kills more people, subjected to terrible violence herself. As her adoptive father, Wolverine grows conflicted about whether his actions have helped or hurt her. The patriarchy "embodies the Western principles of linear rational thought, with its emphasis on order, abstractions, and judgment from above" (Leonard 16). Sometimes the heroine must escape from this restricted hierarchy to discover a new more intuitive way of relating. "Patriarchal thinking—Western rational linear thought—tends to reduce our existence to one extreme: order and control. When we succumb to this reduction of our lives, we lose contact with the reality of our greater human mystery as well as that of the entire cosmos" (Leonard 16).

In fact, this trope of the controlled and remade woman who must break from the patriarchy exists worldwide. In a comic series created by Eli Eshed and Uri Fink, the alien Pinkus kidnaps a little Israeli girl named Lilith and gives her superpowers. She eventually overcomes his brainwashing to do good instead and partner with the superhero the Golem. Cybersix, an Argentinian heroine, is a cyborg transformed by a Nazi in hiding. She conceals herself, through for protection, she takes the male name of Adrian Seidelman during the day. Brazil offers Nova the Gymnoid, another cyborg with superhuman strength and senses, who struggles to express her humanity (*International Catalog*).

Of course, heroines can be remade in other ways. *Winter Soldier: Black Widow Hunt* treats the powerful Black Widow as a victim not even in control of her own body. The comic arc begins with her taken over by a deep layer of conditioning. Certain her time with S.H.I.E.L.D. and romance with Bucky were all a cover, she strikes out and murders a S.H.I.E.L.D. agent. Natasha's allies and friends: Captain America, Bucky, Hawkeye, and Wolverine, set out on their mission to save her from herself. Black Widow is barely seen as the comic is all about their determination and heroism. Bucky even gets conditioned himself and battles Daredevil—as the men fight over the memory of a woman off being mistreated on the other side of the world, they make it all about them. At last, they find her and while the evil Novokov holds her hostage, Bucky insists, "This is between you and me. She doesn't have to be a part of this." Unusually passive here, Black Widow fails to save herself. Instead, Hawkeye shoots her in the leg—once more the men fight over her without consulting her in any way. At last, in S.H.I.E.L.D.'s care, she recovers her memories except for the ones of loving Bucky. He decides on her behalf that they shouldn't try extraordinary measures to recover it, but should leave her incomplete as this will spare her suffering. Through it all Black Widow is the pawn of the men in her life—never acting, only acted upon.

The marginalized and sub-human figure works well, not only as a race metaphor, but also in considerations of women's role in society. Lady Deathstrike is remade as a Wolverine adversary, but she spends the X2 film voiceless, as the villain's controlled creation. She is more computer than X-23, as she is able to cybernetically interface her consciousness with external computer systems and self-repair.

For others, the cyborg also offers a new path to self-expression. "As long as human was the only thing to be, women have had little option but to pursue the possibility of gaining full membership of the species" (Plant 58). In a new world of choices, women can use the new cyborg model to find power in the increasing presence of technology because "while man connected himself to the past, woman was always in touch with the virtual matter of her own functioning" (Plant 6–7). In this way, Laura's claws are artificially added or augmented several times, emphasizing her power to recreate herself.

Liu's *X-23: The Killing Dream* has Wolverine, newly returned from hell, replaced by a demon wearing his skin. Only X-23 knows the truth. This demon tells her, "I wanted to see what it would do to you, being betrayed by the one man you trust most in this world. Maybe you would have felt nothing. You are *so* used to being used, after all. Or maybe ... maybe you would have *liked* it." Laura must struggle with this betrayal by the father even as she remains uncertain whether she's worthy of personhood. Liu explains: "Raised in lab, then pimped out as a whore, now used as a killing machine for the X-Men. She's spent her entire life being used—mostly by men in authority—and she's just beginning to realize what that means, and what a mental trap she's found herself in: this odd circle of power and powerlessness that she keeps returning to" (Richards). Soon after, a dream of Cyclops tells Laura, "Stop resisting the truth! You're a thing! A machine! It doesn't matter what you do ... or what anyone *does* to you! You have no soul!" This message, offered by the vision of the X-Men's leader, is her worst fear brought to consciousness.

After this, however, a glowing blue woman appears. She tells Laura she's "Your true self. The self that lives in a place deeper than your heart, deeper than your silence. I am the part of you the scientists never touched." Voicing the deep thoughts of Laura's soul, she tells Laura she can defeat the demons around her. "All you need to do is *remember* who you are. Know yourself.

Know who you could be" (Liu, *The Killing Dream*). With a childhood anecdote of a puppy, the spirit even proves how Laura was born with empathy before the scientists tried to drive it out of her. It reminds her that she has choices now and will choose the right way if she trusts in herself. Laura wakes to find a star imprinted on her palm. Inspired by this sign, she travels through the underworld and saves Wolverine's soul.

Later, Laura tells Storm, "I want to make my own life. Before someone makes it for me. Again." Storm offers her a blessing but reminds her that the X-Men love her and that she'll never truly be alone. After departing, Laura thinks, "The first thing you learn is how to be alone. You learn or suffer. It is an easy lesson. You suffer more when people are around. People make you feel alone. And loneliness is a quiet wound" (Liu, *The Killing Dream*). Liu concludes: "She's got a long road to travel before she can stand fully on her own. She knows, intellectually, that she can, but actually living that independent life is not as easy as it sounds. Not when she's been conditioned, from birth, to rely on certain power structures" (Richards). This is her most personal challenge.

Described by Donna Jeanne Haraway, author of *Simians, Cyborgs and Women: The Reinvention of Nature*, as "trickster figures that might turn a stacked deck into a potent set of wild cards for refiguring possible worlds" (66), the cyborg is a boundary-breaker, often feared and misunderstood, or sometimes trivialized and victimized. Nonetheless, her perspective is vital in advancing human thought. Cyborg theory considers how women can use technology to liberate themselves and create their own narrative separate from the fiction that society has enforced. Thus, cyborg authors subvert the central myths of origin of Western culture (Haraway 447). In fact, story offers the possibility to "see from both perspectives at once because each reveals both dominations and possibilities unimaginable from the other vantage point" (Haraway 429). In this vein, readers can follow the original story and the possibility of liberation from it.

Gaining superpowers often means becoming a new person. Fatale, heroine of Austin Grossman's novel *Soon I Will Be Invincible*, explains: "You learn to think and move with it. You have to accept that you're not the same person. It doesn't work if you try to be" (31). Everything is strange to her, from "metal teeth and cheek, like a strange metal cup always at my lips" to enhanced senses and reflexes (31). Through it all, she must learn to wield her new body and accept what it means to be superpowered and human, before she can recreate the world.

On *Heroes Reborn*, Hachiro uses his power to bring Katana Girl to cybernetic life so she can protect him. Soseh Mykos and her sister were artificially aged to adulthood by their father on DC's New Earth and subjected to numerous tests to reveal their powers. The Mandarin remakes X-Men's Psylocke as his operative, using her psychic powers to kill. However, all these young women finally rebel, defining themselves as more than their fathers' creations. This is X-23's plotline as well.

Continuing her adventures, Laura meets a hidden community with many child clones like herself. One about her age is reading *Peter Pan*, and X-23 feels a bond with them all and a need to keep them safe. In *The Killing Dream*, she manages to save the children, like rescuing the vulnerable, victimized part of herself and ensuring that, like her, the children have a future. Liu explains, "The greatest enemy one ever faces is one's own self. With Laura, this is taken to a much deeper level, with higher stakes. She must take that first step in becoming her own person, or else risk losing her identity altogether" (Richards). Experimented on again, Laura thinks to herself that this time is much worse. "Because I know better now. I am not an animal. I am not a thing. Why … did no one ever see that? How could they look at me and hurt me like they did? How was that possible?" (*X-23* #9). As she interacts with Damien, another Wolverine clone, she accepts both of their humanity.

The cyborg's split perspective, according to Haraway, provides a deeper understanding of the world by widening perspective—the cyborg can see and understand more by looking from new angles outside of just one species positioning (4). When she wrote, post-feminism was taking over, and women were often convinced that the struggle for rights was unnecessary. However, the culture now is finally rejecting binaries and boundaries. Thus "the cyborgs populating feminist science fiction make very problematic the statuses of man or woman, human, artefact, member of a race, individual entity, or body" (Haraway 178). X-23 is the boundary breaker, the one who questions all the patriarchy's dictates.

Soon after, Laura and the Fantastic Four are sucked into another dimension where Laura must face an ancient creature, one that tried to conquer Earth a million years before but "was defeated by a single man, a prince in possession of a sword that burned with a power of a star." This sword has combined with the hero and created the Enigma Force, Captain Universe. Now Captain Universe tells Laura that everyone is made of stars, but only she has chosen to touch them, as the star on her own palm proves. She returns filled with power and faces the monster. Alone among everyone on earth, she has the willpower to hurt him. She tells him, "You are nothing!" Once the heroine resolves to stand up to authority, it crumbles away before her strength.

He blusters with patriarchal certainty, "I am a king," and "You cannot win," but Laura keeps fighting, retorting, "I can if I choose to." At last, she's learned to claim her personal power and godforce, transforming from victim to teenager and finally to hero.

However, the being takes over the body of the Fantastic Four's child Valeria. Once again, a child is transformed by the patriarchy into a monster. Laura offers herself instead, adding that her presence will give the creature the power to reach earth. It accepts and invades her body, fighting there for control. At last, the dual creature plunges into the portal, telling Valeria's mother Sue Storm that she knows what must be done. Facing the beast, Laura tells it, "You are not the first to try controlling me. I was raised by men to be controlled. I resisted them. You are nothing in comparison." Even lying at his feet, wrists impaled, she maintains composure as he smirks. Her suffering has finally become a superpower. When the creature slices off her hand, Laura is undaunted and insists her sacrifice was worth it to protect the world. She tells it, "I know nothing of signs. I know only action. And death." Her empowered blue soul form takes over and she adds, "I know you will never defeat me." She picks up her hand and reattaches it, literally rearming herself for battle and taking back her personal power. Hands signify agency and a chance to affect the world as their wielders choose. Thus, she becomes Plant's new kind of cyborg, ordering alterations and still fundamentally in touch with her inner goddess. Glowing with blue light, she says, "I know you will never defeat me." The beast's minions cringe as she attacks, filled with radiance. She battles the monster, a shining figure against his darkness. Further, she insists she isn't trapped as she can still see the stars. Since she is made of them, she can always reach them. At last, the star power inside her enables her to fly to the heavens and back to her own dimension. She wakes returned to only Laura, not Captain Universe, with Sue Storm praising her for saving Valeria (Liu, *X-23* #16).

Healed by her journey, Laura finds the child whose parents she once murdered, seeking to atone. She finally heads off to Avengers Academy where she can train in more than killing. In a completely wordless final comic, she goes off into the wilderness and runs with wolves. Inspired by this encounter, she goes on a spirit journey where she battles herself and decides who she wants to become. As the local tribe's matriarch blesses her, Laura gets validation not only for her constructed superhero side, but for the primitive warrior within (Liu, *X-23* #21).

Possessed Heroine: Katana (DC Comics, 2007)

When Katana first arrived in 1984, she had quite a backstory. The lady Tatsu Toro (meaning dragon), a gifted martial artist, weds Maseo Yamashiro, to his brother Takeo's rage. Takeo then joins the Yakuza, getting a pair of mystical fourteenth-century swords as well as their traditional dragon tattoo. At last, he bursts into his brother's house and challenges Maseo for his wife with the words "We shall fight for the prize!" They duel. When a fire starts, Maseo is distracted by the cries of his twin children Yuki and Reiko, and his brother kills him with a mystical sword called Soultaker.

From this, however, a hero is born. Tatsu sees her husband die and attacks Takeo, finally disarming him. When she tries to save her children, however, she hears her husband's voice coming from the sword, telling her they are already lost. "Save yourself! You are all that is left of us. Run!" Grief-stricken, Tatsu escapes and trains as a samurai under the master Tadashi. From there, she emigrates to America to fight for justice and names herself Katana with a red and yellow samurai uniform emblazoned with a sun (Barr, *Batman and the Outsiders* #12). Through her adventures, her sword advises her, though a husband trapped in an inanimate object is a cold substitute. Carrying it is like carrying the burden of the past—the husband and children Katana cannot release. Until then, she is haunted by her lost family, still whispering in her ear. Her husband in her sword is more than a companion but a true spiritual possession, advising her constantly and changing her goals. "I am merely considering the difference between brandishing a weapon … and being one," Katana says in a street fight (Barr, *Batman and the Outsiders* #11).

In the present day, as part of the Outsiders, Katana kills Takeo with the magic blade and takes her revenge. However, this triumph does not bring peace: she now carries around her dead husband and his dead murderer, metaphorically adding to her burden, not lessening it. In several series, as she talks to her sword, those around her believe grief has driven her mad, which isn't far from the truth. Psychologist Carl Jung shows how everyone has a buried killer side, one far more savage and powerful than most people realize:

> The change of character brought about by the uprush of collective forces is amazing. A gentle and reasonable being can be transformed into a maniac or a savage beast. One is always inclined to lay the blame on external circumstances, but nothing could explode in us if it had not been there. As a matter of fact, we are constantly living on the edge of a volcano, and there is, so far as we know, no way of protecting ourselves from a possible outburst that will destroy everybody within reach [*Psychology and Religion* 25].

Takeover by the ancestral soul is a classic part of ancient mythology. Many people originally evoked this by naming the child for a dead ancestor. The Australians saw the dead, the animal spirits, and their personal spirits as all interwoven. Jewish tradition has possessing ghosts called dybbuks that can take over a human, especially a descendent. Jung notes, "Everyone carries a shadow, and the less it is embodied in the individual's conscious life, the blacker and denser it is … if it is repressed and isolated from consciousness, it never gets corrected" (*Psychology and Religion* 131). This shadow lurking under the surface can sometimes last out and subsume the entire everyday personality. The urgings from Katana's sword suggest this shadow—the inner voice she has always ignored, now directing her actions and occasionally taking over her body, encouraging her to lash out.

The Blackest Night event in DC Comics has the dead return, and Katana encounters her husband and children. When she lets her guard down, her teammates must intervene. At last, she duels Maseo, and Soultaker reveals to her the Black Lanterns' plan of destruction. The hero Halo aids Katana, pouring endless light upon the children then the husband and banishing them. Here, Katana's demons metaphorically and literally return to haunt her, and only the boundless optimism of her younger friend can save her (Tomasi, *Outsiders* vol. 4, #24–25).

While Katana appears in the film *Suicide Squad,* all this nuance is missing, replaced by a few images of the nearly personality-free heroine cradling her magic sword. It's an unfortunate reimagining of such a complex character.

Ancestral possession appears in several comics, as White Tiger accepts the amulet of her forbearers, and with it, the weight of the past. In *Runaways: Dead End Kids,* Nico faces her savage ancestor when she travels back in time and trains with her. This great-grandmother is cruel, but trains Nico to perfect her powers. Echo, in the Terry Moore series of that name, absorbs a mysterious compound and with it, the soul of its last wielder, Annie and all her guidance. The Witchblade, too, carries the souls of those who have gone before. All these advise the young heroine, teaching her their wisdom to guide her use of the new powers.

In season four of the show *Smallville,* Lana Lang is taken over by her ancestress Countess Isobel Theroux. The woman is gleefully evil, flaunting her magic and also defending Lana with an adult rage passed down from ancient times. Augmented by this new, darker personality, Lana becomes more perceptive, discovering when people are lying to her and finally learning Clark Kent's secret identity. All this represents the usually helpless Lana taking control over her world and exerting her power as she's always wished to do.

In *The New 52,* Katana gets her own solo comic, written by Ann Nocenti and illustrated by Alex Sanchez. In this reimagining, Katana cuddles her sword and calls it "my love," emphasizing her devotion to the dead husband. Her brother-in-law returns as well, revived as the warrior Sickle, to whom Katana feels drawn. However, she's still divided. When Sickle tends Katana's wound, she protests in fright that Maseo can see them being close. "My husband! His soul! He sees us together!" Sickle retorts that he's "crazy with jealousy." She continues letting the excuse of Maseo hold her back from moving on with her life—in her heart, she's still married to a dead man. Katana continues obsessing over what she once had. Later, Katana confronts her husband's spirit and asks to touch him. When he tells her they can't be together, she retorts, "You could possess someone. Then we could touch."

He protests, "And ruin their life? What kind of life could we build on the corpse of another?"

However, it appears the truth is something different from her original origin story. Now, a widow, she continues choosing her safe, dead husband over a live man, even to the point of forcing herself to forget the truth. In this New 52 version, she recalls being torn between the two brothers and adds, "I was too scared of how you made me feel, Sickle. Maseo made me feel safe. So I chose safety." Her life with Maseo was filled with being a dutiful, perfect wife … to the point of helping Maseo commit murder. Further, Katana describes giving up her martial arts prowess and tomboyish ways after marriage. In this version, Maseo, out of jealousy, killed his good brother. Katana was the one to burn down their house in horror over what her husband had become, killing Maseo. Pushed by Sickle, she finally recalls the truth she's buried and confesses: "I killed you. I killed my husband. I chose Sickle back then."

Maseo tells her, "Just as you choose him now. Goodbye, Tatsu."

She tries being in love with Sickle but finally cannot, as she thinks, "We'll always have my dead husband between us. You can't build love on a corpse." Clearly, the endless burden of her husband continues to confine her.

Nonetheless, she learns enough to pass on one lesson. Katana befriends Shun the Untouchable, whose body is covered in tattooed prophecies. She notes, "What would it be like to have someone else's life written on your skin? The Untouchable has a fiendish horror story etched in her flesh. It was forced on her by officials making decisions about her body." One clan slices off Shan's foot to steal and implement the prophecy there, and the metaphor of the girl's body being used against her will grows brutal.

Shun declares her revenge and attacks her enemies: She decides, "Scar these guys. Don't kill them. Maim them like they did me. Stop just short of killing them. I'll go after every man that marked my body." She shows up to their sword fight with a machine gun and ends it. As she adds gleefully to Katana, "They called me a naughty girl. An untouchable. Call me a bad girl long enough—and I'll be wicked."

Katana, however, stops her. Though Shun insists they share the same need for vengeance eating them from within, Katana retorts, "It *did* drive me. Not anymore. It almost drove me insane. It's not worth it, Shun." With this, she shows she's understood the lesson, that devoting one's life to death will never bring peace. At last, she's starting to let go.

Reclaiming Power

Community Activist: Citlali (Newspaper, 2002–2005)

Joseph Campbell calls a hero "someone who has given his or her life to something bigger than oneself" (Campbell and Moyers 151). All of the JLA and Avengers fulfill this role, emphasizing their unwillingness to simply stand by waiting. Similarly, over at Marvel, *The Inhumans* especially discusses questions of being responsible for lives and trying to live peacefully in a world of differences. The X-Men face similar condemnation from society but keep saving humanity nonetheless.

In her own limited 2014 run, Storm travels the world creating justice. In Santo Marco, she rescues the villagers from a tsunami and, when she's told mutants are forbidden, nearly takes on the soldiers but reluctantly retreats before creating an international incident. Back home, to her surprise, young Marisol Guerra calls her a sellout. Acting like the angry voice from within, Marisol protests, "I need to go *home*. That's where my *community* is. That's who I should be helping." Goaded by the words, Storm returns to Santo Marco, where she picks up trash, rebuilds houses, and brings rain. When soldiers arrive to relocate everyone, Storm takes them on and saves the day (Pak, *Storm: Make it Rain*).

> In general, the same can be said for all superheroes. Their very reason for existing is to stabilize the status quo and to enforce the law. Dittmer refers to superheroes as: "a literary genre that is almost universally about the conservation of the status quo; superheroes are about the protection of life and property and almost never seek to fundamentally revolutionize the system" (2005: 642). In fact, any character that attempts to revolutionize or upset the system is by definition a villain in the superhero universe (see Wolf-Meyer 2003) [Brown, *Modern Superhero* 69].

Some superheroines are even more political. Based in San Antonio, Texas, visual artist and activist Deborah Kuetzpalin Vasquez created "Citlali, La Chicana Superhero" in reaction to the lack of positive images of her people in majority culture. Her name is an Aztec term of reverence meaning "to reach for the stars" and she gains her powers from the goddesses of her people. Her origin story is no accident, but a deliberate creation of a hero to lead the way. Indeed, the archetype of the Crusader is determined to set the world right, knowing in her heart that a world left to its own devices will never repair itself without help. Thus, harnessing her courage and resolution, she obstinately leads the people of her world into battle.

In Citlali's signature opening panel, she's physically exploding like a rocket out of a graffiti-marked map of Texas, her mouth open in a battle cry, emphasizing the suppressed history of her people. The artist describes Citlali as a "combination of indigenous women, their Chicana activist daughters, and the spirit of strong women more generally" (qtd. in Shoemaker 6). As the comic is written in mixed English, Spanish, and Aztec words from Nahuatl. English-only speakers must engage on her terms, even as she expresses her cultural pride. She is the mixed woman, the immigrant, the indigenous, the female guerilla fighter. With long sleeves and pants in bright red and green, cowboy boots, bandana, and a bandolier of bullets, this "macha femme" is tough and transgressive. She breaks all the boundaries of gender while demanding that her message be heard. At the same time, she glories in her beauty and femininity when she tells the reader, "As a woman, my strength does not supplant my sensuality. Chicana lips dark and full, cushioned to kiss away our children's tears, cushioned to ease my lover's anxiety, cushioned to accommodate my loving words, my angered words, my avenging words" (Vasquez).

The comic strip first appeared in 2002 issues of *La Voz de Esperanza*, a monthly progressive publication from the Esperanza Peace and Justice Center in San Antonio, Texas. Art installations at the gallery followed through 2005, leading to more national exhibitions. Certainly, its origin is no coincidence. In the first issue of *Citlali*, the author writes:

> Citlali is the catalyst in exploring issues pertaining to women. Citlali is brown and strong and immersed in San Anto and Tejano culture. The strength of the character is exemplified with a bold use of color, a hybrid representational style, and a straightforward exploration of beautiful and difficult issues. The content of the work is based on historical and contemporary subjects acknowledging that our inner strength and wisdom comes from our indigenous roots.

The series is often painted on rough plywood or printed on cheap newsprint, emphasizing grassroots art as protest. Citlali even calls attention to her art form with quips like "Hey Cabrones! … If you knew anything about Chicano art you'd know that Chicanos negate the forced aesthetics of Western Culture." (Vasquez). "Performing her insurgent role within the space of a typically racist and sexist symbolic imaginary and within the geopolitical realm of Texas, Citlali becomes a subversive modern-day Chicana super hero who re/members her pre- and postcolonial history and culture, challenges stereotypes of women of color, and addresses pressing issues that affect Chicana/os and/or Latinos in their daily lives" (Shoemaker 3).

In a story critiquing San Antonio's "Fiesta" week, Citlali dismisses "Fiesta" celebrations as a multicultural touristic sham and threatens to blow up the revered Alamo as a "symbol of war against our own *raza*" (Vasquez). However, the Alamo, a symbol of oppression now bolstered by a tourist economy, is left standing while the historic meeting place La Gloria is being torn down. A tearful, angry Citlali warns, "Wake up *raza!* Don't be made *pendejos* with the fiesta smokescreen." Pointing a gun at the reader, she forces them to acknowledge the injustice here. "Citlali represents the strategy of creating new narratives when state constructions of justice fail communities of color": Vasquez has joined in protests against social inequality and unfair wages, with banners of Citlali waving proudly (Mata 127).

> Citlali also turns her critique toward her own Chicano community's complacency and its adoption of whitewashed standards of beauty. She takes on the Catholic church and its role in promoting the tradition of *Quinceañera,* an elaborate coming out party for 15-year-old Latinas which constructs them as "pure and chaste" debutantes who give their lives to God (and to men in marriage). She challenges Chicana/os on their lack of knowledge about their shared history. Finally, she mourns the fact that so many Chicana/os eat food that damages their bodies while supporting large agribusiness instead of local growers. She urges her readers to honor and take better care of their bodies in the name of indigenous struggles for social justice and environmental protection [Shoemaker 15].

A similar heroine, the Jaguar by Laura Molina, appeared under her privately owned Insurgent Comix imprint, in response to California's 1994 passage of proposition 187. This proposition established a state-run citizenship screening system and prohibited undocumented workers from using non-emergency health care, public education, and other services. The character Linda Rivera, an East Los Angeles law student, grows up in an alt-world police state. As she explains:

> Racism is alive and well in California and is becoming overt in the politics of this country. Too many took 187 as a license to discriminate ... more people of color are becoming victims of the exploding prison-industrial complex and the corporate culture—creeping into every area of life is leaving us with even less opportunities for free expression. So this book is no corporate sell-out! I intend to use my right to free speech to the fullest.

Thus, she becomes Cihualyaomiquiz, an Aztec name meaning "woman ready to die in battle." Each night, she calls upon her *nahual* (spirit guide) to transform into her alter ego, the Jaguar. Assisted by local activist groups, she combines fighting ability, detective skills and knowledge of the law, all to pursue social justice. As she steals legal documents and intimidates racists, she defends her community while the author criticizes the law.

"A superhero is a man or woman with powers that are either massive extensions of human strengths and capabilities, or fundamentally different in kind, which she or he uses to fight for truth, justice, and the protection of the innocent," Roz Kaveney notes (*Superheroes* 4). She includes those without powers who nonetheless share in the mission. Clearly, all these activists and paragons become superheroes through their acts.

Wonder Woman is such a leader, beginning with her World War II origin as she leads American women in joining the war effort. More recently, she's known for works that better the entire world, especially after her 1987 reboot by George Pérez. On reaching earth, Wonder Woman no longer disguises herself as Diana Prince, war secretary, but becomes an ambassador to the United Nations, changing hearts through her mission. "Rather than battling villains, her first priority and role is diplomatic, changing society through utopian example" (Emad 973). She lives among Americans as herself, Themyscira's champion, not a bumbling, dowdy woman in glasses. Her position as ambassador emphasizes a global mindset as do the events that follow. When Themyscira is eventually destroyed, the women rebuild it, then call on the goddesses of the world, not just of Greece, to restore it. These include Demeter, Artemis, Aphrodite, Hestia, Isis, Mammitu, and Neith (Jiminez, *Paradise Found*). Wonder Woman's new *Sensation Comics* series gives her more international adventures. She saves innocents from a flood near Karachi and participates in Mexican earthquake relief. She wears a hijab in international solidarity. Then in a Wonder Woman spacesuit, she goes up in a shuttle to fix humanity's first permanent extra-planetary settlement (De Campi, "Venus Rising"). She visits Afghanistan to save a girls' school and then aids with Indian hydroponic growing technology (Chu, "Rescue Angel"). *Sensation Comics* #17 by Trina Robbins goes environmental, as Dr. Barbara Minerva arrives to beg help finding the last remaining source of urzkatarga, the plant that supplies the serum that transforms her into the Cheetah. Now it's all that can sustain her life, but the rainforests are quickly perishing. Compassionate Wonder Woman rushes to her aid and the aid of the planet as well.

Many series concentrate on battling supervillains in city-shaking battles or doing tiny acts of kindness like giving pep talks or saving kittens from trees. However, the superheroes' supreme duty truly is to repair the world—making small changes, even in government, that will let them intervene in the terrible human rights crises destroying the earth.

DC's *Outsiders: The Good Fight* begins in the African country of Mali, where boys are recruited to rape and kill in acts of savage terrorism. One military leader, Captain Addana Abioye, protests that their administration is breeding monsters, savages who will never take orders or respect other people. In return she is ordered to go watch the slaughter ... and also ordered to the dictator's bed. Abioye leaves the compound and reveals herself as superhero Thunder, daughter of DC's Black Lightning and now member of the Outsiders. Other heroes on the team include her lover Grace Choi (a "powerhouse" and ex-bouncer), Nightwing, Captain Marvel Jr., Jade, Katana, and Starfire. When the dictator Ratu Bennin discovers the superheroes are helping the villagers, he cries, "We have been *infiltrated*. We have been *raped*," in a pointed inversion of his domineering masculinity. Thunder emasculates him further by kidnapping him out of bed, gloating that she never actually slept with him (it was an endorphin-induced hallucination) and dangling him out of the plane on a rope as she demands information. She and her friends end the mission by dumping him on a deserted island. Superman arrives to protest the Outsiders' high-handed methods of replacing governments. On behalf of the team, Nightwing defends their actions, insisting, "You save the world. I'm trying to save a few corners of it. Corners which your hands are too big to reach." He adds that things need to be done for the common good that the JLA refuses to do. Superman reluctantly agrees.

Striving for real-world social change, Ram Devineni wrote the comic *Priya's Shakti*. A young Indian woman, raped because men felt entitled, endures her family's shaming and leaves. In the jungle, the goddess Parvati fills her with the strength to lead—on a tiger's back, Priya rides around India, changing minds. "Only when society protects all of its citizens equally will we be truly safe," she insists. In an interview, the author revealed he had "basically two goals: one is to challenge those patriarchal views and help create a cultural shift, and the second is to create empathy for rape survivors so that people who have been raped can report it and get justice" (Chatterjee).

In *Champions: Change the World*, the team track kidnapped young women to Lasibad. There, a young activist insists she'll continue opposing the fundamentalists who have taken over her country and insisting on education for young women. As she adds, young women are being murdered in the street for carrying schoolbooks or walking outside without a burka. Kamala Kahn offers to smuggle the young women to freedom, but they insist, "If we run, we accomplish nothing. We give in to extremism" (Waid and Ramos). While Amal and her friends stage a public protest, the Champions take down their attacker but in secret. As Nova points out, "The only ones who will see us down here are some soldiers who'd never admit to being beaten by a 'mere' girl." Departing, Kamala vows they'll spread the camera footage of the young women's heroism. With this, the young women use their identities as much as their personal power to transform the system.

Nature Incarnate: Poison Ivy (Film, 1997)

In this mode, the idealist Pamela Isley (Uma Thurman) begins the film *Batman and Robin* plotting to empower plants to defend themselves. She announces, "If I can only find the correct dose of Venom, these plants will be able to fight back like animals. I will have given flora a chance against the thoughtless ravages of man." Symbolically, they reflect herself, ignored and trampled by her patriarchal boss. However, the evil Dr. Woodrue cannot see a reason to aid the natural world and co-opts her venom samples to construct supersoldiers. When Pamela objects, he throws a rack of poison samples on her and watches as she crumples

She rises from this semi-death, transformed into alluring gorgeousness. Her eyes glow bright green, with red hair flowing and clothes ripped becomingly. As she murmurs sweetly, "Hello, Jason. I think I've had a change of heart. Quite literally. I don't think I'm human anymore." The Doctor is mesmerized as she entices him in and kills him with a poisoned kiss. She adds, "The animal-plant toxins had a rather unique effect on me. They replaced my blood with aloe, my skin with chlorophyll and fill my lips with Venom." She's a hybrid now, a plant monster whose murderous agenda for mankind has only been enhanced by her experience. With poison-enhanced supersoldier Bane at her side (either because he believes in her cause or because he's enthralled as well), she goes after Wayne Industries next.

"By presenting themselves as hybrid creatures, superheroes are able to be simultaneously more and less than human" (Brownie 92). Many heroes become Black Panther or Catwoman, borrowing the savagery of the animal kingdom. Poison Ivy incorporates it in a different way, channeling the toxins but also the anger she perceives in the ravaged forest. All these characters emphasize their connections with nature as they incorporate its tools:

> Carlson (2011, p. 194) observes that animal costumes enable the wearer to outwardly manifest an "inner animal that exists as a kind of primitive substratum." Just as the mask invites freedom from societal constraints, "performing an animal identity provides a way out of human norms that have become unduly restrictive" (ibid., p. 195). As part-animal, the superhero is able to act savagely and aggressively, apparently without compromising the humanity of his alter ego. He may even adopt some of the combat tactics seen in the animal kingdom [Brownie 91].

Bruce Wayne is disturbed by Ivy's methods, pointing out that her plans to ban gasoline will kill millions. She retorts that these are acceptable losses, and when he dismisses her, she launches into the diatribe of her true intentions: "Mammals. So smug in your towers of stone and glass. A day of reckoning is coming. The same plants and flowers that saw you crawl blind from the primordial soup will reclaim this planet. Earth will be a garden again. Somehow, some way, I will bring your manmade civilization to its knees and there will be no one to protect you."

In her book *Sheroes,* Varla Ventura writes, "Whether it is fighting to save gorillas in the mists of Africa or chaining themselves to trees to stop the logging in of old growth forests, women have been at the forefront of the green revolution around the world." As she adds, "Perhaps it is only natural that the nurturing power of women be directed back toward the source of all life—Mother Gaia. At the cusp of a new millennium, we face the continual extinction of species, the razing of precious rainforests—the 'lungs' of the planet—and the scare of toxic oceans, thinning ozone, and global warming." These frightening issues inspire all their readers to do their part to preserve the planet and literally save the world.

Jerusha of *Wild Cards* has a similar, though more benevolent, plant magic. She journeys to Africa where the hotel groundskeeper tells her the many uses of the baobab tree, which he calls the Tree of Life, and gives her a handful of seeds. He emphasizes that she came to the tree because "you could feel the call of the Great Mother in her" (*Suicide Kings* 104). Using the seeds, she creates food for starving villagers, but also grows one tree she uses as a boat to save forty children and another that sinks the enemy as a deadly weapon. Her vines are powerful enough to kill soldiers or tear down strongholds, though they can also form a bridge of safety. When she dies at the end, her plants create a beautiful grove of fruit trees and dazzling flowers. Within are a pair of beautiful intertwined baobabs where birds and animals dwell. "The locals come here for the grove's wild beauty, but they are drawn also, they say, by its magic" (*Suicide Kings* 441). Their fruit can cure the sick and bless married couples starting a new life. Sometimes a woman's voice can be heard there, and that brings the best fortune of all.

In her solo comic, Storm warns the Morlocks, "Nature is beauty. But it is also predation" (Ellis). In a glorious full-page spread, she rains lightning down on them all—such precise lightning that it only incapacitates and doesn't kill. Laster, she saves them all from a bomb with a hurricane that sweeps it out of the Morlock tunnels. She finally brings them to a starving village and sentences them to work the land there and make the place thrive. As she finishes, "And we will be watching. If you harm even one soul there, I will bring my mighty wrath down upon your head."

Meanwhile, the Guardians of the Galaxy face a new supervillain in *Mother Entropy.* This green creation insists, "There is no escaping my loving embrace," and turns all lives she contacts into fungus covered pillars she saps of strength (Starlin and Davis). She is thus the all-controlling devouring mother. With her power, she brings all the cataclysmic force of the mother, leaving the heroes are powerless against her. At last, Groot defeats her by tapping his root structure into the planet and absorbing the ultimate absorber in turn. Only his own nature magic can win against her.

As archetypes scholar Victoria Schmidt says of the Seductress, "Very often the Seductive Muse just wants to be recognized for her brain instead of just her looks.... She wants a true soul mate who sees her for who she is." Certainly, Pamela, like Selina Kyle at the beginning of *Batman Returns*, wants to be seen for her ideas. Only after her transformation to supercreature does she become caught up in her sensuality. Nonetheless, both women fixate on a "perfect man"—respectively Bruce Wayne and Mr. Freeze. "Her biggest motivator is self-actualization. Whether she's publicly recognized or not she has an urge to create. There is a need deep within her soul that drives her to produce things and experience life to the fullest. Without a creative outlet she expresses this drive sexually," Schmidt adds. Ivy has both, and though she seduces the men around her, she clearly cares much more for her plants.

Of course, the movie characters are slow to catch up. When one of the bystanders laughing at her mentions that Batman and Robin will protect them, Ivy sets herself on a mission to destroy them. As Schmidt adds of the Femme Fatale, "She never dirties her own hand when she can manipulate a man into doing the dirty work for her. She will push and tease men, dangling her body in front of them like a golden carrot. Any man who strives for her will end up dead or completely ruined." This is absolutely Poison Ivy's plot. When Batman confronts her for a direct fight, she squirms away, letting Bane provide the physical strength. She tells Batman, "I'm a lover, not a fighter. That's why every Poison Ivy Action Figure comes with him! Try not to make a mess when you die."

At the rainforest ball, lovely ladies in flowery costumes are being auctioned off for charity dates. However, as the music changes, all eyes turn to a dancing figure in an all-concealing gorilla suit. Even clothed thus, she is seductive enough to command everyone's attention. Ivy strips off the gorilla gear and finally reveals herself in her green leotard ensemble. As every man present notices, the Seductress "always adds a touch of uniqueness and class to her outfits and seems totally perfect—hair, nails, and skin all vibrant. She has an inner glow, a 'star quality' about her" (Schmidt). Ivy blows pheromones onto them, and then steps down over the backs of the rainforest acrobats in a mesmerizing entrance. She walks over to Batman and Robin and seduces each in a way that makes them instant rivals: "Why not send junior to bed early," she asks Batman, while she tells Robin, "On the other hand, youth does have its advantages. Endurance. Stamina. Forget the geriatric bat. Come, join me, my garden needs tending." The men are entranced. The rich men present begin bidding for Ivy, but Batman and Robin outbid them, foolishly shouting that they'll spend millions on a date before Mr. Freeze breaks up the party. "You two boys aren't going to fight over little old me, are you?" Ivy smirks, her plan working perfectly.

In fact, Ivy was a Silver Age villainess from a time when many superheroines like Wonder Woman were taking a turn for the wimpy. Created by Robert Kanigher and Sheldon Moldoff, Poison Ivy first appeared in *Batman* #181 (June 1966). A temptress in a leafy bathing suit, she was modeled after Bettie Page, down to the haircut and Southern drawl. When Catwoman had reformed from her evil ways and the rise of feminism pushed comics to add more women, Ivy took a greater role as villainess. Through her adventures, she became obsessed with Batman, the one hero (like Mr. Freeze in the film) that she couldn't control.

After Infinite Crisis, DC Comics rebooted, with Neil Gaiman penning her new origin story in *Secret Origins* #36. This time she was a human-plant hybrid like Swamp Thing. The newly imagined Pamela Isley studies advanced botanical biochemistry under Dr. Jason Woodrue, who seduces her and experiments on her with toxins. She's driven insane, with violent mood swings, and he flees. Of course, this manipulation takes a toll on the heroine. In the "One Year Later" storyline, Batman discovers that Ivy has been feeding people including "tiresome lovers" and "incompetent henchmen" to a giant plant that slowly kills them. This version of her is more hardbitten—she even calls these murders a "guilty pleasure," emphasizing her lack of remorse (Dini and Benitez).

> [Poison] Ivy's transformation from demure female to pheromone-breathing, poison-lipped femme fatale exemplifies the pattern of change common to most female comic book villains. While most male characters like Superman and Batman simply become more powerful when they throw off their alter egos, female comic book warriors like Poison Ivy and Catwoman also become far more sexual and tempting, their dangerous powers acting as an aphrodisiac for men. This increased allure is a manifestation of power, illustrated by the reactions of those around them who are weakened by it [Mainon and Ursini 135].

Batman: Arkham Asylum revamped her to a naked-goddess persona, wearing only an orange prison-issued shirt and foliage panties. She also has a closer link to plants, with green skin and sprouting leaves and vines. In the story, she's tied closely to plants to the point of feeling a maternal bond—in the Penitentiary, she begs to be released from her cell so she can help her "babies"—the island's plants, used to create a terrible drug. At last, when Batman finds her in the garden and threatens her vines, she helps him find an antidote. She's the penultimate boss, blending toughness with a monster nature.

Mentor: Jessica Jones (Marvel Comics, 2005)

Sensation Comics #45 begins with Wonder Woman lightheartedly joining some teens in their race along the beach. When a girl criticizes wonder Woman's fighting crime in a bathing suit, Diana retorts, "Isn't spreading discord and hostility a greater sin than any choice of attire?" She adds, "All bodies are precious. All women should be without shame in regards to their garments." Diana tells them how to be their personal best, a lesson she follows as well. Suddenly, Superwoman from the Crime Syndicate, Wonder Woman's dark mirror all in black, appears in the sky. "Really? You think you're the best?" she asks, grabbing Jodie, the teen who's wearing a starry shirt (Kesel, *Sensation Comics* #45). Wonder Woman saves the teen, while making it clear that she'll always protect innocent lives. She also relies on her community to strengthen her. Wonder Woman exclaims, "My sisters challenged me. Made me stronger, helped me become a champion. I am the result of their training and encouragement strengthening my own dedication to the course" (Kesel, *Sensation Comics* #47). She defeats Superwoman and befriends the teens, offering them the ultimate role model.

Mentoring the next generation often prepares the heroine for becoming a mother herself. The *Alias* comics (roughly corresponding with season one of *Marvel's Jessica Jones*) concludes with Jessica falling pregnant with Luke Cage's child and deciding to build a family with him. Having finished her own story arc, Jessica Jones begins the *Young Avengers* limited series (2005–2006) working for the *Daily Bugle*. There, she tells J. Jonah Jameson she cannot help him identify a brand-new group of teen Avengers-lookalikes. She insists that she was never truly a Young Avenger herself, only "a young idiot who had no business putting on that ridiculous costume in the first place." Her lack of connection with her younger self here emphasizes how unprepared she is for motherhood—soul growth is needed.

"So you'll find the kids, get their story, and practice your mothering skills all at the same time," Jameson smirks.

She retorts, "What mothering skills?" suggesting how far she has to go before she can give birth (Heinberg, *Sidekicks*).

Soon enough, she's understanding the teens' perspective and siding with them against the other adults. Although Captain America and Iron Man plan to order them to give up crimefighting or perhaps tell their parents, Jessica protests, "Well, you can try, but we are talking about teenagers here...." Cap and Iron Man begin interrogating Iron Lad, the team leader. Jessica, however, reaches out in friendship, only to discover he's a fan of hers.

Iron Lad is actually a young Kang the Conqueror fleeing his destiny in the future and determined to become a hero instead. He recruits Hulkling,

Asgardian, Patriot, Ant-Man's daughter Cassie Lang, and talented fighter Kate Bishop. At last, the older Kang the Conqueror locates them, and horrifyingly threatens to kill Jessica's unborn child, representing both her own innocence and the potential of the next generation. Jessica kicks him, adding, "Never threaten a pregnant woman … especially one with powers." As she defends her child, she's once more siding with the Young Avengers against their enemy.

Kang points out that thanks to Iron Lad their timeline is changing. Suddenly Jessica reverts to her old super identity Jewel … without her pregnancy. Fate is testing whether she values the child enough to fight to reclaim it. The other adults cruelly order Iron Lad to surrender to Kang and give up on a future of heroism. Still, the Young Avengers stand by their teammate. At last, Iron Lad sacrifices himself to return to the future and the timeline is restored along with Jessica's baby. Cap ends this arc as he rather naively orders the Young Avengers to turn in their gear and go back to being kids (Heinberg, *Sidekicks*).

After this, Jessica finds herself becoming the teens' confidante. Like her, they have all been stripped of power and are seeking a way to reclaim it through superheroism. Jessica listens to Eli, called Patriot, about his drug addiction, so he suggests that she has more experience with motherhood than she thinks. When Luke pointedly asks Jessica whether she's willing for their baby to be a Young Avenger someday, she replies, "At this point, *I* want to be a Young Avenger" (Heinberg, *Family Matters*). Clearly, she's been won over by the teens and reconnected with her long-lost heroism.

Of course, sometimes women crave support from other women to deal with more personal problems. Cassie confides in Jessica about her unsympathetic mother and stepfather and sends Jessica to intervene—especially awkward as Jessica dated Cassie's father Scott Lang. Jessica also bonds with Kate (Hawkeye) over their dead mothers. Kate finally reveals that they have something else in common: Both were raped (or so the story implies), and both trained afterwards to take back their personal power.

Echoing this arc, in *X-Men First Class: Mutant Mayhem*, Professor X decides Jean needs a specifically female mentor as "she has no peers she can closely identify with, or role models" and invites her to shadow Sue Storm. Certainly, women can be mentored by men, but it's nice that he finds a friend for his sole female student. Sue teaches Jean to play to her strength but also extends powers of invisibility and force fields to help her. Unlike the X-Men, Sue encourages Jean to practice alone, adding that her friends like Cyclops "doesn't know how embarrassing it is to risk failure in front of the others. Especially when you're a woman and everyone doubts your abilities already." They end the pairing happily, with Jean grateful for the girl time and Sue emphasizing how lucky Jean is to have a full-time mentor (Parker and Cruz).

At times, the adult hesitates over being supplanted ... sometimes with good reason. In the 2017 comic *The Unstoppable Wasp*, Janet Van Dyne discovers there's a new Wasp in town and is appalled. Soon enough, however, gets a surprising visit from Nadia, an Eastern European refugee who insists she's Hank Pym's daughter from his first wife. Janet hesitantly begins training the younger woman. At last, Nadia decides she prefers a chosen family over a biological one. Asked to choose a last name, she tells Janet, "Pym makes sense, right? My parents' name. Why wouldn't I choose that. Except I never knew them. and I don't know what they were like, and my last name should mean something to me. And I could only think of one last name that meant anything to me. And it's Van Dyne" (Whitley and Charretier). Honored, Janet accepts, discovering how mentorship can form a closer bond than biology.

Later, Wasp and Ms. Marvel have a delightful team-up with the older heroine Mockingbird, who becomes another mentor. As a child reading her biology reports, Nadia dreamed of being such a "woman who's a super-scientist but doesn't stay locked in a lab all day. She has adventures!" The two scientists drive off together, as Nadia insists, "I want to do everything. I want to fix everything. I want to make a difference." Offering a uniquely feminist approach, Mockingbird tells her of S.H.I.E.L.D.'s list of the smartest people ... and how few women are on it. Inducting the younger girl into a feminist community, she steers Nadia toward Moon Girl, and Nadia begins forming a team of genius girls. "If I'm going to change the world, I'm going to need some help!" she decides.

Just as Jessica defends the Young Avengers to the adults, the Avengers band together to defend her. If her time counseling the teens while heavily pregnant is her trial, going into labor brings the true crisis. While the brutal head of the hospital threatens to throw her onto the street for endangering patients with her superpowered birth, the Avengers all assemble to whisk Jessica off to Doctor Strange. There, surrounded by friends and protectors, she safely births Danielle. This moment signifies Jessica finding wholeness in mythological terms: "While to a woman the birth of the divine son signifies a renewal and deification of her animus-spirit aspect, the birth of the divine daughter represents a still more central process, relevant to the woman's self and wholeness" (Frankel, *Girl to Goddess* 249). The daughter is the innocent side of the self, protected, loved, and created through the power of the mother. "As the mother cares for the infant, she comes to understand the nature of the body, with its vulnerabilities and desires, and thus reaches a greater understanding of the self" (Frankel, *Girl to Goddess* 249–250). After, Luke proposes, emphasizing the creation of a family unit of love and support (Bendis, *The Pulse* #13).

In the next comic, Jessica tells little Danielle a tale of how she gave up her secret identity to comfort lost children, emphasizing how this too was rewarded by meeting Luke and gaining his admiration. However, this moment alerted her that some type of superheroing are too taxing emotionally. Jessica, briefly known as the superhero Knightress, was punching bad guys to make herself feel better. When the villain was revealed to have callously brought his kids along, Jessica unmasked so the police would let her take custody of them for the night. Touched, Luke Cage came over and expressed his praise of her generosity. As she explained simply, "They needed a place." Jessica adds that when her entire family died in an accident, she woke up alone in the hospital, so she understands how much the kids need comforting. However, she decided to give up being Knightress, telling Luke, "I see two kids and I turn to jelly. You gotta have a stiff upper lip for stuff like this." In turn, Luke replied that her emotions were making her a better hero. Jessica concludes the story by believing this lesson and choosing to accept Luke's proposal (Bendis, *The Pulse* #14).

Of course, many children's shows focus on the Mary-Poppins-like teacher. *Burka Avenger* was created to stress the importance of education for girls. Considering that the literacy rate for women in Pakistan is 40.3 percent, she has a valid cause (Neel). Thus, the heroine of the cartoon show is Jiya, a teacher fighting for the oppressed by hurling books and pens. The first episode of *Burka Avenger* ("Girl's School Is Shut") has the heroine defending her school against closure by the villain. Baba Bandook, who's operating under orders from a corrupt businessman in order to steal the school's funds. "This plotline reflects the political realities in Pakistan, which include collusion between business interests, the government, and the Taliban that often result in violence that impacts the population" (Arjana 76). Working alongside her are Ashu, a "very smart, courageous" girl who delivers a powerful monologue about the right to education and a female news reporter who protests, "What will they do next? Stop women from eating?" Using her assertive strength, Jiya protects the children in her charge and ensures that they still have a place to learn. With this, she become a role model to children on the show as well as in the audience.

Antileader: Suicide Squad (DC Comics, 1987–1990)

Amanda Waller is known as the Wall for her massive figure, barely feminized by pink and purple skirt-suits. As she storms through the halls, she actually shoves people aside with just her physical strength. She's also called this for her ruthlessness—she's willing to sacrifice her own team without being affected ... or so it appears. As the author adds, "She's aggressive, confrontational, and known for a no-holds-barred approach. She can also be surprisingly thoughtful" (Ostrander 114). In *Suicide Squad* #31, Amanda's older sister Mary, in charge of Belle Reve's medical facilities, reveals her backstory. "Amanda decided at an early age that unless you could *make* her do something, she didn't have to do it. And she didn't have to listen neither." She describes Waller having three children survive but losing everyone else. As her "Personal Files" in *Trial by Fire* reveal, she married Joseph Waller at age eighteen and they had a large family. However, in the rough part of Chicago, her first child, Joe, Jr., was killed in a mugging, then Damita was raped and murdered, with Joseph killed while killing her attacker. Evicted and miserable with three small children, Amanda went on welfare, losing her pride. Caught in this terrible situation, she vowed, "I'm gonna get me power over my own life! And heaven help the one who tries to take that power from me!" (Ostrander, *Apokolips Now*). Mary concludes that Amanda's toughness has taken her far, but it's finally starting to wear her down.

Amanda swore that the streets would take no more of her family. She worked hard to put all of her other children through college, then she put herself through college and earned a political science degree. She went into politics and finally revived Task Force X as the Suicide Squad under her direction. When her daughter Sereetha shows up, complaining that her linebacker husband is being a jerk, Waller retorts, "I knew that before the wedding," and coldly refuses to let her daughter stay. "I raised you. Made sure you had a college education and a chance to make your *own* life. Now *I'm* making my own life and I ain't got time in it for this kind of nonsense" However, when the husband shows up, she faces him down, though she's about two feet shorter, and tells him, "If you don't straighten up and treat my little girl right, I will quit my job, move in with you, and devote the rest of my life to making your life miserable." He caves (*Suicide Squad: Rogues*). In counseling, she reveals, "There's always lots of pain. Women go through pain on a monthly basis that'd *cripple* most men." She adds that this anger is her strongest weapon to keep her family safe. Her counselor trains her to use it better, but adds, "Rather than confronting and *dealing* with her anger, Amanda now uses it as a *tool*. It has become ingrained, a part of her personality" (*Trial by Fire*).

Beginning with the first collection, *Trial by Fire*, Waller sets up her plan: "What's needed is a covert group of agents—utterly ruthless, totally expendable," she decides. She sets up the Suicide Squad led by Rick Flag with members including Blockbuster, Bronze Tiger, Captain Boomerang, and Enchantress, and fits them with explosive bracelets that demonstrate her lack of trust. When asked about the morality, she has a snappy answer: "All the folks in this project are broken or bent people. They'll get a chance to mend themselves here" (Ostrander, *Trial by Fire*). The Squad's actions are often illegal or immoral but they save lives, creating "the greatest happiness or well-being for the greatest number of people" (Ostrander 115). While she doesn't run a mental health clinic, she does train the team members, all damaged, to contribute and become heroes. She also provides an on-site counselor.

More ruthlessly, over and over she treats the team as disposable and expresses surprise when they survive. She also famously blackmails Batman, threating to expose his secret identity. Still, she defends her team, punching a government official when he calls them expendable as she retorts, "Those are *my* people you're tossing to the wolves" (Ostrander, *Trial by Fire*). With this, she emphasizes that she'll defend her team, like her family. The author explains, "I do not pretend Mrs. Waller is a nice person or even a good one but she *is* making a moral choice. She stands by the consequences of her acts and is willing to be judged by them. Which is more than most politicians seem willing to do" (Ostrander 122).

Her young protégé, her cousin's daughter Flo Crawley, is eager to go on a heroic mission. With square-shaped glasses, this computer tech is an innocent—clever but inexperienced. Waller, of course, protects her while also encouraging her to grow. However, Waller, knowing Flo's in love with one of the teammates, rejects her firmly but kindly (for her), adding "You are a valued member of this team. Stick with what you're good at. End of discussion" (Ostrander, *Apokolips Now*). As she adds to herself, "Young love! Huh! Gives me bunions up the backside!"

Waller begins the *Apokolips Now* arc after being fired. A local minister tells her, "You systematically surround yourself with people who will act as a natural check and balance to you … you count on them to keep you honest—to rein in your nastier side." He asks whether she'll do this again or learn to put the brakes on herself.

In fact, as Waller faces another dark leader, she gets to establish what she stands for. Lashina drags the Suicide Squad to Apokolips, where she smirks that she'll be happy to give their new mission a briefing because "that's one thing I learned from you, Mrs. Waller. Pawns perform better when they know what is expected of them." Once the leader of the Female Furies, she was assigned to rescue Glorious Godfrey from Belle Reeve. However, on the mission, her second-in-command, Bernadeth, attacked her and left her stranded on earth. To reclaim her place, she'll need to kill Bernadeth. With the metal slats of a medieval helmet across her face, she looks more prisoner than soldier. Her breast-cup armor likewise has a bondage gear look, though it fully covers her. Meanwhile, Waller is stuck in a large magenta suit and flats, but is formidable nonetheless, using the clothes as her contrasting armor. With this, they're cast as shadows, inherently similar in their leadership.

Ironically, Lashina has brought the Suicide Squad along to fulfill the same purpose Waller gave them—cannon fodder to distract during her real fight. She condescendingly offers Waller a weapon, adding, "If you can lift the mega-gun, maybe you can use it" (Ostrander, *Apokolips Now*). Waller indeed lifts it, to fire at Lashina, but Lashina has rendered herself immune. Para-demons attack, and Waller orders the Squad, "What are you gaping for? Hit 'em!" Battle commences.

Granny Goodness, trainer of the Furies, arrives, and she and Waller trade brutal blows and quips. As Goodness smirks, "That's all right, Dearie. Granny likes pain," Waller must face another shadow who reminds her of the brutal trainer and dictator she's becoming, cut off from feeling anything. Picking her up to hurl her, Granny smirks, "Tell me, Little Worm—do they regard you as someone strong, someone nasty, in your own world? This is not your world. This is where darkness, where cruelty and power, all are born. You aren't 'nasty' little worm—you're only *human*. We are *gods*. We don't *aspire* to cruelty; we *are* cruelty" (Ostrander, *Apokolips Now*). In the DC universe, Granny is the true monster leader, complimenting her enemies and allies alike when they stab others in the back and telling Nightshade that she should have killed one of her own Furies. Clearly, Granny has no loyalty and only rewards treachery and murder.

She prepares to kill Waller, but the more heroic Barda intervenes. Though Granny blusters that she trained Barda, Barda remains resolute, bragging that she's learned since then. Meanwhile, Lashina faces her own nemesis, Bernadeth, and kills her, reclaiming her place. The supervillain Darkseid applauds her, restoring Bernadeth to life but assuring Lashina she will take precedence. All the women of his realm serve his patriarchal structure in a disturbing metaphor.

Worse yet, Lashina offers Waller's beloved Flo as a gift for Granny to train. She dies in the fighting and Waller mourns. However, when Darkseid offers to return Flo to life, Waller defies him. "I don't think so. Y'see, I've read the file on you. They'd come back your *slaves* and that's no life at all. They've escaped you. I'll let 'em stay free," she retorts, even while cradling her dead cousin. Clearly, she will not capitulate to the patriarchy, even for such a reward (Ostrander, *Apokolips Now*).

She ends the comics arc taking down a New Orleans gang called Loa—and ordering them all shot dead. After, she's put in prison, with the government disavowing knowledge and abandoning her, despite all she's done for the world. She accepts her sentence, with her guilt for all her actions finally catching up to her. While DC Comics celebrate her strength, they also condemn her expedient cruelty. In prison she remains until another story arc calls her forth once more.

Goddess and Ruler: Storm (Marvel Comics, 1975–2009)

"Unlike Jean Grey, who was brought in as the fifth of five students (the other four male), at Xavier's School for Gifted Youngsters, the X-Women who

Goddess and Ruler

were developed in the 1970s were independent thinkers, strong-willed, and tough as nails" (Housel 92). Storm (Ororo Munroe), one of the new team of 1975 X-Men, helped to establish them as multicultural. Hailing from Africa, with one of the team's strongest powers, she established herself as a truly iconic superheroine. In Kenya, she is revered as a nature goddess, and she embraces the part, using her weather control to aid the drought in villages. She calls the people "my children" as the locals cry, "Ororo, great goddess of the storm ... come ease us of our burden!" (Wein and Cockrum). Of course, describing herself as connecting with nature and flying about nude are problematic as they invoke the noble savage trope. "She wears only a skirt and a headdress, and her long white hair covers her breasts—her seminude body is in keeping with those of the villagers who pray before her. An apparent part of her culture, such nudity therefore becomes naturalized within the context of the scene, with only her headdress setting her apart from the others" (Davis 205). Arguably she's sexualized and exoticized, but she's also celebrated. The headdress emphasizes her religious role here and status as goddess before she becomes superhero—a step down by many estimations.

Under Chris Claremont's writing, she grew even more powerful in terms of story and character. "X-Men writers did more than pay lip service to feminism; Storm embodied it in her struggle as an African woman, as a team member, and as an eventual leader of the X-Men," Deborah Elizabeth Whaley writes in *Black Women in Sequence* (108). In the eighties, her mohawk and leather marked her as a punk unwilling to play by the rules. Visually, they signaled that she was tougher, different, remade.

"The 70's were about sensation and pleasure; the 80's craved alienation and suppressed emotion. Storm used her new leather and studs fashion and the accompanying harsher attitude to build a wall around herself, to keep the world out" (Madrid, *Supergirls* 230). As she tells Professor X, "The difference is not cosmetic ... my appearance is an expression of something deep within me.... I find myself casting aside the precepts and beliefs that gave my life meaning—and hardly missing them once they are gone" (Claremont and Smith).

In *Uncanny X-Men* #102 (December 1976), Claremont establishes Storm's backstory: her people, an ancient royal line of white-haired, blue-eyed sorceresses from the Great Rift Valley of Africa, go back to the dawn of humanity. Her mother, Princess N'Dare, rebelled against her role and married an American photojournalist, David Munroe. The pair were killed in Egypt, leaving Ororo to fend for herself as a thief on the streets. Later, on the Serengeti Plain in Kenya, Storm establishes herself as a goddess of the local tribes, who protects them with her weather powers. A goddess appears to her as a shining figure much like herself, and an elderly tribal woman, Ainet, helps her learn how to use her powers. When the mutant Deluge attacks, Storm defeats him and thus attracts the X-Men's attention. Of course, Storm's isolation prepares her for a future as ruler in which she is isolated and ultimately responsible for everything. As Claremont describes her in a novel:

> Ororo'd had no one to teach her, and she'd learned the use and extent—and the price—of her abilities the hard way, with the toll enacted on the very people she sought to help. She's had to learn through experience that when she generated rain in one place, she ran the risk of taking it from somewhere else; a drought easily ended might as a consequence, trigger one elsewhere, and ultimately do more harm than good. Such a harsh lesson for such a young child! [*X-Men: The Last Stand* 69].

After the death of Jean Grey in 1983, Cyclops leaves the team and Storm is appointed team leader by Professor Xavier. She's uncertain at first, but soon rallies. Rebecca Housel writes: "Storm is a born leader, smart and sensitive, with a dedication to duty that produces unparalleled loyalty. In true existential fashion, Storm embraces freedom and responsibility. Despite being orphaned at a young age, trapped with her dead mother under rubble, abandoned and alone on the streets of Cairo, Storm manages to always make the right choices. The reason: She experiences no angst, no temptation to flee from responsibility" (92). She's mature and experienced in a way many of the team are not and thus an excellent feminist statement as leader.

In the *Days of Future Past* storyline, Storm fears she's doing a terrible job. However, when Kitty Pryde saves a senator's life, she takes charge, telling the antagonistic senator, "I am Storm, leader of the X-Men, and I suspect this … child is the person who just saved your life. Mutants, like people, are both good and bad. You would do well to remember that, Senator, before you seek to condemn us *all*" (Claremont, *Uncanny X-Men* #142). As she changes the course of American politics, she establishes herself as formidable.

In another adventure, Storm challenges Callisto, leader of the underground Morlocks, to a deadly fight to save Kitty. Storm notes that she considers Kitty a daughter and takes full responsibility for her loss. However, as she adds, "So long as I am in charge—so long as your lives are my responsibility—I must think of the whole, not the one … whatever the cost." Though suffering from a mutant plague and claustrophobia, she perseveres. After coldly stabbing Callisto through the heart to rescue all her friends, she cradles the rescued Angel in her arms and announces, "If anyone has any objections, they are welcome to challenge me as I did Callisto and risk the same fate." It's an image of power and certainty. Through her victory, Storm finds herself leader of the Morlocks as well. She defends all her new subjects, welcoming them to the mansion for sanctuary (Claremont, *Uncanny X-Men* #169–170).

When Storm and the New Mutants visit Asgard, Loki sees the queenly side of her and offers to make her Goddess of Thunder with Freya's cloak of magic feathers and a mystically enhanced hammer. This would return her to her goddess origins but this time with magic and rulership beyond her gentle villagers. She is tempted, and as she gives in to her dark side, attacks Wolverine. Nonetheless, she overcomes the temptation and returns to earth with her team. There, she challenges Cyclops in a duel for leadership and defeats him. In each of these situations, she steps up, offering a blend of justice and compassion that awakens devotion in those who follow her. She is far more than temporary head—she is the rigid backbone that lends the X-Men their strength and purpose.

On another adventure, Storm is shaken after killing a Morlock girl. She seeks out Wolverine in the forest and confides in him: "Logan, I was forced to cut out a little girl's heart" (Ellis and Dodson). As she adds, she knows it was the right thing to do to save others, as it was attached to a bomb. However, Callisto told her that her bad leadership brought them to this point. "Perhaps if I had been a stronger leader the Morlocks would never have grown into Gene Nation," she worries. As she second-guesses herself, she asks Cable to teach her the Morlock Ceremony of Light to help her atone. Storm apparently dies while performing it, but actually finds herself in another realm where the Morlocks are gaining power. There she battles them but maintains her humanity, thinking, "She doesn't *have* to kill. Not if she chooses otherwise, as she has here." She faces off with their leader, Mikhail Rasputin, who startlingly invites her to become their queen. She rejects the offer, but in the alternate space she is able to consider other paths. She tours the place with Rasputin. "She sees how Mikhail Rasputin can inspire awe. And fear." Finally, she takes him hostage, forcing him to obey her commands. No longer uncertain, she imposes her own will on them all and carries them back to earth, where she eliminates the threat they pose. This rulership through strength and compassion blended suggests a new style of guidance, for the X-Men and the world. With this, she conquers her doubts.

Later, she finds a new role as all powerful queen, as she and Black Panther, king of Wakanda, fall in love. (This was controversial and awkwardly managed at the time, as their "wedding of the century" was staged as a major event, but the characters weren't actually a couple.) Still, the match offers inner challenges of the spirit as well as outer ones. On the verge of her wedding, Storm meets the Panther as a rite of passage and faces who she will become. When she's buried in rubble, she embarks on a dream journey through her subconscious. She talks with her ex-boyfriend as well friends Jean and Kitty, as all advise her to trust herself and find the lost remnants of her family. When animals attack, Ororo thinks, "These beasts spring from the darkness within me and I will not live another day in fear of my own shadow." She finally confronts the Panther Spirit and tells it, "If I accept his proposal I will face him as his equal. And I will be accepted as his equal." She emerges from her spirit journey only to meet her heritage in the flesh: the brutal warlord who has attacked the village is her long-lost uncle Shetani. She also meets her grandmother, who tells her: "I descend from a royal lineage reaching back to the dawn of humanity. The power in our family passes from mother to daughter. Shetani felt left out, so he sought a different sort of power to destroy ours." Having absorbed the voices within and without, Storm accepts their advice and marries the king (Claremont, *X-Men Annual* #1).

> In her new role as an African queen. Storm has been returned to her initial elevated status in her homeland, only this time as royalty rather than as a goddess. Her character design reflects this change, as she now often wears luxurious dresses and other such garments befitting an African queen rather than always wearing her superhero costume. She now also regularly wears her original headpiece again, a symbol of the fact that modern creators have returned the character to her cultural roots, whereby her identity is constructed through ethnic pride rather than by way of her flagrant otherness in American society [Davis 206].

On another adventure, with her husband controlled by evil forces, Storm descends into the spirit world to beseech aid from the Panther God. She challenges the mighty force and returns glowing with power: When all the panthers of Wakanda bow before her, her people acknowledge her as queen once more. Though the Shadow King tries to take over Storm, the Panther God bursts from her mind to defend her, insisting, "No one touches my children." After, Storm's husband admits he has never so inspired the Panther God, and she replies, "We have a connection. You would not understand" (Yost, *X-Men: Worlds Apart*). This bond, too, is more common for the heroic females.

When the X-Men split, she becomes headmistress of the Jean Grey school, devoted to a gentler, less militant path. She could be seen as progressing from leader-protector of her chosen family to the kingdom of Wakanda to the world. As dangerous creatures take over different areas of the planet, Storm transcends her powers to touch the earth's electrical field, manipulating the very force behind the weather. She reaches out to her friends, reminding them that thanks to their nodes they're all still connected. In Dreamspace, she joins hands with her friends and former enemies, and banishes the creatures, as they're linked to a student she once failed to save. After, she thinks, "I'm not a goddess any longer. I'm not even a queen. Instead I'm a part of something so much more." Returning to the school, she thinks, "And this is where I belong" (Pak, *Storm: Bring the Thunder*). She has not only progressed to being a protector of the world, but to understanding the forces she's manipulating and the power she has to do harm or good. Once she flitted around the world, intervening without thought of the global picture, but now she's far more grounded, using the power of home and community to save the larger world. She maintains her status as leader through it all, as perhaps the most famous and beloved superheroine of color, a paragon of what a fierce feminist leader might accomplish.

Supervillainess: Texa (Zip Comics, 1940)

Many supervillains present themselves through the comics. Fans might list the great nemeses: Lex Luthor, the Joker, Doctor Doom, Galactus, Magneto, Loki, Venom, Thanos. Some, like Thanos, Ultron, and Doom, insist they're acting to improve the universe, though their enforced philosophy kills innocents "for the greater good" as they insist. Ra's al Ghul, Magneto, Annihilius, and Kingpin fight for survival. Galactus, like Venom, King Shark, and Killer Croc, are animalistic predators no more evil than a tiger. Still, some like the Joker, Doomsday, and Darkseid evoke no sympathy and offer no moral position within their worldview—they are simply monsters or entropy incarnate. Most have doomed the world on multiple occasions, though their personal strife with the hero makes them even more interesting.

Women are notably absent from this list. One might add Dark Phoenix and Scarlet Witch (complicated by the notion that they're most often beloved heroines) or small-powered seductive criminals like Catwoman, Poison Ivy, Harley Quinn, Elektra, Black Cat, Superwoman, Black Widow, Killer Frost, various Star Sapphires, or Mystique (who tangle with the heroes quite personally and don't offer world-destroying powers). The X-Men have many villainesses, with Cassandra Nova, Callisto, and Lady Deathstrike, among others, fashioned to be perfectly matched nemeses for the heroes. Nebula, Hela, Artemis, Batwoman's Alice, and Blackfire are likewise the evil sisters of heroes, with Silver Swan as evil protégé. Lady Shiva and Granny Goodness are "evil moms," though this is a rare trope in the genre. The most powerful women are the sorceresses: Emerald Empress (nemesis of the Legion of Superheroes), Thor's enemy Enchantress, or Circe and Morgan le Fay, who tangle with Wonder Woman. However, for the true world-conquering megalomanics, it's necessary to travel back to the Golden Age and its particularly fierce women.

> In Golden Age comics, evil women were the ones in charge. They were gang leaders with henchmen and goons to do their bidding, crime queens who commanded armies. In subterranean lairs or secluded hideouts, these women were the absolute rulers. Their very names spoke of their royal status—the Queen of Evil, Baroness Blood, The Crystal Queen, Lady Doom, Ant Queen, Her Highness, the Headhunter Queen. And woe unto anyone foolish enough to oppose one of these mistresses of menace. "I give the orders around here! And since you dare to challenge me … die like the dog you are!" says the dread Lady Serpent, before tossing a dagger into the heart of a rebellious minion. These women reveled in their power, and demanded total obedience. Heroines had normal lives while moonlighting as crimefighters, but villainesses committed themselves fully to evil. They abandoned the everyday world where proper members of society lived, and plunged into the underworld. And there, these women found power and freedom [Madrid, *Vixens* 14].

From her dazzling airship, Texa introduces herself as having "the greatest brain in the world" and planning "the crime of the century" (Novick). First, she captures the Scarlet Avenger by unleashing her tamed pterodactyls to attack his plane, which falls into a net unleashed by her own airship. With it, she has the power to go anywhere, and she rules the skies, with a might far beyond the Avenger's small plane. It's filled with henchmen, emphasizing her queenlike power over men as well. Galen Foresman notes in his essay for *Supervillains and Philosophy*: "Our lists of great supervillains are usually comprised of villains who cause great suffering on the way to achieving their goals. So in some cases a supervillain can be the best of the worst because of their *means* rather than ends" (28).

In her secret lair, Texa paces about, threatening the goody-goody hero. While from the neck up, she sports blonde curls and a bonnet, the rest of her wears a racy halter top and high slit skirt. This hybrid is worn as a costume, defying the conventions of past and present to reinvent herself. As she describes her plan to kill the Avenger, she adds, "I shall rob the U.S. gold bullion which is stored underground ... my magnetic dynamos will soon be finished." Her stealing from the U.S. government itself during a time of war emphasizes her disdain for all that's decent.

> Villains don't want to be part of society. They want the freedom to live their lives unrestricted by laws by which the rest of us abide. Villains are narcissists, slaves to their own greed and lust for power. They are not interested in the welfare of others, only in satisfying their own desires. As a result, villains give no thought to the death and destruction that may result from their nefarious schemes [Madrid, *Vixens* 11].

She is no pacifist or damsel, but acknowledges she's quite willing to kill the hero. In this vein, the spy thriller is far from the lighthearted hijinks of a Superman comic. Coldly, she electrocutes the Avenger, but he is immune and twists the power to aid his escape. Of course, she orders her minions to capture him, but they fail. Back at his home base, the Scarlet Avenger tells his staff of operatives, "We are up against the greatest mind of the age ... we must all work together to frustrate her!" They work night and day to stop the "greatest crime wave in history." Clearly, Texa is no pushover, but a serious antagonist for the hero team. Foresman adds:

> To transform yourself into a true supervillain, you need to get some goals that are big and bad. As we've already pointed out, getting power alone isn't always bad. You need power to reach your ultimate dastardly ends, but it won't be the power that puts you on a list of the great supervillains. Oftentimes, it will be your other dastardly ends that do, like causing others to suffer for no other reason than it makes you laugh, like the Joker. If your only goal is to cause great suffering, then you'd be well on your way to becoming quite the villain. Generally speaking, if your goal is to cause great harm to many people, then you've got the right sort of goal for becoming a great supervillain [28].

The Scarlet Avenger describes Texa as "the greatest mind of our age," and clearly isn't exaggerating. "From her giant zeppelin she could attack the unsuspecting world below with electromagnetic beams or disintegrating rays. Everything about Texa was a mystery. Was she from some lost race or another planet? Where did her incredible powers come from? And why had she chosen a life of crime?" (Madrid, *Vixens* 24). Enacting her plan, Texa sprays the guards at Fort Knox with sleeping gas. Using her Magnetic Dynamos, she actually drags the vault out of the earth, carrying it off in her mighty airship. However, the Avenger wields his "magneutralizing machines" and sends the vault back to where it come from. Using his own ruthlessness to match Texa's, the Scarlet Avenger blasts her airship with liquid flames, attempting to explode the hydrogen tanks and kill her. She shoots back with harmless-looking bubbles … that suddenly blow up his own plane. As he staggers away from his destroyed craft, with her in pursuit, he has thoroughly been bested by the queen of crime. Such villainesses, however, were a bit too powerful for society's comfort, so they tended to make only single appearances before being locked away forever.

Texa was far from an isolated case. The Arthurian hero The Sword battles Axis spy Faye Morgana, Morgan le Fay reborn. Called the Daughter of Death, she combines magic with a terrible whip and low-cut green gown … as well as an imposing red swastika throne. She runs a network of Nazi spies who have infiltrated America. Further, Hitler sends her backup in the form of two goons, "true Aryan warriors" the Hun and the Goth. As a classic female villain, Morgana does have a conscience, however. When the muscled goons attack innocent hostages, she cries, "Enough! Even I can't bear to see any more!" (Da Voren). She and other spy ladies generally avoided direct confrontation and even managed to keep their hands clean most of the time.

Many other evil matriarchs starred in these early pulp superhero comics. Blackhawk and his team of aviators faced the greatest number of lethal female foes, including The Black Tigress, Xanukhara, Miss Danger, Vampira, Eclipse, Satana, Twilight, Spectra, and Madame Double Cross (Madrid, *Vixens* 14). Besides these, Red-haired Kate brandished a whip as a highly fetishized heroine, like Catwoman. The Sorceress of Zoom, who starred in *Weird Comics* between 1940 and 1942, plotted to enslave all mankind. Madam Satan and the Queen of Evil each had their own features back in 1941. In *Champion Comics* (1939), Neptima, Queen of the Deep, plotted to conquer the surface world and battled heroes for three years. Wonder Woman had a long string of villainesses to battle, including Queen Clea, Hypnota, the Saturnian slaver Eviless, Zara the Priestess of the Crimson Flame, Cheetah, Giganta and Doctor Poison, as well as various Nazi spies. However, the men had their female nemeses as well. The original Star Sapphire was a Flash villain, before the one who was an ambiguously moraled love interest for Green Lantern. Plastic

Man battled Madam Brawn, The Figure, Beauteous Bessie, Thrilla, Electra, Madame Serpina, and the Granite Lady. His tiny counterpart Doll Man faced off with the Huntress, The Hag, Little Miss Murder, and Madame Diablo. They were all incredibly glamorous.

Gina Misiroglu, in her critical work, lists supervillain traits as a greedy, antisocial mission, superior powers beyond that of the police with artistic skill at carrying them out, and a mania that leads him or her into obsession. Other tendencies include total selfishness, self-aggrandizement based in a sense of victimhood, and a propensity to monologue (Misiroglu and Eury xvi).

> These women were products of the 20th century, members of one of the first generations of females who could decide what sort of life they wanted for themselves. Embracing a life of crime gave evil women the freedom to live like men. They enjoyed the luxury to do whatever they wanted to do, no matter how cruel or ruthless the act. But since the concept of freedom is intertwined with evil in these stories, the implication is that a woman had to become an outlaw in order to be truly autonomous. Freedom came at the cost of a woman's soul. Still, this freedom was something that most virtuous heroines of the time did not enjoy. Crime-fighting females lived secret lives, while villainesses were able to say and do as they pleased. If anything, the villainesses of early comics were the precursors to the liberated, outspoken, and often combative heroines of the 1970s, like Power Girl and Black Canary [Madrid, *Vixens* 21].

One Silver Age supervillainess was Madame Masque. However, for the new era she's made a bit softer, as the daughter of Count Nefaria, commanded by him to be his successor in the Marvel's Mafia and blackmailed into compliance. With stellar combat skills, she manages her people's underworld operations. She also wears a gold mask to conceal disfigurement by acid.

In season three of 1966's *Batman* television show, Eartha Kitt's Catwoman and Joker join forces. Though he is Batman's number one villain, visually, she holds the cards. She sits on a gold throne while he crouches beside her. While she drives his getaway car, she holds a gun on him. Tellingly, as she faces an enemy beside Joker, he's silent and she gives the orders—to let the singer "Little Louie" bluster until he runs out of breath and then to push him over easily in his nightshirt with a single puff of air. "Let him howl until he springs a vocal cord. Then get him," she smirks to her sidekick (316). For their trial in the next episode, she's the rational one, hiring a brilliant lawyer as the Joker bumbles and blusters. In fact, their lawyer is a criminal who's stacked the jury with his goons. Hanley comments, "Kitt's fierce performance was remarkable for its time. Not only was she a black woman playing a well-known character who had been white since her debut a quarter century before, she also made her stronger and more powerful than she'd ever been" (53–54). Beside her, the Joker appeared little more than a henchman. With this, "the episode featured a black woman in charge of a man who was literally the whitest person on the program ... showing that a black woman not only belonged in the show's hierarchy of villains but excelled among them" (54). She, like many of her early counterparts, dazzled the audience in a way often more memorable than the sweet young heroine's antics.

As different comics eras followed, some of the benevolent heroines went bad. "These formidable women had to be kept in their place somehow, and it turned out the easiest way to do that was to depict female power and sexuality as evil" (Kanayama 39). Superheroines who turned dark wore more revealing outfits, like the Jean Grey clone Madelyne Pryor, who dressed similarly to Emma Frost (herself a reformed villain) but in black. As the Goblin Queen, she had new terrifying powers and could control minds and transform people into demons. "Likewise, when Sue Storm briefly became the villain Malice, Mistress of Hate, she ditched the bright full body jumpsuit for a skimpy black number that was basically a bikini with a loin cloth drape at the bottom, a black hood covered in spikes and a spiked collar. And thigh boots, naturally. The whole ensemble was very S&M chic" (Kanayama 39). Malice used her original force field powers aggressively, carving up her enemies with invisible weapons. "Wanting to gain power is evil, dear readers. That's why Madelyne and Sue had to wear dominatrix gear; it's the same reason Catwoman carries a whip and wears black leather. Only bad women want to be in control, whether sexually, mentally, or any other way" (Kanayama 39).

Dragon Lady: Madame Butterfly (Quality Comics, 1948)

The newspaper strip character that served as the role model for early comic books villainesses was the Dragon Lady. She was introduced in 1934 in Milton Caniff's *Terry and the Pirates*, and her name lives on as the stereotype of the cruel and calculating Asian female. The Dragon Lady was a notorious pirate queen with a horde of fierce cutthroats at her beck and call. Beautiful but heartless, she ruined men's lives. The real source of her villainy came from those qualities that supposedly make men great leaders—a thirst for power, relentless drive paired with a massive ego, and a lack of emotions. The Dragon Lady would do whatever it took to achieve her goals, whether it was seduce an enemy, betray an ally, or kill a man. "No man humiliates the Dragon Lady and lives to tell of it!" she swore. The Dragon Lady was her own creation and set the standard for female villainy [Madrid, *Vixens* 12].

Lai Choi San, Caniff's Dragon Lady, was a breakout character, modeling the "sexually volatile, and mistrustful femme fatale that used her sexuality to manipulate and entrap American heroes" (Whaley). She may have been inspired by an actual female pirate of the time, preying along the China coast and called Lai Choi San, "Mountain of Wealth," though Milton Cardiff attributes her look to a string of models (Caniff 20). The creator further explains that he wanted to create an Eastern villain "who was not a Fu Manchu. Putting this into a woman made it ten times more interesting, an irresistible combination, mean and beautiful" (Caniff 20). Dominating in long, flowing slit skirts and a cape, she coldly menaces scared-looking men with her swords and guns, displaying her beautiful, deadly side. The Dragon Lady has been called one of comics' greatest villainesses. "Fans of the strip immediately recognize the complex and unpredictable relationship the Asian temptress held with the strip's hero" (Misiroglu and Eury 111). By 1938, the Dragon Lady was the nation's leading villainess, with male readers of all ages swept away. "In true fiendish fashion, the exotic bombshell attempted to murder Terry—but she often seduced him, humiliated him, attempted to outwit him, and, interestingly, helped him through the trials and tribulations of puberty" (Misiroglu and Eury 111). *Terry and the Pirates* became a radio show, 1940 film and 1952 live action TV show, with different actresses in the role. When the U.S. and China allied in World War II, the Dragon Lady changed into more of a resistance fighter, though still Machiavellian and selfish.

In this vein, Madame Butterfly, a Japanese lady, menaces the Blackhawks in a 1948 adventure. A successful prospector is found dead and robbed, left with a knife painted with a butterfly. Instantly, the heroes suspect a particular culprit—"the most dangerous woman in the east." She sits on a throne with one of her minions bowing before her, gloating over a treasure map he has found. She and the Blackhawks each head towards the treasure on its mysterious island. The Blackhawks soon discover a ship, but it's covered in a cocoon of green fungus and all the crew have perished. Meanwhile, in her fighter plane, Madame Butterfly shoots at them from above. She and her "caterpillar legion" engage in a dogfight, and the Blackhawks barely escape. "I've never seen anyone fly like her! She's worth twenty of our own pilots!" one thinks. Realizing the other planes are better, however, Madame Butterfly takes a desperate chance and orders her own planes to crash into theirs. A dragon lady in truth, she's heartless about sacrificing her own men.

Critics Allan W. Austin and Patrick L. Hamilton see the dragon lady archetype as "a visual pattern of exotic sexuality and vicious cruelty that demonstrates the West's dualistic impulses of feat and romance, of repulsion and attraction toward the East and the Eastern" (157). She is a figure of forbidden desire as well as an enemy, as she offers "competing valences: threat and danger as well as attraction and allure" (157). This was traditional for all villainesses, of course.

> The evil women in comics were just as duplicitous, cold-blooded and vengeful as evil men were, but with a difference. Because they were women, there was an aura of glamour about their wickedness. Villainesses made being bad attractive, even appealing. Male villains like The Claw, the Joker and Dr. Sivana were a hideous lot,

with faces as horrible in appearance as their depraved souls. But most villainesses were presented as serpentine sirens, with hair cascading over heavy-lidded eyes. They brought an erotic quality to evil. It was no fun for a stalwart hero to be at the mercy of a fiendish male villain. But there was an implied thrill for that same hero to be dominated by a powerful, but evil woman [Madrid, *Vixens* 20].

Subverting this stereotype, Madame Butterfly wears a leotard, butterfly wings, boots, and antennae cap—not terribly seductive apart from the bare legs, as it has more of a Halloween costume look. One of her thugs gets the racist Asian treatment common in comics of the time, but she is drawn as alluring and normally proportioned.

On the island, her caterpillar legion attack once again. Blackhawk wakes in a dungeon with Madame Butterfly there gloating. She tells him, "You are handsome, Blackhawk! I am almost tempted to spare your life! But I have sworn that all white devils must die, and I must keep my vow!" She then tells her tragic story—she once loved the chief of the Japanese Secret Intelligence. However, he died in an American ambush. With this, she exemplifies and reserves the trope of her opera character namesake, who loved and was abandoned by a white man. Now she seeks revenge against all Americans.

She traps Blackhawk underground with the fungus, which will soon multiply, surrounding him in "a cocoon … of death!" This particularly horrific method of killing her victims arguably "plays into the traditional male fear of being smothered by the attentions of a female" (Madrid, *Vixens* 141). Madame Butterfly leaves him tied there and he sets fire to the stuff, then punches his way out. However, even as he beats up her henchmen, he isn't free and clear. She abruptly shoots him in the back. The next scene shows him tied at her feet as she stands over him in a position of power once again. "Your little adventure is ended, Blackhawk! I admire your ingenuity in escaping my cocoon! But now I must use more direct methods…." All seems desperate. However, the Blackhawks team arrive just in time to save him.

Imprisoned in the cavern, Madame Butterfly decides, "Our cause is lost! But they shall never gloat in triumph over Madame Butterfly!" Raising her arms triumphantly and opening the butterfly wings, she stands on the fungus and lets it beautifully wrap its way up her body and consume her. "Appearing four years after the end of WWII, the tale of Madame Butterfly shows that the last vestiges of that war still had story potential for comics. Madame Butterfly chooses to end her villainous career in grand operatic style at the climax of this Blackhawk adventure, which retains the élan of the team's wartime adventures which would sadly diminish in the 1950s" (Madrid, *Vixens* 141–142).

Similar villainesses of the time were just as alluring and deadly. They added to the stereotype, emphasizing that comics women could be foreign … as long as they were also evil. These exotic women were a predatory menace intent on destroying all-American superheroes. Ah Ku (*Top Notch*, 1940) was the crime queen of Chinatown, a "cruel, heartless murderess" who dealt in human trafficking, opium, and other stereotypes. In her three appearances, she masterminded several brutal murders, though she kept her hands clean. She even pretended to be a princess to beguile the hero, Bob Phantom. Echoing this tradition, Madam Klang menaced Spark Stevens in *Wonderworld Comics*.

Even Golden Age Catwoman shared traits with the Dragon Lady: "Comparable to the stereotypical Dragon Lady, The Cat exhibited the cunning, conniving, and potent gesticulations of a slithering, man-eating animal. The similarity in appearance between the two characters is striking as well, as the Dragon Lady and The Cat both have fair skin, almond shape eyes, jet-black hair, high cheekbones, and a pout mouth," Whaley notes. While this figure appears a stereotype, she was designed to appeal to men and women, impressing the latter with her strength. "Women readers would admire the development of the character's beauty, strength, vulnerability, and intelligence. Comparatively, DC believed male readers would respond to Catwoman's exaggerated physio-anatomy, as well as her less than subtle sexual innuendos" (Whaley).

Stereotypes changed with politics: When America entered the war on China's side, Chinese heroines appeared, including Girl Commandos member Mei Ling and Lady Wang "the Eastern Joan of Arc." During the Cold War, however, some of the villainesses rose once again.

"Even in times of comparative peace there is always a little war going on somewhere!" a Blackhawk story explains in 1950 as the hero seeks out an evil tyrant. The aviator team travels to fictional Jinnestan (a name that actually means the "Land of Genies" and emphasizes Eastern exoticism). "Power-mad" Tarya, dressed in a low-cut gown, has conquered this country for the Communists. Of course, she then uses her wiles on the hero. "Am I not beautiful?" she asks as she attempts to seduce him. "Do I not make you forget your silly principles?" These dangerous, seductive beauties continued through spy stories following the war ... until the comics code of 1954 tamed the sexy villainesses and made them far less provocative.

Things changed in the Silver Age ... but not as much as readers might have expected.

> Marvel and DC's Asian heroines evoke every aspect of these feminized versions of the "yellow peril." Like Barnum's Ah Fong Moy [a beautiful woman he displayed], they appeared in similarly "resplendent" and "luxurious" dress and surroundings. Where Mantis first appears, she wears a gold headdress and earrings, as well as a green-and-yellow dress with cutouts above the hips and a skirt slit to midthigh. Lady Shiva, when she arrives in *Kung-Fu Fighter* #5, wears a tight-fitting red dress, open from neck to belly button in a diamond-shaped cutout, with a knee-length skirt featuring slits up to her hip on both sides [Austin and Hamilton].

"Though the arrival of Mantis—and Sunfire and Karate Kid and Shang-Chi and Lady Shiva—may constitute a form of progress in that a greater number of Asian heroes and heroines now populated the comic page, the nature of their representation ultimately ran counter to what their debut might otherwise be said to signify, as their depictions were but thinly veiled versions of other virulent Asian stereotypes" (Austin and Hamilton). Even today, some of the stereotypes live on. In Tom King's *Batman: The Rules of Engagement* (2018), Talia al Ghul perches on a bed filled with her underdressed companions—at least eight, male and female. She sits nonchalantly brushing her hair, leaving the rest of events to the imagination. Her dressing gown has a very plunging neckline, and legs and thighs are casually exposed. Heavy gold jewelry includes a thick necklace extending to her waist, slave bracelet, bangles, collar, and large earrings. It's a picture of total sensuality and decadence. On hearing Batman has arrived, she commands, "Prepare my swords." She faces off with him in a low-necked, midriff-baring costume of crop top and loose pants with wrap skirt in shiny silky fabric. As femme fatale, she orders her men in to "do as they do" and attack Batman and Catwoman. Batman calls her "The most dangerous woman alive," and she in fact brutally impales him with her sword while he tries to negotiate.

In vengeance, Catwoman pulls the sword from her lover's body to duel his attacker. Thus, Talia and Catwoman literally battle over Batman. Talia tells Catwoman she wants him because of all the men in the world, he is her only potential equal. Catwoman, however, sees him more authentically as "broken. All the way, from the start, cracked." She adds that he'll put his childhood vow of fighting crime before everyone. "I'll always be second to a child's idiotic fantasy." However, as she concludes, "He's just the stupid man I stupidly love." She stabs Talia as she did Batman and leaves her to bleed. Afterwards, the injured combatants talk, and Talia tells Batman she likes his fiancée. This is how superheroes, especially the exoticized women, do romance.

Witch Queen: Seven Soldiers of Victory (DC Comics, 2006–2007)

"In a genre where most of the leading characters are still white men, the Seven Soldiers stand out for their diversity. Most of these heroes are either black or female, with only the blue-skinned Klarion [and] gray, cadaverous Frankenstein" even slightly qualifying as mainstream (Singer 223). Of course, with its epic of a separated task force that never meet, culled from the lesser-used DC heroes, this is not the only reason Grant Morrison's *Seven Soldiers of Victory* truly stands out.

The Sheeda, a group of evil creatures often believed to be fairies, attack earth as they have done through the centuries. They target groups of seven, as one such group is prophesized to defeat them. To combat them, the Seven Soldiers are chosen, but for secrecy, this time they must fight separately.

Zatanna, DC's great magician, begins sitting in a support group for superheroes with low self-esteem. There she reveals dreams of locust armies and a queen riding an eight-legged horse. Abruptly, she meets with several magical folk who lead her on a quest through the imaginary realms to regain her lost magic. Across the world, Justin the Shining Knight (in actuality Justina) slays Galahad, who has become a tool of the evil Sheeda queen. Joining her are Frankenstein (always an outsider), the orphaned inventor Mr. Miracle, the Bulleteer, police officer Jake Jordan, and the sneaky Klarion the witch boy. All are outcasts, and none are particularly famous heroes. Nonetheless, all embark on heroic journeys: "All of the Seven Soldiers undergo ordeals of trial and initiation, crises of conscience or of will that force them to examine their principles" (Singer 223). As the ones who have been passed over, who are third string heroes of their universe, they understand the struggles of the tiny folk—the true key to stopping this nemesis.

The Sheeda's queen is Gloria Tenebrae. She is gray-skinned, bald, and horned, a figure of decay like the dried-up Wicked Witch of the West. She wears black, harsh metal and leather collar like a bat's wing. She has come to prey on the innocent of earth, as a particularly chilling trope, the destroyer of life. The young heroines, who represent life incarnate, must battle against her.

She is also a true believer and fanatic like Thanos or Ronan the Accuser from the MCU, certain that they should murder because of their philosophy. Of course, this overcontrol is a traditional path, producing many fanatics. "Evil tyrants act out all the traits of the shadow ruler. They are selfish, narrow minded and vindictive" (Pearson 187). As she comes from the future to destroy mankind, she's a figure of entropy. She explains, "When a civilization reaches its peak, there comes a time of harvest, let's say. After the ripening comes inevitable decay. With predictable and grim implications for your own civilization."

> Some moral monsters choose to do what is evil because they embrace a type of aesthetic perspective that attempts to bring non-moral and higher forms of goodness into the world via acts of cruelty or sadism. Moral monsters who have this type of aesthetic outlook often see the world as completely meaningless and devoid of value, or perhaps they see the world as full of mediocre forms of value [Moseley 131].

Moral monsters of this sort know that they're committing evil acts, but they go ahead all the same. They are not sociopaths, unable to tell right from wrong, but people who revel in wickedness.

In *Birds of Prey*: "Devil's Eyes" (113), Harley Quinn hypnotizes the Huntress to do whatever she says and kill her friends. She is another corrupter of the innocent, turning the good evil—even making kindly Alfred her slave.

Harley then takes over the Birds' clock tower, planning to broadcast the hypnotic signal to every television set in New Gotham and enslave more good people. After Oracle stops her, Huntress reveals that some of the evil came from her—she was the one to open up to her psychiatrist Dr. Quinzell, and people died because of it. This is the true danger of the wicked witch—she evokes the hero's suppressed darkness and sets it loose.

In Simone's *Birds of Prey* comics, Mortis, "goddess of the forgotten dead" as she calls herself, telepathically makes people face their regrets and often drown in sorrow and guilt. She attacks Black Canary, drawing her into a morass of eternal suffering. There, Mortis taunts her with the deaths of her parents and niece, the abandonment of her adopted daughter. Finally, she gloats, "Your friends have dumped you again, haven't they?" This provocation jolts Canary, who insists her friends love her and orders Mortis to "get the Holy Hell out of my brain!" With this, the link is broken (*The Death of Oracle*).

The fairy world is one of dangers as well as good and evil strikingly side by side. "In the topside world, all is interpreted in the light of simple gains and losses. In the underworld or other world, all is interpreted in the light of the mysteries of true sight, right action, and the development of becoming a person of intense inner strength and knowing" (Estés 449). Exploring Gloria Tenebrae's lair, Sir Justin discovers the lovely Olwen abused and dying. The queen adds coldly, "She was passed around my court. And it changed her, as it does." The queen not only destroys innocent civilizations but preys on whichever individuals are too weak to oppose her. As Justin snatches Olwen and flees, Olwen suddenly stabs him, revealing herself as the queen's construct and trap. Once again, the queen reveals that her most insidious power is corrupting her victims and even using them as bait. Without her, Justin flees to earth.

The destroyer of the innocent represents the shadow side of the innocent heroine, all the murderous instincts she's set aside to be kind and loving. At the same time, this dark side offers valuable lessons in strength and ruthlessness for the heroine. Bumblebee's novel in the Super Hero High series by Lisa Yee introduces the wicked Queen Bee. She has made her cousin's son into her minion, Cuckoo Bee, who repeats what he hears. As she lures Bumblebee into her lair by kidnapping her parents, Queen Bee explains that she desires control—her robot bees have showered their own pollen everywhere, making real honeybees sleepy and spreading her own BotBees through the world. When Bumblebee protests that the supervillainess is killing all the crops, Queen Bee smirks, "Disable, distract, and conquer" (156). She has also stolen Bumblebee's technology, preferring to make others work for her instead of inventing on her own. Using it, she can turn herself into the giantess she believes she should be. She will become a queen bee in truth: the queen of the world. Bumblebee defeats her by convincing Cuckoo Bee to abandon her and then sneakily inserting herself inside Queen Bee's helmet, matching her strength with stealth and cleverness.

Squirrel Girl finds a mentor who ends up being a true villainess in North and Henderson's *Who Run the World? Squirrels.* Melissa Morbeck introduces herself as someone who can communicate with all animals, and Doreen is thrilled. However, Miss Morbeck plans to eat her chicken, Alfredo, making her a killer of the innocent and of her own precious pet (despite its suggestive name). Doreen escapes and summons her squirrels, but Miss Morbeck summons her own rats, the most populous animal in New York. She releases cockroaches as well as a mistress of the nastier side of the animal kingdom. She threatens to unleash deadly disease-carrying mosquitos, and Doreen finds herself uncertain how to stop her new nemesis. Miss Morbeck then frames Squirrel Girl—known to speak with animals—and the younger woman finds herself fighting to protect her reputation as well as her friends, from the insidious mentor now determined to destroy both. Her enemy here is her shadow—the perfect counterpart with similar powers, but one who uses them for destruction.

Gloria Tenebrae's lair, Castle Revolving, has mazelike passages built from the bones of her dead enemies. There, she has a cauldron that restores the dead to life, straight from ancient myth. With this and her undead soldiers, she defies the natural order of the life cycle. This is symbolically important, because just as the heroes embody life, she fights for stagnation and sterility. She proclaims, "My glass giants will foul the water supply and enter lethal contagion into the food chain. My harvesters will excavate the earth down to naked barren rock and drain the oceans into our breeding tanks. We are the end result of natural selection, the winner of a savage and bloody struggle for planetary dominion." Her destruction of the world is a battle against nature as she is the force of devastation.

As she nibbles a red apple and once sent a huntsman to destroy her stepdaughter, she seems an ancient memory of Snow White. In fact, young Misty Kilgore, who has apprenticed herself to Zatanna, is related to the evil queen. Zatanna finally tells her, "Let's go take your Momma out."

However, the young hopeful heroine takes Zatanna by surprise and knocks her out, adding, "I've just realized the real reason I asked you to teach me magic. This is why I came to you, Zatanna. So that I could learn to fight my stepmother." She realizes she must take responsibility and save the world all on her own: "There's only one way to stop the harrowing … and that's to take Gloriana's place as the Sheeda queen." She names herself Princess Rhiannon of the Sheeda and her mother's buglike minions dance around her. Clutching her magic dice, she heads into battle. However, she soon realizes, "Beating her's much worse than letting her win! If she falls, I'm the Sheeda queen! I'll have to keep my people alive by preying on the past like *she* did!

I'll have to be like her!" This is the terrible danger of killing the tyrant—ascending to her place and becoming her, and endlessly perpetuating the cycle.

Zatanna tells her, "Don't let anybody tell you what you have to be, Misty, That was *my* mistake." Misty must continue the lifecycle, vanquishing her mother and taking her place as the new queen and symbolic adult, but she can choose to rule benevolently. As Zatanna adds, magic is about doing the impossible and they can save the world together. They cast a spell summoning the Seven Soldiers to unite and defeat the queen, which they do. Dead, Gloria Tenebrae plunges through a portal back to the dark hell she came from. Thus, the youthful heroine representing the strength of the next generation emerges and the ancient witch is purged from the world as well as from consciousness.

Mighty Crone: Spider Widow (Quality Comics, 1942)

Before all comic book heroines were alluring teens in bathing suits, a few writers crafted superheroines that completely embodied the shadow—crimefighters who were vicious, murderous crones. Instead of battling the force of darkness, they unleashed it from within themselves to battle evil.

As the beginning of the *Spider Widow* comic explains, "Beautiful Dianne Grayton wages a private war against crime and un–American activities, by transforming herself from a wealthy debutante into the Spider Widow, the most horrible dispenser of justice at all times!" Dianne is lovely and sweet with coiffed hair, everything a young society woman is supposed to be. Her alter-ego, however, is a wrinkled witch, complete with pointy hat, bulbous nose, and stringy hair.

In ancient times, the crone was a face of terror—Medusa's face embodied female rage, used as a horrific "Keep Out!" sign. There are times when a woman wants to invoke this power, to look tough and dangerous instead of sweet. In her rubber mask, Dianne is "the most horrible dispenser of justice of all time." Through it, Dianne has this ability—and can transform face as well as clothes. In society, girls have the least power—Cinderella takes orders from her stepmother and can only be gentle and meek as the woman domineers over her. The mother is stronger, but defers to the father and often acts cruelly out of frustration at her constraints. The crone, however, is the boss of the three. She is a figure of wisdom, mediator between life and death, filled with ancient secrets. In fact, Spider Widow is called the "Grandmother of Terror" and this is her greatest ability—sweet debutants aren't scary but this woman is.

As Dianne, a man calls her "a cute little mermaid" and dismisses her as harmless. The forceful ship's matriarch Madame Largossi throws her off their ship. Instantly, Dianne suspects a spy ring. When she returns that night as the Spider Widow, she gets a far different reception. "Yow! What a face!" one man cries. When Madame Largossi calls her an old hag and threatens her, the Spider Widow gives her a glare of fury like that of Medusa—terrifying and soul-penetrating. "Mind your tongue, Madame Largossi! You are speaking to the Spider Widow!" The other woman is cowed.

However, the Spider Widow isn't done and follows up her attack by releasing her "insect warriors"—hideous spiders that swarm over the other woman. Clearly, her dark side powers go beyond her mask. "What made Dianne's alter ego such a fright wasn't her costume-shop aesthetic. Through some unexplained process or happenstance, the crime-fighting bachelorette possessed the ability to mentally command black widow spiders to do her bidding" (Morris, *Sidekicks* 96). Madame Largossi leaps over the side of the boat in horror, and the coast patrol picks her up. Spider Widow has broken up the spies and saved the day. Dianne paddles away, having removed the mask but kept the powerful hat, smiling that she has preserved her secret identity—her great source of power in a sexist and ageist world.

Unusually, Spider Widow has an adult male sidekick who is also her love interest. The Raven fights in a purple and green costume and intercepts a trap for Spider Widow, as he's determined to meet her. Their adventure ends with a kiss, unmasked, but with the night concealing both their identities. He fights beside her for a year, but when Phantom Lady arrives, a competitive love triangle develops. At one point, the two women reach the point of fencing with swords. "I told you to stay in the background," Spider Widow exclaims. "Well, dear, if it's going to take you all day to swing into action after all…." Phantom Lady retorts. In response to this competitiveness, the Raven announces naively, "The next time we set out, I'll have these two gals *trained! I* know how to handle women!" (Borth, *Feature Comics* #60). However, the comic ended before the women could resolve their antagonism.

Mother Hubbard, an actual witch with wrinkles and pointy hat, flying broom and striped stockings, has no alter-ego. She is a fairytale character who fights crime and defends children. This juxtaposition feels jarring at first, but considering the Marvel and DC characters like Hercules and Doctor Strange, she isn't such an ill-fit after all. When a criminal boasts, "My leader selected me because of my inhumanity and cruelty," the terrible crone waits to enact justice. She revels in powers that, while used for justice, don't truly seem to be white magic, with "Bat's claws, Madman's blood, and Siren's lure" her potions of choice. "For long, witchcraft has been the power of evil … but I have determined to use it for good, as you are about to see!" she thunders. She bursts into the Torture Room, where Nazis are threatening to brand a little boy to coerce his scientist father to help them. She casts a spell turning them into blind old men—threatening them with a crone's greatest power of terror—the reminder of old age and death. She too sends in giant insects, another gift of the world of occult and terror. On their way, the bugs free the child, emphasizing once more that these powers can be used to protect the innocent. The boy and his father free, Mother Hubbard then burns down the house with the wicked men inside it—apparently the code forbidding supermen to kill has no restraint over her cruelty. "Mother Hubbard's trio of adventures in the early 1940's may have been the most flat-out terrifying superhero stories in the entire genre. Back then, everyone in a cap and cowl fought a few Nazi masterminds. Only Mother Hubbard confronted a race of gnomes who pried the eyes out of children's heads with a crowbar!" Morris comments (*Supervillains* 89).

Meanwhile, Catwoman's first appearance came as the burglar known as The Cat in *Batman* #1 (1940). As Batman chases down a jewel thief on a ship, he and everyone else discount the limping, elderly Miss Peggs. However, when he sees her fleeing with "nice legs for an old woman" he realizes who she is and pulls off the disguise. She is revealed as a beautiful young woman in a long green dress, with the bandage on her leg concealing a half-million-dollar necklace. Though she's a criminal, Batman is enticed enough by her beauty that he allows her to escape. He comments, "Lovely girl! What eyes! Say—mustn't forget I've got a girl named Julie [Madison]—Oh well, she still had lovely eyes! Maybe I'll bump into her again sometime..." (Finger). "Piquing Batman's romantic interest for the first time was a considerable achievement, but even more impressive was the Cat's ability to make Batman forget his commitment to fighting crime" (Hanley 13). Doing so while costumed as a powerful old woman was even more impressive, suggesting a seduction of mind rather than body.

Strangely, another Golden Age hero to dress as an elderly woman and solve crimes was the *male* Richard Stanton, who considered this a clever disguise to draw off attention as he went by Madam Fatal. Mother Goose, likewise actually a costumed man, kills her own three nephews to take a terrible revenge on behalf of the mother they abandoned. Mother Goose murders them with the tools of nursery rhymes, cackling maniacally all the while. She borrows a woman's invisibility, but also the power of the death crone. "Nursery rhymes and fairy tales are fertile ground for creating truly terrifying villains" (Morris, *Supervillains* 88). She finally takes poison, ending the violent story with her demise.

> Not all villainesses were beguiling temptresses. One of the most unique and fascinating was Her Highness. Described as "rough, tough, and nasty," she first appeared as a villain in Hit Comics' "Kid Eternity" series. She was a diminutive old woman with her hair pulled back in a prim, ladylike bun. But a grandmotherly face was offset by the purple man's suit and tie that Her Highness always sported. This old gal's tough demeanor was shaped by the hardscrabble years of the Great Depression, when

people had to fight to survive. Her Highness' partner in crime was a shapely and superhumanly strong young woman named Silk, and the duo proved to be so popular that after twice crossing paths with Kid Eternity, they graduated to their own feature. Despite the fact that she was now the star of her own solo stories, Her Highness never put her criminal ways aside. "Nobody ever got anywhere being legit!" was her motto, and she continued to be a thief and bamboozler in every one of her adventures [Madrid, *Vixens* 19–20].

These Golden Age crones mixed up the superhero genre more than a little. However, as stories shifted to depower strong women, the crone was the first to go: "The patriarchy feared the feminine in connection with her role in birthing and dying even more than in her association with sex. The wise crone transformed into the ugly hag, the death-snatcher" (George 222). The crone represented the realm of death and power over it—a terror to some. She became banished to the underworld as only young and middle-aged women remained in the world's more male dominated pantheons. "To the patriarchy, death is the cutoff to ambition and rule, the final 'debt' that robs men of all they possess. Thus, they cringe from the crone, who is associated with great age, entropy, death, and even doomsday" (Frankel, *From Girl to Goddess* 288). Superhero comics especially sideline and mostly refuse to include older women:

> Older single professional women are portrayed in a less flattering light. They're either terribly stern and hard-boiled, as with Helen Mirren's detective character on the British import *Prime Suspect* or Star Fleet captain Kathryn Janeway (Kate Mulgrew) on *Star Trek: Voyager,* or a bit too much the meddling old biddy, as with mystery writer and sleuth Jessica Fletcher (Angela Lansbury) on *Murder, She Wrote*. It's a subtle way of showing that smart, independent women wind up with the traits of the traditional old maid [Isaacs 130].

Caryn E. Neumann notes in "Babes and Crones: Women Growing Old in Comics": "Comics have long denied the existence of highly capable, attractive, mature women, which also reflects negative Western societal attitudes about aging women" (119). Older men like Lex Luthor or Professor X may have large roles in comics, but women, even ancient ones like Wonder Woman's mother Hippolyte, basically all look young. Superheroines' names stress this as they are called "Batgirl" and "Supergirl," never outgrowing their teens or twenties. Youth, beauty, and goodness are tied together for the women. "In other words, heroes and heroines cannot be old and ugly, because they are good people" (Neumann 121).

More modern comics are reluctant to invoke this creepy trope, but it happens occasionally. One of Chris Claremont's Morlocks is the old woman Plague. With a touch she can make people "sick as a dog" or fatally ill. Among their healers, no one can counter Plague's curses. When the X-Men descend to rescue their friends, she is the one to force them all to surrender, since her power can destroy any or all of them (Claremont, *Uncanny X-Men* #169–170).

In the *Smallville* episode "Abandoned" (1008), Granny Goodness tells Tess Mercer, the CEO of LuthorCorp, that she once trained her and has recently brought her back from the edge of death—she is indeed the goddess of revitalization as well as destruction. On the show as in her original comics, Granny erases the traumatic memories of orphan girls and trains them as ferocious warriors, to aid in Darkseid's conquering of earth. She subverts Green Arrow with her vast mental powers and nearly succeeds in destroying Superman's powers forever in the series finale by corrupting his wedding ring. She is indeed a powerhouse, one that uses feminine symbols to sabotage the next generation.

In *Womanthology*'s "The Wraiths of Roseland," an elderly woman insists on commemorating all the murdered children in the areas with picture-stones. Her neighbors consider this ghoulish and plan to move. However, when their daughter is threatened, the elderly Mrs. Z and the girl's mother invoke the dead children to protect her. As the mother concludes, "Wherever you go, your ghosts are always with you" (Sardina). Fearing death will not help the dead children, but wielding it as a weapon can save the living. Once more, the heroine uses creepy underworld powers, but to save the children of earth with her strength and arcane knowledge.

Conclusion

All these tropes are most evident in comics, television, and team-up films, as the few superheroine films produced tend to be problematic. Stuller notes, "Weak scripts, hurried effects, and one-dimensional characters plagued features such as *Lara Croft: Tomb Raider* (2001) and *Catwoman* (2004)" (82). *Elektra*'s terribly slow, dreamlike filming with slower flashbacks lacks the action expected in a superhero film. Catwoman's plot is shallow, with far more emphasis on how she looks in her suit. The pathos, madness, and hope of redemption of the character in *Batman Returns* is gone. Likewise, Susan J. Douglas in *Enlightened Sexism* describes Lara Croft as "able to leap tall buildings in a single bound and sporting breasts the size of watermelons" (94). This, one assumes, is the main reason to watch.

In a more recent era, *Wonder Woman* (2017) delighted fans, though the heroine had a traditional romance and rather skimpy outfit. *Captain Marvel* (2019), like *Ghostbusters* (2016), enraged many misogynistic fans with its very existence. As Carol Danvers proved herself the mightiest hero of the franchise, destroying the male institutions and dismissing her former mentor's demand for a macho fight, she certainly established her power. She dressed sloppily and didn't bother smiling, showing how uninterested she was in charming her male audience. Following this, *Birds of Prey (and the Fantabulous Emancipation of One Harley Quinn)* delighted fans with five heroines clearly uninterested in dressing for men or finding romance. While pursuing their own goals, they form a triumphant team and definitively squash the patriarchy. Alongside these films, the *Hunger Games* franchise, the *Star Wars* sequels, *Mad Max: Fury Road*, *Ant-Man and the Wasp*, *Black Panther*, *Ghost in the Shell*, *Logan*, *Dark Phoenix*, and *Alita: Battle Angel* all expanded the action women genre of the decade to embrace more powerful and nuanced superheroines.

Even beyond this, the writing of film superheroines is often problematic. In contrast with the beloved Buffy and Xena television shows, superheroines in film rarely crack jokes at all. On *The Avengers*, Black Widow is the "straight man," like the ultra-serious women in the two *X-Men* series and Gamora in *Guardians of the Galaxy*. Unless they're falling in love with the hero, none of them ever seem to be having a good time. In her own film, Catwoman calls herself "fun-deficient." Many "strong female characters" like Hit-Girl end up lacking a personality and being only a living weapon. Wonder Woman in the *Justice League* cartoon movies is hard and uncompromising, without a fun, friendly, or vulnerable side. In 2016's *Batman vs. Superman: Dawn of Justice*, she glows with divine light and traps Doomsday in her gleaming lasso but seems more distant goddess than woman (admittedly Superman has a similar characterization).

Token girls in team-up films have other severe problems. Mystique walks around naked, Emma Frost nearly so. Deadpool's beloved Vanessa is fridged. *X-Men: Apocalypse* has all the women obeying orders as they try to influence the male heroes' battle. Even tough Black Widow runs from the Hulk and interrogates Loki by fake crying (to say nothing of her status as Hulk's "lullaby" and love interest). Marvel also has a trope of women gaining too much power and needing to be deprived of it—not just Dark Phoenix, but girlfriends Pepper Potts (*Iron Man 3*) and Jane Foster (*Thor: The Dark World*).

Progress is coming—slowly but clearly as the heroines on the biggest screens fight for equal screentime and the chance to crack a joke or two. On smaller screens, many more feminist heroes are available, in *Black Lightning, Supergirl, DC's Legends of Tomorrow, Vixen, Batwoman, Agents of S.H.I.E.L.D., Misfits, Marvel's Jessica Jones, Marvel's Agent Carter, DC Super Hero Girls, Marvel Rising, She-Ra and the Princesses of Power, Sailor Moon, Teen Titans, The Umbrella Academy, Star vs. the Forces of Evil, Wynonna Earp, Watchmen, Heroes, Gotham, Powers, Titans, Marvel's Runaways, Inhumans, The Gifted, Cloak and Dagger, Doom Patrol*, and *Raising Dion*. These shows all glow with strong, admirable heroines carving out a place in the world. Meanwhile the new genre of superhero teen novels is breaking down barriers with excellent DC and Marvel tie-ins as well as independent books *Dreadnaught, The Epic Crush of Genie Lo, Vigilante, Not Your Sidekick, Vanished, The Refrigerator Monologues, Renegades, After the Golden Age, Velveteen vs. The Junior Super-Patriots*, and *Danielle: Chronicles of a Superheroine*. Comics are likewise embracing diversity as Marvel heroines from across the world team up to teach genius girls STEM skills. DC, meanwhile, experiments with *Bat Girl and the Birds of Prey, Harley Quinn and Poison Ivy*, and *Doom Patrol* alongside their traditional lines. Cartoons, like *Vixen* and *Marvel Rising*, do not represent the same financial commitment as big budget films, but it's a start. In smaller markets still, independent comics and web comics offer new superheroines of every type imaginable. It's a new world with a new style of storytelling, and the future is looking very heroic.

Primary Sources Cited

Comics and Graphic Novels

Aaron, Jason, and Russell Dauterman. *The Mighty Thor: Lords of Midgard*. Marvel, 2016.
Aaron, Jason, and Russell Dauterman. *The Mighty Thor: Thunder in Her Veins*. Marvel, 2016.
Al-Mutawa, Naif. *The 99*. Teshkeel Comics, 2006.
Azzarello, Brian, and Chris Chiang. *Wonder Woman Vol. 2: Guts*. DC Comics, 2013.
Balent, Jim. *Tarot: Witch of the Black Rose* #1. Broad Sword Comics, 1999.
Barr, Mike W., and Jim Aparo. *Batman and the Outsiders* #11–12. *Showcase Presents: Batman and the Outsiders, Vol. 1*. DC Comics, 1984.
Bendis, Brian Michael, and Michael Gaydos. *Jessica Jones: Return of the Purple Man*. Marvel, 2018.
Bendis, Brian Michael, and Michael Gaydos. *The Pulse* #11–14. Marvel, 2005. Marvel Unlimited. Marvel.com.
Bennett, Marguerite, et al. *Bombshells United. Volume 1: American Soil*. DC Comics, 2018.
Bennett, Marguerite, et al. *Bombshells: Vol. 4: Queens*. DC Comics, 2017.
Borth, Frank M. "The Spider Widow." *Feature Comics* #58. 1942. *Divas, Dames & Daredevils*, edited by Mike Madrid. Exterminating Angel Press, 2013. 90–94.
Borth, Frank M. "The Spider Widow." *Feature Comics* #60. Quality Comics, September 1942.
Brubaker, Ed, and Butch Guice. *Winter Soldier: Black Widow Hunt*. Marvel, 2013.
Brubaker, Ed, and Cameron Stewart. *Catwoman: Wild Ride*. DC Comics, 2003.
Brubaker, Ed, Clay Mann and Michael Lark. *Daredevil: Lady Bullseye*. Marvel, 2009.
Bunn, Cullen, et al. *Uncanny X-Men* #15–17. Marvel, 2017.
Caniff, Milton Arthur. *Enter the Dragon Lady: From the 1936 Classic Newspaper Adventure Strip*. Nostalgia Press, 1975.
Chen, Lynn, and Paul Wei. "You Are What You Eat." Yang, et al. pp. 100–106.
Chu, Amy, and Bernard Change. "Rescue Angel." *Sensation Comics Featuring Wonder Woman Vol. 2*. DC, 2015.
Claremont, Chris, and Allen Milgrom. *Kitty Pryde and Wolverine*. 1984–1985. Marvel, 2008.
Claremont, Chris, and Clayton Henry. *Uncanny X-Men Annual* #1. Marvel, 2006.
Claremont, Chris, and Dave Cockrum. *Uncanny X-Men* #102. Marvel, 1976.
Claremont, Chris, and Frank Miller. *Marvel Team-Up* #100. Marvel, 1980.
Claremont, Chris, and John Byrne. *Marvel Team-Up* #64. Marvel, 1977.
Claremont, Chris, and John Byrne. *Uncanny X-Men* #128–143. Marvel, 1980.
Claremont, Chris, and John Romita. *Uncanny X-Men* #195. Marvel, 1985.
Claremont, Chris, and Mike Vosberg. *Marvel Team-Up* #81. Marvel, 1979.
Claremont, Chris, and Paul Smith. *Uncanny X-Men* #166–170. Marvel, 1983.
Claremont, Chris, and Randall Green. *Decimation: House of M: The Day After* #1. Marvel, 2005.
Claremont, Chris, and Sal Buscema. *Marvel Team-Up Vol 1* #87, Marvel, 1979.
Conner, Amanda, Jimmy Palmiotti and Chad Hardin *Harley Quinn Vol. 5: The Joker's Last Laugh*. DC Comics, 2016.

Conner, Amanda, Jimmy Palmiotti, et al. *Harley Quinn: A Call to Arms.* DC Comics, 2016.
Conner, Amanda, Jimmy Palmiotti, et al. *Starfire* #1–5. DC Comics, 2015.
Conner, Amanda, Jimmy Palmiotti and John Timms. "Tug A' War." 2015. *Harley Quinn's Greatest Hits.* DC, 2016.
Conner, Amanda, Jimmy Palmiotti and John Timms. *Vote Harley.* DC Comics, 2018.
Conner, Amanda, et al. *Harley Quinn: Power Outage.* DC Comics, 2015.
Cornell, Paul, Tom Raney and John Paul Leon. *Black Widow: Deadly Origin.* Marvel Worldwide, 2010.
Da Voren, Earl. *Super Mystery Comics* vol. 3 #3. Ace Magazines, Jan 1943.
De Campi, Alex, and Neil Googe. "Venus Rising." *Sensation Comics Featuring Wonder Woman Vol. 2.* DC, 2015.
DeConnick, Kelley Sue, and Scott Hepburn. *Avengers: The Enemy Within.* Marvel, 2013.
Delany, Samuel R., and Dick Giordano. *Wonder Woman* #203. DC Comics, 1972.
Devineni, Ram. *Priya's Shakti.* Rattapallax, Inc., 2014. http://www.priyashakti.com.
Dini, Paul, and Bruce Timm. "Mad Love." 1994. *The Batman Adventures: Dangerous Dames and Demons.* DC Comics, 2003. 126–190.
Dini, Paul, and Joe Benitez. *Detective Comics* #823. DC Comics, 2006.
Dixon, Chuck, et al. *Birds of Prey: Old Friends New Enemies.* DC Comics: 2003.
Dunn, Ben. *Warrior Nun Areala* #1. Antarctic Press, 1995.
Eisner, Will, and Dan Zolnerowich. "The Legion of Living Bombs: Espionage Starring Black X." *Smash Comics* #14. 1940. Madrid, *Vixens* 27–35.
Ellis, Warren, and Terry Dodson. *X-Men: Storm.* 1996. Marvel, 2013.
Finger, Bill, and Bob Kane. "The Secret Life of the Catwoman." *Batman* #62. DC Comics, December 1950/January 1951.
Finger, Bill, and Sheldon Moldoff. *Batman* #119, *Batman* #122, *Batman* #139, *Batman* #144. DC Comics, 1958–1961.
Fridolfs, Derek, and Federico Dallocchio. "Beloved." *Arkham City Sirens.* DC Comics, 2012.
Gillen, Kieron, and Phil Jimenez. *Angela: Asgard's Assassin: Priceless.* #1–6. Marvel Worldwide, 2015.
Guardineer, Fred. "The Marksman." *Smash Comics* #48. 1943. Madrid, *Vixens* 49–55.
Hall, Barbara. "The Blonde Bomber." *Green Hornet* #7. Harvey Comics, 1942. http://comicbookplus.com/?dlid=31005.
Hall, Barbara. "Girl Commandos." *Speed Comics* #24. Harvey Comics, 1942. http://comicbookplus.com/?dlid=59986.
Hall, Barbara. "Girl Commandos and the Battle for Burma." *Speed Comics* #27. Harvey Comics, 1943. http://comicbookplus.com/?dlid=21083.
Hall, Barbara. "Hawaii Has Termites!" *Green Hornet* #27 November 1945 http://comicbookplus.com/?dlid=33485.
Hall, Barbara. "Pat Parker, Girl Commando." *Speed Comics* #23. Harvey Comics, 1942. http://comicbookplus.com/?dlid=25809.
Hamilton, Edmond, and Sheldon Moldoff. *Detective Comics* #233. DC Comics, 1956.
Hartnell, Andy, and J. Scott Campbell. *Danger Girl: The Ultimate Collection.* Wildstorm Productions, 1997–2001.
Harvey, Alfred, and Barbara Hall. "Origin of the Black Cat." *Pocket Comics* #1 Harvey Comics, 1941. http://comicbookplus.com/?dlid=25734.
Heinberg, Allan, and Jim Cheung. *Young Avengers Vol. 1: Sidekicks.* Marvel, 2006.
Heinberg, Allan, and Jim Cheung. *Young Avengers Vol. 2: Family Matters.* Marvel, 2006.
Hickman, Jessica, et al., editors. *Womanthology: Heroic.* IDW, 2012.
Hopeless, Dennis, and Javier Rodriguez. *Spider-Woman Shifting Gears: Baby Talk.* Marvel, 2016.
Houser, Jody, Nick Roche and Nathan Stockman. *Amazing Spider-Man: Renew Your Vows: Eight Years Later.* Marvel, 2018.
Hudlin, Reginald, and John Romita, Jr. *Black Panther.* Marvel, 2005.
Hudlin, Reginald, and Ken Lashley. *Black Panther: The Deadliest of the Species.* Marvel, 2009.
Isabella, Tony, and Arvell Jones. *Marvel Premiere* #21. Marvel, 1975.

Primary Sources Cited—Comics and Graphic Novels

Jiminez, Phil, et al. *Wonder Woman: Paradise Found* (vol. 2, 171–177). DC Comics, 2003.
Johns, Geoff, and Scott Kolins. "The Search for She-Hulk." 2003–2004. *Avengers: The Complete Collection by Geoff Jones, Vol. 2* (Avengers #64–76). Marvel Worldwide, 2013.
Jones, Geoff, et al. *Supergirl: Candor*. DC Comics, 2007.
Joshi, Kripa. "Girl Power." Yang, et al., pp. 99.
Kanigher, Bob, and Sheldon Moldoff. "Beware Of—Poison Ivy." *Batman* #181. DC Comics, 1966.
Kesel, Karl, and Terry Dodson. *Harley Quinn: Preludes and Knock-Knock Jokes*. DC Comics, 2013.
Kieth, Sam. *Zero Girl*. Homage Comics, 2001.
King, Tom, et al. *Batman: The Rules of Engagement*. DC Comics, 2018.
Kyle, Craig, Christopher Yost and Billy Tan. *X-23: Innocence Lost*. Marvel, 2006.
Larson, Hope, Vita Ayala, et al. *Batgirl: Son of Penguin*. DC Comics, 2017.
Lee, Stan, and Don Heck. *The Avengers* #29–30. *Essential Avengers*. Vol. 2. Marvel Worldwide, 2000.
Lee, Stan, and Don Heck. *Tales of Suspense* #57. Marvel, 1964.
Lee, Stan, and Don Heck. *Tales of Suspense* #64. Marvel, 1965.
Lee, Stan, Don Rico, and Don Heck. *Tales of Suspense* #52. Marvel, 1964.
Lee, Stan, H.E. Huntley and Jack Kirby. *Tales to Astonish* #44. Marvel, 1963.
Lee, Stan, and Jack Kirby. *Fantastic Four* #7. Marvel, 1962.
Lee, Stan, and Jack Kirby. *X-Men* #1. Marvel, 1963.
Lee, Stan, N. Korok, and Don Heck. *Tales of Suspense* #53. 1964. *Black Widow: The Sting of the Widow*, edited by Jennifer Grunwald. Marvel, 2009.
Levitz, Paul, and Joe Staton. *DC Super-Stars* #17. DC Comics, 1977.
Linsner, Joseph Michael. *Cry for Dawn* #1. Sirius Entertainment, 1989.
Liu, Dennis, and Jason Piperberg. *Raising Dion*. Indy Planet, 2018. http://www.indyplanet.us/raising-dion-1.
Liu, Marjorie, and Danni Luo. *X-23* #15–16. Marvel, 2011.
Liu, Marjorie, and Mike Perkins. *Astonishing X-Men: Northstar*. Marvel, 2013.
Liu, Marjorie, and Mike Perkins. *Astonishing X-Men: Weaponized*. Marvel, 2013.
Liu, Marjorie, and Phil Noto. *X-23* #21. Marvel, 2012.
Liu, Marjorie, and Ryan Stegman. *X-23* #9. Marvel, 2011.
Liu, Marjorie, and Will Conrad. *X-23, Vol. 1: The Killing Dream*. Marvel, 2011.
Maggin, Elliot, and Bob Oksner. "The Secret of the Smiling Swordsman." *Shazam* #19. 1975. *Showcase Presents Shazam!* DC Comics, 2006, pp. 346–352.
Mantlo, Bill, and Ed Hannigan. *Peter Parker, the Spectacular Spider-Man* #64. Marvel, 1982.
Marston, William Moulton, and Harry G. Peter. *Sensation Comics* #7. June 1942. *The Wonder Woman Chronicles Vol. 1*. DC Comics, 2010.
Marston, William Moulton, and Harry G. Peter. *Sensation Comics* #22. DC Comics, 1943.
Marston, William Moulton, and Harry G. Peter. *Wonder Woman* #1. *The Wonder Woman Chronicles Vol. 1*. DC Comics, 2010.
Meskin, Mort, and Jerry Robinson. *Black Terror* #23. 1948. Madrid, *Vixens* 72–81.
Miller, Frank. *Daredevil Visionaries—Frank Miller, Vol. 2* (Daredevil #168–182). Marvel, 2002.
Miller, Frank, and Bill Sienkiewicz. *Elektra: Assassin*. Marvel, 2003.
Miller, Frank, and Dave Gibbons. *The Life and Times of Martha Washington in the Twenty-first Century*. 1994–1997. Dark Horse Comics, 2010.
Miller, Frank, and Klaus Janson. *Daredevil* #168, #174, #190. Marvel, 1981–1983.
Milligan, Peter, and Salvador Larroca. *X-Men: Bizarre Love Triangle*. Marvel, 2005.
Moore, Alan, and Brian Bolland. *Batman: The Killing Joke: The Deluxe Edition*. 1988. DC Comics, 2008.
Morrison, Grant, et al. *Seven Soldiers of Victory*, vol. 1–4. DC, 2006–2007.
Newell, Mindy, and J.J. Birch. *Catwoman: Sister's Keeper*. 1989. DC Comics, 1991.
Nocenti, Ann, Alex Sanchez and Cliff Richards. *The New 52: Katana*. Vol. 1: *Soultaker*. DC Comics, 2014.
North, Ryan, and Erica Henderson. *The Unbeatable Squirrel Girl Vol. 6: Who Run the World? Squirrels*. Marvel, 2017.

222   Primary Sources Cited—Comics and Graphic Novels

Novick, Irving. "Death to the Scarlet Avenger." *Zip Comics* #3. 1940. Madrid, *Vixens*, 36–41.
O'Hara, Allan, Alex Blum and Matt Baker. *Fight Comics* #36. Fiction House, 1945.
Ostrander, John, et al. *Suicide Squad: Apokolips Now* (*Suicide Squad* #31–39). 1989–1990. DC Comics, 2016.
Ostrander, John, et al. *Suicide Squad: Rogues. (Suicide Squad #17–25)*. 1988–1989. DC Comics, 2016.
Ostrander, John, et al. *Suicide Squad: The Nightshade Odyssey. (Suicide Squad #9–16)*. 1988. DC Comics, 2015.
Ostrander, John, et al. *Suicide Squad: Trial by Fire. (Suicide Squad #1–8)*. 1987. DC Comics, 2015.
Pak, Greg, Victor Ibañez, and Scott Hepburn. *Storm: Make It Rain*. Marvel Worldwide, 2015.
Pak, Greg, Victor Ibañez, et al. *Storm: Bring the Thunder*. Marvel, 2015.
Parker, Jeff, and Roger Cruz, et al. *X-Men First Class: Mutant Mayhem*. Marvel, 2008.
Pollack, Rachel, and Ted McKeever. "The Teiresias Wars." *Doom Patrol* #75–79. Vertigo, 1994.
Puckett, Kelley, and Mike Parobeck. "*Batgirl: Day One.*" *Batman Adventures* #12. DC Comics, 1993.
Puckett, Kelley, et al. *Batgirl: Silent Knight*. 2000–2001. DC Comics, 2015.
Pulido, Brian, and Adriano Batista. *Bad Kitty* #1. Chaos! Comics, 2001.
Pulido, Brian, Len Kaminski and Adriano Batista. *Chastity: Shattered* #2. Chaos! Comics, 2001.
Rivera, Gabby, and Joe Quinones. *America Vol. 1: The Life and Times of America Chavez*. Marvel, 2017.
Robbins, Trina, and Chris Gugliotti. *Sensation Comics Featuring Wonder Woman* #17. DC, 2015.
Robinson, James, et al. *Scarlet Witch: The Final Hex*. Marvel, 2017.
Rowell, Rainbow, and Kris Anka. *Runaways: Find Your Way Home*. Marvel, 2018.
Rucka, Greg, and J.H. Williams. *Batwoman: Elegy*. DC Comics, 2010.
Sardina, Martel, and Sarah Becan. "The Wraiths of Roseland." Hickman, pp. 26–29.
Sekowsky, Mike. *Adventure Comics* #402. DC Comics, 1971.
Shooter, Jim, and J.G Jones. *Inherit the Earth* (*Fatale* #1–6, *Powers That Be* #1 and *Shadow State* #1–2). Broadway Comics, 1996.
Simone, Gail, and Terry and Rachel Dodson. *Wonder Woman: Ends of the Earth*. DC Comics, 2009.
Simone, Gail, et al. *Birds of Prey: The Death of Oracle*. DC Comics, 2011.
Simonson, Louise, June Brigman, et al. *Power Pack Classic Vol. 1*. 1984–1985. Marvel, 2009.
Slott, Dan, and Paul Pelletier. *G.L.A.: Misassembled*. Marvel, 2005.
Starlin, Jim, and Alan Davis. *Guardians of the Galaxy: Mother Entropy*. Marvel, 2017.
Starlin, Jim, George Pérez and Ron Lim. *The Infinity Gauntlet*. 1991. Marvel Worldwide, 2013.
Taylor, Tom, and Leonard Kirk. *All-New Wolverine: Immune*. Marvel, 2017.
Thomas, Roy, and Don Heck. *The Avengers* Vol. 1 #36–37. 1967. *Essential Avengers*. Vol. 2. Marvel Worldwide, 2000.
Thomas, Roy, and George Bell. *The Avengers* Vol. 1 #43. 1967. *Essential Avengers*. Vol. 2. Marvel Worldwide, 2000.
Thomas, Roy, and John Buscema. *The Avengers* Vol. 1 #76. Marvel, 1970.
Thomas, Roy, and John Buscema. *The Avengers* Vol. 1 #83. Marvel, 1970.
Thompson, Kelly, and Carmen Carnero. *Captain Marvel Vol. 1: Re-Entry*. Marvel, 2019.
Thompson, Kelly, et al. *Hawkeye: Anchor Points*. Marvel, 2016.
Tomasi, Peter, and Fernando Pasarin. *Outsiders* vol. 4, #24–25. DC Comics, 2010.
V, Jennifer, and Sarah "Neila" Elkins. "Spoon Bender." Hickman, pp. 60–63.
Van Lente, Fred, and Gurihiru. *Power Pack: Day One*. Marvel, 2008.
Van Lente, Fred, Ron Lim and Agustin Padilla. *Marvel's the Avengers: Black Widow Strikes*. Marvel Worldwide, 2012.
Vasquez, Deborah Kuetzpalin. "Citlali, La Chicana Superhero." *La Voz De Esperanza*. San Antonio, TX (Feb. 2002): 8–9.
Vaughan, Brian K., and Steve Scott. *JLA Annual* #4. DC Comics, 1997.

Vaughn, Brian K., and Jorge Lucas. *Mystique: Drop Dead Gorgeous (Mystique 1–6)*. Marvel Entertainment: 2004.
Waid, Mark, and Humberto Ramos. *Champions: Change the World*. Marvel, 2017.
Waid, Mark, et al. *JLA: Year One*. DC Comics, 1999.
Wein, Len, and Dave Cockrum *Giant Size X-Men #1*. Marvel, 1975.
Whitley, Jeremy, and Elsa Charretier. *The Unstoppable Wasp Vol. 1, Unstoppable!* Marvel, 2017.
Whitley, Jeremy, and Elsa Charretier. *The Unstoppable Wasp Vol. 2: Agents of G.I.R.L.* Marvel, 2018.
Wilson, G. Willow, et al. *Ms. Marvel: Civil War II*. Marvel, 2016.
Wilson, G. Willow, et al. *Ms. Marvel: Mecca*. Marvel, 2017.
Winick, Judd, et al. *Outsiders: The Good Fight (Outsiders #34–41)*. DC, 2006.
Wolfman, Marv, and George Pérez. *Crisis on Infinite Earths*. DC Comics, 1985.
Wolfman, Marv, and George Pérez. *The New Teen Titans #1–3*. DC Comics, 1981.
Wolfman, Marv, and George Pérez. *New Teen Titans #23–28*. DC Comics, 1982.
Wolfram, Amy, and Karl Kerschl. *Teen Titans Year One*. DC Comics, 2008.
Yang, Jeff, Parry Shen, Keith Chow and Jerry Ma, editors. *Secret Identities: The Asian American Superhero Anthology*. New Press, 2009.
Yang, Jeff, Parry Shen, Keith Chow and Jerry Ma, editors. *Secret Identities Volume 2: Shattered*. New Press, 2012.
Yost, Christopher, and Diogenes Neves. *X-Men: Worlds Apart*. Marvel Entertainment, 2009.
Zolnerowich, Dan, and Bill Quackenbush. *Blackhawk #37*. Quality Comics, 1951.

Film

The Avengers. Directed by Joss Whedon. Performed by Scarlet Johannsen, Robert Downey, Jr., Chris Hemsworth. Paramount Pictures, 2012. DVD.
Avengers: Age of Ultron. Directed by Joss Whedon. Performed by Scarlet Johannsen, Robert Downey, Jr., Chris Hemsworth. Walt Disney Studios Home Entertainment, 2015. DVD.
Batman and Robin. Directed by Joel Schumacher. Warner Bros, 1997.
Batman: Bad Blood. Directed by Jay Oliva. Warner Home Video, 2016.
Batman: The Killing Joke. Warner Bros, 2016. DVD.
Guardians of the Galaxy. Directed by James Gunn. Disney Studios, 2014.
The Incredibles. Directed by Brad Bird. Walt Disney Home Entertainment, 2004. DVD.
The Powerpuff Girls: The Movie. Warner Home Video, 2002.
Son of Batman. Directed by Ethan Spaulding. Warner Home Video, 2014
Suicide Squad. Directed by David Ayer. Warner Bros, 2016.
X-Men: Days of Future Past. Directed by Bryan Singer. 20th Century Fox, 2014.
X-Men: First Class. Directed by Matthew Vaughn. 20th Century Fox, 2011. DVD.
X-Men: The Last Stand. Directed by Brett Ratner. Performed by Hugh Jackman, Halle Berry, Ian McKellan, and Famke Jannsen. 20th Century Fox, 2006. DVD.

Prose

Banas, Danielle. *The Supervillain and Me*. Swoon Reads, 2018.
Cabot, Meg. *Vanished*. Simon Pulse, 2010.
Claremont, Chris. *X-Men: The Last Stand* (novelization). Random House, 2006.
Daniels, April. *Dreadnaught*. Diversion Books, 2017.
Grossman, Austin. *Soon I Will Be Invincible*. Random House, 2007.
Kurzweil, Ray. *Danielle: Chronicles of a Superheroine*. Illustrated by Amy Kurzweil. WordFire Press, 2019.
Lee, C.B. *Not Your Sidekick*. Interlude Press, 2016.
Maas, Sarah J. *Catwoman: Soulstealer*. Random House, 2018.
Martin, George R.R., et al. *Wild Cards Volume 20: Suicide Kings*. Tor, 2009.
Spector, Caroline. "Lies My Mother Told Me." *Dangerous Women*, edited by George R. R. Martin and Gardner Dozois. Tor, 2013, pp. 647–699.
Valente, Catherynne M. *The Refrigerator Monologues*. Saga Press, 2017.
Yee. Lisa. *Bumblebee at Super Hero High (DC Super Hero Girls)*. Random House, 2018.

Television

Adler, Ali, Greg Berlanti and Andrew Kreisberg, creators. *Supergirl* Season 1. CBS, 2015–2016.

Berlanti, Greg, Marc Guggenheim and Andrew Kreisberg, creators. *Arrow.* The CW Television Network. 2012.

Berlanti, Greg, Marc Guggenheim, Andrew Kreisberg and Phil Klemmer, creators. *DC's Legends of Tomorrow.* The CW Television Network. 2016.

Goddard, Drew, creator. *Daredevil.* Netflix, 2015–2016.

Goldsman, Akiva, Geoff Johns and Greg Berlanti. *Titans.* DC Universe, 2018.

Gough, Alfred, and Miles Millar, creators. *Smallville.* The CW, 2001–2011.

Helbig, Grace, and Hannah Hart, creators. *Electra Woman & Dyna Girl.* Sony Pictures Home Entertainment, 2016.

Kalogridis, Laeta, creator. *Birds of Prey: The Complete Series.* Warner Home Video, 2002–2003.

Kring, Tim, creator. *Heroes.* NBC, 2006–2010.

Krofft, Sid, and Marty, creators. *Electra Woman and Dyna Girl.* Krofft Supershow, 1976–1977.

Markus, Christopher, and Stephen McFeely, creators. *Agent Carter Season One.* ABC. 2015.

Prescott, Norm, Lou Scheimer, Dick Rosenbloom, creators. *The Secrets of Isis—The Complete Series.* 1975–1977. Bci/Eclipse, 2007.

Rashid, Aaron Haroon, creator. *Burka Avenger.* Nickelodeon Pakistan, 2013–2016. Television.

Ross, Stanley Ralph, creator. *Wonder Woman.* ABC and CBS, 1975–1979.

Semple, Lorenzo, Jr., and William Dozier, creators. *Batman.* ABC, 1966–1968.

Sugar, Rebecca, creator. *Steven Universe.* Cartoon Network, 2013–2019.

Timm, Bruce, Paul Dini and Mitch Brian, creators. *Batman: The Animated Series.* Warner Brothers, 1992–1995.

Whedon, Joss, creator. *Buffy the Vampire Slayer:* The WB and UPN, 1997–2002.

Secondary Sources Cited

Alaniz, José. *Death, Disability, and the Superhero.* University Press of Mississippi, 2014.
Aldama, Frederick Luis. *Latinx Superheroes in Mainstream Comics.* University of Arizona Press, 2017.
Alexander, Dorian L. "Faces of Abjectivity: The Uncanny Mystique and Transsexuality." *Gender and the Superhero Narrative,* edited by Michael Goodrum, Tara Prescott-Johnson, Philip Smith. Univ. Press of Mississippi, 2018.
Amash, Jim, and Eric Nolen-Weathngton, editors. "Part One: Meet Matt Baker: Baker of Cheesecake: An Appreciation of Matt Baker, Good Girl Artist Supreme." *Matt Baker: The Art of Glamour.* TwoMorrows Publishing, 2012. http://www.twomorrows.com/media/MattBakerPreview.pdf.
Andrivet, Sébastien. "Janissary—Turkish Super-Hero," *Writeups,* 16 July 2013, https://www.writeups.org/janissary-dc-comics-turkish-hero.
Arjana, Sophia Rose. "Muslim Women in Western Popular Culture," *Veiled Superheroes: Islam, Feminism, and Popular Culture,* Lexington Books, 2017, pp. 1–22.
Austin, Allan W., and Patrick L. Hamilton. *All New, All Different? A History of Race and the American Superhero.* University of Texas Press, 2019.
Bajac-Carter, Maja, Norma Jones and Bob Batchelo, editors. *Heroines of Film and Television: Portrayals in Popular Culture,* Rowman and Littlefield, 2014.
Bardugo, Leigh "We Are Not Amazons." Mignogna, pp. 151–161.
Barr, Marleen S., editor. *Future Females, the Next Generation.* Rowman and Littlefield, 2000.
Barsamian, Edward. "Actress Letitia Wright on Transforming Into a Superhero for *Black Panther.*" *Vogue,* 18 Jan. 2018. https://www.vogue.com/article/letitia-wright-black-panther-vogue-february-2018-issue.
Baumgardner, J., and A. Richards. *Manifesta: Young Women, Feminism and the Future.* Farrar, Strauss and Giroux. 2000.
Beard, Jim. "WonderCon 2012: Captain Marvel." *Marvel,com,* 17 Mar. 2012. http://marvel.com/news/ comics/ 18290/ wondercon_ 2012_ captain_ marvel.
Black, Bill. *Golden-Age Greats Volume Six: Fighting Females of the Golden Age of Comics.* AC Comics/Paragon Publishers, 1995.
Bolen, Jean Shinoda. *Goddesses in Everywoman.* Quill, 2004.
Bradley, Allison Mae. "Pin-ups and the DC Bombshells: Reenlisted." 47th Annual Pop Culture Association-American Culture Association, 12–15 April 2017, Marriott Marquis Marina, San Diego, CA. Conference Presentation.
Brown, Jeffrey A. *Dangerous Curves: Action Heroines, Gender, Fetishism, and Popular Culture.* University of Mississippi, 2011.
_____. *The Modern Superhero in Film and Television.* Taylor & Francis, 2017.
_____. "Supermoms? Maternity and the Monstrous-feminine in Superhero Comics." Gibson, Huxley and Ormod, pp. 185–196.
Brownie, Barbara. *The Superhero Costume (Dress, Body, Culture).* Bloomsbury, 2015.
Bullock, Lauren. "The Killing Joke: My Trauma Is Not Your Punchline." Black Nerd Prob-

lems, 15 Mar. 2016. http://blacknerdproblems.com/the-killing-joke-my-trauma-is-not-your-punchline.

Busnardo, Rachel. "*Steven Universe*: A Gender Fusion Buffet on Cartoon Network." *The Thought Erotic*, 2 Mar. 2016. https://thethoughterotic.com/2016/03/02/steven-universe-a-gender-fusion-buffet-on-cartoon-network.

Campbell, Joseph, with Bill Moyers. *The Power of Myth*, edited by Betty Sue Flowers. Doubleday, 1988.

Caniff, Milton. *Milton Caniff: Conversations*, edited by Robert C. Harvey. University Press of Mississippi, 2002

Captain Marvel: The Official Movie Special. Titan, 2019.

Carter, Lynda, et al. "Beauty, Brawn, and Bulletproof Bracelets: A Wonder Woman Retrospective." *Wonder Woman: The Complete First Season*. Warner Home Video, 2004.

Casey, Joe. "Playing God and Discovering My Own Mutanity." Wein.

Cavna, Michael. "RIP, Yvonne Craig: As Original Batgirl, She Smartly High-kicked Her Way to Stardom." *Washington Post*, 19 Aug. 2015. https://www.washingtonpost.com/news/comic-riffs/wp/2015/08/19/rip-yvonne-craig-as-original-batgirl-she-smartly-high-kicked-her-way-to-stardom.

Chatterjee, Rhitu. "India's New Comic Book Hero Fights Rape, Rides on the Back of a Tiger." *NPR*, 16 Dec. 2014. http://www.npr.org/sections/goatsandsoda/2014/12/16/371209381/indias-new-comic-book-hero-fights-rape-rides-on-the-back-of-a-tiger.

Cink, Lorraine. *Powers of a Girl*. Illustrated by Alice X. Zhang. Marvel, 2019.

Coggan, Devan. "Brie Larson, Samuel L. Jackson Blast to the Past with EW's Captain Marvel Issue." *EW*, 28 Feb. 2019. https://ew.com/movies/2019/02/28/captain-marvel-issue-brie-larson-samuel-l-jackson-90s.

Cook, Marcy. "Ten Rules for Making a Modern Transgender Superhero." *The Mary Sue*, 9 Jan. 2015. http://www.themarysue.com/modern-trans-superhero.

Cotton, Mike. "Last Call: Preparing for Retirement, Alan Moore Reflects on His Accomplishments." *Wizard Universe*, 11 May 2006. http://www.wizarduniverse.com.

Cronin, Brian. *Was Superman a Spy?* Plume, 2009.

Davis, Blair. "Bare Chests, Silver Tiaras and Removable Afros: The Visual Design of Black Comic Book Superheroes." *The Blacker the Ink: Constructions of Black Identity in Comics and Sequential Art*, edited by Frances Gateward and John Jennings. Rutgers, 2015, pp. 193–214.

DeCandido, Keith R. A. "Pryde and Joy." Wein.

DiPaolo, Marc Edward. "Wonder Woman as World War II Veteran, Camp Feminist Icon, and Male Sex Fantasy." *The Amazing Transforming Superhero! Essays on the Revision of Characters in Comic Books, Film and Television*, edited by Terrence R. Wandtke. McFarland, 2007, pp. 151–173.

Disbrow, Jay. *Alter Ego*, vol. 21, no. 3, Feb 2003.

Douglas, Susan J. *Enlightened Sexism*. Times, 2010.

Dyer, Ben, editor. *Supervillains and Philosophy: Sometimes, Evil Is Its Own Reward*. Open Court, 2009.

Emad, Mitra C. "Reading Wonder Woman's Body: Mythologies of Gender and Nation." *the Journal of Popular Culture*, vol. 39, no. 6, 2006, pp. 954–984.

Erhart, Itir, and Hande Eslen-Ziya. "Janissary: An Orientalist Heroine or a Role Model for Muslim Women?" Bajac-Carter et al.

Ewing, Al, Kenneth Rocafort and Christian Ward. *The Ultimates: Start with the Impossible*. Marvel, 2016.

Faludi, Susan. *Backlash: The Undeclared War Against American Women*. 1991. Three Rivers Press, 2006.

Florence, Brandi L. "Busting Out All Over: The Portrayal of Superheroines in American Superhero Comics from the 1940s to the 2000s." M.S. thesis. University of North Carolina at Chapel Hill, April 2002.

Foresman, Galen. "Making the A-List." Dyer, pp. 23–30.

Framke, Caroline. "Why Shuri, Black Panther's Teen Girl Genius, Is Marvel's Most Promising Character in Ages." *Vox*, 16 Mar. 2018. https://www.vox.com/culture/2018/2/20/17030266/black-panther-shuri-letitia-wright-best.

Frankel, Valerie Estelle. *Buffy and the Heroine's Journey*. McFarland, 2012.
_____. *From Girl to Goddess: The Heroine's Journey Through Myth and Legend*. McFarland, 2010.
_____. "Introduction." *Fourth Wave Feminism in Science Fiction and Fantasy: Volume 1. Essays on Film Representations, 2012–2019*. McFarland, 2019, pp 1–10.
Gallagher, Ashley. "Strong in the Real Way: *Steven Universe* and the Shape of Masculinity to Come." *BitchFlicks* 24 June 2015. http://www.btchflcks.com/2015/06/strong-in-the-real-way-steven-universe-and-the-shape-of-masculinity-to-come.html.
Galvan, Margaret. "From Kitty to Cat: Kitty Pryde and the Phases of Feminism." *The Ages of the X-Men: Essays on the Children of the Atom in Changing Times*, edited by Joseph J. Darowski. McFarland, 2014, pp. 46–59.
Gatta, Oriana. "Comic Convergence: Toward a Prismatic Rhetoric for Composition Studies." Ph.D. dissertation, Georgia State University, 2014. http://scholarworks.gsu.edu/english_diss/130.
George, Demetra. *Mysteries of the Dark Moon: The Healing Power of the Dark Goddess*. HarperCollins, 1992.
Gianola, Gabriel, and Janine Coleman. "The Gwenaissance: Gwen Stacy and the Progression of Women in Comics." *Gender and the Superhero Narrative*, edited by Michael Goodrum, Tara Prescott, and Philip Smith. University Press of Mississippi, 2018, pp 251–283.
Gibson, Mel, David Huxley and Joan Ormrod. *Superheroes and Identities*. Routledge, Taylor & Francis Group, 2015.
Gillis, Stacy, Gillian Howie and Rebecca Munford, editors. *Third Wave Feminism: A Critical Exploration*. Palgrave Macmillan, 2007.
Gleiberman, Owen. "Film Review: Captain Marvel." *Variety*, 5 Mar. 2019. https://variety.com/2019/film/reviews/captain-marvel-review-brie-larson-samuel-l-jackson-1203154542.
Goulart, Ron. *Comic Book Culture*. Collectors' Press, 2000.
_____. *Great History of Comic Books*. Contemporary Books, 1986.
Guzzo, Gary. "How Are Heroes Born?" *JimShooter.com*, Jan. 2012. http://jimshooter.com/2012/01/more-about-broadway-and-fatale.html.
Haines, Rebecca C. "Power(Puff) Feminism: The Powerpuff Girls as a Site of Strength and Collective Action in the Third Wave." *Women in Popular Culture: Representation, Meaning, and Media*, edited by Marian Meyers. Hampton Press, 2008, pp. 211–235.
Hanley, Tim. *The Many Lives of Catwoman: The Felonious History of a Feline Fatale*. Chicago Review Press, 2017.
_____. *Wonder Woman Unbound: The Curious History of the World's Most Famous Heroine*. Chicago Review Press, 2014.
Haraway, Donna Jeanne. *Simians, Cyborgs and Women: The Reinvention of Nature*. Free Association, 1991.
Harris, Anita. *Future Girl: Young Women in the Twenty-First Century*. Routledge, 2004.
Helford, Elyce Rae, Shiloh Carroll, Sarah Gray, Michael R. Howard, editors. *The Woman Fantastic in Contemporary American Media Culture*, University Press of Mississippi, 2016.
Housel, Rebecca. "X-Women and X-istence." Housel and Wisnewski, pp. 85–98.
Housel, Rebecca, and J. Jeremy Wisnewski, editors. *X-Men and Philosophy: Astonishing Insight and Uncanny Argument in the Mutant X-Verse*. John Wiley and Sons, 2009.
Hudson, Laura. "DC Introduces First Transgender Character in Mainstream Comics." *Wired*, 10 Apr. 2013. http://www.wired.com/2013/04/transgender-dc-comics-batgirl.
Inness, Sherrie A. *Tough Girls: Women Warriors and Wonder Women in Popular Culture*. University of Pennsylvania Press, 1999.
The International Catalog of Superheroes. 2002. http://www.internationalhero.co.uk.
Isaacs, Susan. *Brave Dames and Wimpettes: What Women Are Really Doing on Page and Screen*. Ballantine, 1999.
Jankiewicz, Pat. "Quinn-tessentials. Arleen Sorkin Gets a Kick Out of Being the Joker's Wench." *Starlog*. http://harley-quinn.com/oldsite/ainterview.html.
Jarema, Kerri. "Gabby Rivera Brings Latinx Superheroine America Chavez to Life in New Marvel Series." *Bustle*, 1 Mar. 2017. https://www.bustle.com/p/gabby-rivera-brings-latinx-superheroine-america-chavez-to-life-in-new-marvel-series-exclusive-interview-40982.
Jehanzeb, "The Objectification of Women in Comic Books." *Fantasy Magazine*, 2008. http://

www.fantasy-magazine.com/non-fiction/articles/the-objectification-of-women-in-graphic-novels.

Jung, Carl. "Psychological Aspects of the Mother Archetype." *Collected Works* vol. 9, pt. 1, 2nd ed., translated by R. F.C. Hull. Princeton University Press, 1968, pp. 75–112.

____. "Psychology and Religion: West and East." *Collected Works* vol. 11, 2nd ed., translated by R. F.C. Hull. Princeton University Press, 1968, pp. 113–147.

Kaklamanidou, Betty. "The Mythos of Patriarchy in the X-Men Films." *The 21st Century Superhero*, edited by Richard J. Gray II and Betty Kaklamanidou. McFarland, 2011, pp. 61–74.

Kakoudaki, Despina. "Pinup and Cyborg: Exaggerated Gender and Artificial Intelligence." Barr 165–195.

Kanayama, Kelly. "Women in Comics." *Comic Heroes*, 2017, pp. 34–43.

Karras, Irene. "The Third Wave's Final Girl: Buffy the Vampire Slayer." *Thirdspace*, vol. 1 no. 2, March 2002.

Kaveney, Roz. *Superheroes! Capes and Crusaders in Comics and Films*. I.B. Tauris, 2008.

Kirkpatrick, Ellen. "TransFormers: 'Identity' Compromised." *Cinema Journal*, vol. 55, no. 1, Fall 2015, pp. 124–133.

Klein, Alan M. *Little Big Men: Bodybuilding Subculture and Gender Construction*. SUNY Press, 1993.

Knight, Gladys L. *Female Action Heroes: A Guide to Women in Comics, Video Games, Film, and Television*. Greenwood, 2010.

Kowalska, Monika. "Interview with Rachel Pollack." *The Heroines of My Life*, 15 Dec. 2013. https://theheroines.blogspot.com/2013/12/interview-with-rachel-pollack.html.

Kyle, Catherine Bailey. "Her Story, Too: Final Fantasy X, Revolutionary Girl Utena, and the Feminist Hero's Journey." Bajac-Carter et al., pp. 131–146.

Lavigne, Carlen. "'I'm Batman' (and You Can Be Too): Gender and Constrictive Play in the Arkham Game Series." *Cinema Journal*, vol. 55, no. 1, Fall 2015, pp. 133–141.

Lee, Stan. *The Superhero Women*. Simon & Shuster, 1977.

Leon, Melissa. "How Brie Larson's *Captain Marvel* Made Angry White Men Lose Their Damn Minds." *The Daily Beast*, 6 Mar. 2019. https://www.thedailybeast.com/how-brie-larsons-captain-marvel-made-angry-white-men-lose-their-damn-minds.

Leonard, Linda Schierse. *Meeting the Madwoman: Empowering the Feminine Spirit*. Bantam, 1994.

Madrid, Mike. *The Supergirls: Fashion, Feminism, Fantasy, and the History of Comic Book Heroines*. Exterminating Angel Press, 2009.

____. *Vixens, Vamps & Vipers: Lost Villainesses of Golden Age Comics*. Exterminating Angel Press, 2014.

Mann, Nicola. "From SuperOther to SuperMother: The Journey Toward Liberty." Helford et al. pp. 101–118.

Marston, William Moulton. *Emotions of Normal People*. Harcourt, Brace, 1928.

____. "Letter to M.C. Gaines Feb. 20, 1943." *MS. Wonder Woman Letters*, 1941–1945. SILD-LHST.

____. "Women: Servants for Civilization." *Tomorrow*, Mar. 1942: 42–45.

Mata, Irene. *Domestic Disturbances: Re-Imagining Narratives of Gender, Labor, and Immigration*. University of Texas Press, 2014.

Maverick, Chris. "Oracle of the Invisible: Sexual Assault and Rape in *The Killing Joke*." 47th Annual Pop Culture Association–American Culture Association, 12–15 April 2017, Marriott Marquis Marina, San Diego, CA. Conference Presentation.

Mignogna, Lisa, editor. *Last Night, a Superhero Saved My Life*. Thomas Dunne Books, 2016.

Misiroglu, Gina. *The Superhero Book: The Ultimate Encyclopedia of Comic-Book Icons and Hollywood Heroes*. Visible Ink Press, 2004.

Misiroglu, Gina, and Michael Eury. *The Supervillain Book: The Evil Side of Comics and Hollywood*. Omnigraphics, 2006.

Morris, Jon. *The League of Regrettable Sidekicks*. Quirk Books, 2018.

____. *The League of Regrettable Superheroes: Oddball Criminals from Comic Book History*. Quirk Books, 2017.

____. *The Legion of Regrettable Supervillains: Oddball Criminals from Comic Book History*. Quirk Books, 2017.

Morrison, Grant. *Supergods: What Masked Vigilantes, Miraculous Mutants, and a Sun God from Smallville Can Teach Us About Being Human*. Spiegel & Grau, 2011.
Morse, Ben. "The X-Perts: Kitty Pryde. Jason Aaron, Kieron Gillen, Victor Gischler, Christos Gage and Nick Lowe Discuss the Heart of the X-Men." *Marvel.com*, 10 Nov. 2011. http://marvel.com/news/comics/17040/the_x-perts_kitty_pryde.
Moseley, Daniel. "The Joker's Comedy of Existence." Dyer, pp. 127–136.
Muir, John Kenneth. *The Encyclopedia of Superheroes on Film and Television*. McFarland, 2004.
Murray, Ross. "The Feminine Mystique: Feminism, Sexuality, Motherhood." Gibson, Huxley and Ormod, pp. 173–184.
Neel, Aly "Burka Avenger, Pakistan's New Superhero." *The Washington Post*, 8 Jan. 2013. https://www.washingtonpost.com/blogs/she-the-people/wp/2013/08/01/burka-avenger-pakistans-new-superhero/?noredirect=on&utm_term=.ec1f0f118116.
Neumann, Caryn E. "Babes and Crones: Women Growing Old in Comics." *Aging Heroes: Growing Old in Popular Culture*, edited by Norma Jones and Bob Batchelor. Rowman & Littlefield, 2015, pp. 119–127.
Neuwirth, Allan. "Whopping Some Cartoon Ass, Powerpuff Style." *Makin' Toons: Inside the Most Popular Animated TV Shows and Movies*. Allworth Press, 2003, pp. 12–13.
Nicholson, Hope. *The Spectacular Sisterhood of Superwomen*. Quirk Books, 2017.
O'hara, Helen. "Captain Marvel Review." *Empire Online*, 5 Mar. 2019. https://www.empireonline.com/movies/captain-marvel/review.
Ormrod, Joan. "*Body Issues in Wonder Woman 90–100*." Helford et al., pp. 159–176.
Ostrander, John. "New Wars, New Boundaries." Dyer, pp. 113–123.
Packer, Sharon. *Superheroes and Superegos: Analyzing the Minds Behind the Masks*. ABC-Clio, 2010.
Pearson, Ben. "Director Ryan Coogler Talks *Black Panther*'s Unbroken Casino Fight Shot, Obama's Influence, and More." *Slash Film*, 15 Feb. 2018. https://www.slashfilm.com/black-panther-interview.
Pearson, Carol S., and Katherine Pope. *The Female Hero in American and British Literature*. R.R. Bowker, 1981.
Peterson, James Braxton. "Graphic Black Nationalism: Visualizing Political Narratives in the Graphic Novel." *The Rise and Reason of Comics and Graphic Literature: Critical Essays on the Form*, edited by Joyce Goggin and Dan Hassler-Forest. McFarland, 2010, pp. 202–221.
Plant, Sadie. *Zeros and Ones: Digital Women and the New Technoculture*. Fourth Estate, 1997.
Pulliam-Moore, Charles. "The Hero of This Comic Is a Single Black Mother Raising Her Superpowered Son." *Splinter News*, 27 Aug. 2015. https://splinternews.com/the-hero-of-this-comic-book-is-a-single-black-mother-r-1793850363.
Riesman, Abraham. "The Hidden Story of Harley Quinn and How She Became the Superhero World's Most Successful Woman." *Vulture*, 17 Feb. 2015. http://www.vulture.com/2014/12/harley-quinn-dc-comics-suicide-squad.html.
Riviére, Joan. "Womanliness as Masquerade." *Formations of Fantasy*, edited by Victor Burgin, James Donald, and Cora Kaplan. Methuen, 1986.
Robbins, Trina "Babes in Arms." San Francisco Comic Con, 2–4 Sept. 2016. San Francisco, CA.
_____. *The Great Women Superheroes*. Kitchen Sink Press, 1996.
Robinson, Lillian S. *Wonder Women*. Routledge, 2004.
Sarkeesian, Anita. "Damsel in Distress (Part 1) Tropes Vs Women." *Feminist Frequency*, 7 Mar. 2013 http://feministfrequency.com/2013/03/07/damsel-in-distress-part-1.
_____. "Damsel in Distress (Part 2) Tropes Vs Women." *Feminist Frequency*, 28 May 2013. http://feministfrequency.com/2013/05/28/damsel-in-distress-part-2-tropes-vs-women.
Schmidt, Victoria. *45 Master Characters*. Writer's Digest Books, 2007.
Shoemaker, Deanna. "Cartoon Transgressions: Citlali, la Chicana Super Hero as Community Activist." *Liminalities: A Journal of Performance Studies* vol. 7, no. 1, 2011. http://liminalities.net/7-1/Citlali.pdf.
Sims, Chris. "*Tarot #63* Explains What Breasts Are for to Naked Lady Werewolves." *Comics Alliance*, 19 Aug. 2010. http://comicsalliance.com/tarot-63-naked-werewolves.
Singer, Marc. "Time of Harvest." *Grant Morrison: Combining the Worlds of Contemporary Culture*. University Press of Mississippi, 2012, pp. 221–250.

Stasia, Cristina Lucia. "My Guns Are in the Fendi: The Postfeminist Female Action Hero." Gillis et. al, pp. 237–249.
Stevens, J. Richard. "Of Jungle Queens and Amazons: Marvel's She-Hulk as Poststructuralist Feminist Icon." Helford, et al., pp. 13–38.
Stryker, Susan. "Transgender Feminism." Gillis et al., pp 59–70.
Stuller, Jennifer K. *Ink-Stained Amazons and Cinematic Warriors*. I.B. Tauris, 2010.
Sullivan, R. Lee. "Batman in a Bustier." *Forbes*, vol. 157, no. 7, 1996, pp. 37–38.
Taylor, Tosha. "The Dragon Lady of Gotham: Feminine Power, the Mythical East, and Talia Al Ghul." Helford et al., pp. 61–81.
Thurm, Eric. "The New *Powerpuff Girls* Is So Self-Conscious About Its Feminism That It Forgets What Made the Original Great." *Slate*, 4 Apr. 2016. http://www.slate.com/blogs/browbeat/2016/04/04/the_new_powerpuff_girls_leans_so_hard_into_self_conscious_feminism_that.html.
Ventura, Varla. *Sheroes*. Red Wheel Weiser, 1998.
Vidal, Ava. "'Intersectional Feminism.' What the Hell Is It? (And Why You Should Care)." *The Telegraph*, 15 Jan. 2014.
Wein, Len, editor. *The Unauthorized X-Men: SF and Comic Writers on Mutants, Prejudice, and Adamantium*. BenBella, 2005. Kindle Edition.
Wertham, Fredrick. *Seduction of the Innocent*. Rinehart and Co, 1954.
Whaley, Deborah Elizabeth. "Black Cat Got Your Tongue? Catwoman, Blackness, and the Alchemy of Postracialism," *Journal of Graphic Novels and Comics*, vol. 2, no. 1, 2011, pp. 3–23, DOI: 10.1080/21504857.2011.577280.
"Why *Supergirl* Has Earned a Second Season." *TV Guide*, 18 Apr. 2016. http://www.middletowntranscript.com/article/ZZ/20160418/entertainment/304189885.
Wilson, Matt D. "DC and Palmoitti Respond to Criticism of Harley Quinn Contest Page." *Comics Alliance*, 13 Sept. 2013. http://comicsalliance.com/dc-comics-jimmy-palmiotti-respond-criticism-harley-quinn-contest-page.
Woerner, Meredith. "*Steven Universe Guidebook* Spills the Secrets of the Crystal Gems." *io9*, 14 May 2015. http://io9.gizmodo.com/steven-universe-guidebook-spills-the-secrets-of-the-cry-1704470546.
Wolfe, April. "*Captain Marvel* Film Review: Brie Larson Packs a Punch in Effective, Sometimes Obvious, Marvel Saga." *The Wrap*, 5 Mar. 2019. https://www.thewrap.com/captain-marvel-film-review-brie-larson-avengers-mcu.
Woolsey, Angela. "I Need a Hero: How *Supergirl* Could Rescue the DC Cinematic Universe." *The Mary Sue*, 18 Apr. 2016. http://www.themarysue.com/supergirl-batman-v-superman.
Wright, Katheryn. "Her Potential Lies Within: Zoey Redbird's Remarkable Tattoos." *The New Heroines: Female Embodiment and Technology in 21st-Century Popular Culture*. ABC-Clio, 2016, pp. 27–45.
Wright, Megan. "*Steven Universe*: A Superhero Team We Can Believe In." *BitchFlicks*, 26 June 2014. http://www.btchflcks.com/2014/06/steven-universe-a-superhero-team-we-can-believe-in.html.
Yabroff, Jennie. "Holy Hot Flash, Batman!" *Newsweek*, 5 Jan. 2008 http://www.newsweek.com/holy-hot-flash-batman-87089.
Zeisler, Andi. *Feminism and Pop Culture*. Seal Press, 2008.

Index

A-Force 156
abuse 19, 32, 46, 71, 74, 145, 149, 150, 209
adoption 148
Africa 5, 6, 8, 102–106, 126, 168, 169, 182, 185, 195, 198
African-American 58, 73, 163, 202, 203
Agent Carter 3, 158, 217
Alex Danvers 40, 113, 115, 123, 124, 177
Alfred Pennyworth 9, 15, 21, 44, 106, 136, 208
Alysia Yeoh 98
Amanda Waller 2, 191, 192
America Chavez 3, 156–159
amnesia 12, 18
ancestor 176–177; *see also* spirit journey
Angela Asgard's Assassin 108
Ant-Man 3, 17, 18, 189
AntMan and the Wasp 216
Apokolips 192–194
Aquaman 119, 162, 163
Araña 113, 164
Areala the Warrior Nun 37
Argentina 171
Arkham Asylum (game) 109, 150, 151, 187
Arkham City (game) 151
Arrow (TV) 28, 124
Artemis 33, 42, 182, 199
Asian 8, 154, 168, 203–207
assimilation 131, 166
The Atom 45, 155
The Avengers 1, 2, 17–19, 26, 64, 80, 135, 143, 144, 167, 170, 175, 179, 188–190
The Avengers (British) 22
The Avengers (2012 film) 216
Avengers: Age of Ultron 2

bad girl 2, 26, 33–37, 81–87, 90, 178
Bad Kitty 38
Baker, Matt 9
BatGirl (Betty Kane) 15–16
Batgirl (Barbara Gordon) 79, 115, 116, 119, 133

Batgirl (Cassandra Cain) 41, 44- 46
Batgirl (1966 TV) 17, 21, 22
Batman 1–3, 9, 11–17, 21, 28, 30–34, 41–46, 58, 68, 73, 79, 83, 84, 92, 106, 115, 116, 121, 122, 133, 136, 141, 145–151, 154, 155, 162, 163, 176, 186, 187, 193, 202, 207, 213, 217
Batman (1966 TV) 79, 84
Batman and Robin (film) 44, 115, 184
Batman and the Outsiders 41, 176; *see also The Outsiders*
Batman Begins 45
Batman Returns 84, 92, 186, 216
Batman v Superman 2, 65, 121, 122, 216
Batman Year One 152
Batsuit 21, 44, 115
Batwoman (Kate Kane) 3, 4, 13–16, 50, 71, 98, 120, 134, 146, 199, 217
beautiful 1, 5, 9, 13, 15, 23, 44, 67, 79, 82, 85–88, 99, 109, 139, 142, 143, 158, 167–169, 180, 181, 185, 204, 206, 213, 214
Bechdel Test 35, 82
Bendis, Brian Michael 60, 190, 191
Big Barda 79, 194
Big Bertha 168
bikini 37, 81, 87, 125, 131, 132, 145, 203
The Bionic Woman 22, 26
biracial 55, 164, 180
Birds of Prey (comic) 4, 42, 209, 217
Birds of Prey (film) 216
Birds of Prey (TV) 3, 44, 108, 208
bisexual 96, 98, 156
Black Canary 12, 28, 42, 44, 117, 202, 209
Black Cat 66, 67, 199
Black Lightning 3, 183; *see also* Thunder
Black Panther 3, 47, 49, 51, 101–104, 119, 184, 197, 216; *see also* Shuri
Black Widow 1, 134, 142–144, 171, 199, 217
Blackest Night 176
Blackfire 119, 120, 199
Blackhawk 201, 205, 206
Blaxploitation 77

231

Index

Blonde Bomber 69
body image 54, 94, 96, 167, 168, 169; *see also* overweight
bra 5, 24, 33, 35, 38
Brazil 71, 170, 171
breasts 8, 33–38, 73, 82, 132, 146, 193, 195, 216
broken back 33, 37, 42, 82
bronze age 1, 24, 27–29, 31, 78
Bucky 6, 101, 105, 171, 172
Buffy the Vampire Slayer 2, 39, 44, 50, 65, 134, 216
Bumblebee 209
burka 160, 183
Burka Avenger 160, 191

Callisto 196, 197, 199
Campbell, Joseph 179
Captain America 2, 34, 47, 53, 64, 75, 144, 156, 158, 171, 188
Captain America: The Winter Soldier 2
Captain Marvel 3, 47, 48, 50, 52, 53, 61, 124, 135, 183, 216
Captain Marvel (film) 47–53, 216
Carter, Lynda 22, 40, 132
Cat Grant 121, 124
catsuit 1, 21, 22, 81, 82, 85, 91, 142, 144, 146, 152
Catwoman (golden age) 12, 206, 213
Catwoman (1966 TV) 22, 202
Catwoman (Selina Kyle) 10, 12, 13, 38, 68, 79, 83, 84, 86, 92, 100, 116, 141, 152, 184, 186, 187, 199, 201, 203, 207, 216
Catwoman (2004 film) 3, 45, 47, 216, 217
The Champions 183
Charlie's Angels 22, 26, 40, 41, 44, 82
Chastity Marks 37
Cheetah 10, 182, 201
Chinese 68, 206
Chrysalis 170
Circe 199
Citlali 179, 180, 181
Claremont, Chris 19, 60, 78, 88, 109, 111–113, 117, 118, 130, 148, 195, 196, 198, 214, 215
Clayface 164
Cloak and Dagger 114, 217
The Clock 141
Coagula 93–95
Cold War 1, 82, 206
Colleen Wing 1, 77, 78
college 25, 26, 34, 39, 111, 134, 157, 192
computer game 151
Conner, Amanda 131, 140, 151
costume 10–19, 21, 24, 33, 34, 38, 45, 46, 49, 64, 67, 68, 73, 85, 86, 95, 96, 104, 115–117, 131, 132, 133, 136, 139, 143, 150, 152, 154, 159–164, 184, 186, 188, 198, 200, 205, 207, 212

Crisis on Infinite Earths 28, 124
crone 211–214
cross-dressing 99, 213
cyborg 159, 170–175, 184
Cyclops 17, 19, 172, 189, 196, 197

Damien Dahrk 155
Damien, son of Wolverine 174
Damien Wayne 146, 147
damsel 5, 6, 18, 20, 21, 29, 48, 77, 106, 145, 150, 200
Danger Girl 2, 81
Danielle Cage 59, 60, 190
Danielle, Chronicles of a Superheroine 125, 217
Daredevil 2, 24, 25–27, 152, 171
Dark Angel 40, 44
The Dark Knight (film) 28
Dark Phoenix 3, 109, 199, 217
Dark Phoenix (film) 216
date 12, 15, 72, 156, 163, 187
daughter 9, 10, 17, 30, 50, 51, 59, 60, 104, 107, 113, 117, 119, 129, 145, 153, 155, 156, 169, 170, 183, 189–193, 196, 202, 209, 210, 215
Dawn 37
Dawnstar 164
DC Bombshells 4, 70, 98, 164
DC Super Hero Girls 3, 209, 217
DC's Legends of Tomorrow 3, 10, 155, 217
Deadpool 3, 123, 217
Dini, Paul 149, 187
disabled 4, 27, 31, 46, 78, 94, 130
diversity 8, 43, 53, 73, 93, 94, 207, 217
Doctor Poison 201
Doctor Strange 123, 190, 212
Doctor Who 8, 58
dominatrix 12, 154, 203
Doom Patrol 3, 28, 93–97, 217
Doomsday 65, 199, 217
Dragon Lady 1, 154, 203–206
Dreadnaught 100, 217
dresses 1, 6, 11, 22, 34–39, 41, 55, 67–69, 82, 91, 99, 101, 104, 119, 140, 142, 145, 146, 153, 168, 198, 206, 207, 213
Dust 160
dystopian 24, 47, 72, 111

Echo 177
education 191
Electra Woman and Dyna Girl 22, 133–140
Elektra 1, 24–26, 33, 45, 199
Elektra (film) 3, 47, 216
Ellen Ripley 26, 110
Emma Frost 11, 130, 134, 203, 217
empowerment 4, 24, 39, 41, 50, 80, 156, 165
evil son 147

exotic 9, 82, 85, 86, 105, 160, 161, 162, 195, 204, 205, 207
Exterminatrix 154
fangirls 158

Fantastic Four 16, 17, 20, 118, 174; *see also* Invisible Woman
Fantomah 10
Fatale 33–36
father 6, 17, 18, 25, 26, 30, 31, 43, 55, 57, 59, 63, 65, 72, 91, 92, 100, 115–120, 123, 125, 129, 130, 146, 147, 150, 153–155, 171–173, 189, 211–213
Female Furies 193
feminine 6, 7, 10, 12, 18, 20, 22, 23, 25, 26, 35, 39, 41, 43, 44, 55, 61, 62, 65, 66, 68, 71, 85, 90, 127, 129, 141, 143, 149, 167, 180, 214, 215
feminism 1, 2, 10, 12, 20, 22, 23, 27, 29, 33, 39–44, 48–52, 61, 62, 64, 67, 71, 79, 80, 82, 94, 97, 101, 102, 108–112, 121, 125, 170, 174, 187, 190, 195, 196, 198, 217
femme fatale 13, 24, 25, 85, 86, 89, 143, 146, 186, 187, 203, 207
Fiction House 5, 7, 8, 10, 66, 70
Flamebird 16, 134
The Flash 117, 122, 201
fourth wave feminism 43, 47, 49, 51, 99, 101, 102, 104
Fraulein Halunke 145
freedom 2, 24, 29, 62, 67, 68, 72, 75, 76, 79, 86, 126, 145, 183, 184, 196, 199, 200, 202
Freya 64, 65, 196
fridging 27, 29, 31, 32, 217
friendship 10, 44, 78, 96, 125, 140, 188

gadgets 13, 14, 21, 82, 95, 102, 106, 136–139
gender-flipping 2, 48, 55, 91
gender roles 16, 21, 56, 75, 78, 84, 114, 144, 146
genocide 155
Ghostbusters (2016 film) 47, 49, 50, 53, 216
Girl Commandos 66–69, 206
girl power 39, 40, 43, 44, 121
G.L.A. 168
glasses 94, 122, 160, 182, 193
global mindset 40, 134, 161, 182, 183, 185, 198
goddess 37, 62, 65, 79, 129, 175, 180, 182, 183, 187, 195, 196, 198, 209, 215, 217
golden age 8, 17, 66–69, 86, 87, 107, 113, 134, 135, 145, 199, 203, 204, 206, 213, 214, 217
good girl 2, 6, 7, 9, 29, 30, 67, 68, 149, 154
Gotham Girls 100
government 2, 20, 27, 71, 74, 75, 77, 88, 89, 164, 182, 191, 193, 200
grandmother 148, 157, 159, 163, 168, 177, 198

Granny Goodness 194, 199, 215
Green Hornet 69
Green Lantern 27, 161, 201
Guardians of the Galaxy 52, 170, 185, 217
gun 7, 13, 38, 60, 61, 68–70, 81, 85, 95, 116, 119, 138, 142, 154, 178, 181, 193, 202, 204
Gwen Stacy 17, 28, 29

hair 6, 8, 9, 11, 34, 35, 40, 43, 69, 73, 91, 92, 99, 104, 105, 112, 122, 132, 136, 142, 144, 148, 152, 154, 184, 186, 195, 200, 205–207, 211, 213
Haraway, Donna 173, 174
harem outfit 33, 68, 91, 145, 154
Harley Quinn 2–4, 71, 83, 108, 115, 116, 131, 134, 140, 141, 148–151, 199, 208, 209, 216, 217
Harley Quinn (cartoon) 3
Hasmat 170
Hawkeye (Clint Barton) 3, 18, 142–144, 166, 171, 172
Hawkeye (Kate Bishop) 157, 189
headscarf 159, 161, 182
Her Highness 199, 213, 214
Heroes Reborn 173
Hippolyte 107, 214
HitGirl 65, 217
Hitler 158, 201
hotness 168, 169
House of M 44, 130
housewife 14, 20, 21, 31
Hulk 2, 11, 165, 166, 167, 217
Huntress 42, 44, 108, 202, 208, 209
husband 2, 14, 19, 59, 64, 79, 85, 86, 138, 144, 176–178, 192, 198
hypnotize 87, 208

Identity Crisis 45
The Incredibles 2, 59
Infinite Crisis 187
The Inhumans 119, 179, 217
inner voice 158, 159, 172, 175, 176
innocent 37, 59, 75, 76, 90, 115, 150, 155, 163, 164, 182, 188, 190, 199, 201, 208–210, 213
intersectionality 51, 99; *see also* fourth wave
intuitive 126, 171
Invisible Woman (Sue Storm) 1, 12, 20, 21, 60, 189, 203
Iron Fist 77, 78
Iron Man 4, 47, 64, 102, 106, 124, 142, 167, 188
Israeli 171

Jade 183
Jaguar 181
Janissary 159, 160, 161, 162, 163
Japanese 68, 69, 70, 71, 164, 204, 205

Index

Jean Grey 1, 16, 19, 20, 109, 189, 194, 196, 197, 198, 203; *see also* Dark Phoenix
Jessica Jones 2, 59, 130, 188
Jessie Drake 98
joke 2, 18, 40, 44, 102, 103, 122, 132, 151, 166, 217
Joker 30, 31, 32, 46, 149, 150, 151, 199, 200, 202, 204
Jung, Carl 127, 128, 176
Justice League (cartoon) 65, 217
Justice League (comic) 10, 43, 94, 117, 136, 159, 162, 163, 179, 183
Justice Society 20, 70

Kanigher, Robert 15, 187
Karma 117–119
Katana 2, 173–178, 183
The Killing Joke (comic) 27–32
The Killing Joke (2016 cartoon) 32
kiss 16, 19, 20, 32, 34, 43, 56, 63, 86, 87, 111, 114, 116, 124, 132, 154, 166, 180, 184, 212
Kitty Pryde 2, 109–114, 133, 148, 196, 197

Lady Bullseye 152
Lady Deathstrike 172
Lady Satan 68, 70
Lady Shiva 47, 199, 206, 207
Lara Croft 39, 40, 81, 216
Larson, Brie 53
Latin American 156, 157, 164, 179–181
Layla Miller 130
Lazarus 4, 146, 169
leather 14, 44, 49, 50, 64, 195, 203, 208
Lee, Stan 17, 18, 20, 34, 80, 142
Legion of Superheroes 97, 199
The Lego Batman Movie 3
The Lego Movie 45
legs 8, 11, 35, 37, 42, 65, 70, 82, 147, 172, 205, 207, 213
lesbian 10, 16, 56, 71, 91, 96, 98, 130, 183
Lex Luthor 199, 214
lipstick 14, 34, 58, 86, 154
Liu, Marjorie 118, 170–175
Lois & Clark 40
Lois Lane 2, 45, 79
Loki 65, 91, 119, 196, 199, 217
love triangle 125, 212
Luke Cage 130, 188, 191

Mad Love 149, 151
Madam Butterfly 1, 203–205
Madam Doom 84, 144
Madam Fatal 1, 213
Madam Masque 202
Madam Satan 87, 201
Madelyne Pryor 203

madness 31, 32, 72, 93, 146, 149, 150, 166, 176, 178, 187, 206
Magneto 88, 199
makeup 21, 39, 41, 45, 92, 112
Man of Steel 121
Mantis 206–207
Maria Rambeau 50–51
Marston, William Moulton 23, 106, 107, 109
Martha Washington 2, 71–77
Marvel Cinematic Universe 47, 101, 103, 106, 119, 208
Marvel Rising 3, 217
Marvel's Jessica Jones 3, 188, 217
Marvel's The Defenders 78
Mary Jane Watson 2–3
Mary Marvel 7, 68, 113
mask 13, 24, 35, 37, 66–68, 70, 95, 112, 115, 143, 150, 153, 160, 163, 184, 202, 211, 212
Masquerade 97, 143
matriarchy 56
mean girls 126, 127, 128
mentor 47, 48, 50, 94, 112, 116, 135–138, 161, 176, 189, 190, 195, 210, 216
Mexican 164, 182
Middle Eastern 8, 154
Millennials 158
mind-control 123, 147, 155
misogyny 23, 27, 36, 43, 62, 81, 94, 125, 166, 167, 216
Misty Knight 1, 77, 78
Mockingbird 190
Monet 167
monster 10, 12, 17, 19, 59, 104, 109, 111, 115, 117, 129, 133, 136, 147, 158, 164–169, 174, 175, 184, 187, 194
Moon Girl 3, 158, 190
Morgan le Fay 199, 201
Morlocks 113, 114, 148, 185, 196, 197, 214
Morrison, Grant 98, 207
mother 2, 10, 13, 19, 25, 30, 35, 50, 51, 55–61, 64, 72, 99, 103, 107, 109, 113, 118, 119, 123–125, 130, 135, 140, 141, 146, 147, 153, 157, 169, 170, 175, 185–190, 195, 196, 198, 210, 211–215
Mother Goose 1, 213
Mother Hubbard 1, 212, 213
Ms. Marvel (Kamala Khan) 3, 48, 64, 80, 160, 163, 164, 183, 190
multiculturalism 159
Muslim 134, 160–163
My Super Ex-Girlfriend 44–45
Mystique 1, 20, 87–93, 130, 199, 217
mythology 22, 176

naked 11, 30, 31, 36, 38, 73, 78, 83, 87, 88, 132, 187, 210, 217
Native American 164

Index

nature 6, 63, 88, 91, 97, 118, 126, 128, 159, 164, 170, 184, 186, 187, 190, 195, 207, 210
Nazi 5, 23, 66, 68, 70, 73, 82–84, 145, 158, 171, 201, 212, 213
Nebula 119, 170, 199
Netflix 25, 58, 78
Nick Fury 50, 62
Nightwing 146, 183
1940s 1, 8, 11, 22, 23, 67–69, 86, 109
1950s 1, 12, 14, 21, 71
1960s 1, 10, 12, 17, 18, 23, 26, 79, 84, 109, 115, 143
1970s 1, 18, 22–26, 44, 48, 77–79, 110, 136, 195, 202
1980s 24, 26, 27, 82, 108–110, 113, 133, 134, 152, 158, 195
1990s 2, 27, 33, 34, 38–40, 49, 82, 94, 97, 98
The 99 134
Nora Dahrk 155–156
Not Your Sidekick 134, 135, 217

Odin 63–65
Oracle 4, 27, 44, 45, 134, 209
The Outsiders 182; see also *Batman and the Outsiders*
overweight 68, 168; *see also* body image

Pakistan 71, 160, 163, 191
Palmiotti, Jimmy 131, 140, 151
Paradise Island 23, 131
patriarchy 2, 16, 29, 41, 46–48, 51, 52, 62, 65, 76, 79, 90, 97, 130, 143, 152, 165–171, 174, 183, 184, 194, 214, 216
Pepper Potts 217
Pérez, George 182
perfection 17, 18, 21, 30, 42–46, 48, 51, 73, 75, 89, 92, 94, 104, 114, 122, 127, 128, 145, 150, 153, 166, 186, 210
persona 65, 74, 85, 88, 99, 166, 168, 187
Phantom Lady 9, 212
pink 13, 39, 55, 82, 88, 136, 139, 148, 152, 153, 191
pinup girl 1, 9, 11, 67, 71
Plague 214
Platinum 170
Poison Ivy 15, 44, 83, 115, 116, 149, 184, 186, 187, 199, 217
postfeminism 80, 82
Pow-Girl 19
Power Girl 42, 202
Power Pack 109, 113–116, 148
Powerpuff Girls 2, 38–43
pregnant 31, 45, 61, 188–190
princess 3, 9, 18, 71, 102, 105, 116, 131, 153, 206
privilege 58, 73, 75, 83, 97
Priya's Shakti 183

professional 78, 131, 161, 214
Professor X 19, 89, 109, 111, 119, 130, 189, 195, 214
Psylocke 93, 173
Pussycat 145

queen 87, 101, 103, 109, 110, 197, 198, 203, 206, 208–211
queer 7, 90, 99

racism 8, 10, 94, 163, 180, 181, 205
rainforests 74, 182, 185
Raising Dion 3, 4, 57, 217
rape 26, 30, 31, 45, 80, 125, 182, 183, 189, 192
Red-haired Kate 201
The Refrigerator Monologues 29, 217
Rivera, Gabby 156–158
Robbins, Trina 20, 33, 182
Robin 3, 6, 12–17, 21, 46, 58, 129, 131, 133, 136, 145, 146, 149, 184, 186, 187
Rogue 2, 92, 125
romance 1, 12, 13, 16, 25, 40, 47, 49, 55, 69, 79, 80, 84, 87, 102, 141, 149, 155, 171, 204, 207, 216
Runaways 3, 91, 148, 177, 217

Sailor Moon 2, 40, 217
Sarah Connor 26, 110
The Sarah Jane Adventures 58
Sarkeesian, Anita 28, 108, 109
savage 5, 6, 9, 11, 105, 111, 121, 165, 176, 177, 182, 195, 210
Scarlet Witch 18, 44, 45, 80, 165, 166, 199
scientist 102, 125, 190
second wave feminism 40, 80
The Secrets of Isis 22
Seduction of the Innocent 10
seer 130, 164
Señorita Rio 1, 66, 70
Sensation Comics 106, 109, 182, 188
Seven Soldiers of Victory 98, 207
sex 7, 23, 32, 34, 36, 38, 41, 44, 85, 91–94, 97, 166, 214
sexism 26, 33, 50, 52, 64, 125, 145, 170, 180, 212
sexuality 10, 12, 32, 34, 35, 41, 82, 86, 93, 167, 203, 204
sexualized 2, 4, 6, 23, 26, 36, 40, 71, 170, 195
shadow 12, 22, 75, 135, 153, 154, 167, 176, 189, 194, 197, 208–211
She-Hulk 2, 3, 11, 165–167
She-Ra 40
Sheena the Jungle Girl 5–10, 67
S.H.I.E.L.D. 171, 172, 190
Shuri 3, 51, 101–106
sidekick 4, 16, 27, 38, 66, 69, 87, 99, 115, 134–141, 152, 202, 212

Index

silver age 1, 16, 17, 19, 21, 187, 202, 206
Simone, Gail 21, 27, 28, 94, 98, 125, 209
sister 23, 37, 38, 44, 54, 66, 71, 79, 101–105, 113–115, 119, 120, 123, 126, 131, 134, 135, 154, 163, 173, 192
skin 5, 6, 8, 9, 11, 24, 34, 36, 37, 49, 67, 88–92, 114, 167, 172, 178, 184, 186, 187, 206
Sky Girl 5, 70
Smallville 3, 44, 177, 215
smiling 50, 52, 53
Soon I Will Be Invincible 173
Sorceress of Zoom 201
South Sea Girl 9
speech 9, 50, 53, 124, 131, 140, 148, 181
SpiderGirl (Mayday Parker) 113
Spider-Man 1, 2, 3, 41, 60, 78, 79, 113, 114, 117, 118
Spider-Man: Into the Spiderverse 3, 51
Spider Widow 211–212
Spider-Woman 3, 22, 60, 61
spirit guide 175, 176, 181
spirit journey 175, 197
spy 17, 22, 24, 71, 84, 90, 143, 144, 145, 200, 201, 206, 212
Squirrel Girl 3, 210
Star Sapphire 201
Star Trek 22, 214
Star Wars 49, 216
Starfire 11, 80, 108, 119, 129, 131, 133, 183
Stature (Cassie Lang) 189
stereotype 24, 146, 151, 203, 205, 206
Steven Universe 3, 54–58, 99
Storm 47, 64, 103, 111, 158, 173, 175, 179, 185, 194–198
suicide 144, 148
Suicide Squad 2, 3, 4, 10, 153, 154, 177, 191–193
Supergirl 1, 3, 4, 11, 12, 21, 28, 42, 45, 80, 120–124, 134, 214, 217
Supergirl (film) 3
Supergirl (TV) 114, 120, 122, 123
Superman 2, 10, 17, 28, 34, 40, 45, 52, 65, 68, 73, 121, 122, 123, 124, 183, 187, 200, 217
Superman v Batman 121–122
Superman's Girl Friend Lois Lane 79
supervillain 2, 52, 95, 123, 137, 140, 143, 145, 154, 155, 171, 185, 194, 200, 202
Supervillain and Me 155
Superwoman 45, 188, 199
Suzie Su 98
sword 33, 34, 37, 38, 40, 54, 78, 107, 113, 155, 161, 162, 174–178, 204, 207, 212

Talia al Ghul 1, 91, 92, 145–147, 154, 155, 207
Tank Girl 39
Tarot 2, 37–38
Teen Titans 108, 119, 129, 131, 133, 135, 153, 170
Teen Titans (cartoon) 3, 129, 217
teenager 69, 100, 103, 106, 110, 134, 174
Terra 133
Terry and the Pirates 91, 203–204
Texa 199–201
Thanos 170, 199, 208
third wave feminism 39, 41
Thor 3, 18, 62–65, 91, 119, 154, 199, 217
Thor (female) 61–65
Thunder 41, 183
Titans (TV) 153
torture 31, 145, 154, 158
transgender 2, 57, 91–99
trauma 30, 31
trickery 15, 42, 150, 154
trickster 90, 91, 173
Turkey 159–163
2000s 2, 38, 44, 45

underwear 36, 122; *see also* bikini

Veda the Cobra Woman 1, 84–86
veil 1, 24, 159–161, 163, 207
Veil 171
Vixen 3, 10, 156, 217
vulnerability 18, 58, 63, 78, 102, 134, 149, 171, 206

War Nurse 7, 67, 68
Wasp (Janet Van Dyne) 3, 12, 16–20, 47, 80, 190
Wasp (Nadia Van Dyne) 190
weak 1, 63, 118, 165, 166, 209
wedding 13, 21, 192, 197, 215
whip 9, 12, 54, 79, 84, 152, 201, 203
White Tiger 177
Wild Cards 168, 169, 185
Witchblade 2, 40, 44, 177
Wolfman, Marv 28, 108, 120, 129
Wolverine (Laura Kinney) 2, 123
Wolverine (Logan) 130, 133, 170, 171, 172, 197
Womanthology 129, 215
Wonder Girl 20, 134, 135, 164
Wonder Woman 3, 4, 5, 7, 9–11, 19–24, 26, 33, 40, 42, 45, 47–49, 61, 65, 69–71, 79–81, 91, 106–109, 125, 131, 132, 134–136, 160–164, 182, 187, 188, 199, 201, 216, 217
Wonder Woman (film) 47, 49
World War II 4, 7, 9, 66, 67, 70, 107, 144, 182, 204, 205

X-Men 1, 2, 3, 16, 17, 19, 87, 92, 93, 109–113, 117, 119, 120, 130, 148, 158, 167,

170, 173, 179, 189, 195, 196, 198, 199, 214, 215, 217
X-Men (2000 film) 2, 47
X-Men: Apocalypse 50, 217
X-Men: First Class 88
X-Men: The Last Stand 88
X2 (film), 172
X-23 169–175

Xavin 91
Xena 40, 50, 65, 134, 216

Young Avengers 156, 188–190
Young Romance 80

Zatanna 20, 208, 210, 211
Zero Girl 126–129

www.ingramcontent.com/pod-product-compliance
Ingram Content Group UK Ltd.
Pitfield, Milton Keynes, MK11 3LW, UK
UKHW041943140426
5217IPUK00014B/634